DEMYSTIFYING DIGITAL TRANSFORMATION

NON-TECHNICAL TOOLSETS FOR BUSINESS PROFESSIONALS THRIVING IN THE DIGITAL AGE

Attul Sehgal

Apress®

Demystifying Digital Transformation: Non-Technical Toolsets for Business Professionals Thriving in the Digital Age

Attul Sehgal
London, UK

ISBN-13 (pbk): 978-1-4842-9498-7   ISBN-13 (electronic): 978-1-4842-9499-4
https://doi.org/10.1007/978-1-4842-9499-4

Managing Director, Apress Media LLC: Welmoed Spahr
Acquisitions Editor: Shivangi Ramachandran
Development Editor: James Markham
Project Manager: Jessica Vakili

Distributed to the book trade worldwide by Springer Science+Business Media New York, 233 Spring Street, 6th Floor, New York, NY 10013. Phone 1-800-SPRINGER, fax (201) 348-4505, e-mail orders-ny@springer-sbm.com, or visit www.springeronline.com. Apress Media, LLC is a California LLC and the sole member (owner) is Springer Science + Business Media Finance Inc (SSBM Finance Inc). SSBM Finance Inc is a Delaware corporation.

For information on translations, please e-mail booktranslations@springernature.com; for reprint, paperback, or audio rights, please e-mail bookpermissions@springernature.com.

Apress titles may be purchased in bulk for academic, corporate, or promotional use. eBook versions and licenses are also available for most titles. For more information, reference our Print and eBook Bulk Sales web page at http://www.apress.com/bulk-sales.

Any source code or other supplementary material referenced by the author in this book is available to readers on the Github repository: https://github.com/Apress/Demystifying-Digital-Transformation. For more detailed information, please visit https://www.apress.com/gp/services/source-code.

Paper in this product is recyclable

Contents

About the Author

Attul Sehgal is an award winning entrepreneur, innovator, and speaker. Attul possesses a rare combination of technical expertise and business acumen, enabling him to seamlessly navigate the complex landscape of digital transformation within organizations at varying stages of digital maturity. Academically trained as an electrical engineer, he has a unique balance between launching digital products in some of the world's leading organizations and developing his own ventures. He has consulted and collaborated on digital with major global brands across diverse sectors encompassing technology giants, conglomerates, telecommunications firms, financial institutions, and utility companies worldwide. Today he is using his unparalleled wealth of experience set to provide fresh proposition thinking to traditional enterprises, mentor burgeoning start-ups, and contribute to academic programs and accelerators through the consultancy Red Octopus Innovation. His expertise positions him as a valuable catalyst for businesses seeking to transcend their traditional boundaries and embrace the evolving landscape of digital transformation.

Acknowledgments

The author extends gratitude to Helene Panzarino, Ruchi Bahl, Daniel Willoughby, Simone Frahm and Peter Wilson for their support over the duration of this book.

Preface

We find ourselves in a period of rapid social and economic change, driven by the transformative power of digital technology over the past three decades. However, our ability to smoothly adapt to this change has been a challenge.

In the fast-paced realm of digital innovation, businesses often struggle to navigate the best path forward. Despite the enormous potential of digital and big data, recent reports have highlighted alarmingly high failure rates of digital transformation efforts, ranging from 72% to an astonishing 94% amongst leading firms.[1]

These failures come at a significant cost and are detrimental to our businesses. To address this, we must find ways to adapt more seamlessly to the changing landscape. We need to learn from our mistakes, make better decisions, and embrace new ideas and approaches. Collaboration, transparency, and openness about our plans are crucial. Above all, we must be mindful of the impact our decisions have on our customers, employees, and communities.

Many business owners today struggle to keep up with the rapid advancements in technology, fearing that inaction will lead to their downfall but at the same time confused with the pace of innovation. Critical decisions are often made without fully grasping the potential consequences, driven more by hype than a clear vision for achieving optimal business outcomes and effectively collaborating with data teams.

There are several reasons why digital transformation efforts fail. Firstly, many senior executives mistakenly believe they understand what digital transformation entails, viewing it simply as the automation of tasks using technology. However, it encompasses much more. Secondly, people tend to underestimate the complexity of digital transformation. It involves not only implementing new technology but also changing the mindset and work practices of individuals, transforming the organizational culture, and reimagining how data is utilized. Thirdly, people narrow the scope of building new skills to the technical and marketing departments. It has to include non-technical business executives building up a practical digital understanding too.

---

[1]https://www.forbes.com/sites/forbescoachescouncil/2022/03/16/12-reasons-your-digital-transformation-will-fail/.

Amidst the obsession with digital delivery and working with data science, business owners routinely overlook the long-term societal and ethical implications, particularly in the absence of comprehensive regulations. The allure of digital transformation and new technologies can blind us to these vital considerations.

Consequently, we misinterpret our customers' needs and violate their trust, underestimate the costs of digital transformation, struggle to collaborate effectively with data scientists and partners, and fail to articulate our future roadmaps clearly. Moreover, we often underestimate the impact that this change will have on our human values and the importance of being responsible citizens.

To succeed in the digital age, we need to address these challenges. This is where this book comes in, providing a solid foundation for non-technical executives to gain a deeper understanding of digital transformation. Its purpose is to empower the commercial organization to engage fully with their data teams regardless of their technical background and successfully navigate the complex world of digital innovation.

Through compelling classic case studies, user-friendly tools, and a simplified explanation of data, this book opens doors for business owners to work effectively with their digital and data counterparts, enabling them to ask the right questions and gain a much-needed reality check on the complexities of digital transformation.

The book comprises ten chapters, each addressing a crucial aspect of the digital transformation journey:

1. The first chapter lays the foundation by defining digital transformation and exploring its profound effects on customers, competition, innovation, value creation, and data utilization.

2. Building on the first chapter, the second chapter demystifies data, explaining how it can be harnessed to uncover valuable insights using simple statistical techniques accessible to anyone.

3. The third chapter provides practical tutorials on user-friendly digital tools that significantly enhance business productivity and build confidence in using data. It offers practical solutions for immediate implementation.

4. The fourth chapter focuses on problem-solving and offers an outcome-based approach to ensure that digital investments remain on track and yield the desired results.

5. Chapter five delves into the key innovations that have propelled digital transformation, offering readers a glimpse into the game-changing forces at play.

6. Going deeper, the sixth chapter explores the intricacies of data mining, examining various algorithms and artificial intelligence, while highlighting effective ways to collaborate with data analysts and scientists.

7. In Chapter seven, we introduce no-code/low-code tools that enable business owners to experience machine learning algorithms and data mining methods firsthand, as discussed in the earlier chapters.

8. Chapter eight sheds light on understanding technology roadmaps and effectively incorporating emerging technologies into product plans, ensuring businesses stay ahead of the curve and not consumed by the hype.

9. Shifting focus, Chapter nine addresses the societal and ethical challenges associated with digital transformation. It explores how algorithms can influence our behavior and provides strategies for proactive addressing of these concerns.

10. The final chapter synthesizes the learnings from the previous chapters, illustrating how these insights can be applied in our day-to-day operations moving forward.

By offering valuable insights and practical tools, this book equips business owners with an invaluable toolkit for leading the charge in the digital transformation space. It bridges the gap between non-technical executives and data teams, fostering collaboration and empowering businesses to thrive in the era of digital innovation.

Written for readers with no technical background in mind, this book enables you to gain a deeper understanding of digital concepts, empowering you to be effective in a digital transformation environment. It provides the knowledge and primary skills necessary to understand and implement digital transformation within your own business.

So, what are you waiting for? Let's embark on this transformative journey together!

Before we embark on this digital transformation journey, let's take a moment to assess our current position by reflecting on the questions below:

Where Do You See Yourselves on the Digital Transformation Journey?

Instruction

Review the following survey categories and choose the response (1, 3, 5, where 1 = nascent, 5 = best in class) that best suits you or your business. If you find yourself in between two responses, use either 2 or 4.

a. **Business led digital roadmaps**

1 = IT pushing solutions, but business is not engaged

3 = Lots of good experimentation with digital, but no transformative impact

5 = Business leaders own the digital transformation and are accountable for the transformative impact

b. **Digital talent**

1 = We outsource our development needs

3 = We have attracted some digital talent

5 = We have a deep set of digital talent and know how to attract, grow, and retain them

c.   **Agile delivery**

  1 = We are considering launching agile teams

  3 = We have a few agile teams running successfully

  5 = We are driving agile at scale

d.   **Technology stack and retooling**

  1 = Traditional large system environment with long evolution times

  3 = Adoption to cloud to expose data from legacy systems

  5 = High software development productivity enabled by cloud-based platform, API, and automation

e.   **Data management**

  1 = Data is a continuous challenge to all our efforts

  3 = Systems in place to show single source of truth and expose data to cloud and API

  5 = Process and governance in place to enrich data to support digital value creation

f.   **Adoption and operating model change**

  1 = Digital solutions are stuck in the pilot stage

  3 = Customers adopt new digital solutions, but full value not achieved because business operations model has not adapted

  5 = Digital solutions adopted at scale, and business model evolves to maximize value from technology

By submitting your answers to the survey on the GitHub directory, you can compare your answers against other respondents.

Introduction to Digital Transformation

Digital transformation (or DX) is the total integration effort for rewriting the rules for customers, innovation, competition, data, and value propositions. The speed of customer insight, internal decisions, empowered workforces, creativity and understanding new market forces ensured digitally empowered companies stay ahead.

This chapter looks at the working practices of organizations, which can give a first clue into the real challenges that large companies have in the face of competition from new digital competitors.

We'll speak about the empowered customer; data as a continuous stream of information; innovation being cheap; competition as fluid; and how value propositions must evolve to be relevant.

In this chapter, you'll see how digital transformation is the push to integrate these elements into an organization.

© Attul Sehgal 2024
A. Sehgal, *Demystifying Digital Transformation*,
https://doi.org/10.1007/978-1-4842-9499-4_1

Setting the Stage

Using digital techniques to improve our productivity is nothing new – it has been happening for decades, but success is not guaranteed. Practically every company has embraced some form of digital or digitalized technique to simplify and/or optimize its operations.

Yet, while conducting our day-to-day operations, something else quite radical is taking place with these digital tools that has lopsided the fortunes of many companies. To stay ahead, our ways of working need to be re-evaluated considering the wholesale digital evolution taking place. It is imperative that we reconsider how we manage customer relationships, respond to competition, foster innovation, shape value propositions, and utilize data.

Within the pages of this book, we will delve into a number of case studies spanning different industries and digital tools, all aimed at illuminating the journey toward achieving business success through digital transformation. By examining the interplay between data mining, algorithms, digital technology, regulation, and our ethical values, we will uncover their pivotal roles in shaping the landscape. We will navigate through potential pitfalls and engage in discussions about the future of business. Moreover, we will equip you with valuable insights to help you stay ahead of the curve and ensure the prosperity of your business in this digital age. To commence, let us embark on an exploration of the origins of the digitally driven world we currently inhabit.

Great to Gone

There are numerous starting points to choose from, but to show what's at stake, let's rewind to the year 1995 and focus on an electronics retail store situated near a typical shopping mall in the United States as it managed its business to the end of the first decade of the millennium. As we will see in this book, the first decade of the millennium were the pivotal years in digital transformation.

This store happens to be Circuit City, one among many spread across the country. At first glance, Circuit City appears rather ordinary, adopting a "warehouse style" layout where products are prominently displayed for customers to peruse and purchase at service tills (refer to Figure 1-1). Even if you have never set foot in a Circuit City store, you might still recognize its familiar store design, as the mall locations followed a standardized blueprint in your own country. It served as the preferred destination for a wide range of electronic devices, including televisions, video recorders, computers, and video games.

Figure 1-1. Circuit City Store. Source: parkescompanies.com

As a major retail player in 1995, Circuit City was competing against large electronic retailers such as Radio Shack and Best Buy throughout the 1980s and 1990s. Typically, the retailers would have stores relatively close to each other – often near malls, thereby competing directly for customer footfall.

The Circuit City brand grew steadily over many decades through the acquisition of smaller independent electronics stores, and by building deep customer understanding, they dominated the US electronics market in the 1990s, and into the new millennium. The employees at Circuit City were always willing to help, and they knew their stuff.

If you were looking for a new TV, they could tell you the difference between a plasma screen and an LCD. If you were looking for a new computer, they could tell you the difference between a Pentium 2 and a Pentium 3 processor. And if you were looking for a new video game, they could tell you the difference between a Nintendo 64 and a Sega Dreamcast.

This retailer acquisition model was just not limited to the United States, it played out across many regions and sectors around the world. However, wide product inventories, coupled with brand recognition and value nurtured over many decades, created a prominent and profitable business.

The year 2008 saw the emergence of some of the most successful tech companies of the 21st century like Waze, Uber, Slack, the Apple app store, Google Chrome, Android, Bitcoin, Airbnb, and Spotify. It was also the year that Circuit City went bust.

The classic story of Circuit City's demise is salutary.

Due to high volume sales, Circuit City was able to offer products at lower prices and offer service incentives such as home delivery and in-store repairs. By 1990, it had sales of over $2Bn. It was so successful that it went public in 1990, experiencing an 8000% stock growth within six years. By 2001, industry recognition peaked when it was profiled in a well-respected business management book entitled *Good to Great* by Professor Jim Collins (`https://en.wikipedia.org/wiki/Good_to_Great`) which sought to discuss some of the greatest companies that were set to dominate the new century. *Good to Great* was cited by members of the *Wall Street Journal* as the best management book they'd ever read at the time and sold over 4 million copies.

In his book, Jim Collins stated company greatness is not a function of company outlook, or even that of the sector, but rather is a function of the company's conscious choice and discipline.

How could Circuit City go from "Good to Great" to "Great to Gone" in eight years? What went *so* wrong, *so* quickly?

A digital presence was low on the list of reasons. Circuit City is an electronics company and the IBM personal computers had been available since 1981 and the World Wide Web (Internet) available for public use in 1991. It took advantage of these developments as well as the process of transferring documents and images in digital form, called digitalization, which was widespread since the 1980s – although this is not to be confused with digital transformation. It is important to make a distinction between the computing practices over time. We had computers at our desks and created digital content which was stored locally on drives and we were actively digitalizing our content too. Digitalization is the mechanism of taking printed matter and putting it onto computers. These are not areas where Circuit City was ever excluded.

In fact, Circuit City was digitally active. It launched its e-commerce site in 1999. Figure 1-2 shows its online growth for the years from 2004 to 2009.

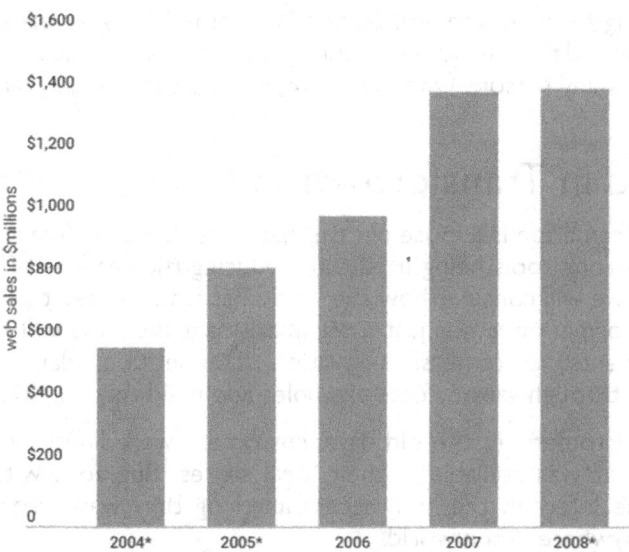

How CircuitCity.com fared before bankruptcy
web sales in $millions, 2004-08

Figure 1-2. www.digitalcommerce360.com/2018/01/16/circuit-city-comeback-consumer-electronics-changes/ *Internet Retailer Estimate, Source: Internet retailer top 500

However, while online retail was expanding rapidly in the early millennium, Circuit City was focused primarily on revamping "brick and mortar" stores, negotiating terms for its on-floor sales teams, and mitigating the threats posed by new vertical players such as Home Depot who were increasingly broadening their electronic appliance offer.

As a result, Circuit City failed to take note and effectively respond to Amazon's online category killer strategy which focused on dominating a particular product category by offering a wide selection of products, competitive prices, and a convenient shopping experience (www.liveabout.com/category-killer-2890178#:~:text=E-commerce%20giant%20Amazon%20could%20be%20considered%20an%20online,impossible%20for%20a%20smaller%20e-commerce%20company%20to%20match).

Circuit City is not alone, many other respected brands succumbed to the same fate. Do you remember your local Blockbuster video store, eToys, Tower records, the Borders Books on the high street or the shopping mall, and the Toys "R" Us at the out-of-town retail park? They all had an online presence too but have all disappeared.

Could these companies have survived by responding more fully to, and embracing, online retailing, or is there something more complex at play? Are there any more parallels from other sectors?

Before moving forward, can you think of any brands in your area that were prominent around the same time in your region that have now just disappeared? Can you recall any reasons why this occurred? Do you see any parallels?

A World in Transformation

Digital transformation is a loose phrase that if we do not define it clearly can lead to the wrong tools being used thus reducing the chances of success. In this chapter, we will consider how the world has transformed through digital. Digital transformation is not just a technical makeover. We will look at five key components: customers, innovation, competition, data, and value propositions through various case examples and build the definition:

- Customers: In the old days, customers were limited to what was available in their local stores. But now, with the Internet, they can access anything they want, from anywhere in the world.

- Innovation: In the past, innovation was slow and expensive. But now, with digital techniques and the Internet, it's much faster and cheaper to develop new products and services.

- Competition: In the past, businesses had a lot of control over their markets. But now, with digital channels, it's much easier for new businesses to enter the market.

- Data: In the past, data was collected by businesses and stored in internal databases. But now, data can be also collected from a variety of external sources to create deeper volumes of intelligence.

- Value: Think of a value proposition simply as a short, clear statement on why a customer should buy your product or service. In the past, businesses competed on price and quality. But now, with digital technology, they can also compete on the total package including brand, and customer pain points addressed.

By understanding these components, we can better understand what digital transformation means and how it can impact our businesses and daily lives.

Customer

No company is immune to the effects of digital transformation – not even a company as powerful as McDonald's in 2012. To understand this, let's look at the back story of this mighty brand.

McDonald's was founded in 1940 as a small restaurant and had a very simple menu – just burgers, French fries, and beverages such as "Triple Thick Milkshakes."

In 1948, the McDonald brothers revolutionized the fast-food industry by introducing a new business model that focused on low prices, quick service, and a limited menu. They sold their burgers for just 15 cents, which was half the price of the competition. They also eliminated waiters and waitresses by using service counters, and they cooked their burgers ahead of time and kept them warm under a heat lamp. This allowed customers to get their food in record time.

The McDonald brothers' business model was a huge success, and by 1961, they had trademarked the now-ubiquitous overlapping, double-arched "M" logo. Two years later, they introduced Ronald McDonald, the Hamburger-Happy Clown, to represent their family-oriented brand personality.

McDonald's has continued to invest heavily in marketing and advertising, and by 2014, they were spending $800 million on promotion and advertising globally. In addition to traditional media channels, such as television, radio, and print, McDonald's has also sponsored key global sporting events, including the Olympics and the FIFA World Cup, of which according to Forbes, they sponsored for around $15–20m each year since 1994.

These sponsorships have helped McDonald's become one of the most successful fast-food brands in the world.

This suite of one-way communications has enabled McDonald's to become the largest restaurant chain by revenue, serving over 69 million customers daily in more than 40,000 outlets worldwide and one of the world's most recognized brands.

Furthermore, customer feedback was carefully addressed with any negative media being actively managed in a timely fashion through an effective PR "machine."

Then, in January 2012, McDonald's got a shock when it used new digital media to ask its customers to share their positive stories about the company on Twitter with the hashtag #McDStories (Figure 1-3). This channel was expected to provide community feedback focusing on what customers found great about McDonald's.

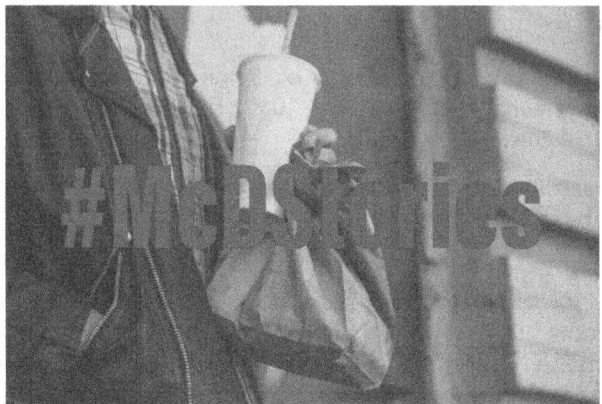

Figure 1-3. Marketing Promotion of #McDStories

Given its customer base and brand strength, the company assumed everyone had a positive perception of their food and restaurant experience and thus did not account for the posting of any negative reactions. However, they quickly learned that this wasn't the case.

Instead of rave reviews, and nostalgic, fun memories, the campaign spurred a proliferation of jokes about obesity, horror stories from customers about the food, service, and restaurant experience in addition to complaints of poor treatment by ex-employees (Figure 1-4).

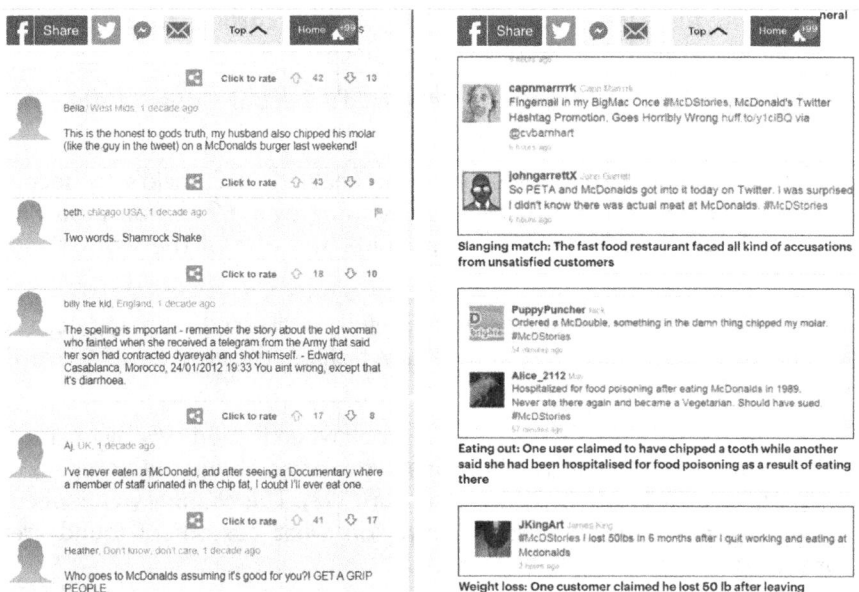

Figure 1-4. Twitter Messages from Customers. Source: Daily Mail

McDonald's was forced to withdraw a promotion after just two hours due to a deluge of negative comments and insults. This backlash would have been impossible just a few years earlier, when negative feedback was more easily contained. However, the rise of social media and smartphones gave customers a new platform to voice their opinions, which could not be ignored or suppressed. This episode is a reminder of the power of the empowered customer, and how companies need to be prepared for feedback that they may not like. McDonald's has since learned from its mistakes, but this was a wake-up call for many businesses about the new world of digital transformation.

Since then, we have moved from a world where customers can be considered as a mass market, who can be broadcasted to via traditional media-based advertising. We can no longer operate on the premise that by customers receiving brand messages they will buy the product or services, enabling companies to increase market share and economies of scale.

Although complaint channels were always available, they were not widely used by customers because of the friction involved in using them.

Today digitally enabled customers are increasingly in a two-way dynamic relationship with brands. Thus, when brands have products or services to launch, they must consider the message and its real value to potential customers. Even the most traditional companies have been forced to rethink and, in some cases, re-invent themselves to survive.

However, open feedback loops were not a concept engineered by the brands, but rather the way that consumers developed their relationship with digital technology and apps over time. Instead of using mobile phones to purely communicate, customers were buying smartphones and downloading apps such as Facebook, Twitter, and WhatsApp to communicate, and form social circles, to share their thoughts with their audience, and at the same time respond to everyday brand communication, and their values through their own experiences.

Furthermore, an ongoing challenge for brands is in growing the number of social media apps available to customers, especially young influencers, to express their thoughts. From Facebook and Myspace, we have now moved to YouTube, Instagram, Telegram, and TikTok as well as online consumer sites, making it difficult to exert message control.

In this digitally transformed age, brands need to understand that value flows both ways. The messages that a brand sends out today can be responded to by customers in real time in social media feedback and customer reviews, and this creates a new relationship built on economies of customer value. Today, consumable items now go through social media trial to prove its worth as part of the course. Figure 1-5 summarizes the key transitions in the brand/customer relationship.

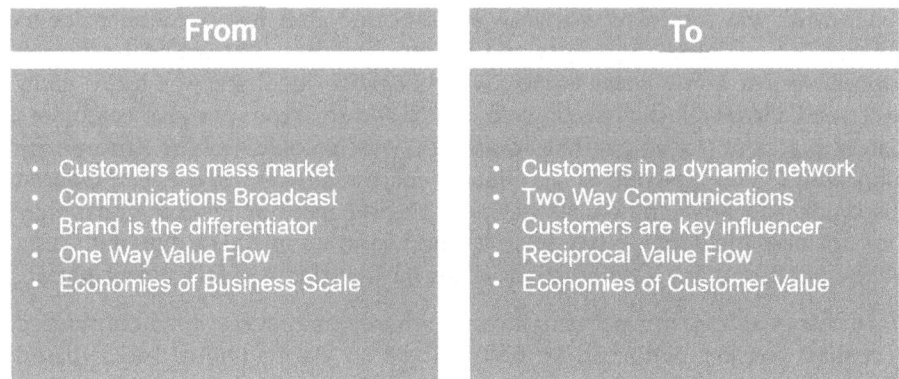

From	To
• Customers as mass market • Communications Broadcast • Brand is the differentiator • One Way Value Flow • Economies of Business Scale	• Customers in a dynamic network • Two Way Communications • Customers are key influencer • Reciprocal Value Flow • Economies of Customer Value

Figure 1-5. Evolution of the Customer Relationship in the Digitally Transformed World

However, for less nimble and/or large organizations, it can be challenging to manage this transition. So where does that leave established brands? Are they all slowly treading the path followed by Circuit City, Blockbuster Video, Borders, Toys "R" Us, and numerous others by not adapting effectively to the challenges and opportunities of digital transformation?

Having said all that, if, in 2004, you invested $1000 into either Amazon, Google, Apple, Meta (Facebook), or Domino's Pizza, which brand would give you the highest return in 2018?

Answer: Domino's Pizza. Figure 1-6 shows the trend over the period. Of the FAANGs (Facebook, Amazon, Apple, Netflix, and Google), only the Netflix share price grew more rapidly.

Figure 1-6. Stock Price Growth of Domino's Pizza vs. Big Tech Through Leadership of J Patrick Doyle, CEO

So, let's look at Domino's Pizza, the well-known Pizza chain for some clues of how to not only survive but thrive through the leadership CEO J. Patrick Doyle, who guided Domino's from near bankruptcy to become one of the industry's most enviable brands before departing in 2018.

Domino's Pizza Driving over 2500% Growth (2004–2018) Through Digital Transformation

From 2006 to 2008, Domino's experienced a consecutive decline of 10% in same-store sales at its domestic locations. This downward trend was accompanied by a decrease in revenues, which dropped from $1.5 billion to $1.4 billion during that period. Additionally, the company found itself burdened with $1.7 billion in debt. As a result of these challenges, Domino's had to let go of several franchisees, leading to a reduction of over 100 domestic locations by 2008, leaving just over 5000 locations in operation. The company's stock value also suffered, plummeting below $3 per share in November 2008.

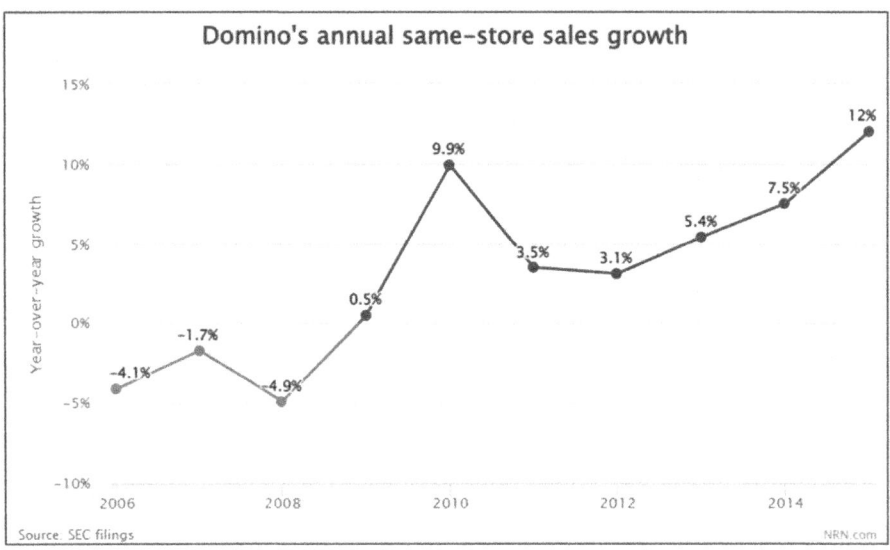

Figure 1-7. *Dominos Same-Store Sales Growth*

During this period, various industries, including retail banks, were also grappling with the integration of digital media into their operations while staying within their comfort zones. In the United Kingdom, NatWest (National Westminster Bank), a prominent high street bank, faced particular challenges. Following the 2008 financial crash, if someone conducted a Facebook search for "Nat West Bank," the top result was often a Facebook group called "I hate Nat West." Despite this negative sentiment, NatWest chose to adopt a strategy of monitoring social media activity without actively engaging or responding to it.

For Domino's, customers also took to social media to brand Domino's Pizza as having flavorless, bland, chewy, and cardboard-like textured pizzas. These negative reviews had a detrimental impact on the company's market share. If Domino's had remained solely focused on their traditional methods of serving customers, they could have faced a situation similar to Circuit City in the mid-2000s, where the company encountered significant challenges and ultimately suffered negative consequences.

In a proactive approach, Domino's Pizza directly tackled the social media feedback and utilized the gathered data to initiate significant changes in their products, services, and brand image.

Recognizing the impact of negative influencers on various social networks, Domino's reached out to them and responded to their comments in a manner that conveyed active listening, consideration, and a commitment to bringing about positive change. Moreover, the company actively collaborated with these influencers to enhance its product offerings by incorporating their direct feedback. This partnership extended to testing new products and services, utilizing the influencers' insights and opinions.

For example, one common complaint expressed on social media was the extended delivery times beyond the promised 30 minutes. In response, Domino's introduced a mobile application called "Pizza Tracker," enabling customers to track the progress of their pizza's preparation and delivery in real-time through their smartphones. This innovative solution significantly improved customer satisfaction and heightened the overall experience.

By actively engaging with customers and leveraging social media influencers, Domino's Pizza successfully addressed the concerns raised online and transformed their product, services, and brand perception to enhance customer satisfaction.

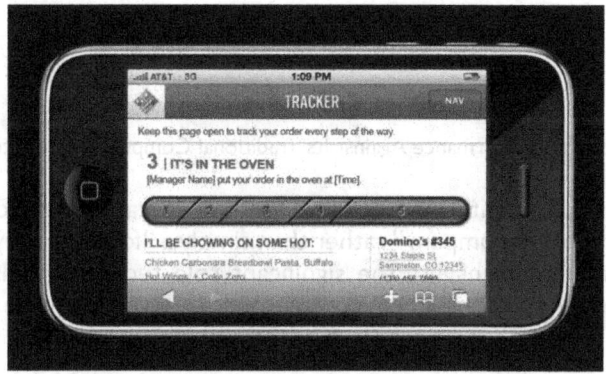

Figure 1-8. Domino's Pizza Tracker. Source: Dominos

Riding on the success of the "Pizza Tracker," Domino's Pizza further enhanced the customer experience by introducing convenient features to their iPhone app. They integrated the capability for customers to place orders and make payments through their "Pulse" platform.

This strategic move not only improved customer perception but also contributed to fulfilling the company's core business objectives. By developing customer-centric digital technologies, Domino's not only reversed its decline but also positioned itself for growth in market share, revenues, margins, and overall profitability. Figure 1-9 shows its stock price performance compared to its traditional competitors.

Domino's change in stock price compared to its competitors

During CEO Patrick Doyle's tenure

Source: FactSet · Created with Datawrapper

Figure 1-9. Dominos Performance Against Its Traditional Competitors. Source: FactSet

As a testament to its digital innovations, Domino's Pizza now proudly identifies itself as a "technology company" rather than simply a "food delivery" company. This transformation highlights the significant role technology plays in their operations and underscores their commitment to leveraging it for continued success.

Similar to Amazon and other big tech companies, it has a "fail fast" business culture of testing new ideas through a team of data scientists who gather customer data, mostly from the company's online and mobile app but also from its point-of-sale (POS) system, to analyze results and determine if ideas will work. Here is an idea it tested for a delivery car with a warming oven in 2018.

Figure 1-10. Source Prototype Dominos Delivery Car with Warming Oven

McDonalds, also saw the need to address digital as a focus for growth. In 2020 as part of the 'Accelerating the Arches', M-C-D strategy it emphasised the need to use digital to tailor better client store experiences and targeted offers. For 2024, it announced a partnership with Google to connect stores via their cloud technology.

However, digital transformation is not limited to commercial ventures.

In the arts sector, museums have traditionally offered a physical experience where visitors enter the museum or gallery to observe artifacts. Typically, they would walk through an art exhibition, exit through the shop, and perhaps purchase gifts, enjoy a coffee, and then depart. However, according to the American Academy of Arts and Sciences, between 2002 and 2012, there was a significant decline of approximately 7 million visitors to museums in the United States. This decline, coupled with limited state funding, evolving needs in the digital age, and customers' willingness to pay, created an uncertain future for traditional museums.

Fortunately, the advent of digital transformation techniques has revolutionized how these challenges are being addressed. Museums are now embracing digital tools not only to raise awareness but also to enhance operational efficiencies and increase funding from visitors. For instance, in 2013, the Dallas Museum of Art (DMA) introduced the DMA friends program, aimed at improving visitor engagement by offering perks such as store discounts and free parking in exchange for customer data. Within two years, over 100,000 members had joined the program, leading to a significant increase of more than 20% in donations.

During the same period, the Louvre in Paris utilized Bluetooth technology to track people's movements within its galleries and analyze visitor preferences. This data was then used to alleviate congestion within the museum. The Museum of Modern Art in New York took digital transformation even further by appointing a Chief Digital Officer to integrate digital technology into the museum's overall strategy. Working with all departments, the Chief Digital Officer employed digital tools to transform the visitor experience. This included improving website viewing to increase digital traffic, developing mobile apps for museum navigation, organizing remote events where visitors could access curator collaboration sessions and interact directly with curators. Additionally, they even offered the opportunity to view or participate in live art restoration, making for a captivating experience.

Numerous other museums have effectively partnered with digital experts to broaden the accessibility of their exhibits. The British Museum, for example, collaborated with Google Arts and Culture to create "The Museum of the World." This interactive platform allows users to explore and engage with exhibits in ways that were unimaginable just a few decades ago.

The benefits of digital transformation are not limited to large institutions alone. The Black Country Living Museum (BCLM), a small open-air museum recreating an early industrial landscape in Britain, faced significant challenges following the 2020 lockdown. Visitor numbers dropped from the typical 350,000 to 90,000, resulting in losses of £5.5 million. Most of the staff were furloughed, and volunteers were unable to provide their usual support. The museum had a tradition of employing entertainers to portray historical roles against the backdrop of the museum, but they were left without a role due to the circumstances.

To adapt, the museum turned to digital platforms and became the first museum to join TikTok. They experimented with sharing performances online, which proved to be a success. The museum's TikTok channel reached 30 million people globally and currently boasts 1.3 million followers. Notably, the majority of these followers are individuals under the age of 30, many of whom had never previously interacted with a museum on social media. Since the easing of lockdown restrictions, the museum has witnessed an upsurge in young people visiting in person (`www.ftstrategies.com/en-gb/insights/ the-digital-future-of-the-arts-and-culture-sector`).

This example once again demonstrates that by embracing digital transformation comprehensively, any business can undergo a radical transformation.

Let's now move to innovation.

Innovation

In 1939, Joseph Schumpeter, an Austrian economist, provided a definition for invention and innovation. He characterized invention as an act of intellectual creativity devoid of consideration for its potential economic implications, while innovation occurs when companies transform inventions into constructive changes within their business models.

The process of introducing new technology to the market has undergone significant changes with the emergence of digital transformation. To comprehend these changes, let's examine the traditional approach to innovation, which typically revolves around qualitative and quantitative market research of a potential market proposition, often with the final decision influenced by the "Highest Paid Person's Opinion" (HIPPO) approach.

Traditionally, the process involves the following steps, as summarized in Figure 1-11:

1. Craft a brief to commission market research.

2. Collaborate with an agency to determine the research methodology.

3. Conduct the research activities, analyze and consolidate the data.

4. Present the findings and engage in discussions.

However, this traditional market research method is slow, expensive, and time-consuming. It involves challenges such as securing budgets, shortlisting agencies, planning feedback sessions, and preparing reports, which could take up to six months to share the insights.

Consequently, market research was conducted relatively infrequently. Today, digital techniques enable companies to test quickly, inexpensively, and frequently. Crucially, this approach allows for easy iterations in response to evolving data or factors like competitor launches.

As a result, digital market research provides targeted and continuous pulse checks on customer behavior and desires, replacing delayed snapshots. Adopting continuous digital market research has become a crucial differentiating factor for businesses.

Figure 1-11. Market Research Stages

A case in point is the evolution of the Clinical Research sector requiring the rapid innovation of vaccines through digital techniques during the recent COVID-19 pandemic.

Pre-covid, the average cost of developing a vaccine and bringing it to market was $2Bn with an average duration of 7.5 years. A breakdown of the costs from clinical research.io is given in Figure 1-12:

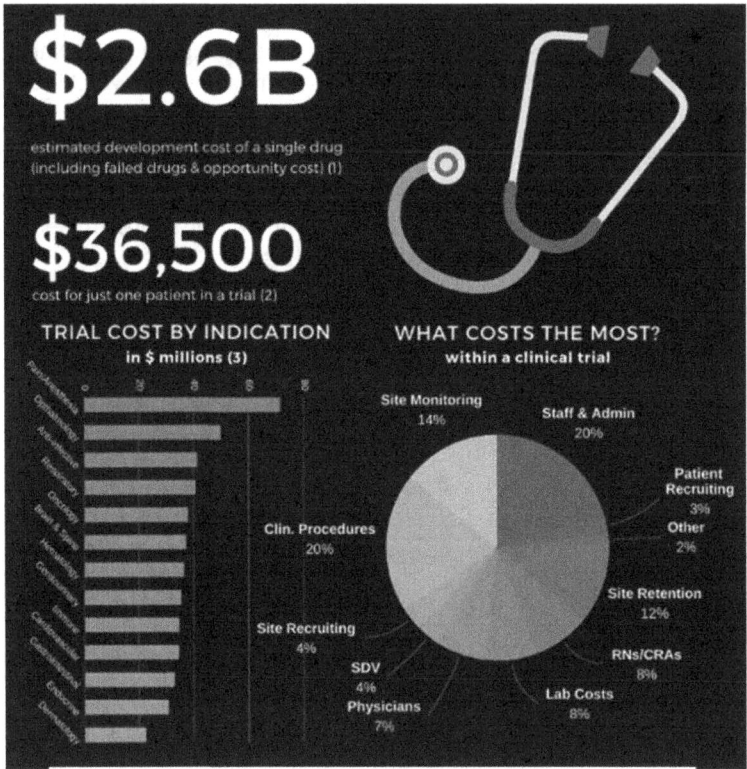

Figure 1-12. Costs of Clinical Trials Source Clinical Research.io

(1) Tufts Center for the Study of Drug Development (CSDD) 2014
(2) Battelle Technology Partnership Practice and PhRMA, Biopharmaceutical Industry-Sponsored Clinical Trials Impact on State Economies. March 2015
(3) Sertkaya et al. Key cost drivers of pharmaceutical clinical trials in the United States. 2016

clinical research

powerful, all-in-one eSource & CTMS

One of the main cost challenges is in the setting up of the sites, patient identification, and recruitment. The chances of trialists not ultimately fitting the criteria for the trial can be as high as 90% (Examination of Clinical Trial Costs and Barriers for Drug Development | ASPE (hhs.gov)).

If we carried on this mode of operation during COVID-19 pandemic, we would still be searching for a vaccine in 2023!

The status quo had serious questions to address

- Ways to reduce the time to make test sites operational?

- Improvements in time to trial completion?

- Identifying the right trial participants, in the right cohorts, doing the relevant test

How did this occur? Faced with the pandemic challenge, clinicians had to move away from the traditional pharmaceutical company approach trial participants recruitment through contact databases with known case histories and prioritize digital means.

From	To
Print Advertising	Social Media
Word of Mouth	Websites
Direct Mail	Email
Telephone Calls	
In Person Recruitment	

Figure 1-13. Evolution of Patient Recruitment Methods

Based on research conducted by the Tufts Center for the Study of Drug Development, traditional methods of patient recruitment for clinical trials come with an average cost of $1000 and take around six months to complete. In contrast, employing digital methods for patient recruitment in clinical trials carries an average cost of $100 and can be accomplished within two months. These findings indicate that digital recruitment methods offer a potential cost reduction of up to 80% and a time-saving of up to 80% compared to traditional approaches.

The drug firms used social media and through riding the wave of "wanting to help" clinical trials were started within seven months with the right participants. The intelligence gained from using digital methods was then leveraged to help the Clinical Research firms to rapidly and efficiently identify those priority groups for the vaccine.

From a position of concerns of privacy of customer data, lack of awareness, investment and resources for the digital tools available, digital transformation played a major role in the fight against the pandemic.

They also used digital tools to help constantly track the spread of the virus, to monitor people who were at risk, to provide care to people who were sick, and through social media educate the public about the virus.

Furthermore, knowing where those priority groups are based helped to target optimal operational vaccination sites, leading to rapid mass vaccination deployment. By intelligently using data, vaccination services were brought to the patient, not the other way around, while building direct contact relationships with each of the trialists, enabling tracking of implementation and local variations being reported in real time.

The use of artificial intelligence also allows powerful dashboard summarization of data to track trends and discrepancies without human intervention, as shown in Figure 1-14.

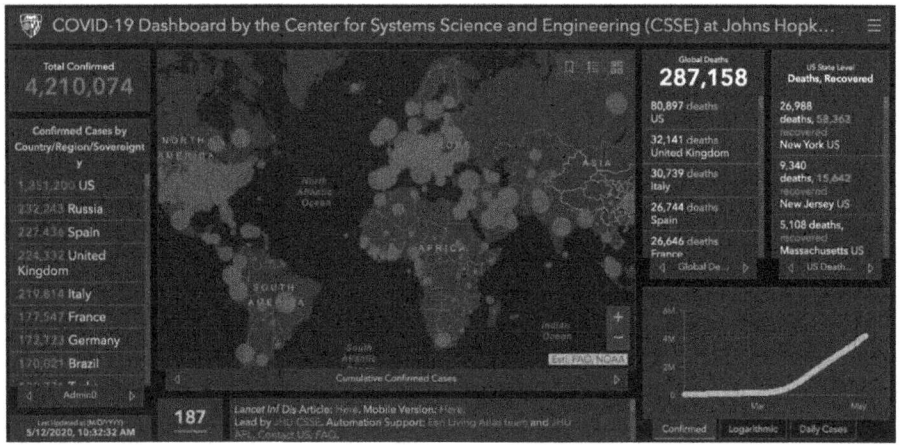

Figure 1-14. Johns Hopkins Center Interactive Map. Source: Johns Hopkins Centre

As shown earlier, although the clinical outcomes remain consistent, the methods of delivering these outcomes have undergone significant changes. Previously, recruitment was typically handled by a briefing agency, but now there is direct contact with each trial participant. Studies are actively designed and conducted with real-time data, utilizing the power of remote learning to swiftly process and analyze data, as well as enhance data visualization.

Through the implementation of these digital techniques, patient data processing and sharing have become faster, leading to a remarkable improvement in service provided to the community. Consequently, these advancements have also resulted in enhanced business outcomes for the clinical research companies. Figure 1-15 summarizes the transition that took place through digital transformation.

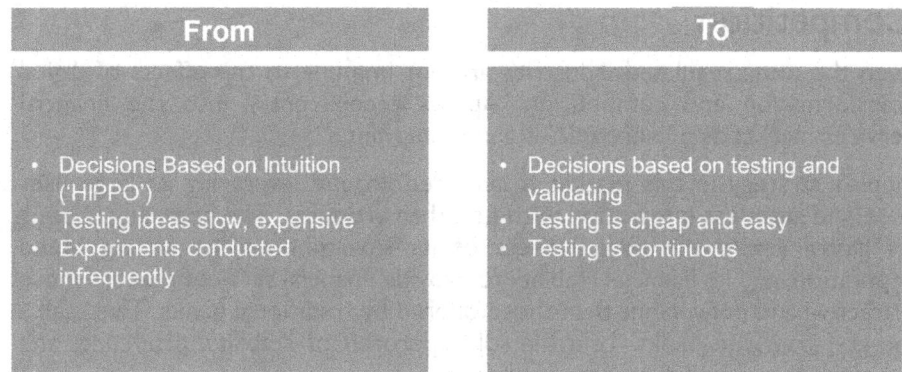

From	To
• Decisions Based on Intuition ('HIPPO') • Testing ideas slow, expensive • Experiments conducted infrequently	• Decisions based on testing and validating • Testing is cheap and easy • Testing is continuous

Figure 1-15. Transition of How Innovation Takes Place Through Digital Transformation

Why didn't this approach happen earlier? Traditionally, value propositions are defined by an industry that would execute that same trusted value proposition each time. Big Pharma firms focused on developing new drugs and bringing them to market. That was the priority and there was a way of doing this. While digital tools were known, they were not a priority. The efforts to convince the regulatory of the benefits were probably very complicated and the general lack of investment into building digital resources and expertise into the area were real challenges too.

For clinical trials, there was an established way that "Big Pharma" companies were doing trials and this approach was accepted. With the onset of the COVID pandemic, society needs and the regulatory environment suddenly adapted to the new reality and the established process was revisited with digital driving successful outcomes. Today, digital is helping pharmaceutical firms to improve efficiency, reduce costs, and improve the quality of their products.

At the same time, digital tools were used by commentators to create a backlash around the pandemic. Do you think we are really ready to use these tools and apply them to other illnesses outside a pandemic situation without a regulator?

Is regulation playing an important role in the speed of delivery of new propositions? Do you think we are moving so fast today that regulators cannot keep up, thereby giving digital innovators an unfair advantage?

We will discuss this further later on in Chapter 9, but in the meantime, let's look at how competition has evolved.

Competition

Even the most regulated industries are not immune to the effects of digital transformation and competition. Apple's recent entry into the financial services market as a "neobank" is a case in point.

Apple's strategy in this market is centered around leveraging its large user base and seamless integration with its other products. The company is using its global reach, the addictiveness of its smartphones, its strong brand reputation, and its financial stability to provide financial services that are more attractive and convenient than those offered by traditional banks. This is all a far cry from the banks' centuries-old approach of stability, prudence, and governance to build customer confidence.

Apple's journey into the finance sector has been gradual. It began in 2014 with the introduction of Apple Pay, a mobile payment service that allows users to make purchases with their iPhones. Over 75% of iPhone users have Apple Pay activated, and the service has generated huge revenues for Apple. It subsequently launched a "buy now pay later" service as well as Apple Card to keep people in the Apple eco-system.

Apple's entry into the financial services market has raised concerns about fair competition. Some critics argue that Apple is using its market power to gain an unfair advantage over traditional banks. Others argue that Apple's financial services are not subject to the same regulations as those offered by traditional banks, giving Apple an unfair advantage to lever its reputation and customer knowledge in different ways.

It is too early to say what the long-term impact of Apple's entry into the financial services market will be. At the same time, the incumbent banks have carried out extensive digital transformation engagements themselves. However, it is clear that Apple is a major player in the digital transformation of the financial sector, and its actions will have a significant impact on the future of banking.

To comprehend the effect digital transformation on competition has on existing sectors, let's revisit the case of Circuit City and its relationship with Amazon. Amazon launched its e-commerce site on July 16, 1995, with the sale of a book titled *Fluid Concepts & Creative Analogies: Computer Models of the Fundamental Mechanisms of Thought*. At the time, the idea of purchasing something online and having it safely delivered to one's home was quite daunting for most people, especially when it came to electronic goods.

While the online concept was still taking shape, Amazon adapted its customer proposition by observing shifts in buying behavior and expanding its product range to include music compact discs (CDs) and digital video discs (DVDs). By 1999, Circuit City, an established electronics retailer, was reporting $10 billion in sales and decided to partner with Amazon to sell their products online in 2001. During that period, Amazon's revenue in the US electronics, tools, and kitchen category was recorded at $111 million, representing a modest 21% increase from the previous year. This growth rate fell short of what was expected from Internet companies. Additionally, Amazon incurred a $41 million loss on those sales.

The partnership between Circuit City and Amazon allowed customers to purchase certain products online from Amazon and pick them up at local Circuit City stores. In the traditional retail model, Circuit City occupied the customer end of the value chain, while Amazon functioned as a reseller, earning commissions on the sales. The relationship resembled a typical retailer/supplier dynamic.

Circuit City did not view the Amazon channel as a significant threat, primarily due to its extensive market understanding, long-standing reputation, and trusted brand built since its establishment in 1949. Selling electronics online was not perceived as having substantial potential, especially considering that Buy.com had been delisted from Nasdaq in the same year. Circuit City primarily saw itself competing with Best Buy in physical stores.

However, Amazon had previously formed similar partnerships with Borders and Toys "R" Us and was actively seeking more collaborations. The potential for Amazon to compete with well-known brands was underestimated. Amazon excelled at understanding customer behavior and capitalized on the convenience and competitive pricing offered by online shopping. Furthermore, by avoiding the costs associated with maintaining physical stores, Amazon was able to secure better deals and offer more competitive prices.

The situation highlighted how digital transformation, coupled with Amazon's astute understanding of evolving customer preferences, disrupted traditional retail models. The convenience, pricing advantages, and ability to adapt quickly to changing market dynamics gave Amazon a competitive edge over well-established brands like Circuit City.

In 2005, despite experiencing rapid sales growth through their partnership with Amazon, Circuit City, confident in their relationship with customers, decided to revamp their own website and create their own online offering. As part of this shift, they terminated their agreement with Amazon.

In January 2005, Circuit City's website attracted 6.7 million visitors, a significant increase of 46% compared to the previous year, as reported by comScore Networks. Similarly, Best Buy witnessed 11.8 million unique visitors, marking a 28% rise from the same period the previous year. However, Amazon.com far surpassed both retailers with a staggering 41.5 million visitors in January, showing a 9% increase from 38 million in the previous year. Amazon's success was attributed to its partnerships with various retailers such as Nordstrom, Target, Office Depot, and many others.

Despite the growth in their online presence, Circuit City's decision to terminate their partnership with Amazon meant relinquishing access to the vast customer base and reach that Amazon offered. It showcased the inherent challenges traditional retailers faced in competing with an e-commerce giant that had established numerous successful collaborations (www.marketwatch. com/story/circuit-city-ends-relationship-with-amazoncom#:~: text=In%20an%20effort%20to%20drive%20consumers%20to%20 its,president%20of%20Circuit%20City%20Direct%2C%20in%20a%20 release).

"I wonder If I Can Get This Cheaper Online"

However, digital transformation did not stop with online providers offering a better purchase experience than established companies. Digital channels also evolved with the growth of the smartphone. By 2006, you could walk into a store with your phone, assess the products you might want to buy, search for it on your phone, and locate a cheaper price elsewhere. This change led to the demise of Circuit City in 2009 and countless others across sectors such as DIY, health, sports, and clothing.

Figure I-16. Summary of the Circuit City /Amazon Partnership0

If we take a step back, we can see how competition has evolved.

Previously, competition was within well-defined sectors. Thus, a company such as Circuit City would, in addition to its own market research, look at key competitors, for example, Radio Shack, Home Depot, or Best Buy to understand broader market activity. This, over time, was complemented by insight from delivery/logistics partners, including Amazon.

With the onset of digital, the distinction between partners and rivals blurred. The carefully guarded knowledge assets built inside companies no longer held the currency they once had. However, at the time, companies like Circuit City were still thinking, "well, we've only got three other competitors, so let's focus on them."

Amazon, in contrast, developed a whole new service model that could take intelligence and apply it across sectors as it learnt that the dynamics of selling books was not fundamentally different from selling electronic goods and a host of other product sectors. It was a big challenge to drill down on excelling in the online customer experience for a suite of industries could overturn the heritage of these traditional brands.

Addressing this challenge, coupled with a uniquely scaled competency set and growing brand presence, meant they could rapidly and effectively move up the value chain.

A key skill was that Amazon understood how to leverage the digitally generated knowledge sets of consumer behavior to not only deliver for today's customers but to predict future customer behavior independent of product sector. This ability became the key game changer in winning customers. We will later look at some of the key algorithms they revolutionized in their path to success.

By facilitating a wide product set with huge stocks, their platforms evolved to be product agnostic – through engaging with partners who could exchange value regardless of product type. Amazon's offer proposition was to provide better services and features from their platform based on the "I can get whatever I want here" principle.

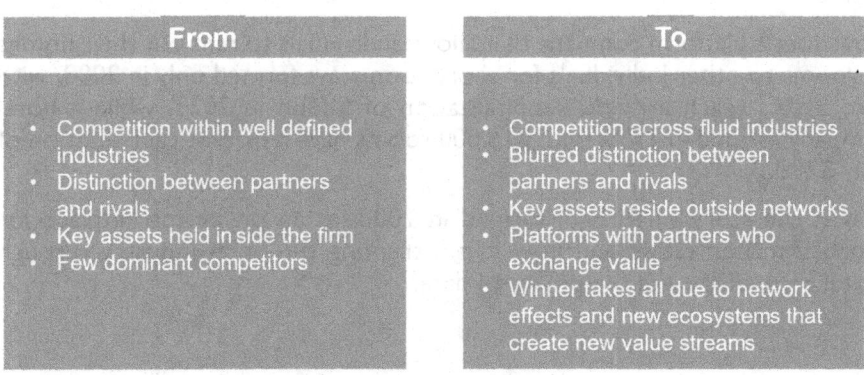

Figure 1-17. Digital Transformation of Competition

The key lesson is that regardless of who you are or where you start from, if you can get the customer experience correct, you can move in almost any consumer market, allowing the building of your brand to a level that can challenge the incumbents.

It is clear digital unreadiness contributed to the demise of Circuit City, but there were other factors like

- Slowness to adapt internally

- Failure to understand the changing customer mindset

- Failure to respond to the rapid growth of technology such as the smartphone

- Incomplete understanding of the competitive space

- Slowness to understand the real potential of digital

One way to survive is to elevate the value of the direct relationship with the customer and how they are perceived, including overall store experience, friendliness of staff, customer care, or smooth returns policies.

Applying some the lessons from the Circuit City scenario, can you think of ways that Apple's foray into financial services could play out?

In all cases, the advantage that digital natives gained was in being able to effectively drill down on customer behaviors through mining customers data to provide the best experience and acting on the learnings. The way that they have been able to use data has given rise to the phrase data as "the new oil."

Data

How does a platform company that allows individuals to rent out their homes or rooms to other individuals for short-term stays formed only in 2008, with zero assets reach a market capitalization of $86Bn in 2023, while a hotel company formed in 1959, with 216,000 rooms have a market capitalization of only $29Bn?

This is the story of Airbnb, formed in 2008, as an online marketplace for short-term homestays and how it is disrupting the hotel industry through digital technology and the power of data.

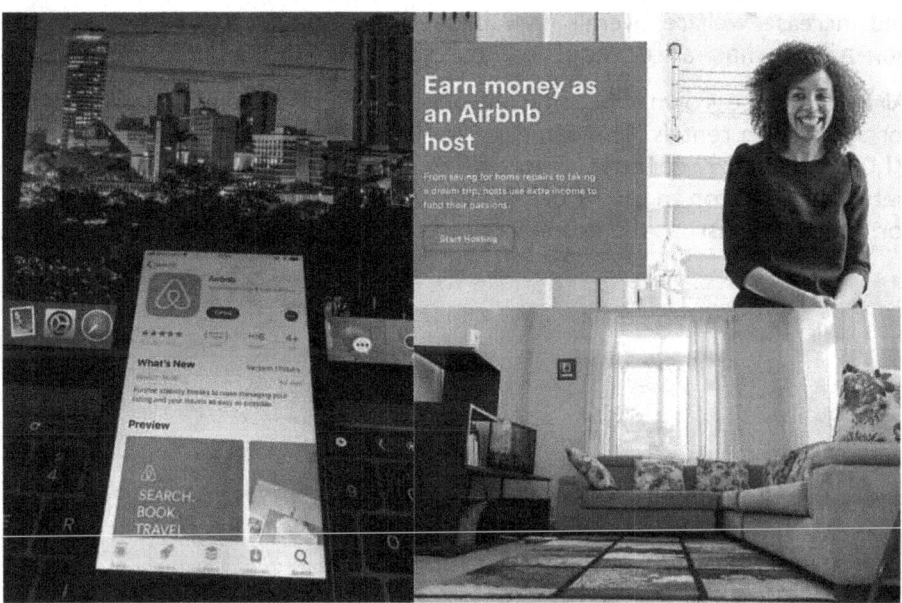

Figure 1-18. Airbnb: https://stavica.com/how-to-make-money-as-an-airbnb-host-in-kenya/

In their own words, Airbnb describes their unique value proposition as "Airbnb exists to create a world where anyone can belong anywhere, providing healthy travel that is local, authentic, diverse, inclusive and sustainable." Through its use of data, it has transformed the hospitality sector with positive and negative outcomes.

In 2014, a study by the National Bureau of Economic Research found that Airbnb reduced hotel profits by up to 3.7%. However, the study also found that Airbnb generated $41 of consumer surplus per room per night and $26 of host surplus per room per night.

The study found that the impact of Airbnb was concentrated in locations and on dates where hotel capacity was most constrained. For example, in New York City on New Year's Eve, Airbnb bookings were estimated to have reduced hotel revenues by 14%.

A more recent study, conducted in 2018, found that hotel revenues would be 1.5% higher without the presence of Airbnb. However, the study also found that between 42 and 63% of these additional bookings would not have resulted in hotel bookings if Airbnb were not available.

In other words, Airbnb has both positive and negative effects on the hotel sector. On the one hand, it can reduce hotel profits by increasing competition. On the other hand, it can also generate consumer surplus and host surplus and increase welfare overall (www.bls.gov/opub/mlr/2018/beyond-bls/how-airbnb-has-affected-the-hotel-industry.htm).

Airbnb has since grown to become one of the most popular online marketplaces for short-term rentals. The company now lists over 6 million listings in over 81,000 cities in 192 countries. Figure 1-19 compares the hospitality experience between the Hilton and an Airbnb homestay. So how did an online marketplace for homestays disrupt the hospitality sector so rapidly?

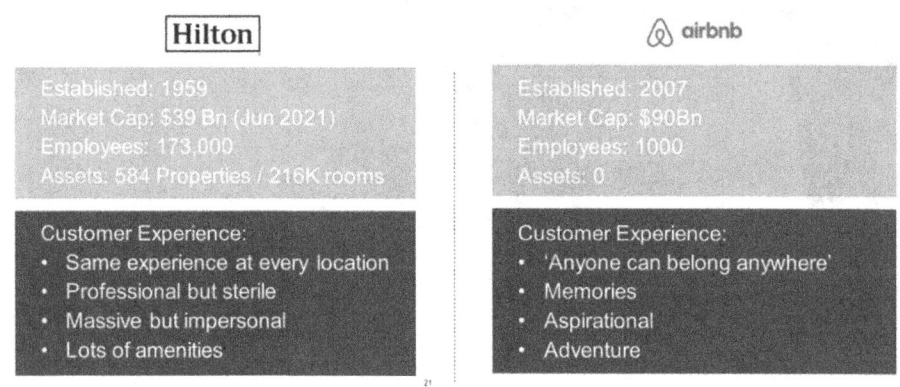

Figure 1-19. Data Platforms Transforming Hospitality Experiences (Data as of 2022)

Airbnb achieved its success through its platform and the innovative way it manages data captured through it. The platform allows hosts and guests to exchange housing accommodations for money. Throughout the application process, hosts and guests can find reviews and social media connections to build trust among users in the marketplace. This helps to build a community among its members.

In the early days, the founders would meet with all the guests and hosts to improve the service. However, as the number of guests grew, this became impractical. Instead, they adopted a vision of data as the "customer's voice" and data scientists as "interpreters." A data scientist, a person who collects, analyzes, and interprets data, interacts directly with other business functions, not only to fully understand the problem to be solved but also to make sure decision-makers fully understand the result of their analysis and can, therefore, act upon them.

In 2015, the Airbnb Head of Data Sciences described elements of the Airbnb data gathering process when he spoke about the platform. He said that Airbnb "tries to recreate the sequence of events that you do so that when they learn from it, they can provide you with the relevant things that are relevant for you." Airbnb keeps records of the number of beds, transaction history, photo images, location data, and customer feedback to provide a unique experience for customers. It could use this intelligence to define a new category of travel based on your unique preferences and experiences.

You may have already seen this if you use the Airbnb platform. If you search for a property without signing in, you often get different options than if you login with your account. The platform also has the ability to seamlessly translate images sent such as a photograph and gain intelligence from them using algorithms that understand unstructured data, which we will discuss in a later chapter. It also analyzes your booking behavioral characteristics, including transaction price ranges and price sensitivity, and feeds them into an algorithm to give you a targeted range of options.

What is key to Airbnb is that these data points are not factors defined by the data scientists, but rather those that help to address the objectives of the business owners. This is critical as if you're looking for the reasons why some businesses are more successful than others, we can be easily led astray by statisticians and the data scientists doing projects with unclear business outcomes. We will discuss more in Chapter 3.

Market surveys can provide structured data such as sex, age group, location, nationality, to help in customer profiling. However, there are severe limitations to this data capture. How do you categorize and market to someone who's 50 who behaves like a 20-year-old? You just can't see this with the normal structured data you would see in a customer registration form. Data is also produced in departmental silos, so if you had the marketing department producing data, and the customer service department producing their own data sets, it is difficult to integrate this data. In contrast, Airbnb captures real-time "raw" data that can be shared and exploited across departments without any restrictions.

Having data in its raw or unstructured tabular form allows not only data sharing across departments but the construction of an organizational 360 degree view. This possibility unleashes the power of the data allowing a digitally transformed organization to use its data platform to optimize its business and add value to the customer experience seamlessly.

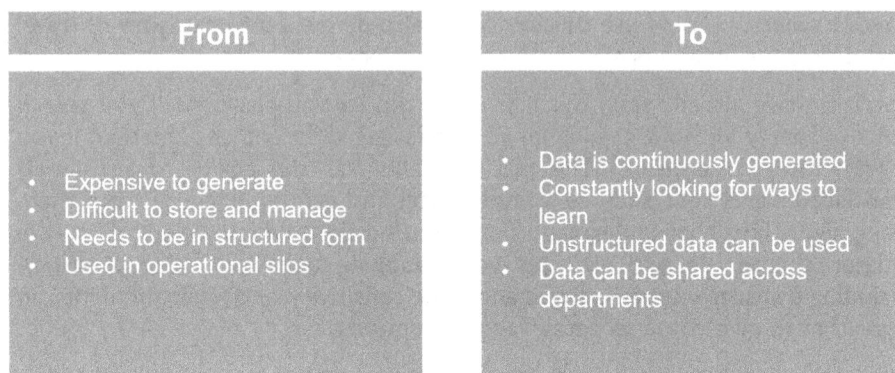

Figure 1-20. Summary of How Data Has Transformed Through Digital Transformation

If it is just purely exploiting data intelligence, could Airbnb use their platform expertise to move into other sectors such as car sharing? Could they compete with Uber?

We have discussed the challenge of established businesses to embrace digital transformation. While it may seem an enormous challenge for any established company to completely rewire itself into the data mindset of a digital native, it has been achieved quite successfully in one of the most complex and regulated sectors – retail banking space with DBS bank formed around the same time as Hilton hotels, through a fundamental digital transformation rethinking processes, people, and strategy that led to huge success

DBS the 22,000-Person Start-Up

Singapore-based DBS is a major financial services group in Asia, and a leading consumer bank in Singapore and Hong Kong, serving more than 4 million, including 1 million retail customers. Founded nearly 50 years ago as the Development Bank of Singapore, DBS was the catalyst to Singapore's economic development during the nation's early years of growth post-independence (https://sloanreview.mit.edu/case-study/redefining-performance-management-at-dbs-bank/; https://link.springer.com/chapter/10.1007/978-3-030-48950-2_22).

Figure 1-21. Source DBS Bank

In 2009, DBS encountered efficiency issues and initiated a digital transformation of its 28,000-employee business. The primary objective was to dominate the digital realm by leveraging data, embracing social media, and adopting a mobile-first approach. This entailed more than superficial changes like creating a website or Facebook page; it necessitated a comprehensive re-evaluation and reimagining of the organization's fundamental operations to deliver a distinct service experience.

To instill inspiration and align teams with digital pioneers, the project was named GANDALF. This acronym represented various principles: Open Source akin to Google, running on Amazon cloud platforms, Personal Recommendations like Netflix, Design influenced by Apple, Continuous Learning resembling LinkedIn, and fostering a more collective approach like Facebook. The inclusion of the letter "D" symbolized DBS Bank's digital identity, encouraging employees to view themselves as part of an elite group.

DBS launched a range of digital services while concurrently optimizing internal processes within the organization.. The timeline is shown in Figure 1-22.

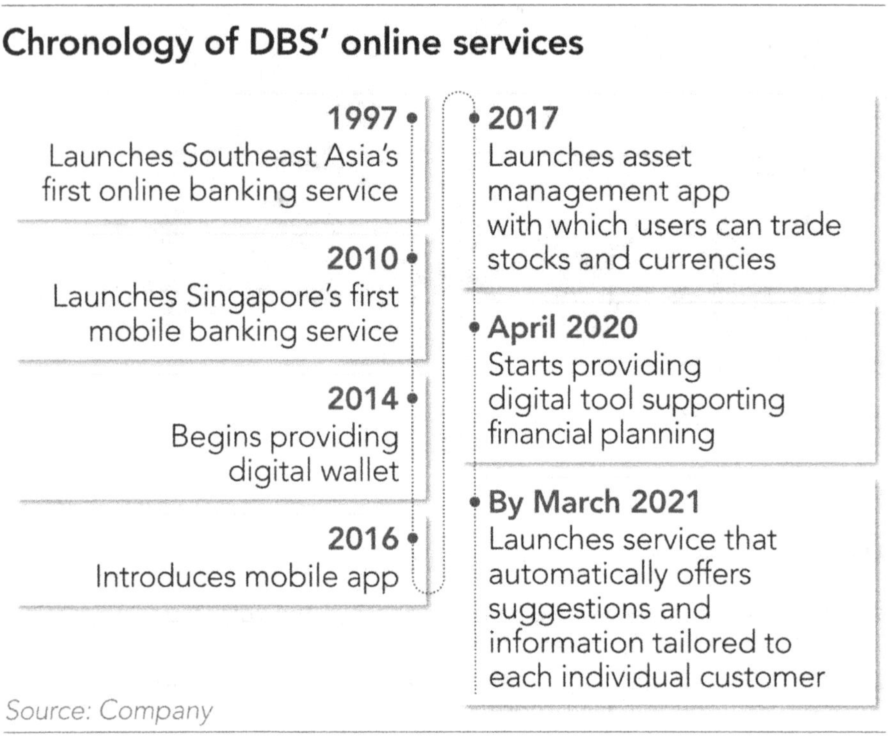

Chronology of DBS' online services

1997
Launches Southeast Asia's
first online banking service

2010
Launches Singapore's first
mobile banking service

2014
Begins providing
digital wallet

2016
Introduces mobile app

2017
Launches asset
management app
with which users can trade
stocks and currencies

April 2020
Starts providing
digital tool supporting
financial planning

By March 2021
Launches service that
automatically offers
suggestions and
information tailored to
each individual customer

Source: Company

Figure 1-22. Timeline (Source DBS)

During its initial transformation phase until 2015, DBS accomplished a remarkable 9% compound annual growth rate (CAGR) in income and a 13% CAGR in net profit. In 2018, the bank disclosed that it generates twice as much income from its digital customers compared to traditional customers.

The Digital ATM team at DBS collaborated with data scientists to develop predictive models using data analytics methodologies. These models focused on preventive maintenance and cash recycling, leading to a significant reduction in ATM downtimes from 20% to almost negligible levels. This achievement resulted in approximately $20 million in savings for the bank.

Moreover, by employing predictive analytics, DBS gained insights into the frequency of ATM usage, enabling them to determine the optimal number of ATMs and to establish efficient reloading schedules.

Additionally, one of the key challenges faced by banks is the effective and efficient assessment of risk and creditworthiness for individuals and businesses. At the start of the 21st century, this process relied heavily on manual labor, lacked standardization, and operated in an ad hoc manner. It was more of an art than a science, and most importantly, it was not well-performing. The process relied on questionnaire responses and lacked integration with customer data or any data-driven intelligence.

The COVID-19 pandemic served as a catalyst for DBS' transformation, expediting the adoption of digital services. In the period June–August 2020, the number of customers enrolling in DBS' smartphone-based financial service skyrocketed by 216% compared to the previous year. Additionally, transactions involving asset management products conducted through smartphones experienced a remarkable increase of 217% during the same period.

Within their digitally transformed landscape, there is an increased reliance on remote access, bringing forth new challenges related to technology resilience. Following a string of service outages that impacted customers in 2023, they have committed to investing $60 million to enhance this aspect through-out 2024.

There is no doubt that the pandemic has digitalized many processes. Can you think of ways how your enterprise or your daily life is using data intelligence to simplify processes post pandemic?

With the disruptive forces taking place today, how do successful companies stay relevant in the customer? We will look at the ways companies define their value.

Value

In 2023, Apple received the accolade of being the most valuable brand worldwide. The success is grounded in customer loyalty because people wanted to join the exclusive club of iPhone, Macs, iPad, etc. Figure 1-23 shows how the Apple brand value, which is the monetary worth of a brand if it was to be sold, has increased over the years.

(in billion U.S. dollars)

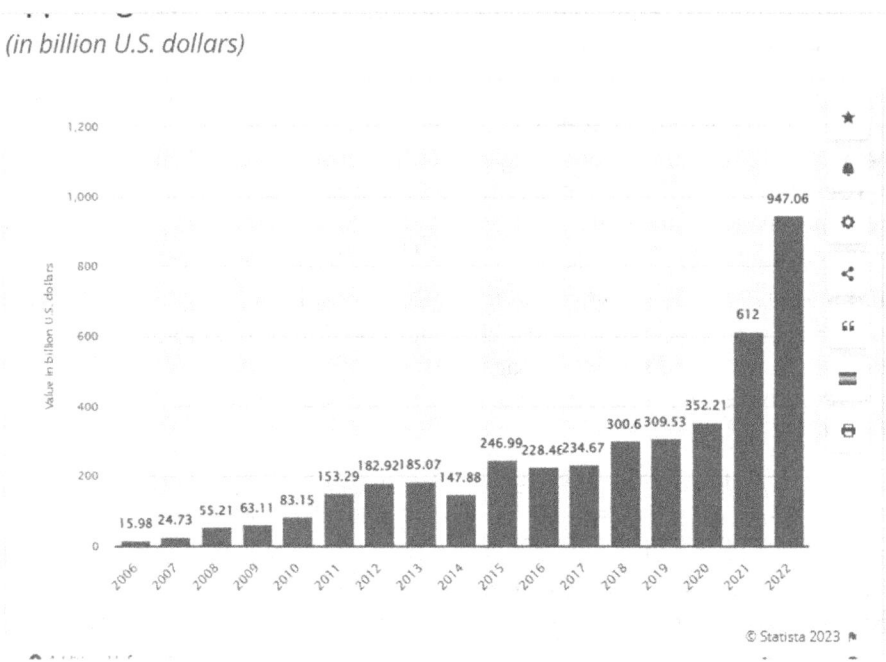

Figure 1-23. Apple's Global Brand Value from 2006 to 2022 Statista

To understand the importance of value in digital transformation, let's look deeper into the story of Apple. In 1993, Apple was very successful with their Mac computer building its market share and the management decision at the time was to focus purely on this one proposition. However, Apple released a number of the innovators from the senior management team and brought in new members to focus on growing this particular proposition. By 1997, the company faced stagnation, with retention of existing Mac customers as a business priority as the share price plateaued.

In 2002, Apple brought back innovators into the management team and started to build a suite of winning products that we know as the iPod, iPhone, iPad, and iWatch. While each innovation possessed different adoption curves, they have all contributed to profitability and providing greater brand value to Apple. Figure 1-24 shows the current revenue by operating segment.

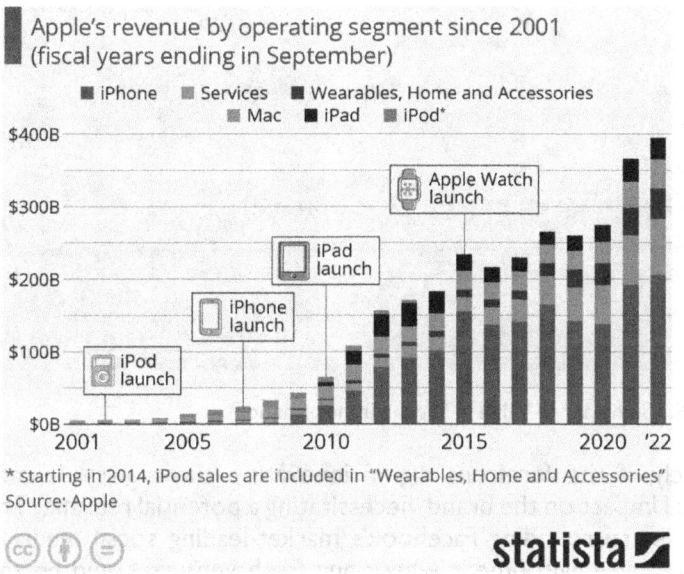

Figure 1-24. Apple Revenue by Operating Segment (www.statista.com/chart/17862/ apples-annual-revenue-by-operating-segment/)

Daniel Tello provides a detailed review of the Apple product adoption curves to 2013 on his blog page, http://aaplmodel.blogspot.com/2012/10/ long-term-apple-segmented-revenue.html. While the different products have different adoption curves, the iPod, despite not being revolutionary technology (very similar to the pre-existing MP3 players), had a very steep adoption curve and drove value to iTunes as the platform to acquire music content. The iTunes platform also had a steep adoption curve for two years, but then flattened as Google and other data sharing providers entered, or gained prominence in the market.

The iPad also had an impressive adoption curve despite warnings that it was simply a large screen iPhone, but it created a market by facilitating computer-like use away from the desktop.

What is clear is Apple's determination to generate value through continuous innovation by embracing digital transformation techniques and swiftly embracing new ideas. Apple recognizes that complacency poses a threat to the success of digital transformation, and therefore, prioritizes a proactive approach to drive constant innovation.

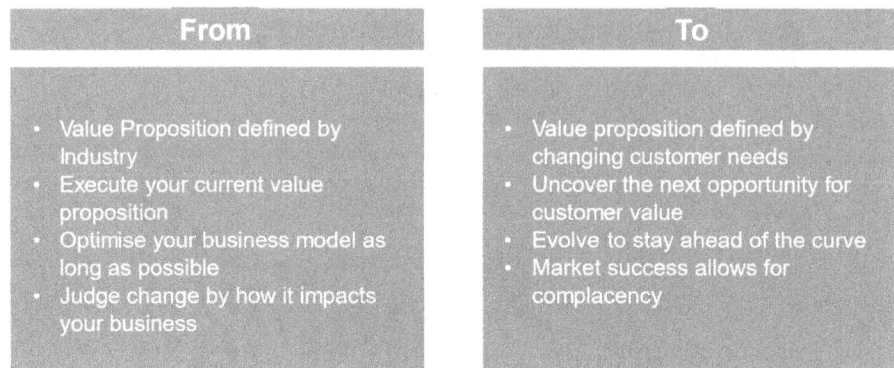

From	To
• Value Proposition defined by Industry • Execute your current value proposition • Optimise your business model as long as possible • Judge change by how it impacts your business	• Value proposition defined by changing customer needs • Uncover the next opportunity for customer value • Evolve to stay ahead of the curve • Market success allows for complacency

Figure 1-25. Summary of Value in Digital Transformation

Alternatively, if the forefront digital innovation turns awry, it can have a detrimental impact on the brand, necessitating a potential rebrand. The recent controversies surrounding Facebook's market-leading social media platform have created an environment where any fresh venture could be tainted by association with the Facebook name. This toxic reputation has had adverse effects on the company's workforce, making it challenging to attract and retain employees. By rebranding as Meta, the company aims to appeal to a younger demographic and capitalize on its new lineup of products.

Conclusion

Digital transformation is the total integration effort for rewriting the rules for customers, innovation, competition, data, and value propositions. In the digital world, customers are empowered, innovation is fast and cheap, competition is fluid, data is in abundance, and value propositions must evolve. In order to comprehend the concept of digital transformation, we have examined various case examples that vividly illustrate its profound impact on society and the subsequent reshaping of business norms. No industry remains immune to the effects of digital transformation and therefore must take proactive measures to avoid complete disruption. While the process of transformation is challenging, when executed correctly, it holds the potential to greatly enhance the fortunes of companies, even those established prior to the digital age.

We have analyzed how Domino's Pizza and DBS Bank undertook significant restructuring to improve their fortunes, defying the conventions of their traditional competitors. Nevertheless, even the most admired brands, such as Apple, cannot afford to rest on their laurels. In the digital realm, customers wield considerable power, competition is dynamic, innovation is so cost-effective, and data serves as a driving force behind creativity. Consequently, value propositions must continuously evolve. The objective of digital transformation is to seamlessly integrate these elements into an organization.

Regrettably, many companies are heavily investing without reaping the anticipated rewards. Despite substantial financial commitments, numerous digital transformation initiatives fail to meet business expectations, while several data projects end up as mere experiments that fade away.

While there exist various pitfalls to avoid, it is indeed feasible to identify, mitigate, and chart a successful path toward transformation. But there is also a knowledge gap that business owners can fill. Subsequent chapters will delve into building a deeper understanding of data, explore strategies to navigate the realities of digital transformation, and acknowledge the common challenges faced by most companies in their pursuit of digital objectives. We will also provide valuable insights and tactics for non-technical business owners to enhance their effectiveness in executing digital transformation initiatives. Additionally, we will examine the technologies that propel digital transformation and introduce digital data tools that even non-technical executives can use to optimize project success and reduce costs.

In the next chapter, we will dig deeper into data.

Unleashing the Power of Data

Introduction

It is often said that the second most recognized phrase in the world, after "OK," is "Coca Cola." Now, imagine the impact of a single gesture from Cristiano Ronaldo, with his massive following of 550 million on various social media sites, during a press conference after Portugal's opening match at UEFA Euro 2021. Ronaldo chose to drink water instead of the Coca Cola soft drink, resulting in a 1.6% drop in Coca Cola's share value, according to Nasdaq. The Twitter images are shown in Figure 2-1. Despite the millions Coca Cola had invested in tournament sponsorship, the market capitalization dropped by over $4Bn. How could this happen?

© Attul Sehgal 2024
A. Sehgal, *Demystifying Digital Transformation*,
https://doi.org/10.1007/978-1-4842-9499-4_2

Figure 2-1. Ronaldo Says "Drink Water." Source: Twitter

A negative response from a footballer on a pre-match TV interview regarding a world famous soft drink was shared to 550M followers on social media and generated a lot of column inches in online media that triggered a sharp negative reaction in the share price in just a matter of days. There were clearly other factors at stake, but clearly a backlash was felt on the Coca Cola brand globally for a period. (www.theguardian.com/media/2021/jun/18/coca-colas-ronaldo-fiasco-highlights-risk-to-brands-in-social-media-age)

Coca Cola, although taken by surprise, responded quickly and the share price did recover, but this incident is just an example of how digital transformation, or DX, can have a strong sudden reverberating effect on established brands that was never seen previously.

Many established companies in recent times have been casualties to the effects of digital transformation on their business.

Let's go back to 1994, when Blockbuster Video was valued at $8.4 billion. They operated over 3000 physical stores and generated revenue primarily through video rentals and late return fees. However, three years later, a new player emerged: Netflix, with a business model, centered around digital subscriptions. Despite the growing popularity of digital subscriptions, Blockbuster failed to respond quickly enough to the changing digital landscape. Eventually, in 2010, Blockbuster went bankrupt, even though they had invested over $200 million in Blockbuster Online as a belated effort. As we saw, this pattern of digital disruption leading to downfall was evident in the case of Circuit City as well. In 2005, Circuit City, a renowned US retailer, terminated a four-year e-commerce partnership with Amazon, fearing a loss of customer ownership. Unfortunately, in 2009, Circuit City went bankrupt, and Amazon went on to become the largest electronics retailer in the United States.

Other companies have recognized the challenges posed by digital disruption and attempted to respond, but their reliance on outsourcing their digital initiatives has led to significant setbacks. For instance, Hertz is engaged in a huge multimillion-dollar legal battle with Accenture over the latter's failure to deliver a digital platform for a seamless digital experience across all Hertz brands and digital channels.(www.theregister.com/2019/04/23/hertz_accenture_lawsuit/)

Given the numerous examples of digital disruption, one might believe that digital success is primarily limited to the innovative digital natives and established firms will struggle to adapt. It was no surprise then that in a 2023 survey by Boston Consulting Group (BCG), they identified the five most innovative firms globally as Apple, Tesla, Amazon, Alphabet, and Microsoft. (www.visualcapitalist.com/most-innovative-companies-2023/)

However, there are established companies that we can learn from who have taken bold and decisive steps to transform their businesses and have achieved significant success.

We discussed how Domino's Pizza, an established Fortune 500 company, founded in 1960, faced similar disruptive challenges to Blockbuster and Circuit City. By 1998, it had expanded to over 6000 stores. In the early 2000s,

Domino's Pizza faced declining revenues due to perceived weak product lines, inconsistent delivery times, and slow inventory cycles. By the end of 2008, their stock was trading at a mere $3.85 per share. Instead of sticking with outdated methods, Domino's Pizza executives embraced a radical business transformation approach. They engaged with their critics through digital channels and invested in new technologies to enhance the customer experience, including ordering, inventory management, and delivery, while also improving the employee experience.

By 2018, Domino's Pizza provided customers with over 15 digital ordering options. Their stock value had skyrocketed by over 2500%, surpassing even Google's growth during the same period.

Unlike its counterparts, Domino's Pizza successfully embraced digital technology and the power of data and witnessed direct improvements in its business outcomes. This achievement is truly remarkable given the dismal success rate of digital transformation efforts by Fortune 500 companies.

Despite the projection that digital transformation spending would surpass $2 trillion by 2023, a staggering 87% of companies have yet to fully realize the impact of their digital investments. It makes one wonder why anyone would undertake a digital transformation initiative.

According to David Mounts, a former Executive Vice President at Domino's Pizza, the underlying issue lies in the fact that digital transformation is not merely a technology problem but a mindset problem. There are gaps in our ability to gauge our efforts and efficiently coordinate seamless digital experiences, leading to a failure to realize the full potential of our substantial investments. If business owners continue to fail to ask the right questions, these investments will lead them in a downward direction. Source: Forbes – "Digital Transformation Is Not a Technology Problem" (www.forbes.com/sites/forbestechcouncil/2021/07/21/digital-transformation-is-not-a-technology-problem/)

The article in Forbes, published in 2021, emphasizes the importance of understanding that digital transformation goes beyond implementing technology. It requires a fundamental shift in mindset and strategic thinking. Only when businesses adopt the right mindset and ask the right questions can they truly leverage the potential of digital transformation and achieve successful outcomes.

This all does spark some fundamental questions:

- Why have so many companies struggled to reinvent themselves in the digital age?

- With such high failures for digital transformations, why do we continue to invest in these high-risk projects?

- What are the competency gaps that we should fill so that we do not become digitally irrelevant, but winners in the future?

Let us dig deeper into the new digital market environment and find out.

The New Market Environment

As we discussed in Chapter 1, customers are empowered, innovation is rapid and cheap, propositions must continuously evolve, and data is the "new oil" for future prosperity. Figure 2-2 summarizes DX.

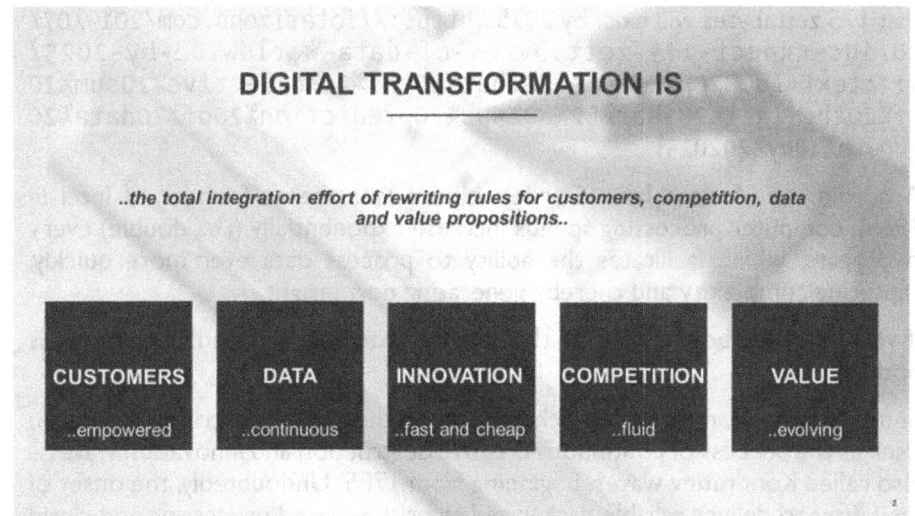

Figure 2-2. Summary of Digital Transformation

The key driver behind this change is data. Data has always existed, but now data has evolved to become a new tool due to faster machine processing, bigger storage, advanced analytics, intelligent algorithms, and better ways to visualize information. Today it is the power of data that drives deep market intelligence, predicts future outcomes, and creates new revenue streams.

Businesses around the world are aggressively adapting their processes to accommodate data intelligence, knowing that failing to tap its maximal potential could result in their demise. We call it "Big Data."

In the next section, we will look at how this situation arose but before moving further, look around yourself and identify ways that digital innovation has transformed the ways you work from how you did things differently, from say, 15 years ago. How much does data drive this?

How Did We Get Here?

It is the rise of data, the ways it can be distributed, and the speed of data processing that has fueled this wave of innovation.

The volume of data produced in the world is growing rapidly.

Just a few years ago, a Gigabyte (1 Million bytes) was considered a huge amount of data. With the onset of new digital services, we are now living in a world of zettabytes – which is 1 followed by 21 zeroes or a trillion gigabytes.

From approximately 33 zettabytes of data in circulation today, it is predicted that 175 zettabytes will exist by 2025. (https://iotarizona.com/2019/07/16/idc-expect-175-zettabytes-of-data-worldwide-by-2025/#:~:text=IDC%20predicts%20that%20the%20collective%20sum%20of%20the,last%20year%E2%80%99s%20prediction%20of%20data%20growth%20by%202025)

According to Moore's law, (Gordon Moore was the co-founder of Intel in 1965), computer processing speeds increase exponentially (i.e., double) every two years, which facilitates the ability to process data ever more quickly, capturing complexity and thereby generating new insight.

If you have not been aware of this change, don't be alarmed! Innovation is nothing new.

In fact, the economist Joseph Schumpeter, in the 1940s, described capitalism itself as the process of continuous creative destruction and innovation waves – also called Kondratiev waves, beginning from 1785. Undoubtedly, the onset of new ways to deliver reliable data, rapid algorithm-based processing and cloud storage, and creation of new products and services has accelerated the cycle process.

If we review some innovation cycles from the past, we can extract some lessons on how our ancestors had reacted to change and how we can position digital transformation (DX) in our lives today.

One thing is clear, as we moved from one innovation wave to another, frequently the tool sets we had used became obsolete as we embraced new ones. The digital wave is an extension of that process.

A key challenge is that earlier innovation waves were relatively gradual – until even recently, taking approximately 50–60 years to transpire. This gave us time to adapt our tool sets for the new wave. But today's digital wave is moving far more rapidly in an unrestrained way and established firms are not adjusting sufficiently quickly. We need to embrace and exploit new tool sets much faster to compete with digital natives.

Welcome to the new norm!

Before we move on, try to think of three things that we were doing in the last 20 years that we have subsequently abandoned with the development of digital technology and how we made the adjustment.

Examples could be on how you use maps, tell the time, record movies on TV, call your friends, or even manage your household finances.

What Are These Waves of Innovation?

Capitalism is fundamentally an evolutionary process of continuous innovation and creative destruction

—Joseph Schumpeter

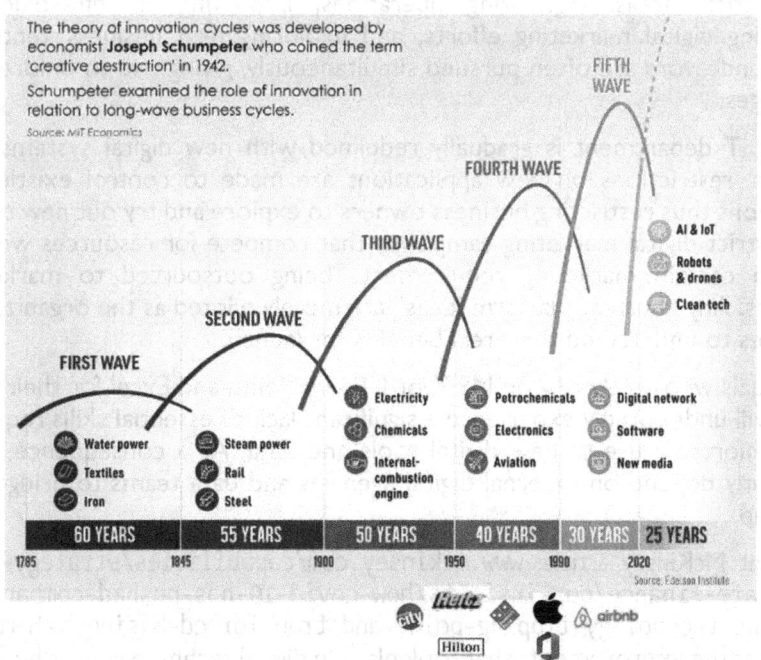

Figure 2-3. Innovation Waves with the Founding Periods of Some Leading Companies
Source: MIT Economics

The Soviet economist Nikolai Kondratiev was the first to bring these waves to international attention in 1925. Based on this, Joseph Schumpeter, in 1939, posited of the first key innovation wave, or Kondratiev wave, starting around 1785; we have now progressed through six radical innovation waves to where we are today, as shown in Figure 2-3. (www.visualcapitalist.com/the-history-of-innovation-cycles/) Waterpower, steam power, electricity, and then electronics characterize the first four waves, with digital networks and AI being key for the fifth and sixth that are currently taking place. When we study the transitions between the waves, it's almost laughable to think that the same skills from tool sets built from previous waves will be sufficient to be competitive today. The overlap of the fifth and sixth wave really questions whether the tools and ways of working used in the fourth wave really make sense and how relevant the new business tools being used in the 4th wave will be in the near future.

Indeed, as innovation cycles are becoming ever shorter, it becomes easier to recall the companies that formed, prospered, and demised from earlier cycles. To avoid such demise, it is critical that companies re-evaluate their processes, invest in new tool sets, build expertise, and review their operations to transform to the digital world.

Based on years of extensive first-hand experience with various companies undergoing digital transformation, the investment focus is directed toward four critical areas: digitalizing operations, improving IT infrastructure, enhancing digital marketing efforts, and exploring new business ventures. These endeavors are often pursued simultaneously, giving rise to unforeseen challenges.

As the IT department is gradually redefined with new digital systems and skillsets, restrictions on new applications are made to control existing IT operations thus restricting business owners to explore and try out new digital tools, strict digital marketing campaigns that compete for resources with IT lead to certain marketing requirements being outsourced to marketing agencies. Any "burning platform ideas" are merely piloted as the organization struggles to understand their real benefits for launch.

Individuals who solely rely on MS Word, PowerPoint, and Excel for their daily tasks will undoubtedly experience a significant lack of essential skills required for comfortable use of new digital tools and data. As a consequence, they frequently depend on external digital agencies and data teams to bridge the skills gap.

A recent McKinsey article, www.mckinsey.com/capabilities/strategy-and-corporate-finance/our-insights/how-covid-19-has-pushed-companies-over-the-technology-tipping-point-and-transformed-business-forever, highlights the improvements that took place in digital technologies for business decision-making post the pandemic, but still an acceleration needs to take place to bring these skills in-house to reduce costs. See Figure 2-4. Even for simple tasks like making videos. Companies in the UK are very happy to spend up to £25,000 to make a short video when they could do the work themselves using simple digital tools for a fraction of the cost.

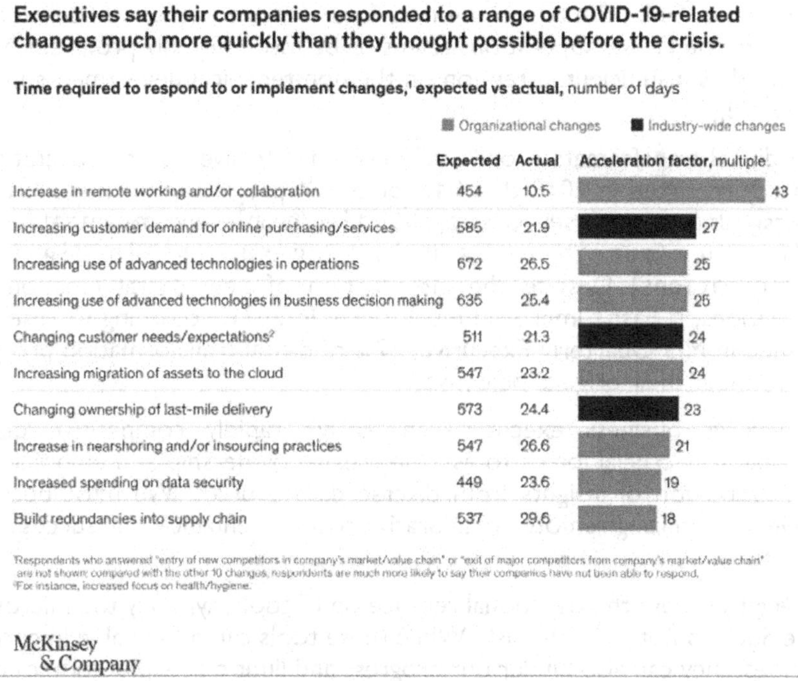

Executives say their companies responded to a range of COVID-19-related changes much more quickly than they thought possible before the crisis.

Time required to respond to or implement changes,¹ expected vs actual, number of days

■ Organizational changes   ■ Industry-wide changes

	Expected	Actual	Acceleration factor, multiple
Increase in remote working and/or collaboration	454	10.5	43
Increasing customer demand for online purchasing/services	585	21.9	27
Increasing use of advanced technologies in operations	672	26.5	25
Increasing use of advanced technologies in business decision making	635	25.4	25
Changing customer needs/expectations²	511	21.3	24
Increasing migration of assets to the cloud	547	23.2	24
Changing ownership of last-mile delivery	573	24.4	23
Increase in nearshoring and/or insourcing practices	547	26.6	21
Increased spending on data security	449	23.6	19
Build redundancies into supply chain	537	29.6	18

¹Respondents who answered "entry of new competitors in company's market/value chain" or "exit of major competitors from company's market/value chain" are not shown; compared with the other 10 changes, respondents are much more likely to say their companies have not been able to respond.
²For instance, increased focus on health/hygiene.

McKinsey
& Company

Figure 2-4. Use of Digital Pre- and Post-pandemic; (www.mckinsey.com/capabilities/strategy-and-corporate-finance/our-insights/how-covid-19-has-pushed-companies-over-the-technology-tipping-point-and-transformed-business-forever)

Naturally, getting used to familiar and reliable tools and work methods, especially if they have resulted in past success, can make it challenging to embrace any new digital tools. This hesitance, lack of awareness, or slowness to change internally can significantly impede effective digital transformations, acting as a major bottleneck to success in the organization.

Can you think about any digital technologies you were presented with, the hurdles that were encountered in its introduction, and how long it took for the transformation to take effect?

Innovation Effects on Our Day-to-Day Processes

Current innovation cycles render it imperative for us to be adaptable with the way we work. Sadly, the typical business focus tends to center on developing the role of the IT and Operations teams to be more digitally proficient, with less, and thus insufficient, attention on the non-technical departments in the organization.

Most, digital transformation or "DX" efforts fail to live up to expectations. McKinsey reported in 2018 that 84% of all DX programs fail to reach their businessgoals.(www.mckinsey.com/capabilities/people-and-organizational-performance/our-insights/unlocking-success-in-digital-transformations) Despite the introduction of new digital functions in organizations, it hasn't improved much since. In 2021, according to research published in MIS Quarterly Executive, 87% of digital transformation projects failed to meet their original objectives.

However, as business executives in today's rapidly competitive digital landscape, it is crucial for us to assume greater ownership and embrace the direct extraction of insights from diverse data sources. We must become proficient in utilizing remote collaborative tools to enhance our success and productivity.

Breaking free from the traditional reliance on IT tools, typically the Microsoft Office Suite, is not a simple task. While these tools can be valuable in certain capacities, they can also hinder our progress and limit our exploration of new digital alternatives. The absence of awareness regarding available digital innovations, coupled with uncertainty about how to leverage them effectively, has prompted a rush toward outsourcing. However, the traditional outsourcing model heavily relies on external parties to execute digital initiatives. This approach has often resulted in reputable firms failing to adopt and capitalize on the benefits of digital transformation (DX). In some cases, these firms have incurred significant losses, diminished sales, and even faced complex and costly legal disputes with their partners as a consequence of their DX endeavors.

The tool sets we rely on today, such as MS Word, PowerPoint, and Excel, possess considerable power when wielded by skilled individuals. However, they possess inherent limitations in terms of speed of execution and their ability to handle the voluminous data processing required to support the rapid decision-making, implementation, and evaluation demands of the present era.

Fortunately, a new generation of tools allow even non-coders to define and become proficient performing some of the most involved digital tasks. An immersion into these simple tool sets will empower you to work more effectively with your digital counterparts and open the door to DX success.

Can you think of examples where companies have outsourced digital expertise to third parties?

Examples could include creating promotional videos, developing prototypes, or sourcing and analyzing data. Try and list some examples and the challenges that took place in their implementation.

Let's look at a fictional case example based on a real digital transformation engagement failure and see how we can better address some of the tasks internally with a few simple digital tools and save money.

Case Example: Landis Car Hire – Digital Front-End Redesign

Landis Car Hire is a 100-year-old hire firm in the Fortune 500 with branches and sub-brands around the world. Figure 2-5 shows a sample logo I produced with the logo app Looka. You can try it for free yourselves at www.looka.com.

Figure 2-5. Landis Car Hire Logo Developed Using www.looka.com

In 2016, it is seeing real threats from new digital players and decides to develop a compelling digital front end to align its channels to improve its brand perception, drive higher customer engagement, and subsequently build revenues and profits.

It assigns a well-known digital consultancy, Blue30, who it has seen as being a trusted technical partner over many years to carry out the digital transformation engagement described. With its day to day operational concerns to worry about, it even gives the responsibility of the product ownership for the engagement to the integrator. The product owner is responsible for representing the interests of all the stakeholders and ensuring that the digital development team delivers value to the customer. Both parties agree the project would take 18 months to complete.

Blue30 prepares the product requirements document for approval from Landis Car Hire. However, due to the rapid pace of digital innovation, Blue30 take a calculated risk by recommending and deciding to use a new software version of the approved user interface platform. The intention is to enhance their own skill set and knowledge capability at the same time once the project is approved and underway.

Although the software doesn't meet the initial performance expectations, Blue30 persists with the implementation. This decision is driven by their business relationship with Landis, which is based on expensing resource time and materials used in new feature development charged by the day.

Unfortunately, Landis citing huge delays to the agreed timelines and unreasonable fees pulls out of the engagement and replaces Blue30 with a new system integrator fueling further costs.

Three years later, Landis, goes into a public litigation with Blue30. It cites unreasonable costs like over "$100,000 charged by Blue30 to build the visual style guide for the IPAD." The actual litigation dispute for the failed digital front-end design was totaled at an astounding $36M!

So, what went wrong?

- Why did Landis give so much control of the engagement to Blue30?

- Could Landis have developed front-end elements – like the IPAD – themselves and just outsourced the back end?

- Could the Landis marketing team have crafted the overall vision and look and feel for the whole digital experience themselves?

Do you have examples of how you may have come unstuck with a DX engagement? What were the barriers in not doing some of the digital work inhouse?

For this digital engagement to end up in such a large litigation, there are major lessons to be learnt. Let's take a step back and try to understand what happened.

The project began in 2016 and it was in the fifth innovation wave. Landis was using an outdated approach. Given that Landis outsourced the product ownership to the supplier tells us that perhaps they probably misconceived the project as more of a technical exercise than a digital transformation (DX) exercise. This is a problem in many companies in how digital transformation is perceived even by the most senior management. The term used in a "lax" way that could imply a "technical makeover" or a "digitalization" engagement. In the past, many companies have relied on outsourced system integrators to carry out their technical work and from the previous innovation cycles, this would be standard practice. As we can see, the consequences were more than just a technical mishap.

The outsourcing relationship seems to have created a total dependency on the supplier to deliver the digital solution for Landis. But with the onset of DX, old relationships must change. The speed of digital innovation meant while Landis was confused about what was going on with DX in general, things even got out of control for Blue30. Given how central the project was to Landis' future operations, they really lacked the internal know-how to really understand what was at stake if things went wrong. Instead, they took their eye off the ball and let their supplier do the experimentation. Landis really needed to understand digital and get more involved with the engagement by leading some of the digital improvements themselves. This would have helped them manage the digital wave more easily in the future. By being aware of simple digital tool sets available, Landis could have avoided the delays, some of the high costs, and heavy reliance on the supplier.

As a legacy from the previous wave of innovation, the adoption of MS Office (Word, PowerPoint, and Excel) as the de facto digital tool in organizations has restricted companies from evolving their business tool sets to empower their teams to do some of the digital work themselves. By investigating a few simple digital tools, Landis could have saved a lot of time, resource effort, costs, internal headache, and achieved some digital transformation success on this engagement.

Further, these "alternative" tool sets have now been simplified in such a way that you don't need to be a proficient coder to create videos, manipulate data, or even develop a prototype.

Let's explore some tools that have become more accessible and could have empowered Landers Car Hire to take a leading role in their own digital transformation (DX) efforts, enabling their integrators to work for them rather than just with them. A case in point is in the design of the front end for the IPAD which cost over $100K. Could Landis have designed this themselves at a fraction of the cost?

In the following section, I will describe some digital tools to execute the work , and then in the next chapter, we will use them in a detailed tutorial to design a mobile/IPAD front end. Later on, after the chapters that focus on data mining and algorithms, we will take a step further and apply some simple tools to experiment with some data visualization and machine learning techniques.

As business owners, instead of relying solely on PowerPoint, we can consider using video-making tools to enrich and simplify our messages to get executive buy-in. Instead of using expensive UI data designers to simulate the user experience, we can create simple wireframes and prototypes for these apps ourselves using no-code tools. We can even understand data sets without relying solely on data analysts and even manipulate them without depending on data scientists through simple digital platforms.

Before we continue, take a moment to think about the tools you currently use and the capabilities you outsource to your partners. Imagine the potential time and cost savings and increased team engagement if you could handle some of the work internally. Are there any restrictions imposed by your firm that prevent you from exploring different digital tools?

When initiating the process of conceptualizing the IPAD using innovative digital toolsets, a pragmatic approach involves experimenting with various whiteboarding tools. By analyzing the Landis Car Hire front-end challenge, it becomes evident that collaborating on idea generation with business teams proves highly effective in shaping the optimal customer journey and significantly expediting the successful development of the application.

Let's start by looking at the tools for this.

Introducing Simplified Tools for Whiteboarding, Video Making, Wireframing, and Data Analysis

In today's market, there are numerous whiteboarding tools available. One highly practical tool I recommend is Miro (www.Miro.com). It belongs to a new generation of remote collaboration tools that facilitate idea sharing and real-time collaboration. With Miro, you can invite colleagues to collaborate with you, visually representing their focus on the screen.

These tools typically offer a free basic version for download, with additional subscription options for advanced features. Other tools with similar functionalities include Mural (www.mural.co), Invision (www.invisionapp.com), Lucidspark (www.lucidspark.com), and Whiteboard Fox (r5.Whiteboardfox.com). I encourage you to explore them when you have the time. The key limitations usually revolve around collaboration options and the number of simultaneous projects you can engage in.

Now, let's consider a scenario where Landis Car Hire assigns us the task of redesigning the front-end user journey for their messaging service, specifically for a mobile app. Once we have the desired look and feel, it becomes easier to guide developers in creating the "live experience."

One highly useful app for creating front-end prototypes and demonstrations is Marvel Apps. It belongs to a new breed of collaborative design platforms that allow wireframing, designing, prototyping, collaboration, and even whiteboarding. Other prototyping tools worth mentioning are Balsamiq, Invision, Figma, and Sketch. Limitations may vary in terms of collaboration options, specific prototyping features, image libraries, or the number of prototypes you can create. Many design platforms provide access to image libraries where you can search and download images for your prototype. Marvel Apps offers a user-friendly prototyping screen.

Video has been shown to increase content recall rates by up to 75% compared to traditional slideware. There are several video-making platforms available, operating on either a free subscription or a monthly fee basis. One of the best and simplest video-making tools I use is Lumen5 (www.Lumen5.com). Lumen5 falls under the category of low-code/no-code video-making tools, enabling you to present content typically found in PowerPoint presentations (such as problem statements, market opportunities, revenue projections, and business benefits) in a dynamic form using video imagery and simple text. Its plug-and-play benefits stem from its menu structure and its library of ready-made videos and graphic images courtesy of Unsplash (www.unsplash.com), which adds a professional touch to your presentations. Lumen5 also allows you to upload your own images and content through its interactive front-end, without requiring coding or video editing skills.

Working with data is crucial for effectiveness in a data-driven world. While MS Excel remains the go-to tool for data work, it does have limitations when handling large datasets and producing visualizations like dashboards. Fortunately, there are numerous low-code solutions available that reduce reliance on dedicated data scientists, enabling you to upload large datasets and create compelling visualizations for dashboards.

Among the many data visualization tools on the market, one I find particularly useful is MS Power BI. If you have a Microsoft Office 365 package, you should be able to try it for free.

Before moving forward, have a look at the links and play with these tools. In the next chapter, we will apply these tools to the Landers Car Hire example to develop the IPAD front end as well as look at ways to better visualize data.

Let's now dig deeper to understand what is data, why it is so important how it will play a central role in all our digital transformation (DX) fortunes.

Introducing Big Data, Data Warehousing, and the Data Lake

In the past 20 years, the way we store, manage, and analyze data has changed dramatically. We have moved from a world of mainframes and data warehouses, which were designed for structured (tabular) data and "what happened" analysis, to a world of cloud computing, unstructured data, and "what will happen" analysis. The main driver of this is the emergence of the data lake, which is a centralized repository for all of an organization's data, regardless of its format or structure.

The increase in computer-processing power, cloud-storage capacity and use, and network connectivity have led to a tidal wave of data being generated by businesses and individuals. This data is so large and complex that it cannot be processed using traditional methods. This new type of data is called "big data." Big data is being generated from a variety of sources, including social media, sensor data, and machine logs. This data can be used to gain insights into customer behavior, optimize business processes, and make better decisions. To understand the size of this "tidal wave," Figure 2-6 gives some figures for WhatsApp, Google searches, Facebook videos generated against the amount of information humans can process each day. This data is just the tip of the iceberg. The amount of data being generated is growing exponentially. In the next few years, we will see even more data being generated from new sources, such as self-driving cars, and smart machines.

Application	Size
WhatsApp Messages	41M messages/min
Google Searches	6 Bn /yr
Facebook Videos Posted	2.7M Videos / Yr
Total information a human processes each day	34GB/day

Figure 2-6. Examples of Speed of Data Generated by Internet Services Against the Amount of Data Humans Can Process Each Day

The question then becomes where is the best place to store and harness such the data? A laptop typically can hold around 32 GB of memory. Even a typical server in a data warehouse can only hold around 2 Terabytes of data. Therefore, it is difficult for data warehouses to keep up. The sheer volume and variety of this data, the speed at which information is generated and transmitted and its ever shorter currency – that is, utility for a defined period of time – within internal and external networks has necessitated new ways to store, retrieve, and harness data.

Therefore today, over 80% of all data processing takes place in remote servers away from the traditional company offices and premises. These mega data centers can hold many "000"s of servers and together form the basis of "The Cloud."

We are now liberated in the sense we don't need to know where the data is physically located – as long as it is secure. One critical change has been the creation of data lakes. A phrase first coined in 2011 to describe a repository of data stored in its natural (or raw format), which can include data originating in diverse forms, including email, real-time sensor readings, financial transactions, images, videos, and audio files. This capability has led to the development of concepts such as digital twins.

Figure 2-7. What a Data Warehouse Looks Like. Source: `https://datablog.zeus.vision/2017/06/02/que-es-data-warehouse/`

Unlike in a data warehouse shown in Figure 2-7, where information is structured, the data lake allows data to be stored in its raw form – rendering it more economical and efficient for storing and accessing large data sets. Figure 2-8 highlights the differences between the two.

	Data Warehouse	Data Lake
Data Structure	• Transformed, cleaned, and integrated before being loaded • Follows a relational database model	• Data stored in its raw, unprocessed form • More flexible for exploration and analysis by data scientists
Data Processing	• Uses an extract, transform and load process that fits into a predefined schema	• Uses an extract, transform and load where the data is stored as is and processed as needed
Data Usage and Analytics	• Suitable for BI tools and traditional reporting	• Raw data form enables data scientists to carry out more flexible ad-hoc tasks and queries
Data Governance and Security	• Stricter governance since data is pre-processed into a schema	• Looser data governance as data can be stored in many formats
Storage cost and Scalability	• Expensive to scale as data volumes increase	• Can take advantage of cost-effective storage solutions, such as distributed file systems and cloud based storage options

Figure 2-8. Data Warehouse vs. Data Lake Comparison

Businesses and Consumers lease memory space on these servers as it is cheaper and more effective than housing and managing the data locally.

To plan for future growth, build new products and revenue streams, rationalize operations, and compete in evolving markets, we need to embrace the data not only within our businesses but also from big data sets across the web.

Given its vital importance, let's look at the fundamentals of data.

What Does Data Look Like?

Each file, video, document, and image in our laptops, phones, smartwatches, etc., can be and is represented by a (very long) series of numbers. We store this data in binary digit form of 0's and 1's. This is called the bit system. The way value is associated with each 1 or 0 is based on their position in a sequence. So any number or character can be represented as a sequence of 1's and 0's. A typical character on a keyboard is composed of 8 bits which is called a byte. These are summarized in Figure 2-9.

For example, the number "1" is 00000001; the number "10" is 00001010; the number "100" is 01100100 in bits, respectively.

In Chapter 4, we will look at an emerging digital technology, quantum computing, which uses a different mechanism, called qubits, that enhances computing power further.

Data Fundamentals

Data Storage
- Smallest increment of data information is a bit.
- 8 bits make a Byte.
- A character like 'A' is made up as a Byte

Network Speed
- Measured in bits per second
- Typical unit is Mbps (Mega bits per second)

Figure 2-9. Summary of the Data Fundamentals

How Does It Build into a Data Lake?

Network speeds are measured in bits per second. The higher the bit rate, the more data can be transferred (e.g., downloaded or uploaded). The typical unit of network data transfer speeds is Mbps (Megabits per second).

To understand the data velocity, consider the waterfall of data being posted from Google, Facebook and how much information we as humans process each day. See some examples in Figure 2-10.

Data Velocity

Application	Size
WhatsApp Messages	41M messages/min
Google Searches	6 Bn /yr
Facebook Videos Posted	2.7M Videos / Yr
Total information a human processes each day	34GB/day

Figure 2-10. Data Velocity

For context, a streamed Netflix movie takes up 4 GBytes of data (4 billion bytes) if it is stored locally. Also, Facebook messages generated 4 Peta Bytes of data per day in 2020.

Data Volume

Application	Size
Typical Netflix Movie	4GB
Total Social Media Messages Posted in 2020	4PB
Human Memory Storage	2.9PB
Expected Total Data in the World by 2022	74 ZB

Figure 2-11. Data Volume

Another component is the variety of data forms. We categorize data into three types: structured data that we typically see in tables; unstructured data that we see in images; and data that is in between the two termed semi-structured, where unstructured data has some form identifier such as a date stamp. Approximately 85% of all data we use is in the unstructured form. Figure 2-12 gives some examples.

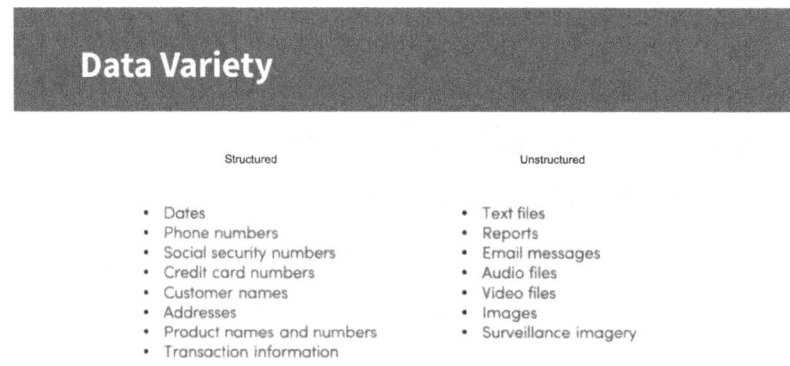

Data Variety

Structured
- Dates
- Phone numbers
- Social security numbers
- Credit card numbers
- Customer names
- Addresses
- Product names and numbers
- Transaction information

Unstructured
- Text files
- Reports
- Email messages
- Audio files
- Video files
- Images
- Surveillance imagery

Figure 2-12. Structured vs. Unstructured Data

The ability to use data science to not only describe what happened but use predictive tools to understand why it happened, to then predict what will happen to then dictate how to make something happen is the level of maturity of the digital leaders. Figure 2-13 expands on how data is used to achieve this. We look in more detail at the algorithms that allow us to make data predictions from these data types in a chapter on data mining and algorithms.

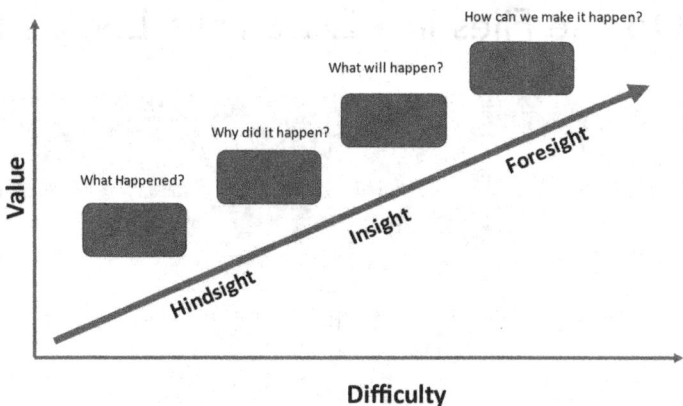

How can we make it happen?

What will happen?

Why did it happen?

What Happened?

Value

Foresight

Insight

Hindsight

Difficulty

Figure 2-13. Evolution of Data Analysis

Today the way companies use the data lake is key to how to succeed in business. The most successful companies in recent years have been termed "big data" firms from the way they managed to utilize the data lake components to drive business success. While these firms have had an advantage – it doesn't mean that traditional companies cannot successfully change their mindset and create value using data.

However, many companies that have either done nothing or have been slow to react to big data have struggled to grow with many failing and going out of existence.

The ways we can use data to help out decision-making is not just confined to business, we use data-driven decisions tools in our everyday lives. Anyone with a smartphone should be able to provide some examples.

Can you think of applications in your daily life that provide intelligent recommendations, saving you time and effort?

We have looked at the power data has to provide unique insights to help us analyze, predict, and advise and on how to be successful, even business owners need to be more conversant with using data. To build insight, we need to mine and extract data sets from the data repository, and the formats are different. For the non-technical business owner, big data and data lakes may sound like challenging new concepts – in size and complexity, but we don't need to be afraid of the information that is contained therein.

Let's take a look.

What Do the Files in a Data Lake Look Like?

Data Formats

Application	Example
Documentation and Scripts	.htm, html, .xml, .txt, .pdf, odt, .doc/docx, .xls
Video	.mp4, .jp2, .mj2
Audio	.mp3, .wav
Quantitative Tabular Data	.csv, .tab, .xls, .mdb, ods
Image	.pdf, .tif, .jpeg
Data Retrieval	.JSON, ORC, AVRO

https://guides.library.oregonstate.edu/research-data-services/data-management-types-format – toc=Data%20Types%20%26%20File%20Formats%20%20TYPE_Hyperlink%20%30 %20%20%20man%20rows %20

Figure 2-14. Information Types in a Data Lake

There are many types of data stored in the data lake. Some of the data files we receive will be familiar like pdf, .doc, etc. Figure 2-15 summarizes the types. Some files like JSON, ORC, AVRO have specific data retrieval and storage benefits, but the key data type more business users need to be aware of is the .CSV file.

A Comma Separated Values (CSV) file is a plain text file that contains a list of data. These files are often used for exchanging data between different applications. For example, databases and contact managers often support CSV files.

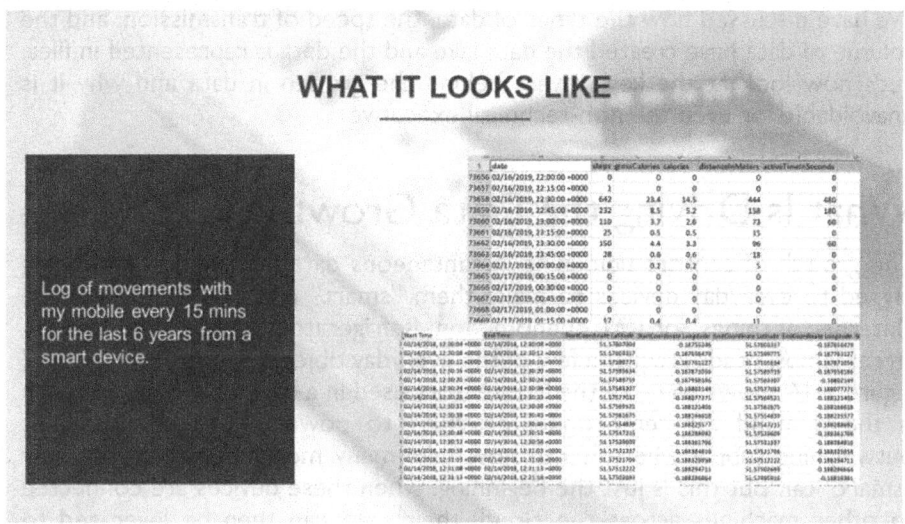

Figure 2-15. Sample CSV File

Figure 2-15 shows an extract from a CSV file. CSV files may also be called Character Separated Values or Comma Delimited Value (or files). Most commonly the comma character is used to separate (or delimit) data, but others such as semicolons can be used. The key thing with CSV files is you can easily export complex data from one application, and then import the data into another.

A CSV file has a simple structure. If we assume a contacts list is separated by commas, you'd get a file containing text like this:

> Name,Email,Phone Number,Address
>
> Bob Smith,bob@example.com,123-456-7890,123 Fake Street
>
> Mike Jones,mike@example.com,098-765-4321,321 Fake Avenue

The first line is usually the headers, but this is not essential, and some may use quotation marks to surround each bit of data.

The resulting data is human-readable, within passive text editors such as Notepad, or spreadsheet programs such as Microsoft Excel.

In the Landers Car Hire case example, there is a .csv file tutorial that allows the reader to download and view via the GitHub link. Try and take a look at some of the fields and upload into MS Power BI for the tutorial.

We have discussed how the types of data, the speed of transmission, and the volume of data have created the data lake and the data is represented in files. Let's now look at the key drivers behind the growth in data and why it is unavoidable for even the non-technical executive.

What Is Driving the Data Growth?

The growth of sensors uploading instantaneous data information and being tagged to everyday devices to make them "smart" is the first stage of the "Internet of things" or IOT phenomenon. Refrigerators, cars, coffee makers, street lamps, roads are just a few of the everyday objects being made "smart." Figure 2-16 shows some of the IoT sensors used in a smart building. So much is the demand for semi-conductor chips to power these devices, it is outweighing supply where it can now take many months to receive a new "smart" car. But this is just the beginning; when these devices are connected to other machines across the cloud, their data can then be leveraged to provide even further value and fuel even more data.

In 2023, every second, 127 new IOT devices connect to the Internet. Today there are approximately 27 billion devices connected to the Internet. By 2030, this figure will rise to 100 billion devices. The amount of data generated by IoT devices, further fueling the data lake. (Source: www.mckinsey.com/ industries/semiconductors/our-insights/whats-new-with- the-internet-of-things)

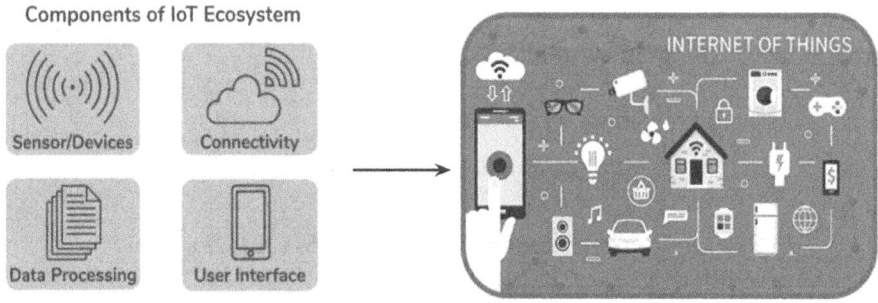

Figure 2-16. Smart Devices. Source: https://dmexco.com/stories/thats-why-the- internet-of-things-needs-artificial-intelligence/

In cities, for example, sensors can report on various environmental conditions such as air quality, traffic congestion, lighting, and even communicate with consumer devices such as cars to guide decision-making.

Sensors are also being used to replicate the behavior of physical objects digitally. This digital representation is called a digital twin. Enterprises today can replicate very complex machines such as oil rigs and wind turbines and simulate their performance without having to use the actual equipment themselves, thus saving huge costs and time if there is a failure.

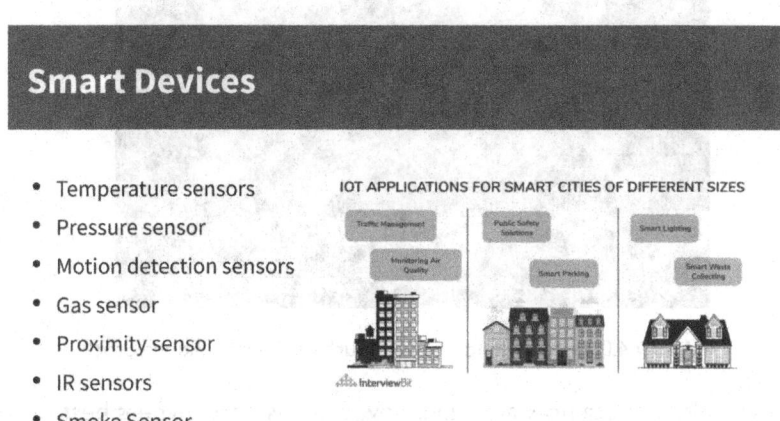

Smart Devices

- Temperature sensors
- Pressure sensor
- Motion detection sensors
- Gas sensor
- Proximity sensor
- IR sensors
- Smoke Sensor

Figure 2-17. Examples of Devices in a Smart Building

A new sub-category of IOT is Industrial IOT (IIOT). IIoT focuses specifically on industrial applications such as manufacturing or agriculture. Smart machines with simulations are being used in predictive maintenance to reduce costs and improve overall operational efficiency, fueling a new revolution termed Industry 4.0. Figure 2-18 shows a digital twin of a turbine that allows a user to simulate exact scenarios on the turbine remotely without affecting operations.

Figure 2-18. Industry 4.0 digital twin for a Smart Turbine. Source: Adobe Stock

With this wealth of data now available, how can business owners best process this data and derive insights without being reliant on a data analyst or a data scientist?

Introducing Data Visualization

In parallel with the growth of big data has been the growth of data visualization techniques. Data visualization is the representation of data through the use of graphics, such as charts, plots, infographics, and even animations. Visualizations can help you find insights in your data that are difficult, or impossible, to extract by viewing the raw data.

In a short time, visualization has evolved from the simple graphs that can be generated in MS Excel to trend sparklines and dynamic dashboards. Fortunately, you don't need to be a data expert or statistician to derive such data insights.

There are some very good sites such as Statista (www.statista.com) and Visual Capitalist (www.visualcapitalist.com) that provide ready-made visual content that you can use.

Here are some examples of the ready-made visuals or data files you can download.

Number of monthly active Facebook users worldwide as of 1st quarter 2023
(in millions)

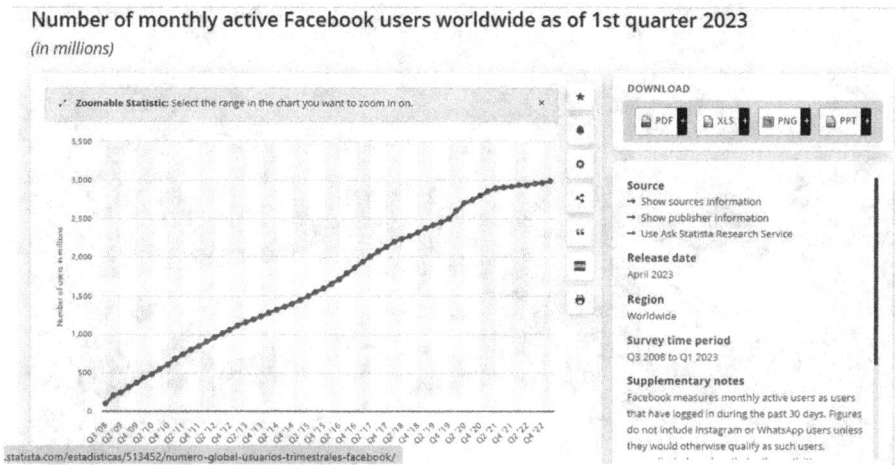

Figure 2-19. Number of Facebook Users: Source Statista

Visualcapitalist.com allows users to use the visuals for free if you present them in their original form. The following visualization compares the market cap of Apple compared to GDP of countries.

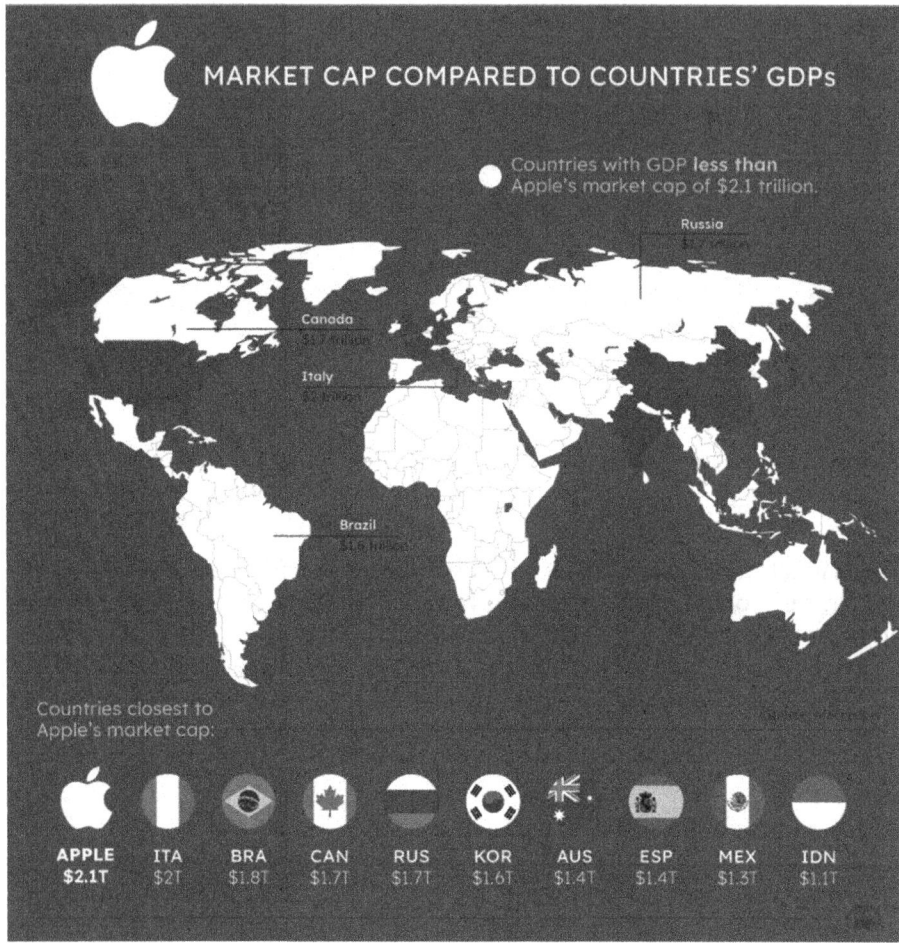

Figure 2-20. Market Cap of Apple Compared to Countries. Source: Visualcapitalist

We can also create visualizations ourselves. In Chapter 3, the case study guides the reader through simple visualizations using Power BI. A key aspect when working effectively with data analysts and scientists on your own data is developing an approach that permits definition and address of simple questions that are possible to be addressed with the available data that generates insight that may challenge assumptions. Getting carried away and focusing on the best-looking visualizations rather than the question, as well as taking the time to check the data and the approach generating the visualization can easily lead to issues that could be critical. Not all new visualizations available add value. They must assist in answering a question – rather than create new ones. It is critical to ensure you understand a visualization – whatever it is.

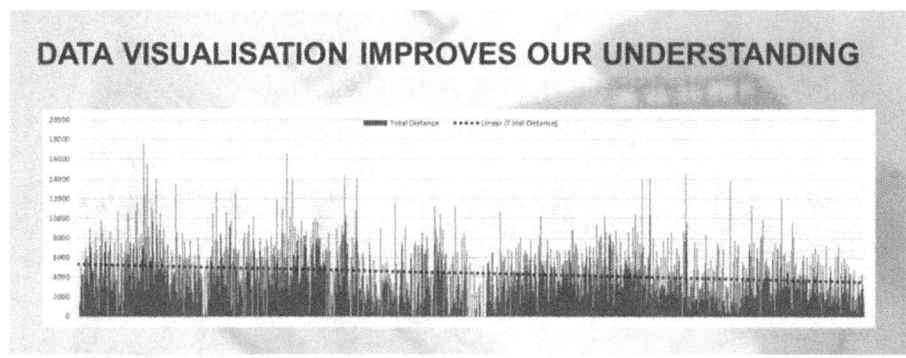

Figure 2-21. Visualizing Data sets

Figure 2-21 shows a data profile of movements over many years with a trendline showing the average daily movement. Through the use of visualization, we can see that there are gaps in the data which can lead us to ask different questions than a data scientist that could be vital to a successful operation. For example, Why was the sensor showing "zero" on these days? Does the trendline ignore the gaps? Is there a problem with the sensor? We will revisit the Landers Car Hire example and derive some questions on the data set received.

On the other hand, there is the old adage, "lies, damned lies, and statistics" and similarly bad or misleading data can be hard to uncover when the visualization is attractive and unchecked. Even a visualization cannot disguise bad data.

A classic example of this was the use of Google Maps by the Nicaraguan Army in 2013 that incorrectly identified territory, leading to Nicaragua invading a Costa Rican Island! (www.cnet.com/tech/mobile/google-maps-mishap-leads-to-nicaragua-inadvertently-invading-costa-rica/) See Figure 2-22.

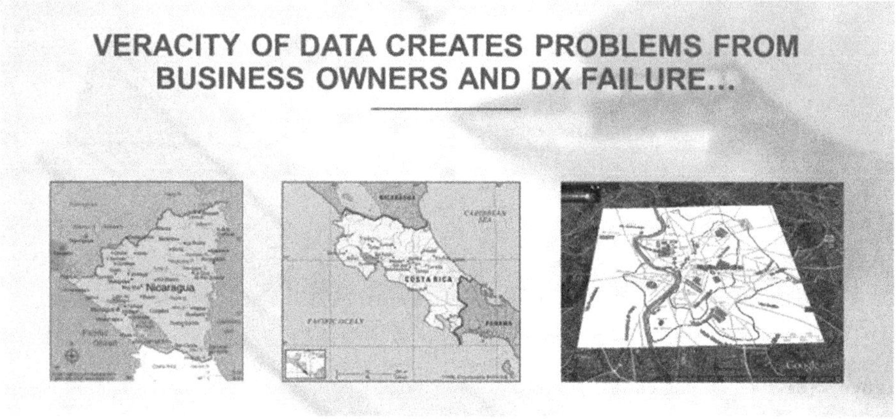

Figure 2-22. Nicaragua/Costa Rica Border According to Googlemaps and Bing

There are some core principles we can apply to integrate any visualization:

Harvard Kennedy School has produced design guidelines to help in presenting a visualization (www.hks.harvard.edu). In essence, the rules are that the visualization must

- Be truthful to the data presented (baselines start from zero, no misleading trendlines)

- Target the information to the audience (expertise, key questions addressed)

- Choose the right chart

- Present the right insights and key facts

Before moving forward,

- Do you recall any great data visualizations?

- Can you remember what elements made it compelling?

- Did you feel any need to challenge the data?

How Can Business Owners Best Challenge Assumptions Driven by Data Scientists?

As we will uncover in Chapter 4, the approach to digital transformation efforts has been led by data analysts and engineers looking for business initiatives. An overreliance and belief that data visualizations and data outputs driven by data analysts are inherently correct has been a major root cause of digital transformation failures.

We need to turn this around and let the businesses, through a more insight-driven approach, drive the technology.

For any delivery, the data analyst plays a crucial role as a key collaborator in the visualization delivery process. Their primary responsibility is to understand the business insights needed and lead the transformation of raw data into valuable information for decision-making purposes. This involves various functions such as gathering business requirements, collecting, processing, and cleaning the data. The ultimate goal is to extract insights from the information by presenting it in a visual format. Therefore, the decision on how the information is presented becomes essential in conveying the desired message effectively. With the onset of no-code/low-code tools, we don't need to fully outsource this responsibility but can become partners in checking the data is valid, the messages and insights are correct.

By knowing the purpose of what we want to do with the data and knowing how important each data component is, we can direct the analysts to what visualization works best for the question at hand. There are some guidelines on when to use a visualization. Let's take a look. Figure 2-23 shows some of the graphs.

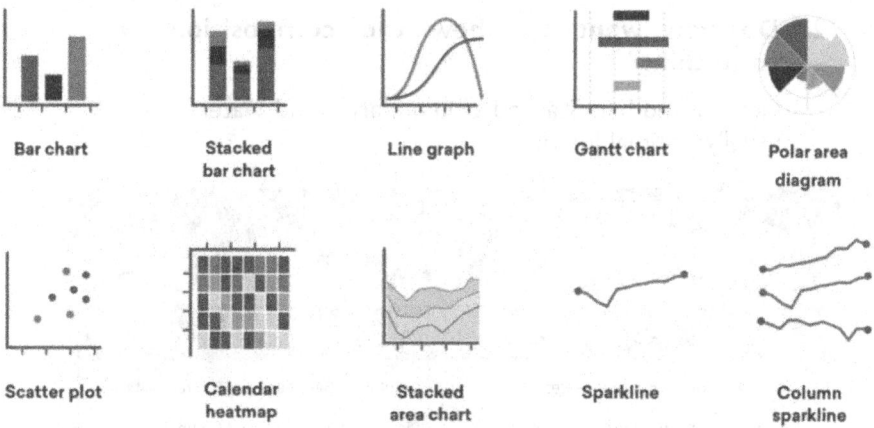

Figure 2-23. A Plethora of Data Visualizations. Which Graph to Use?

Here is a quick description of the most common types:

- Bar charts: Perhaps the most common misconception about charts is that more is better. Bar charts are a simple and effective way to look at cohort analyses, comparisons, and trends that most people understand.

- Line charts: A line chart is an effective graph formed from a series of data points connected by the eponymous line. They are often used to show developments over time and identify trends.

- Tables: Tables are great for detailed information with different units of measure, which may be difficult to represent easily in a graph or chart that needs attention.

- Area charts: Area charts are ideal for multiple data series with part to whole relationships, or for individual series representing a physically countable set.

Once you know the purpose of the visualization, the data analyst can better do the collecting, cleaning, and processing of the data to answer your business questions.

When deciding which visualization to use, here are some questions to ask:

1. **Are you comparing values?**

   Column, bar, pie, line, and scatter plots are usually optimal for this.

2. **Do you want to show the composition of something?**

   Pie, stacked bar. Stacked column, area, and waterfall are usually optimal for this.

Key Questions

Header	Header
Are you comparing values?	Column, Bar, Pie, Line, Scatter Plots
Do you want to show the composition of something?	Pie, Stacked Bar. Stacked Column, Area, Waterfall
Do you want to know the distribution of your data ?	Scatter plots, line, column and bar
how a data set performed during a specific time period?	Line and Column charts
Do you want to better understand the relationship between value sets?	Scatter, Bubble charts or line charts

Figure 2-24. Summary of Key Questions

3. Do you want to understand the distribution of your data ? Scatter plots, line, column, and bar work are usually optimal for this.

4. Do you want to know more information about how a data set performed during a specific time period?

   There are specific chart types that do extremely well. Line and column charts are usually optimal for this.

5. Do you want to better understand the relationship between value sets? Relationship charts are suited to showing how one variable relates to one or numerous different variables. You could use this to show how something positively affects, has no effect, or negatively affects another variable. Scatter, bubble charts, or line charts are usually optimal for this.

   Figure 2-25 has a decision-making flowchart to help decide which graph to use.

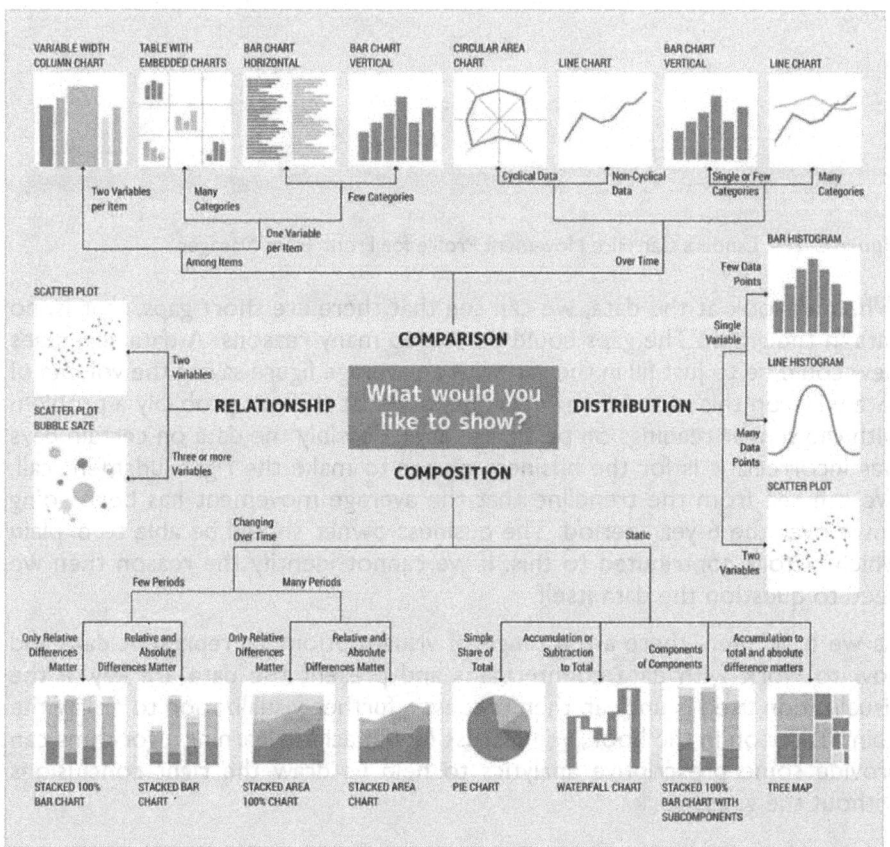

Figure 2-25. Which Graph to Use. Source: https://alexgonzalezc.dev/posts/data-visualization-principles.html

As we saw earlier, seeing gaps in the data, creating trendlines, and performing basic stats, that is, Measures of Central Tendency: (Mean, Median, Mode); Measures of Dispersion: (Variance and Standard Deviation)

Measures of Position: (Quartiles, Quantiles, and Inter-quartiles) you can discover if the data set makes sense. We will look further into these tools to help you ensure the data outputs have a sound grounding later on in the chapter.

Let us now return to our case example of Landers Car Hire and see if we can derive insights from the data.

Case Example – Landers Car Hire

Let's take a look at the movement profile of the Front Team Manager from Landis Car Hire. This data file is located in the GitHub directory.

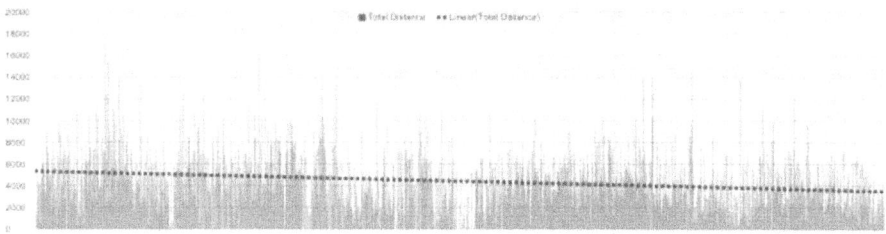

Figure 2-26. Landers Car Hire Movement Profile for Front Team Manager

When we look at the data, we can see that there are short gaps, that is, no data in the graph. The gaps could be due to many reasons. A data scientist's view could be to just fill in the gap with an average figure saying the volume of data will iron this out. An engineer may say that there is probably a problem with the sensor readings on particular days. Possibly the data on certain days was incorrect. It is for the business owner to make the right judgment call. We can see from the trendline that the average movement has been going down over the 6-year period. The business owner should be able to explain which factors contributed to this. If we cannot identify the reason then we need to question the data itself.

As we have seen, there are a range of visual options to represent data and how to work with data counterparts and present the data are key. If the visualization used is unclear, then request a further visualization to clarify the point. Later on in the book, will discuss how machine learning algorithms can provide some prescriptive analytics to help us draw the right conclusions without the guesswork.

Have you come across departments with different interpretations of the same data set? It could the data team, marketing, sales, or operations. How do you make the decision call on which viewpoint is right?

We touched on trendlines and gaps in data giving us clues, but a knowledge of basic statistics can really help.

Introducing Basic Statistics

Statistical analysis is an important part of quantitative research and is a powerful tool to inform and validate data interpretation. The term statistics may bring back memories of math lessons at school dealing with the collection, analysis, interpretation, and presentation of masses of numerical data. Simply put, statistics is the field of mathematics that can be used to characterize data.

Mean, Mode, and Median

The most simple statistics are those that describe an average – termed *descriptive statistics*:

> Mean: The mean or average is the sum of all elements (values) divided by the number of elements (values).

> Median: The median is the middle value, such that there is an equal number of values above and below it in a given data set.

> Mode: The mode is the value that appears most frequently in a given data set.

Figure 2-27 gives some examples of their use.

- Human Resources: Use **mean** salaries from data sets to know salary to offer new employees
- Estate Agents: Use **median** house prices to get a idea of a typical house price as the median is less influenced by super expensive homes in the neighbourhood
- Marketers: Calculate the **mode** of an ad format (newspaper, internet, TV, radio, etc) used to know which ad types companies use the most.

Figure 2-27. Uses of Mean, Median, and Mode

Standard Deviation and Quartiles

Standard deviation is the variation or dispersion of a set of values from the mean of those values. It gives an idea of stability of a data set around a mean The further the data points are away from the mean, the higher the standard deviation. Figure 2-28 shows the standard deviation.

Standard Deviation : Spread of

   numbers from the mean

Higher spread: Greater data dispersion

   from the mean

Lower spread: Lower data dispersion

   from the mean

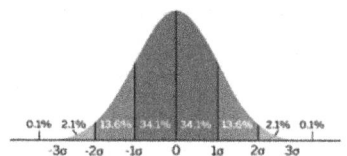

Figure 2-28. Standard Devation

Quartiles and the interquartile range provide information about the central tendency and spread of the data. Quartiles divide a dataset into four equal parts, representing the distribution of the data. The three quartiles are denoted as Q1, Q2 (which is the median), and Q3. The interquartile range (IQR) measures the spread of the middle 50% of the data and is calculated as the difference between the third quartile (Q3) and the first quartile (Q1).

- Quartiles, Quantiles,
   or interquartiles can
   assist in decision
   making

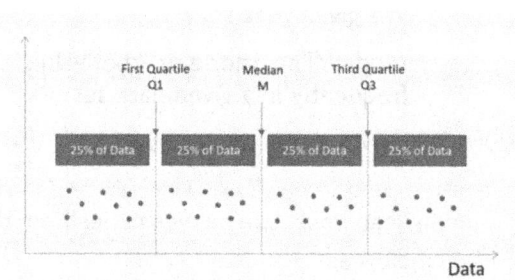

Figure 2-29. Quartiles

In human resources, departments use quartiles to benchmark themselves against other companies. For example, the median company pay for a given position is set at the first quartile of the top 20 companies in that region.

Statistics and Parameters

It is crucial to distinguish between the terms "statistics" and "parameters," as they are sometimes used interchangeably by data experts.

A statistic refers to a specific data point derived from a subset of your overall population, known as a sample. It represents a numerical value calculated from the sample data. On the other hand, a parameter represents a characteristic or attribute of the entire population. It is a piece of data that pertains to the entire population rather than just a subset.

In most cases, it is impractical or impossible to collect data from the entire population. Therefore, analysts rely on samples taken from the population to make informed estimations about the population as a whole. By analyzing the sample data, they can calculate statistics and use them as proxies for the corresponding population parameters. These statistics serve as educated guesses or estimates about the population parameters, helping to draw conclusions or make predictions about the larger population based on the available sample information.

Introducing Business Intelligence and Data Management

Business intelligence or BI is the process by which enterprises use strategies and technologies for analyzing historical or current (real-time), with the objective of improving decision-making and thus providing a competitive advantage.

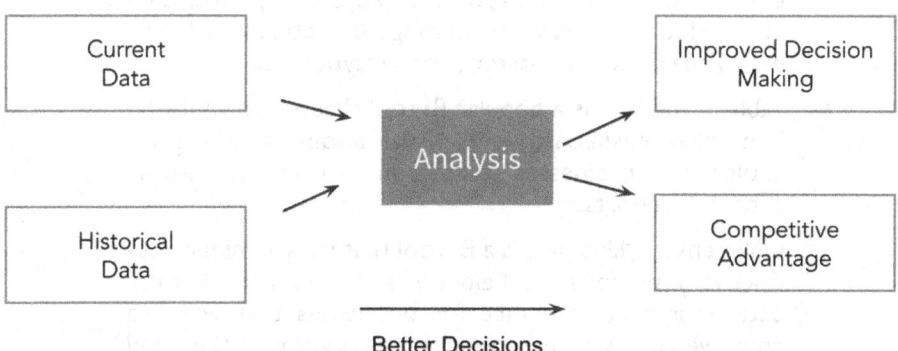

Figure 2-30. BI Intelligence Rationale

The need for BI was derived from the concept that managers with inaccurate or incomplete information will tend, on average, to make poorer decisions than if they had better information.

BI tools and software come in a wide variety of forms. Let's take a quick look at some common types of BI solutions.

- Spreadsheets: Spreadsheets like Microsoft Excel and Google Docs are some of the most widely used BI tools.

- Reporting software: Reporting software is used to report, organize, filter, and display data.

- Data visualization software: Data visualization software translates datasets into easy-to-read, visually appealing graphical representations to quickly gain insights.

- Data mining tools: Data mining tools "mine" large amounts of data for patterns using classical statistics and increasingly artificial intelligence/machine learning. We will look at some of these later in the book.

Online Analytical Processing (OLAP) is a type of business intelligence (BI) software that allows users to analyze data from multiple perspectives. OLAP systems are designed to handle large amounts of data and to provide fast response times. For example, a sales manager might use an OLAP system to analyze sales data to see which products are selling well and which regions are generating the most sales. This information can then be used to make decisions about marketing, product development, and pricing.

There are many BI tool sets on the market today, each with its own strengths and weaknesses. Some of the most popular BI tool sets include:

- Microsoft Power BI: Power BI is a cloud-based BI tool that is easy to use and can be deployed on-premises or in the cloud. It offers a wide range of features, including data visualization, reporting, and analytics.

- Tableau: Tableau is a popular BI tool that is known for its interactive dashboards and visualizations. It is a good choice for businesses that want to create visually appealing reports.

- Qlik Sense: Qlik Sense is a BI tool that uses a unique data discovery platform to help users find insights in their data. It is a good choice for businesses that want to empower users to explore their data without the need for technical expertise.

- SAP BusinessObjects: SAP BusinessObjects is a suite of BI tools that offers a wide range of features, including data integration, data warehousing, and analytics. It is a good choice for large enterprises that need a comprehensive BI solution.

- IBM Cognos Analytics: IBM Cognos Analytics is a BI tool that offers a wide range of features, including data integration, data warehousing, and analytics. It is a good choice for large enterprises that need a comprehensive BI solution.

For the scope of this book, we will look at Power BI and its differences to MS Excel and the reasons it makes sense to try new BI tools.

Microsoft Excel has been the go-to reporting tool for businesses for many years. In 2015, Microsoft released Power BI – a "business intelligence" tool that offers more powerful analytics and reporting features. It makes it easier to visualize and understand complex data. Business users have gradually started to gravitate to its benefits in how they analyze and present their data.

Power BI is designed specifically for systematically analyzing data and sharing insights. Thanks to its ability to carry out faster experimentation with visualizations, managing calculations and statistical functions across extensive datasets, it is clear that if used appropriately, Power BI delivers far greater insights into data than Excel.

- Excel is used to organize data, transform it, and perform mathematical operations and calculations. On the other hand, Power BI was conceived as a business intelligence and data visualization tool for businesses.

- Excel has limitations in the amount of data it can work with and slows down with large data files. In contrast, Power BI can handle much larger amounts of data.

- Power BI can connect to a large number of data sources, while Excel's connectivity capacity is limited. Also, unlike Excel, Power BI can be easily used from mobile devices.

- Power BI has faster processing than Excel. Power BI dashboards are more visually appealing, interactive, and customizable than those in Excel.

- Power BI is a more powerful tool than Excel in terms of comparison between tables, reports, or data files.

- Power BI is more user-friendly and easy to use than Excel.

Dashboarding

If you want to convey crucial information to decision-makers in the easiest and most effective way possible, you need to embrace the power of interactive dashboards and learn how to create a dashboard. A dashboard offers at-a-glance insights based on key performance indicators (KPIs) and is an intuitive and visually pleasing way to engage and interpret data. Critically, they facilitate the evaluation of real-time data and offer a more dynamic approach than MS PowerPoint or the numbers-without-a-story approach of MS Excel.

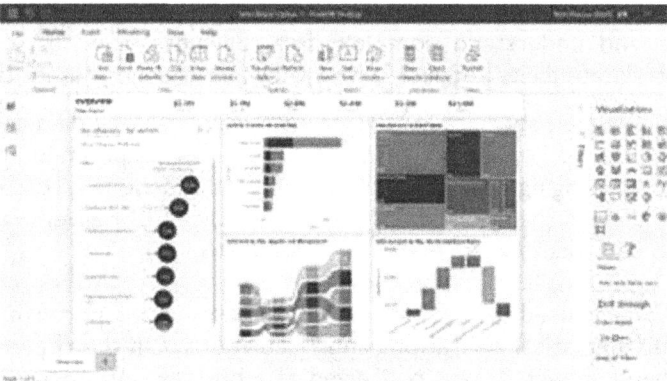

Figure 2-31. Sample Data Visualization

Let's summarize with some general rules of thumb of what to do and avoid when considering how to create dashboards:

DO'S

- DO build dashboards that focus on the needs of your audience.

- DO keep your dashboards as simple, clean, and minimalist as you can, while also including all of the most important KPIs.

- DO make sure that your final dashboard is better than your audience's previous method of viewing their KPIs.

- DO tell a story, as stories are the easiest way to make sense of data.

DON'Ts

- DON'T clutter your dashboard with too much data. This is the number one rule to follow! Too much data = too hard to use = waste of time.

- DON'T use colors that are very similar in brightness to your main colors – color-blind people won't be able to use your dashboard.

Conclusion

In Chapter I, we introduced the concept of digital transformation and explored some of the key drivers behind it. In this chapter, we took a closer look at one of the most important drivers of digital transformation: data.

Data is the fuel that drives digital transformation. It is used to understand customers, identify new opportunities, and improve operational efficiency. In today's digital world, businesses are generating more data than ever before. This data can be used to gain insights into customer behavior, identify trends, and make better decisions.

However, data is only valuable if it can be used effectively. This requires a strong understanding of data analytics and business intelligence tools. Non-technical executives can play a key role in ensuring that data is used effectively by understanding the basics of data analytics and business intelligence.

By understanding data analytics and business intelligence, non-technical executives can ask the right questions, make informed decisions, and track the progress of digital transformation initiatives. They can also communicate the value of data clearly to stakeholders and partners.

By studying the tutorial in Chapter 3, we can bring digital tools to life and see practically how they can help you be more data centric in your day-to-day endeavors. In Chapter 4, we will discuss how to put the problem before the technology and align business outcomes to digital transformation projects to ensure we can succeed with our digital endeavors.

Improving Productivity with New Digital Toolsets

In Chapter 2, we explored the rapid pace of innovation and various digital tool sets that enhance our comprehension of big data, digital principles, and data manipulation. Building a mentality of acquiring new skills and shedding outdated knowledge is fundamental to being effective in this space. Being comfortable with new digital tools and exploring and practicing with new tool sets should be integral to other day-to-day activities to succeed. In the following chapters, we will apply some simple tool sets to develop a mobile app loyalty solution for the Landis Car Hire case example we discussed in Chapter 2. We will harness the sensor data from Landis Car Hire, as provided in the Appendix, to extract valuable insights regarding the showroom and forecourt facility's staff utilization. By using this data we hope to enhance the efficiency of showroom operations and the performance of our staff.

© Attul Sehgal 2024
A. Sehgal, *Demystifying Digital Transformation*,
https://doi.org/10.1007/978-1-4842-9499-4_3

In this chapter, we will look at ways to

- Carry out brainstorming with teams using Miro
- Create wireframes using Marvel
- Make Video Summaries using Lumen5
- Mine Data using Power BI
- Create Data Visualizations using Power BI

In a later chapter, we will explore low-code AI tools to help us build further competencies. So let's get started!

Whiteboarding Using Miro

To begin, let's utilize the Miro tool (www.miro.com) for brainstorming ideas. Anyone can access its basic functions for free by registering for an account. Additionally, there's a Miro app available for use on smartphones for brainstorming when on the move.

Upon opening Miro, you'll find an impressive splash of free board templates, such as Mind maps, flowcharts, 2:2 Prioritization matrix, and Kanban frameworks (Figure 3-1) and various strategy templates, which can greatly aid the brainstorming process. The standout feature of Miro is its real-time board-sharing capability, enabling virtual brainstorming with all team members contributing, and their inputs visible to the entire team. Now, let's delve deeper into the specific tools we'll use to craft our solution.

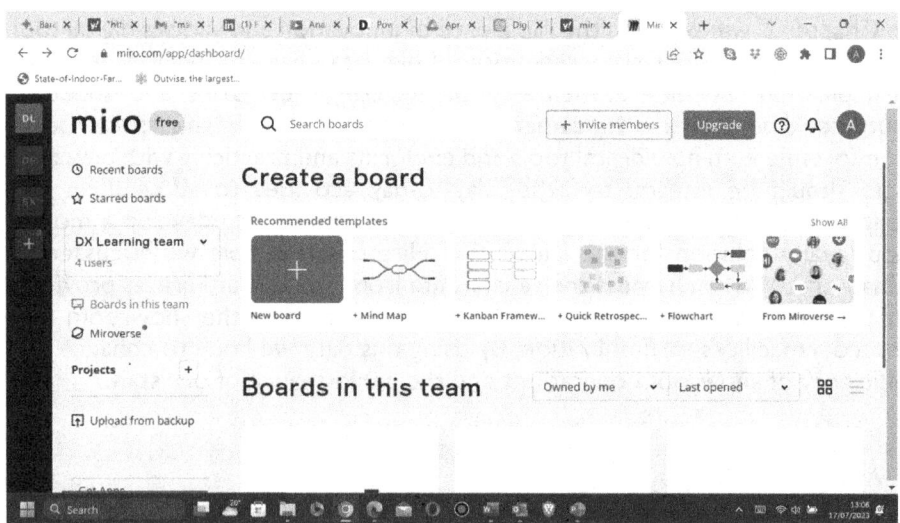

Figure 3-1. Miro Opening Screen

When we move to the "Create a Board" screen with our cursor and select a new board on the Miro tool, we see a screen page as shown in Figure 3-2. On the left side, there are a number of features that we can select to create our user experience. If you move your cursor on to them they provide details of what each icon can do. The second icon from the bottom, as shown in Figure 3-3, has a number of wireframing elements and standard icons that a lot of mobile apps use when you select the icon from the submenu.

Figure 3-2. Miro New Project Screen

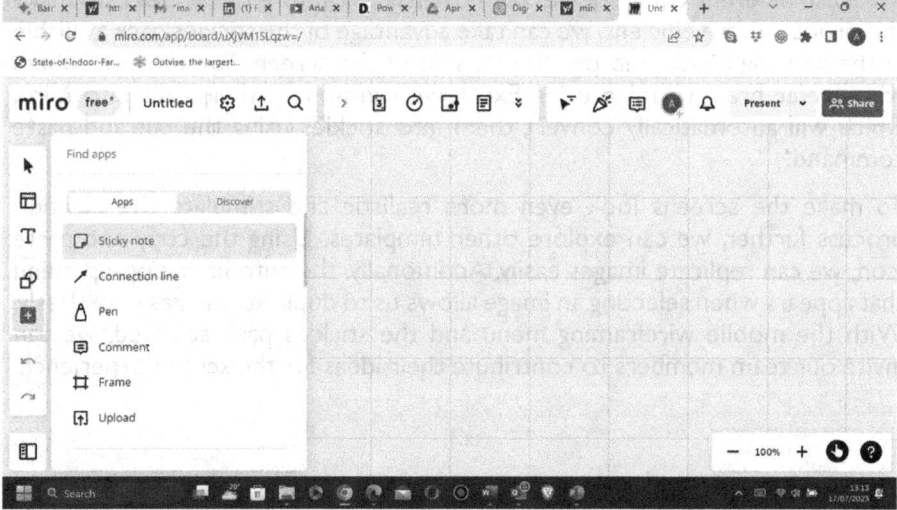

Figure 3-3. Miro Apps Menu

In our illustration, we will employ the tool set and pre-designed building blocks to construct the front-end concepts for the Landis Car Hire loyalty tool mobile app. Our design will encompass a sign-in page, a welcoming page, a menu options page, and finally, a community chat page. These components will form the foundation of our app, offering a seamless and user-friendly experience for the customers.

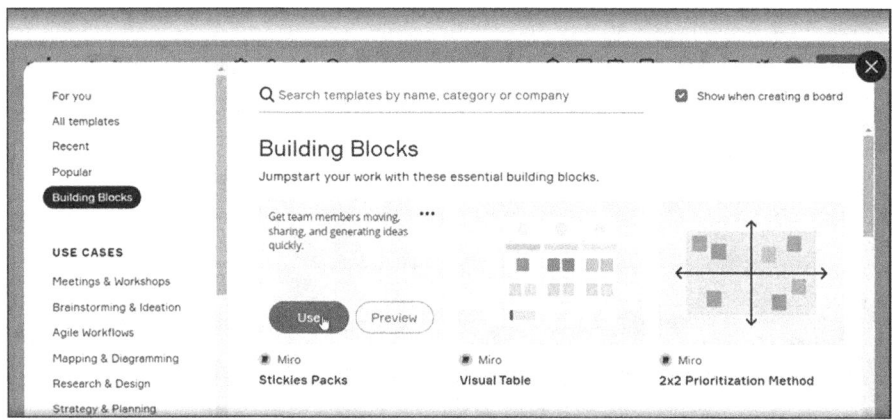

Figure 3-4. Ready-Made Building Blocks – Stickies Pack

To begin crafting the front-end mobile app experience, specifically the screen journeys for the loyalty tool, we'll start by selecting the mobile app wireframing elements icon and using an iPhone icon as a starting point for brainstorming.

Next, we'll create a collaborative space where our team can share their ideas. We'll use different color stickies (or Post-Its) to capture these ideas. To make this process more efficient, we can take advantage of the stickies pack available in the building blocks tab on the left side of the screen. For team members who prefer brainstorming using Excel, we can import their cells into Miro, which will automatically convert them into stickies using the cut and paste command.

To make the screens look even more realistic and stimulate the ideation process further, we can explore other templates. Using the copy and paste icon, we can replicate images easily. Additionally, the automatic pop-up menu that appears when selecting an image allows us to duplicate images effortlessly. With the mobile wireframing menu and the stickies pack selected, we can invite our team members to contribute their ideas for the screen experience.

In Figure 3-5, we can see three iPhones displaying various stickies of different colors, showcasing the collaborative ideation process in action.

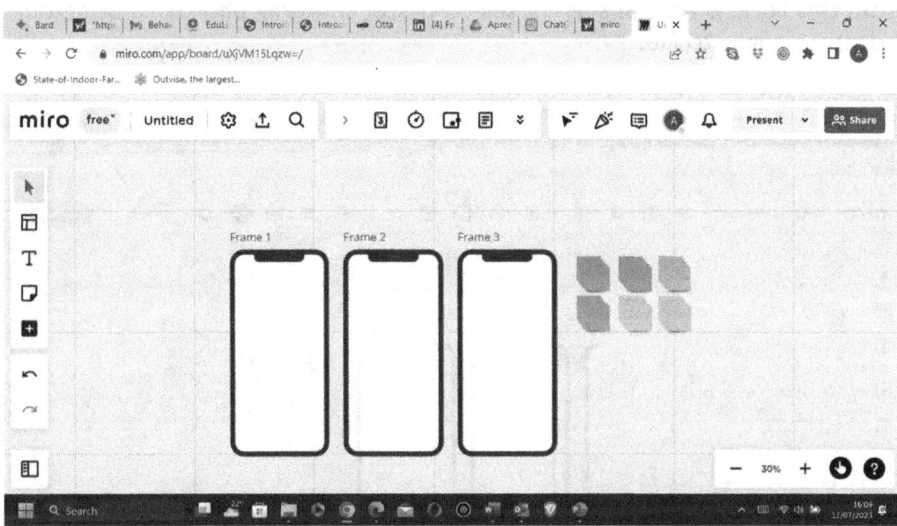

Figure 3-5. Brainstorming Page in Miro with Stickies and Three Mobile Journeys

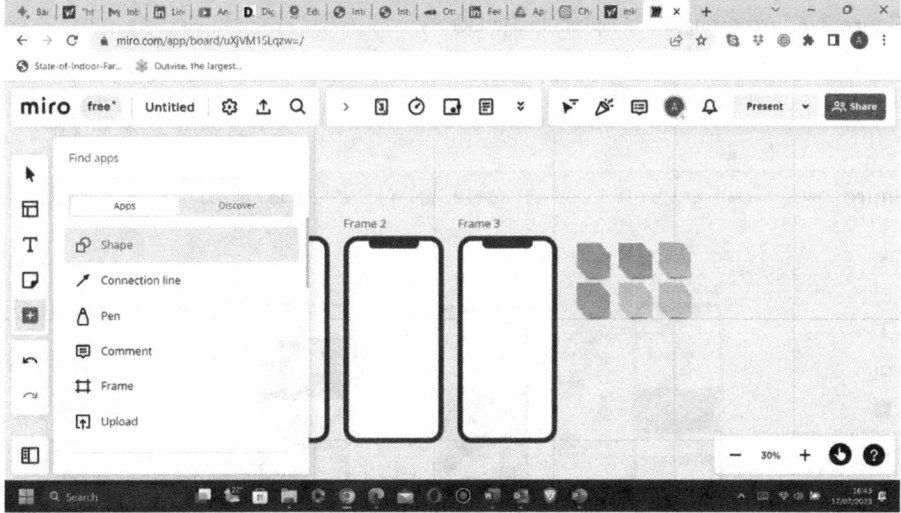

Figure 3-6. Sub-menu to Access Images Through "Upload" Icon

If you select on the left screen menu the discover field and scroll to the bottom icon, you will be able to access the photo library through the Unsplash photo library. Figure 3-7 shows how to access library from the left menu. From this library, we can search, select, paste, and drag photos to bring our prototype pages to life.

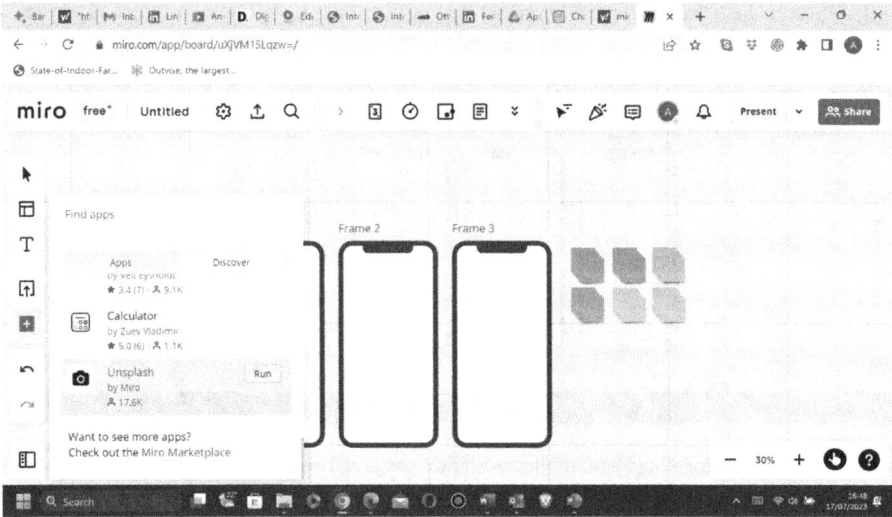

Figure 3-7. Accessing the Unsplash Image Library

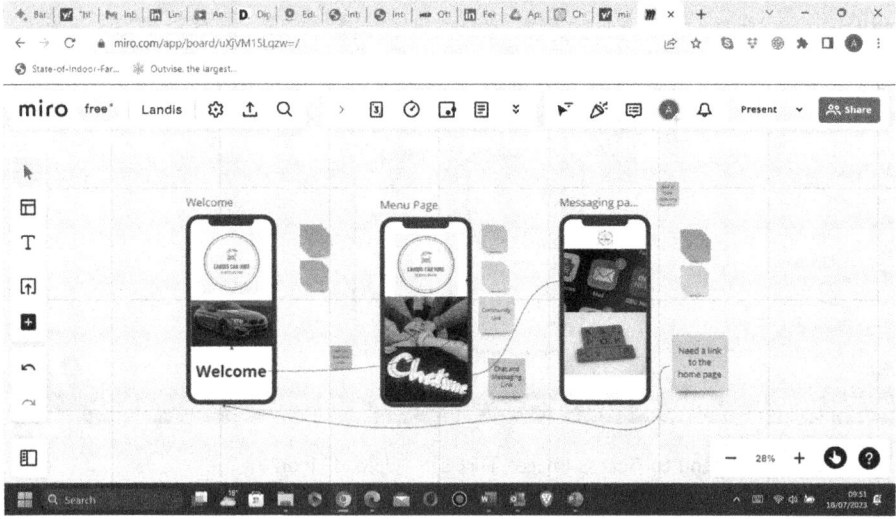

Figure 3-8. Building the Mobile App via Whiteboarding

Figure 3-8 shows how we can quickly create a first cut of the prototype experience for the design teams. Through the upload icon, we can also upload images from our own directory like the Landis Car Hire logo. Through the icons at the top left of the screen, we can share, present for brainstorming with our other team members allocating post-its for an interactive experience. Once we are comfortable with the journeys, we follow up and direct our user experience teams to create the framework for the Mobile Screen experience.

By playing with the whiteboarding, you will discover very practical ways to bring your ideas to life, saving time and money and resources and ensuring you lead to the engagement and not rely on third parties.

If you are a true novice and are really stuck for ideas, some of the ready-made templates can also assist. Figure 3-9 shows the Miro App Wireframe feature in the research and design template library that can accelerate your creation of the mobile experience by simply deleting and repopulating the fields.

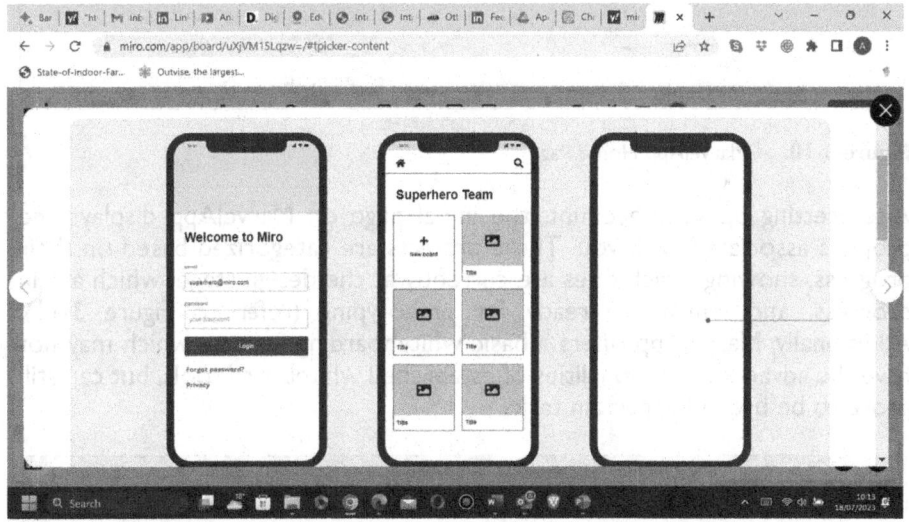

Figure 3-9. Miro Standard App Wireframes

To give life to these ideas, we can utilize an intuitive low-code prototyping tool known as MarvelApp (www.marvelapp.com). With this tool, we can transform enabled icons on the virtual screen into interactive buttons, allowing us to quickly create functional prototypes.

Prototyping Our Solution Using MarvelApp

Figure 3-10 displays the Marvelapp home page, where you have the option to register for a free account, enabling you to create prototypes. To access the registration page, visit the following link: `https://marvelapp.com/features/prototyping`

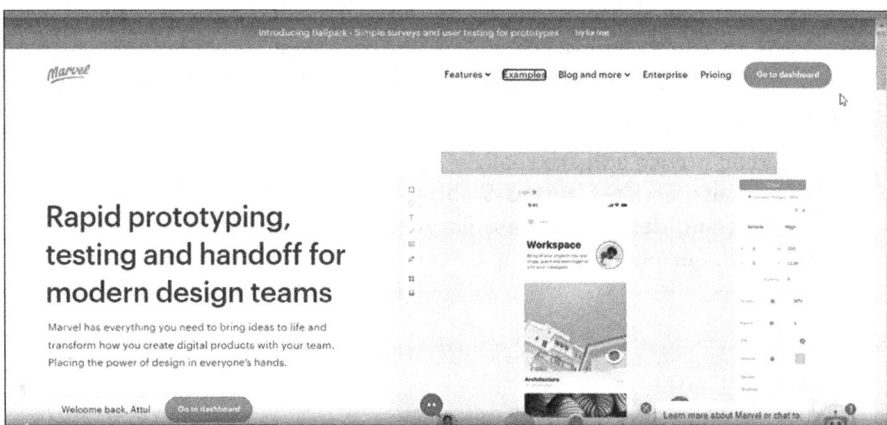

Figure 3-10. – MarvelApp Home Page

After setting up your account, the initial page on MarvelApp displays the projects associated with you. These projects are categorized based on their progress, showing which ones are currently at the design stage, which are in progress, and which are ready for prototyping (refer to Figure 3-11). Additionally, MarvelApp offers a basic whiteboarding feature, which may not have the advanced functionalities of established whiteboard tools, but can still prove to be useful for certain tasks.

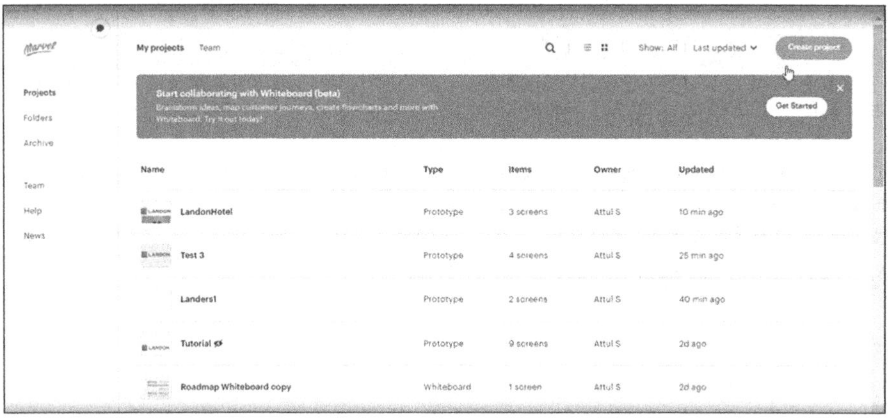

Figure 3-11. MarvelApp list of Projects in Progress with Status

When you start a new project, MarvelApp asks you to name it and select the prototype project type (see Figure 3-12). Select with the drop-down menu the iPhone option which ensures the images will be scaled to fit a mobile screen.

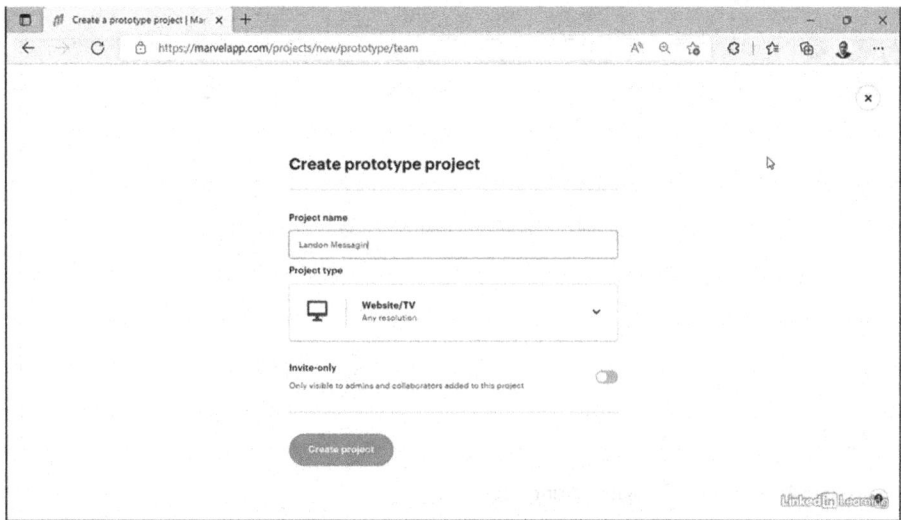

Figure 3-12. Marvel Media Selection Page

Once you have selected your prototype project name and media type for your video, you will then automatically move to the designs page once the project is created (Figure 3-13).

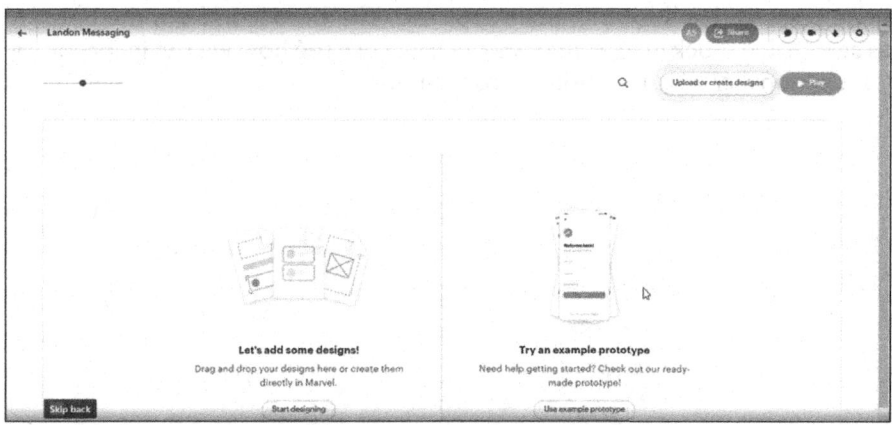

Figure 3-13. – Marvel Designs Page

There is an assisted design-making screen option on the right side of the screen, but let's select the left side (start designing) option to create designs from scratch (Figure 3-13). This will then open up the design-editing screen, as shown in Figure 3-14.

Figure 3-14. – Marvel Designs Editing Page

On the left-hand side of the marvel designs editing page (Figure 3-14) are a number of icons that we can select to create our user experience. The bottom icon on the left has a library of ready-made icons that we could use or reuse from earlier designs. Figure 3-14a shows the logo for Landis Car Hire uploaded locally with the menu for wireframing elements. This is the second icon from the bottom and contains a number of wireframing elements or standard phone screens that a lot of mobile apps use. The third icon from the bottom has searchable stock images that we can use. Let's see how we can incorporate this functionality into our mobile prototype.

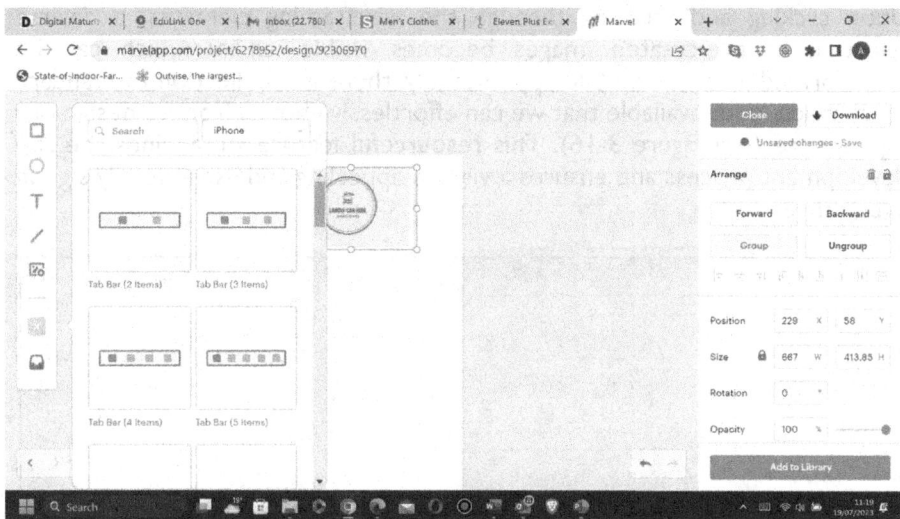

Figure 3-14a. Design Screen with Uploaded Logo and Menu Open for Iphone Wireframes

For our loyalty tool mobile app from the Miro whiteboarding tool, we want to create the prototype messaging app with three screens, starting with a welcome page (Figure 3-15).

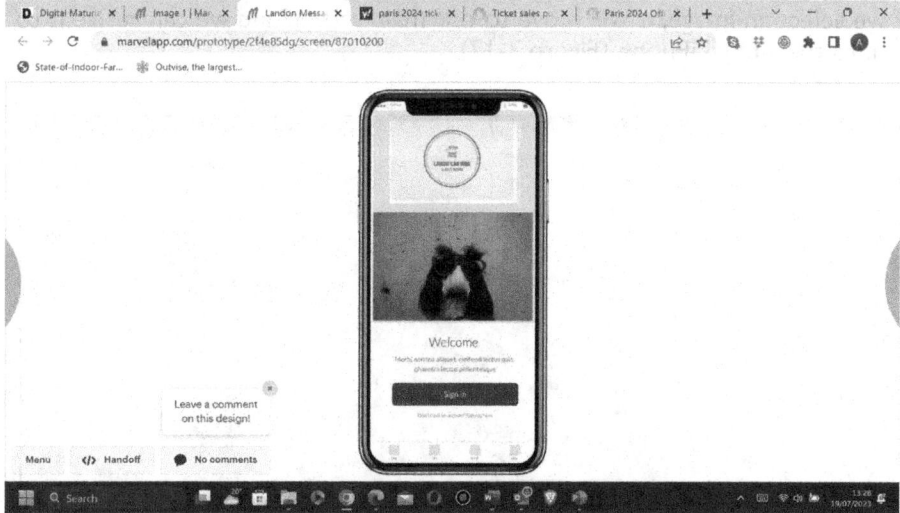

Figure 3-15. Landis Car Hire Loyalty Tool Mobile App Welcome Page

Upon clicking and scrolling through the wireframing elements, a diverse selection of pre-created images becomes visible, all of which can be incorporated into our mobile app. Notably, there is a collection of standard ready-made icons available that we can effortlessly choose from to design our sign-in page (see Figure 3-16). This resourceful feature streamlines the app development process and ensures a visually appealing and user-friendly sign-in experience.

Figure 3-16. Marvel Selection of Standard Icons from the Sub-menu

If we select an image, it will move to our main screen and we can resize it to fit into the virtual iPhone (Figure 3-17).

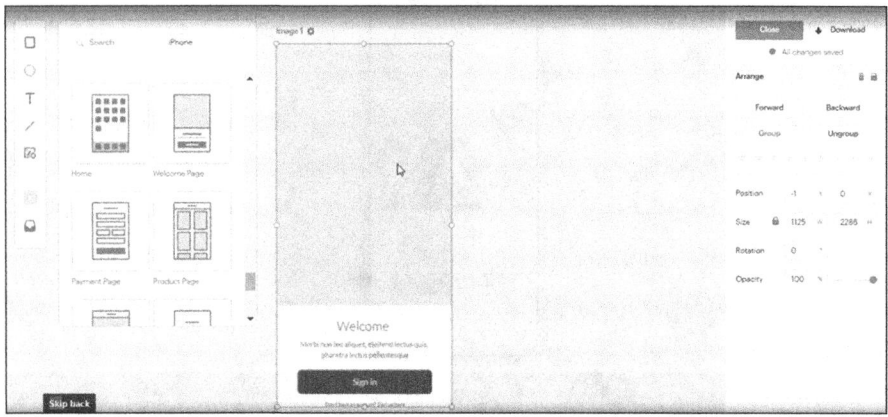

Figure 3-17. Marvel Selecting Images and Icons for the Welcome Page

Naturally, any welcome page will require a logo which we can simply upload as a JPEG or PNG image to our libraries menu and see it on the on the left-hand side sub menu.(Figure 3-18).

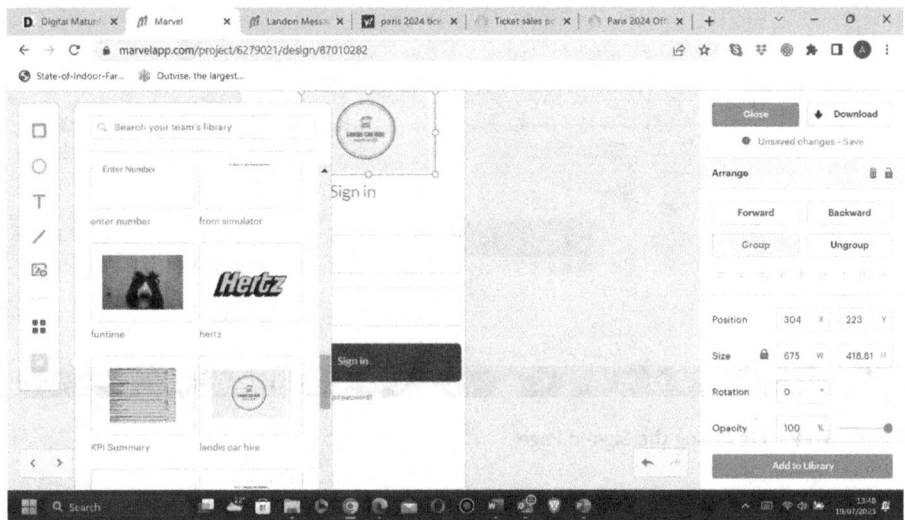

Figure 3-18. *Marvel Selecting and Uploading Saved Images*

To give our app a mobile feel, we can begin by incorporating a tab bar at the top of the homepage. When searching for tab bar options, we'll find a variety of iPhone tab icons to choose from. The status bar, displaying battery power and coverage, comes as a standard feature, but there are numerous other options available for customization.

In addition to the top tab bar, we also require a bottom menu bar with multiple tabs. Scrolling through the menu list, we'll discover pre-used images tailored for the bottom bar. By selecting and positioning these images accordingly, we can easily create the welcome page for our app, as demonstrated in Figure 3-15.

Next, we'll proceed to design the sign-in page (Figure 3-19). By clicking on "New design" in the bottom left menu and following the same selection and positioning process as we did for the welcome page, we can effortlessly create the sign-in page for our app, as depicted in Figure 3-19.

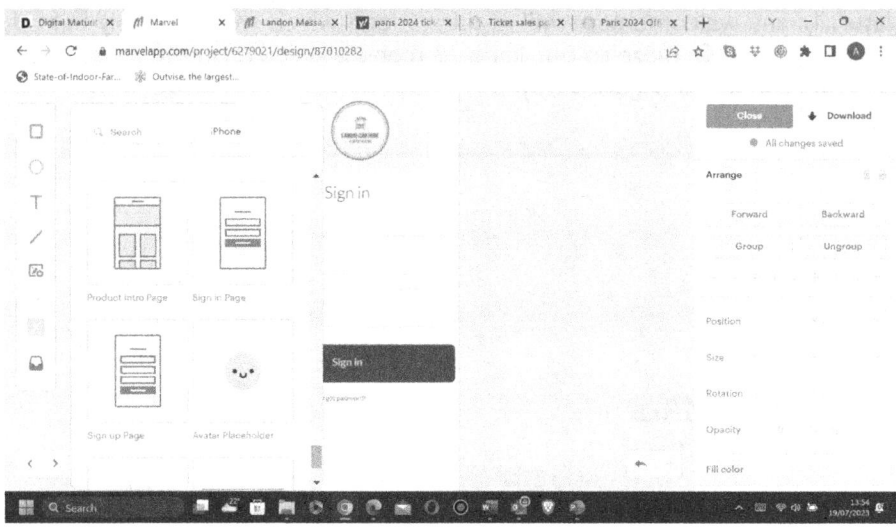

Figure 3-19. Designing the Sign-in Page

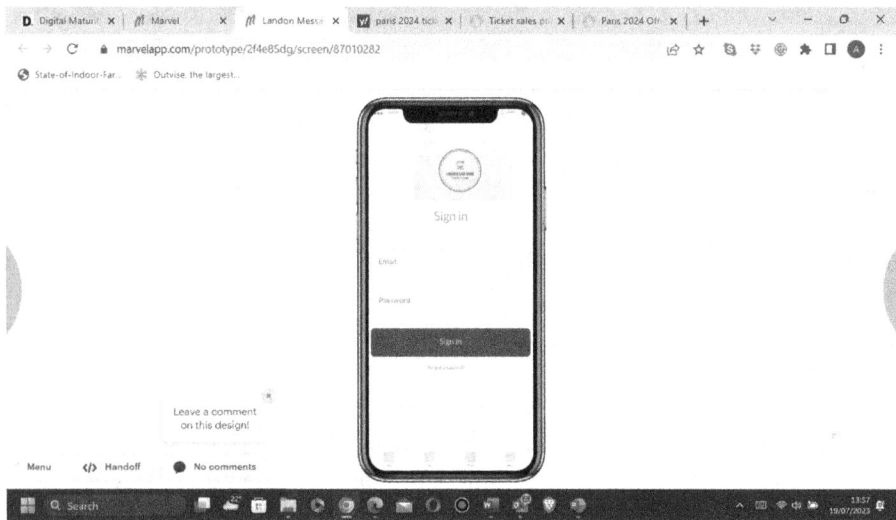

Figure 3-20. Completed Sign-in Page

To create the third page, which displays menu options leading to the chat, I have uploaded pre-loaded images from the image library. These images will serve as visual icons for each menu option.

Among the selected menu items, there is one menu image called "Chattime" (Figure 3-21) that will be utilized to represent messages within the chat. This design has been finalized and can be observed in the completed screen (Figure 3-22).

Figure 3-21. Uploading Menu Screen

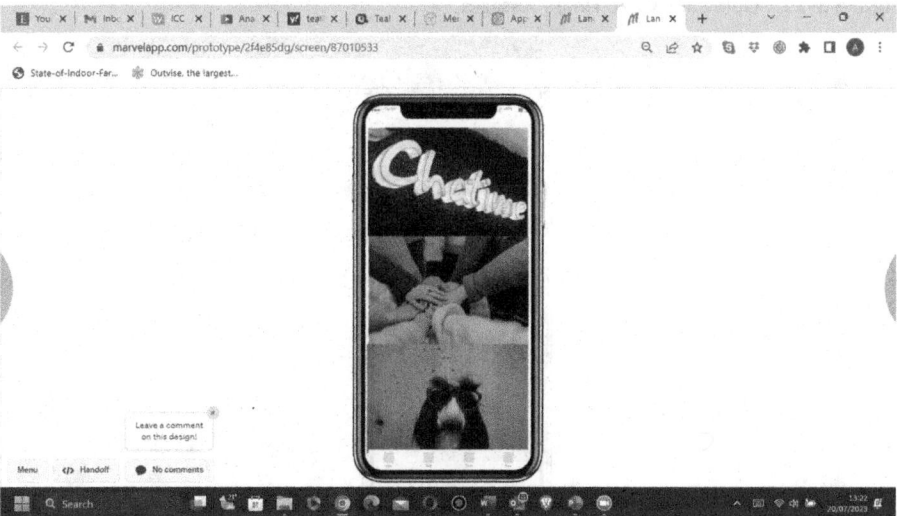

Figure 3-22. Completed Menu Screen

After crafting a few example messages, I can seamlessly choose and include them in the screen journey as a 4th screen by uploading them as PNG files (Figure 3-23). To enhance the user experience, I will also add a navigation tab at the top, enabling easy access to the chat feature (Figure 3-24). This way, users can smoothly navigate through the chat and interact with the example messages we've created, making the app more engaging and user-friendly.

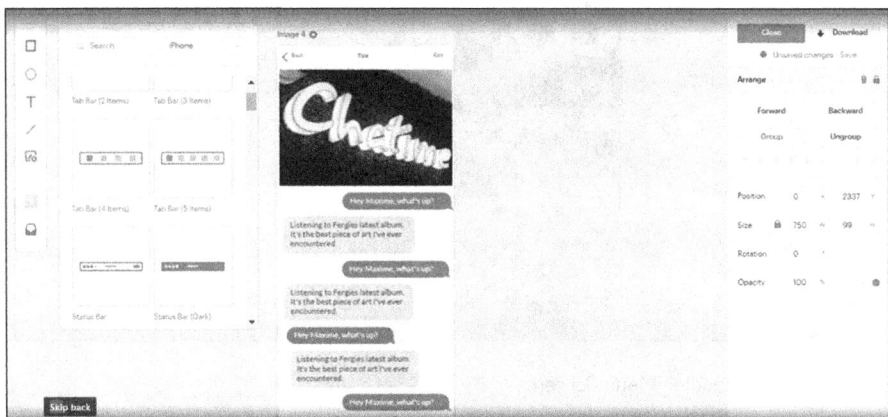

Figure 3-23. Uploading Chat Time Messages

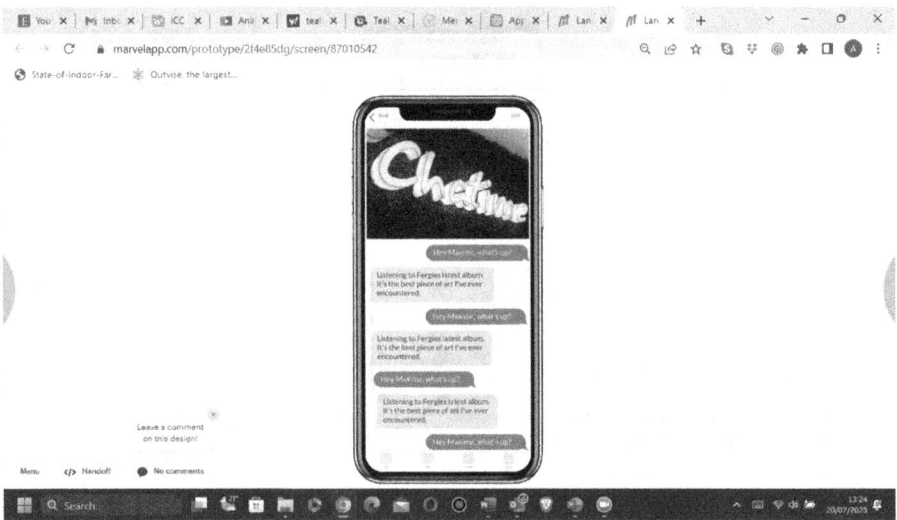

Figure 3-24. Uploaded Chat Messages

With these images, we have the prototype for the community site.

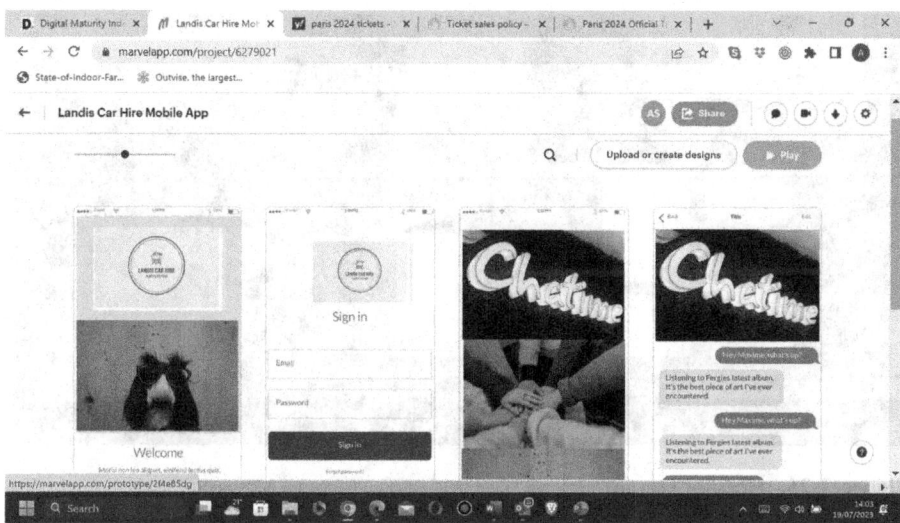

Figure 3-25. Final Screen Images

To create a seamless screen journey resembling an actual user experience, we'll connect the images together using the prototype icon. When you select the prototype icon, you can easily choose the specific area on the screen that you want to be clickable, creating "hotspots" that lead to the next or previous page. This interactive feature allows users to navigate through the app just as they would in a real scenario, providing a more immersive and dynamic experience.

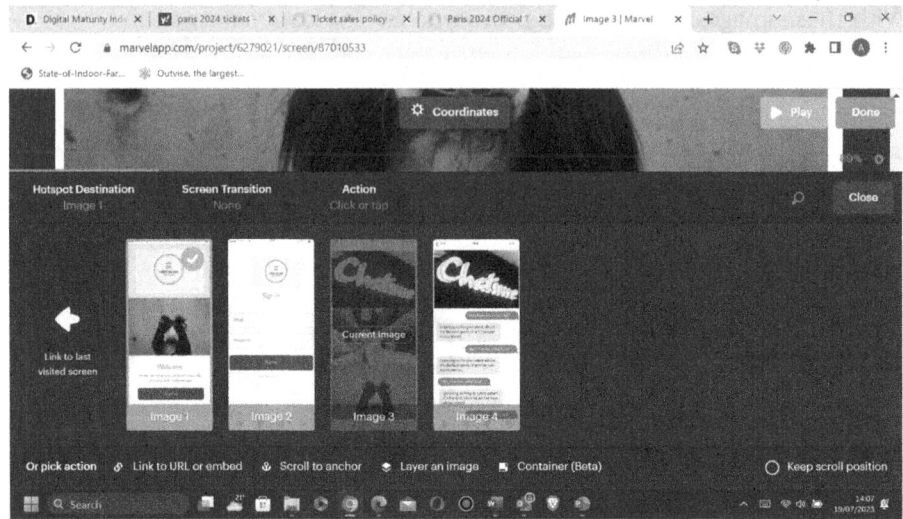

Figure 3-26. Hotspot Feature

Using the hotspot command, when you highlight a specific area on the screen, it will direct the user to another screen once they click on it (Figure 3-26). This allows for seamless navigation between different screens within the app.

Next, we can follow the same steps with the next screen, where selecting "Chattime" on the menu will take the user to the images in the chat.

Once the design is complete, we can click on the "PLAY" button located on the top right of the prototype menu. This action initiates the customer journey, enabling us to experience the entire app flow, starting from the initial screen and leading all the way to the final screen. This interactive playback provides a comprehensive view of how the app will function and helps identify any potential user experience improvements.

Figure 3-27. Activating the Back Image as a Hotspot

Once we reach the end screen, we naturally want to return to the start page. In Figure 3-27, we can observe the process of using the back buttons on the prototype to navigate back through the app.

To achieve this, we select the back button in the status bar as a hotspot and direct the link to the earlier screen, effectively taking us to the preceding page. By selecting the "Done" button at the top right, each step of the journey is saved, allowing us to repeat the process until we reach the start page.

Now, when you play the prototype, you will witness the complete mobile app experience. Users can seamlessly navigate through the app, from the start page to the end screen and back, replicating the actual user journey and ensuring a smooth and interactive app flow.

By using this approach, we can rapidly create prototypes and share with our design experts.

Video Creation Using Lumen5

It is said that video can increase the recall rate of content by up to 75% compared to traditional slideware. One of the simplest and best video-making tools currently available with a free subscription is Lumen5 (www.Lumen5. com). The homepage is shown in Figure 3-28.

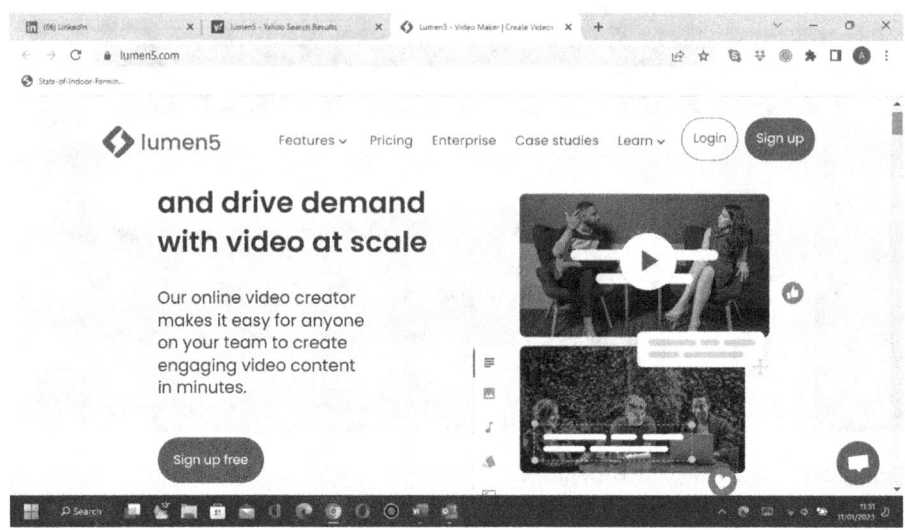

Figure 3-28. X

Lumen5 is an innovative low-code/no-code video-making tool that empowers users to present their content, which could typically be found in an MS PowerPoint presentation, in a highly dynamic and engaging video format. This includes elements such as the problem statement, market opportunity, revenue projection, and business benefits, all conveyed through captivating video imagery and straightforward text.

As a low-code tool, Lumen5 offers a free subscription model with basic functionality, making it accessible to a wider audience. Its plug-and-play benefits stem from its user-friendly menu structure, allowing for effortless navigation and swift creation of videos.

One of Lumen5's notable strengths lies in its vast library of royalty-free, ready-made video and graphic images courtesy of Unsplash (Figure 3-29). This extensive collection empowers users to enhance their ideas and presentations with a polished and professional appearance, without the need for extensive design skills.

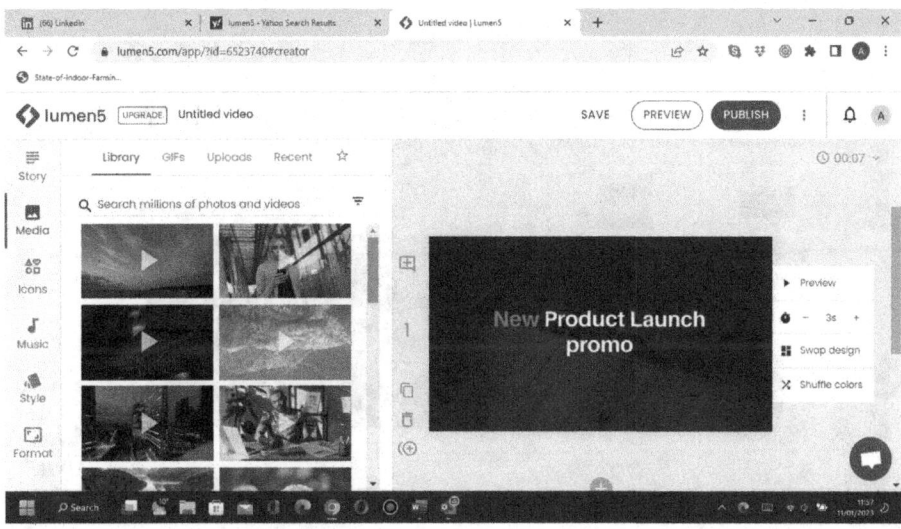

Figure 3-29. Lumen5 Video Image Library

Lumen5 further extends its capabilities by enabling users to seamlessly upload their own images and video content through its interactive front-end. This means you can easily incorporate your unique visuals without the need for coding or video editing skills.

Now, let's leverage Lumen5 to present our proposition for the Landis Car Hire loyalty mobile app. After brainstorming with the whiteboarding tool and designing the UI using the wireframing tool, our next step is to create a compelling video to pitch our front-end prototype for the iPhone/iPad. To begin, it's beneficial to sketch the storyline that we want to convey through the video. This helps to organize our thoughts and structure the content in a way that effectively communicates the value of the app and its features to potential stakeholders.

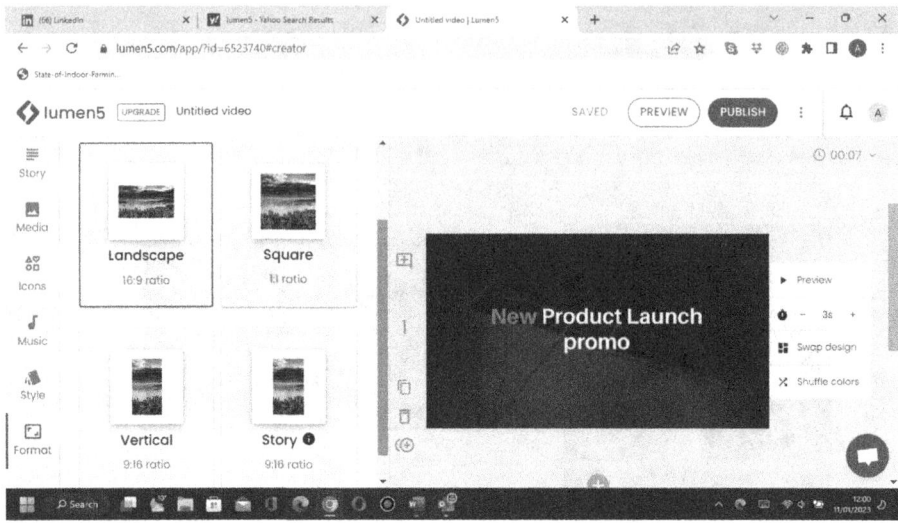

Figure 3-30. Video Option Menu

Upon accessing the Lumen5 dashboard, navigate to the left-side menu where a variety of options for starting your project can be found (Figure 3-30). As you scroll down, you'll come across the "video format" icon, which presents numerous video formats to choose from. While I recommend the YouTube option, which is ideal for PCs, feel free to experiment with other formats based on your preferences.

Upon selecting the YouTube format, the images will automatically adjust to fit the screen size. Simultaneously, a text box will appear, allowing you to input text. To build our narrative effectively, we can utilize the "STORY" feature and the text box on the right to complement and edit any visual images we wish to include (Figure 3-31). This ensures a cohesive and engaging storytelling experience for our viewers.

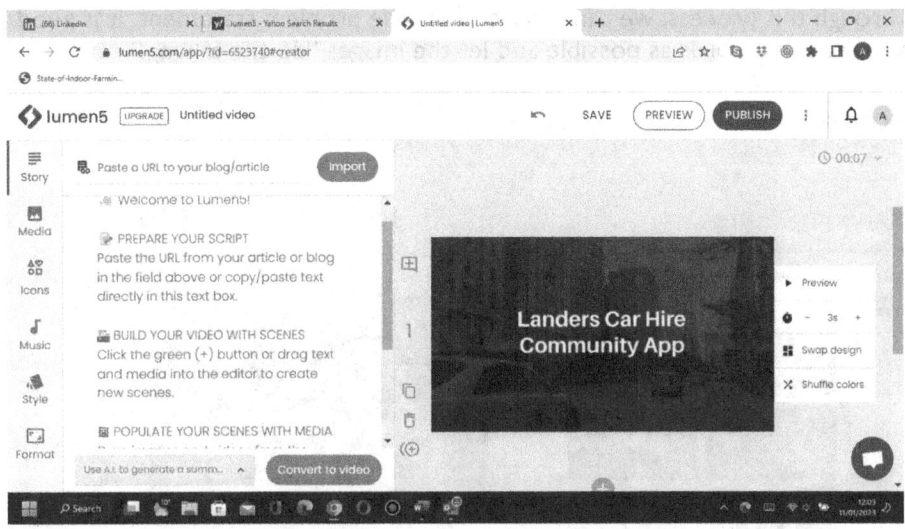

Figure 3-31. Using the STORY Feature

By selecting the MEDIA icon on the left menu bar, the search bar appears from which we can search the video gallery for images that can relate to our problem statement (Figure 3-32). There are thousands of images in the video library which, once selected, can be dragged to the image editor to create the visuals for our story board having added key words for context.

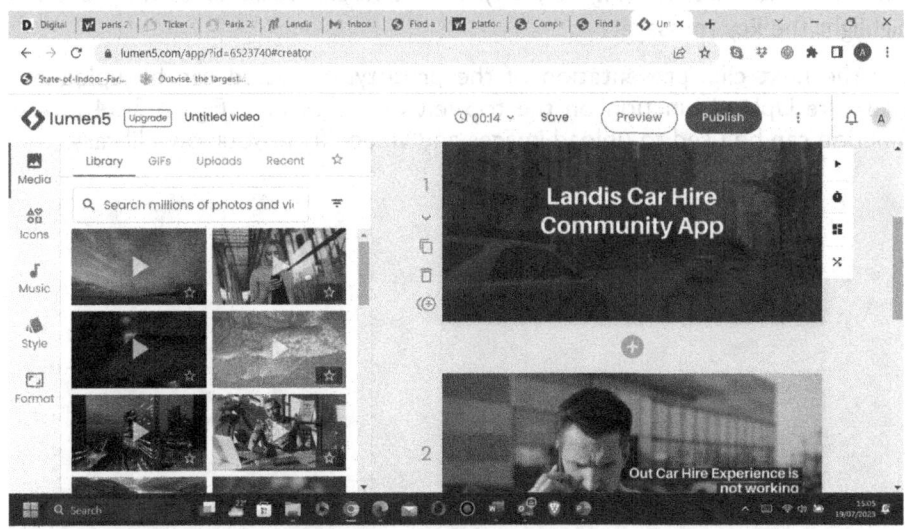

Figure 3-32. Using the Image Library to Create the Story

Through this process, we can start crafting the problem statement. It is good to use as few words as possible and let the images "do the talking."

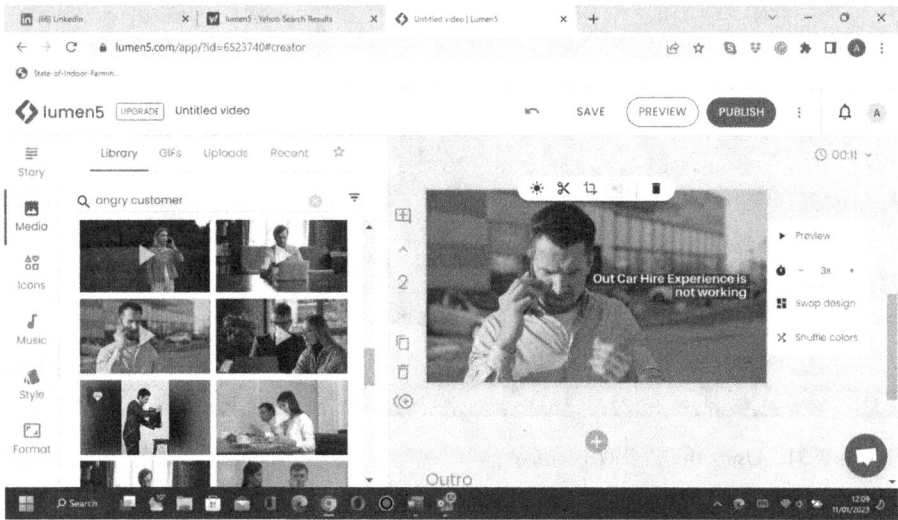

Figure 3-33. Using the Key Word Search for the Right Type of Video Image

For the opening screen, I searched the video library for an "ANGRY CUSTOMER" and a selection of thumbnail images of video was returned from which one was selected (Figure 3-33). Then text can be added to the video to highlight the key message.

For the next clip, presentation of the prototype created can be uploaded using the Upload function on the top left of the screen (Figure 3-34). This function can be used to upload images and videos from your own library.

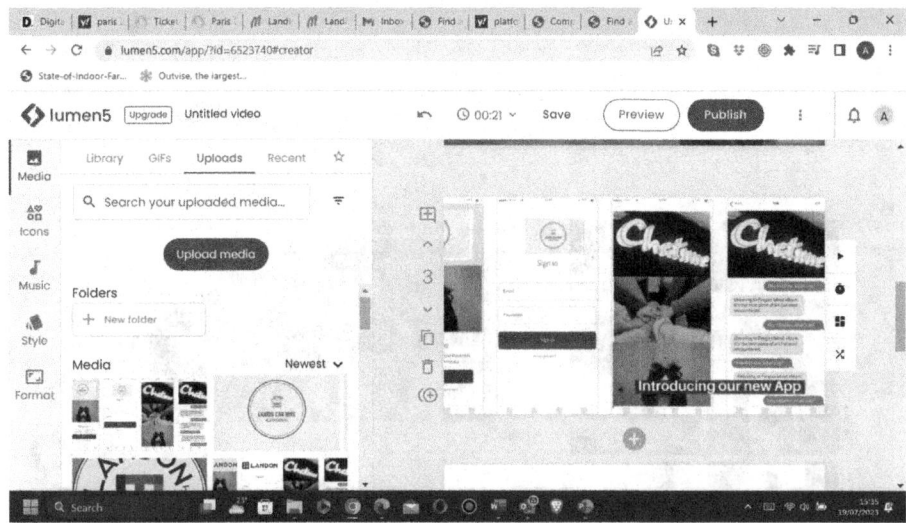

Figure 3-34. Uploading Screenshots from MarvelApp

Once an image is uploaded, you can use them for other projects too. Again, if you select an image, you can drag it onto the right side of the screen to add to a storyline. By repeating these steps, you can quickly build up a story line.

Having created a draft storyline, it can be reviewed and images easily swapped by dragging new images over the old ones.

By selecting the image editor menu on the main screen, you can adjust the position of the text in addition to text characteristics such as font size, color, boldening, italicization, and paragraphing to ensure any text complements the image (Figure 3-35.).

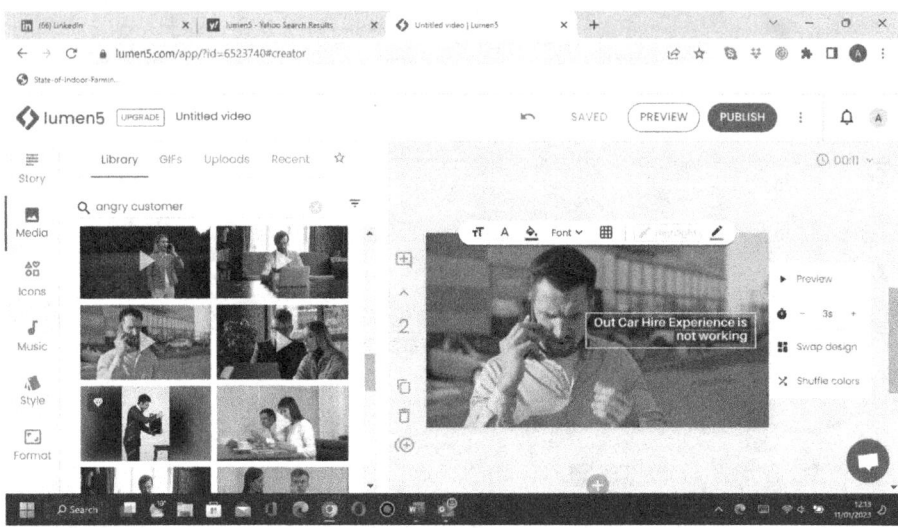

Figure 3-35. Editing the Text Position and Font Size on the Image

It's essential to consider how the video directly applies to your audience. Tailoring the story to resonate with them is crucial, and doing so with as few words as possible presents a challenging yet rewarding task. Don't hesitate to edit and re-edit the text, aiming for maximum clarity and impact in the message. Crafting a concise and compelling narrative will captivate your audience and ensure that the video delivers its intended message effectively. Remember, striking the right balance between brevity and impactful content will create a memorable and engaging experience for your viewers.

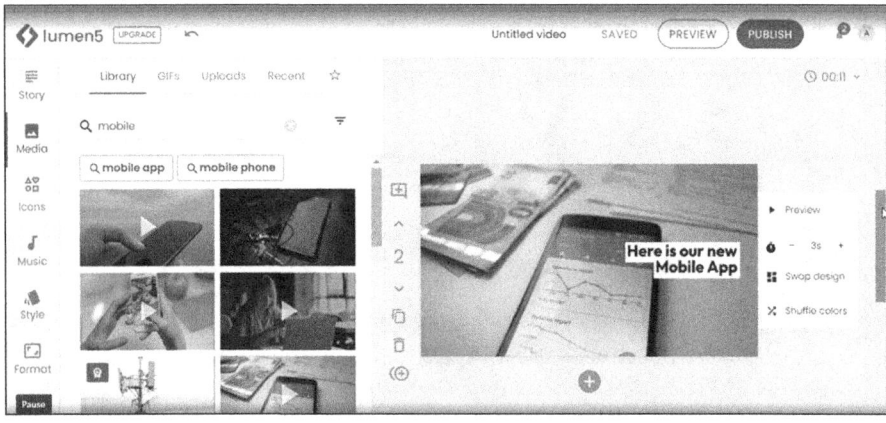

Figure 3-36. Using as Few Words as Possible on Each Slide Is Key

A notable feature of Lumen5 is the ability to adjust the length of each scene, allowing you to emphasize different aspects of the storyline effectively. By selecting the timer icon in the right menu next to the image, you can control the duration of each scene, setting it anywhere from 3 to 30 seconds.

To maintain audience engagement and impact, I would recommend keeping the videos within a maximum length of 90 seconds. Longer videos can often lose their effectiveness and are less likely to be shared.

To enhance the video's impact further, consider incorporating background music. By clicking on the MUSIC icon in the left-side menu, you can preview and choose from a variety of ready-made tracks. Alternatively, you have the option to upload your own music (Figure 3-37). Focus on the mood you want to convey, and let that guide your search for the perfect music piece rather than fixating on a particular track.

By skillfully adjusting scene lengths and adding suitable background music, you can create a captivating video that conveys your message with precision and leaves a lasting impression on your audience.

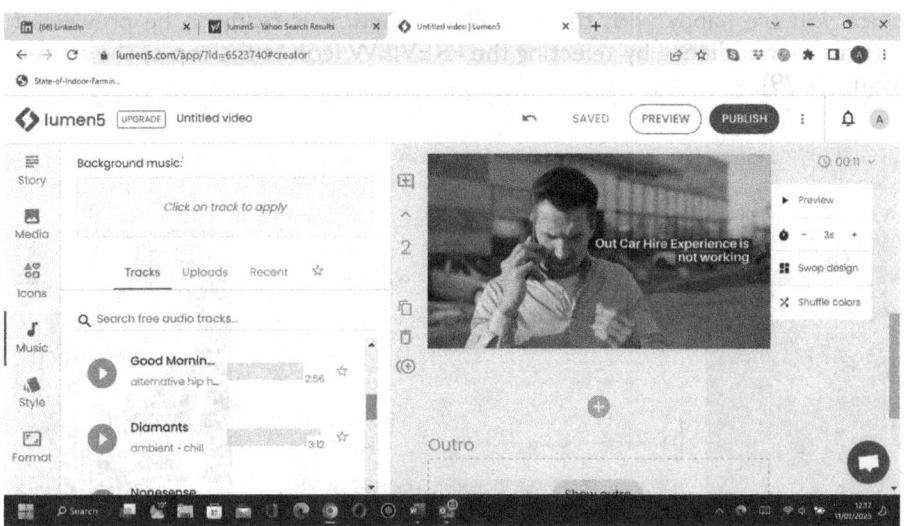

Figure 3-37. Lumen5 Music Menu

Finally, add your logo at the end to close your presentation in the outro by uploading it locally with any follow-on text (Figure 3-38).

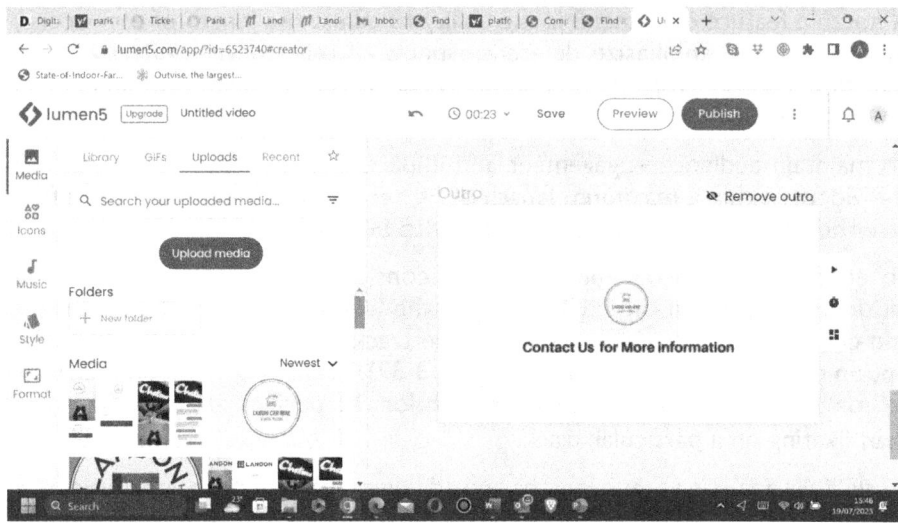

Figure 3-38. Adding a Logo to the Outro

Once you are happy with the overall storyline, it is ready to be previewed with a wider audience by selecting the PREVIEW icon at the top of the screen (Figure 3-39).

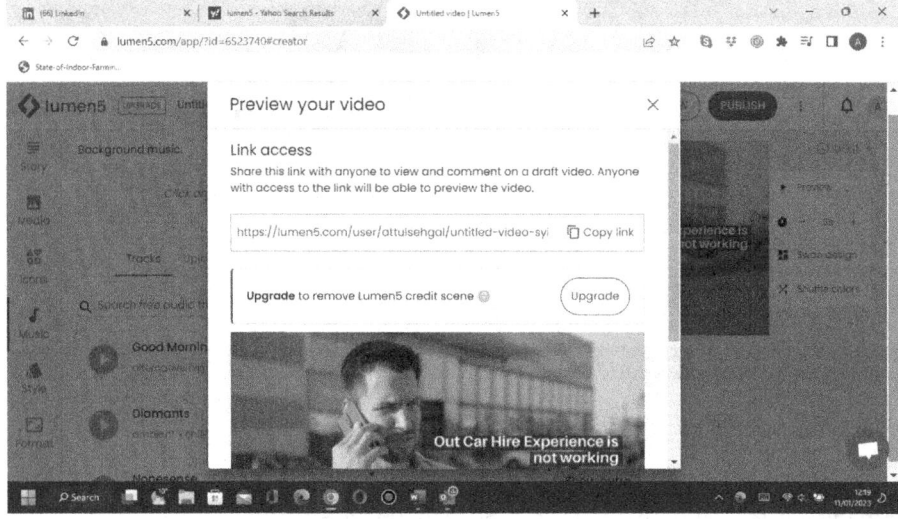

Figure 3-39. Preview Link for Sharing

Your colleagues can also share comments on slide duration, key messages, caption positioning to provide a compelling video for your audience (Figure 3-40).

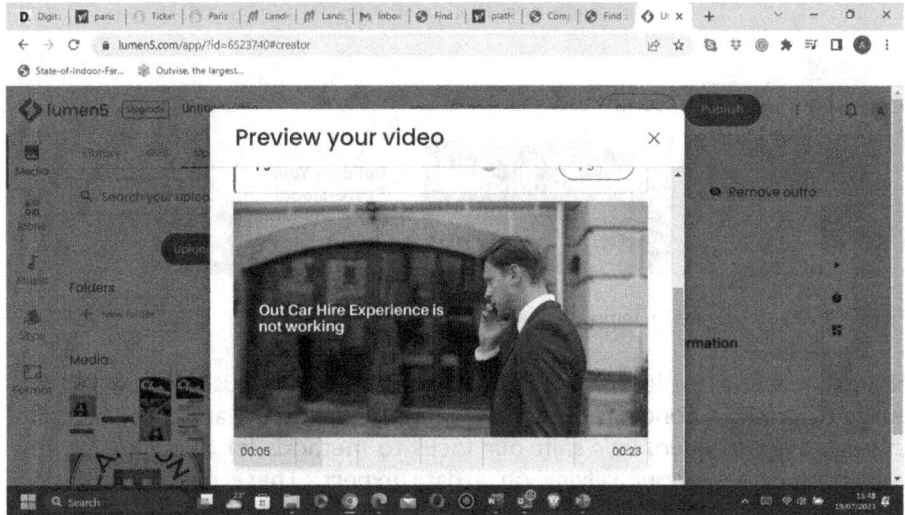

Figure 3-40. Share and Review with Colleagues

When you are happy, select the publish icon and the pitch will be packaged into an MP4 video that can be shared.

Try to make a one-minute video of your own. If you need further help on getting, try one of the ready-made templates on the platform. Once you get used to the platform, you would never want to go back to produce endless PowerPoint slides.

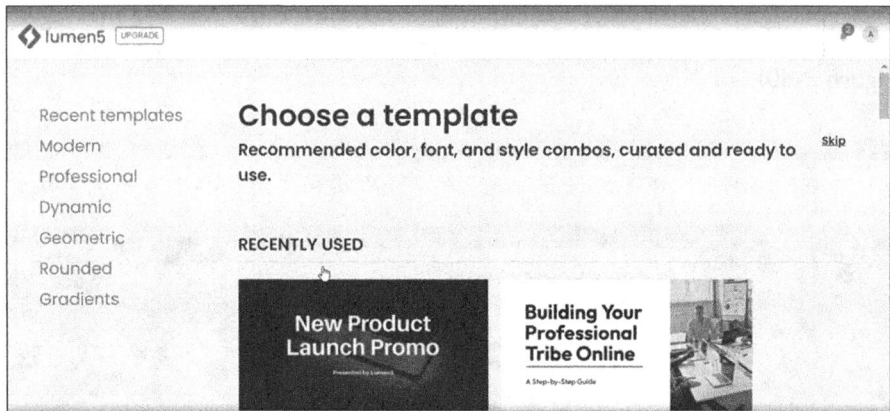

Figure 3-41. Ready-made Templates

Now that we've explored three digital tools that any business owner can utilize to create a concept, design a wireframe prototype, and bring it to life through a short video, let's shift our focus to methods for manipulating and visualizing data without relying on a data expert. These data visualization techniques empower business owners to gain valuable insights and make informed decisions, even without specialized technical knowledge in data analysis.

Manipulating Large Datasets Using Microsoft Power BI

In today's data-driven world, working with data is crucial for effective decision-making. While Microsoft Excel (or MS Excel) serves as a standard tool for data manipulation, it does have limitations when dealing with large datasets and creating comprehensive visualizations like dashboards. Fortunately, there are various low-code solutions available that reduce the reliance on dedicated data experts and allow you to upload vast datasets and generate compelling visualizations, making them ideal for presenting extensive data independently.

Among the many data visualization tools in the market, one tool I find particularly useful is Microsoft Power BI (or MS Power BI). If you have a Microsoft Office 365 package, you can try the online version for free.

As you might recall from Chapter 2, there was some data from a .csv file that was uploaded from a movement sensor. The data file consisted of approximately 133,000 rows across six columns. Now, let's explore how we can create a simple dashboard to analyze and present this data effectively. With Power BI, we can transform this raw data into actionable insights and visually appealing visualizations to facilitate better decision-making.

If we look at the .csv file in its raw form in MS Excel, the data (with the column headers in row 1) looks like Figure 3-42.

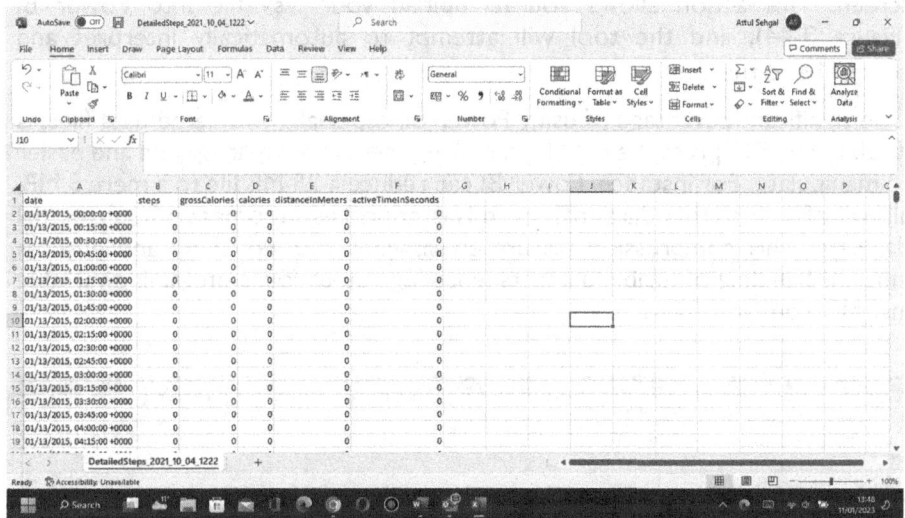

Figure 3-42. Data Extract from .csv file

If we move to the bottom of the file, we see that it contains many rows and so it is hard to derive any immediate insights. Furthermore, it can take a long time to prepare the data to use within the charts function in MS Excel.

We can import this data directly into Power BI. Figure 3-43 shows the home screen.

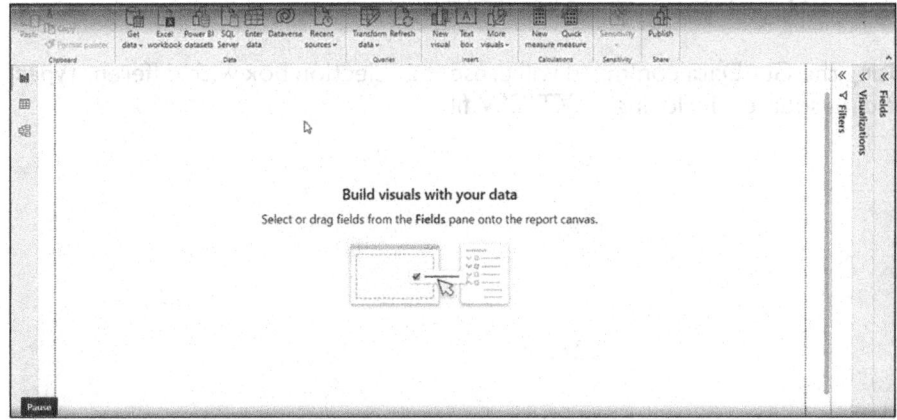

Figure 3-43. Power BI Home Screen

Upon setting up a free account in MS Power BI, you gain access to an interface that facilitates data visualization. To begin working with your data, click on the "GET DATA" command located at the top left of the menu bar on the home screen. This action allows you to upload your .csv file into Power BI (Figure 3-44), and the tool will attempt to automatically interpret and comprehend the data.

One significant advantage of using Power BI, especially with large data files, is its ability to compress the data files, making them more manageable and easier to manipulate. For instance, Power BI can reduce a 25 MB file to a mere 3 MB, allowing for smoother data analysis and faster processing times with substantial datasets. This compression feature streamlines the workflow and ensures efficient handling of sizable datasets, enabling you to focus on gaining valuable insights from your data.

Figure 3-44. Get Data Command with the TXT/CSV Sub-menu

Using the Get Data command will present a selection box with different types of data sources, including TEXT/CSV files.

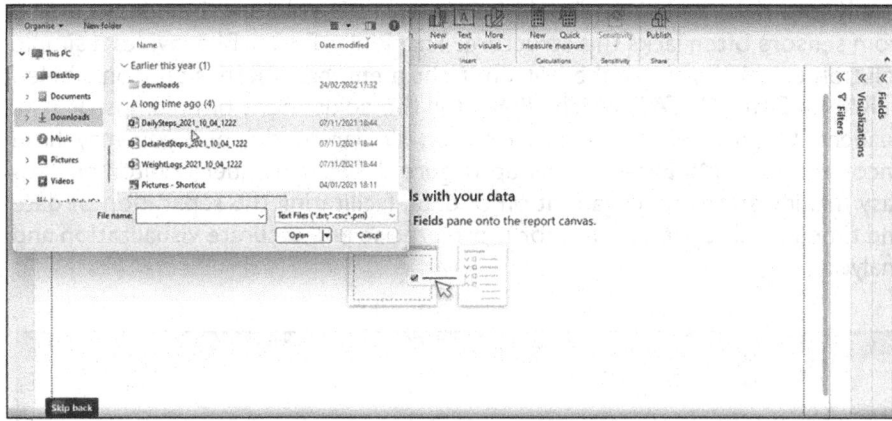

Figure 3-45. File Upload

Once imported as shown in Figure 3-45, Power BI automatically shows a preview of the data set (Figure 3-46). From inspection of the data, it should be evident that it contains sensor readings that have a frequency of response every 15 minutes.

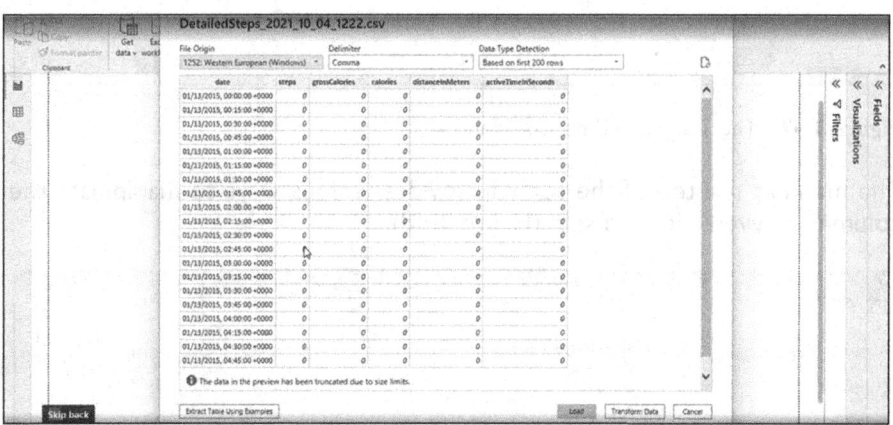

Figure 3-46. Snapshot of Data File

The most straightforward method to visualize the data is by using a line profile graph. However, a common challenge arises when dealing with a substantial amount of data, as seen in our example.

Ideally, the date and time should be in separate columns, but data coming from sensors often lacks this structure. Thankfully, Power BI provides a simple solution to this issue. At the bottom right menu bar, there is an icon labeled "TRANSFORM DATA," which allows for the adjustment of columns or row headers. Upon selection, a query editor, similar to the one you may have encountered in MS Excel, opens up (Figure 3-47). This query editor enables easy manipulation and organization of data, facilitating the separation of date and time into distinct columns for more precise and accurate visualization and analysis.

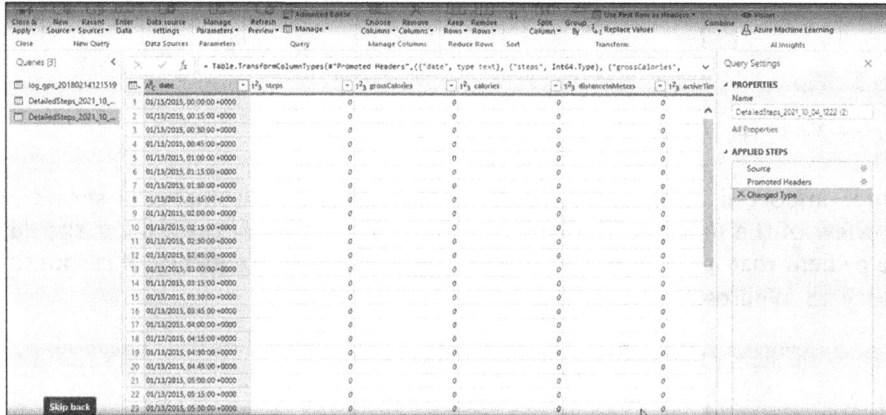

Figure 3-47. The Transform Data Command

The menu at the top of the screen provides various ways to manipulate the columns or even add data sets (Figure 3-48).

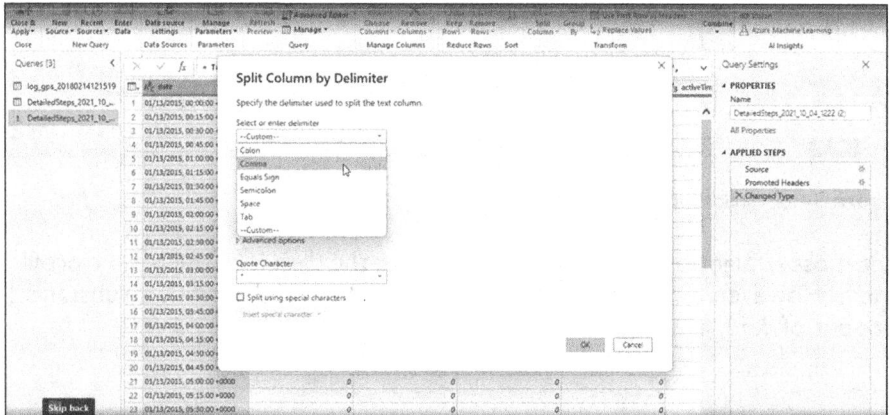

Figure 3-48. The Split Function

One option is the SPLIT column function, which allows you to select the delimiter option that is used to separate the data according to characters or spaces on the row. As there is a comma, selecting the delimiter as COMMA creates a new column with the amended content, with all information from the left of the comma.

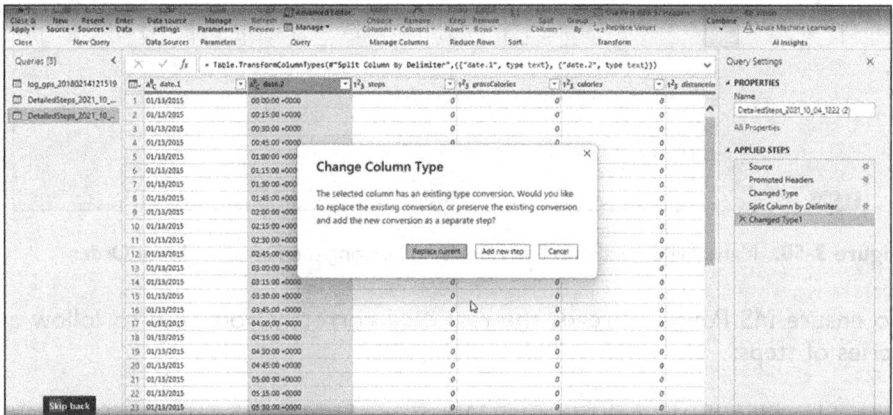

Figure 3-49. Changing Column Type from Text to Date Column

With the data successfully separated into two columns, one for data readings and the other for time, you can now rename the latter column as "TIME." Utilizing time as a variable allows for efficient tracking of the data.

However, there might be an issue with the Date format, and changing the column type is proving challenging. It's crucial to be mindful of this when working with time zones from territories outside the United States, as the day, month, and year formats may differ. To ensure accurate data representation and analysis, take into account the potential variations in date formats and make the necessary adjustments accordingly. Being aware of these differences will prevent any inconsistencies in the data and lead to more reliable insights.

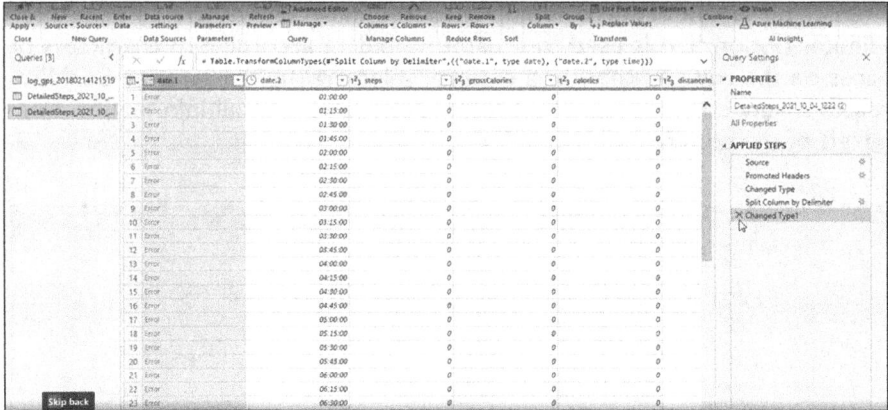

Figure 3-50. Managing Errors with Data Fields – Changing the Day and Month Order

To ensure MS Power BI reads the real date correctly, you need to follow a series of steps:

1. Identify the column type: When you highlight the column type on the row header, it may be recognized as a text column. If you attempt to convert this column into a number, for instance, for day, month, and year, you may encounter an ERROR warning.

2. Utilize APPLIED STEPS: While editing columns, MS Power BI helps you keep track of any changes through the screen on the right called APPLIED STEPS. This feature allows you to view and manage the modifications you've made. If the last step is removed, you can use the SPLIT command to break down the elements of the day, month, and year and then rearrange them in the US date format of month, day, and year before merging them.

3. Split and rearrange columns: By splitting the columns again and breaking down the month, day, and year, you can then switch around the month and day columns using the "/" as the delimiter. This reorganization will ensure the date is correctly formatted in the US style, eliminating any issues with date recognition and facilitating accurate data analysis.

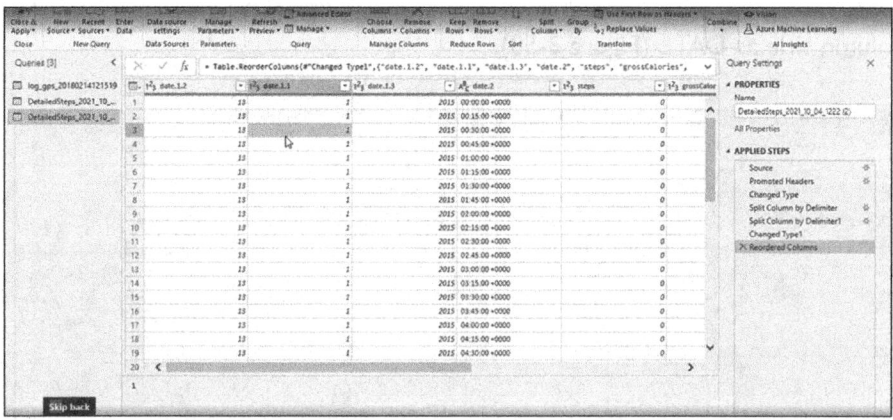

Figure 3-51. Splitting the Columns

Now that the three data sets have been successfully separated (Figure 3-51), you can proceed to merge them back together using the MERGE command. However, to distinguish the fields clearly, a hash line can be used as a separator (Figure 3-52). This merging process will consolidate the data sets into a unified structure, making it easier to work with and analyze the combined data effectively. The hash line acts as a visual aid, ensuring that each dataset's boundaries are discernible within the merged dataset, facilitating better comprehension and interpretation of the information.

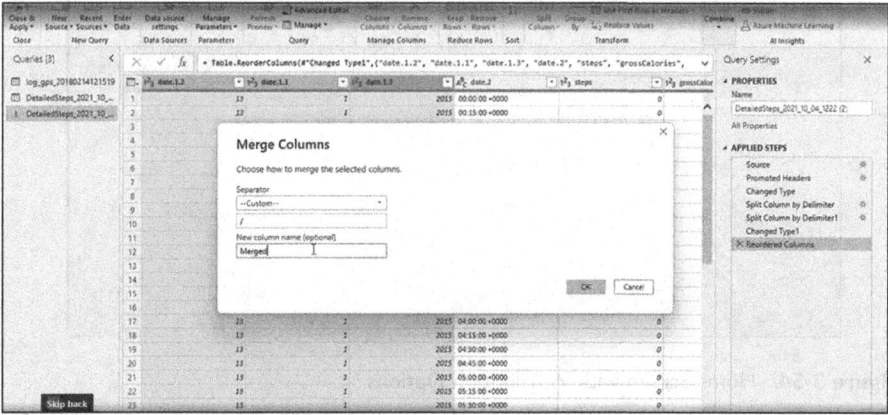

Figure 3-52. The Merge Function

If we try to convert the column once again to "Date." It now accepts the column title as DATE (Figure 3-53).

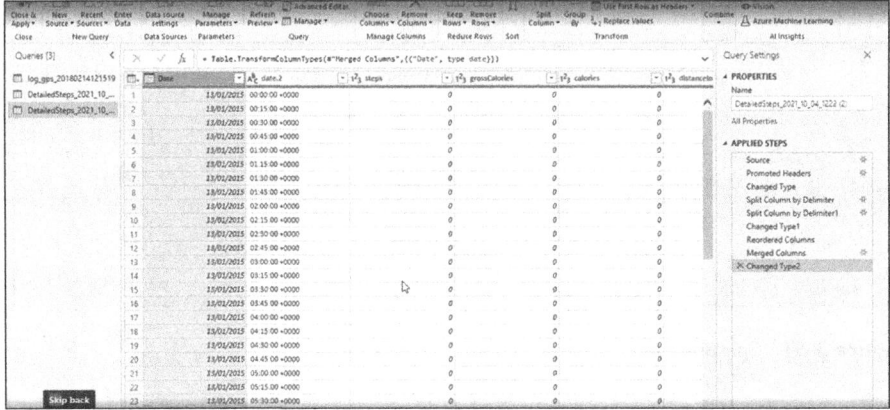

Figure 3-53. Formats Updated

After closing the query editor and having selected APPLY, the file upload can be seen in the correct format with the HOME screen showing the visualization options on the left side (Figure 3-54).

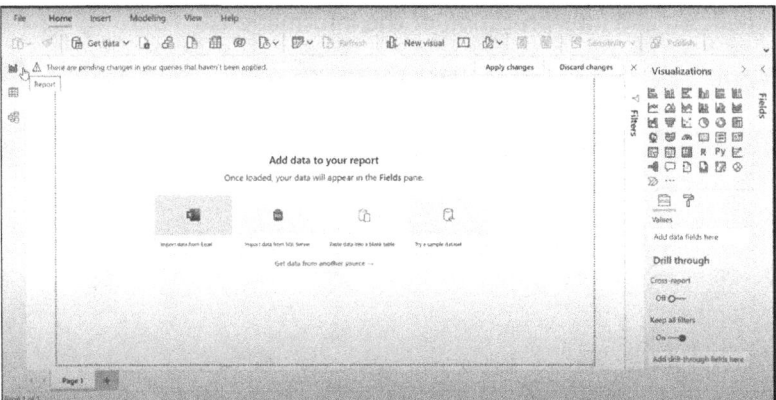

Figure 3-54. Home Screen with Visualization Options

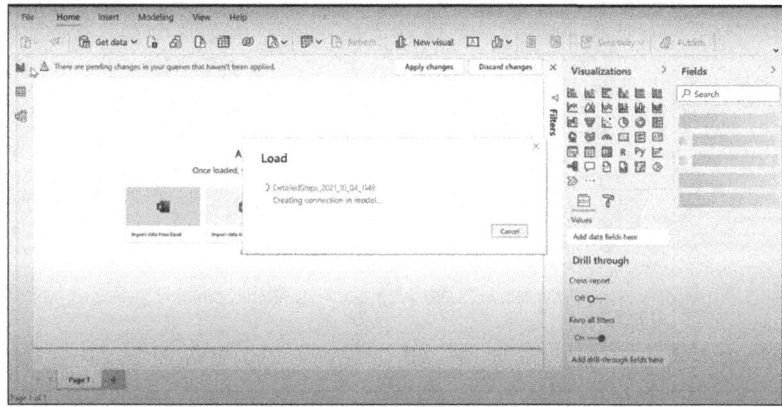

Figure 3-55. Feeding the Editor with the Updated Ffile

The data is now imported into the Power BI file (Figure 3-56).

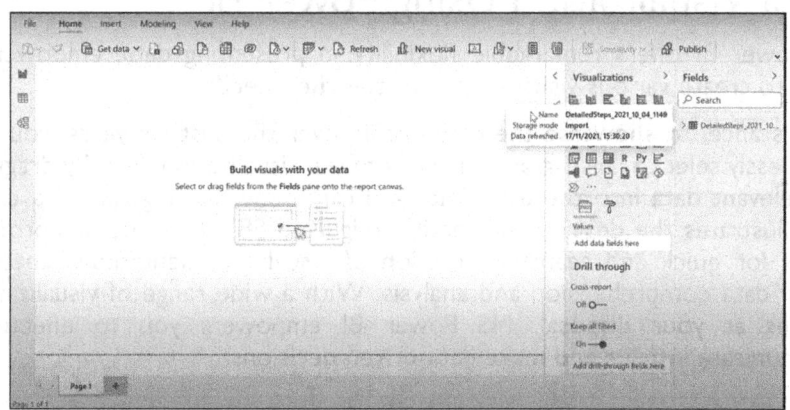

Figure 3-56. Data File Uploaded to the Power BI Editor

On the right side of the screen, the data file is now visible and using the visualizations tab on the left side, data visualizations can be created. By selecting the fields from our data file and the type of visualization, we can show the data in a graphical form.

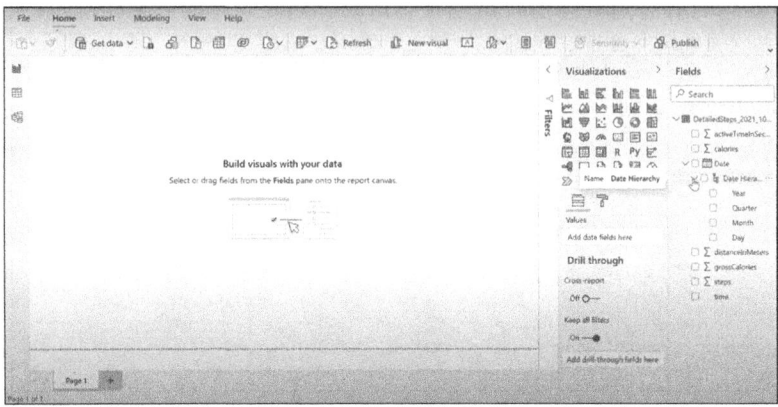

Figure 3-57. Selection of Graph Options with Fields

Data Visualization Using Power BI

MS Power BI offers remarkable flexibility in presenting data, empowering users to create various visualizations to suit their needs.

For instance, to showcase the data profile over the past six years, you can effortlessly select a "histogram" chart from the visualization field. By dragging the relevant data into the data field, you can immediately generate a chart that illustrates the desired information (Figure 3-58). This intuitive process allows for quick and seamless creation of visual representations, enabling better data comprehension and analysis. With a wide range of visualization options at your disposal, MS Power BI empowers you to effectively communicate insights and make data-driven decisions.

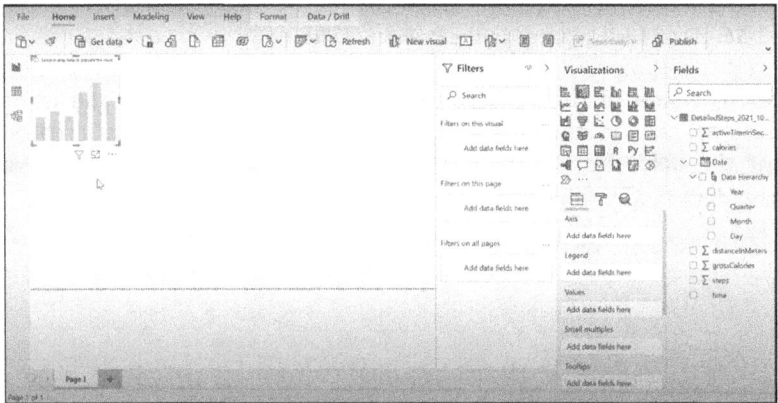

Figure 3-58. Selecting and Dragging a Histogram from the Visualizations Field

By selecting the date and the date hierarchy with the check box and then dragging this information in the date fields area on the screen with the y axis variable, in this example "STEPS," the profile of the data shows sensor movements over the time period (Figure 3-59).

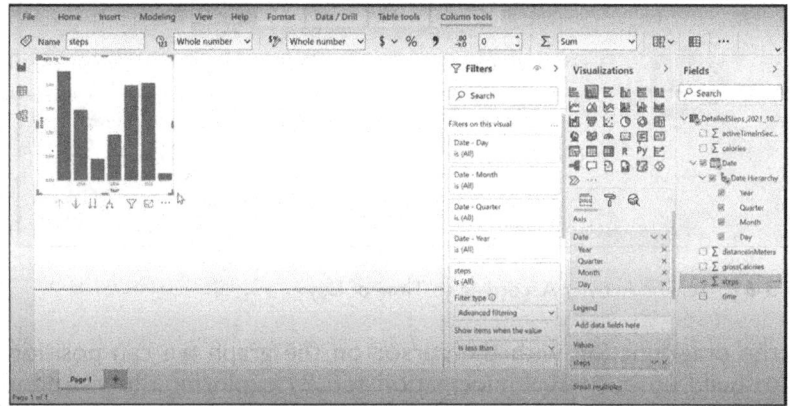

Figure 3-59. Total Movements for Each Year

With the date hierarchy field, one can drill down further, for instance, by quarter, month, or even by day (Figure 3-60) to derive more data insight.

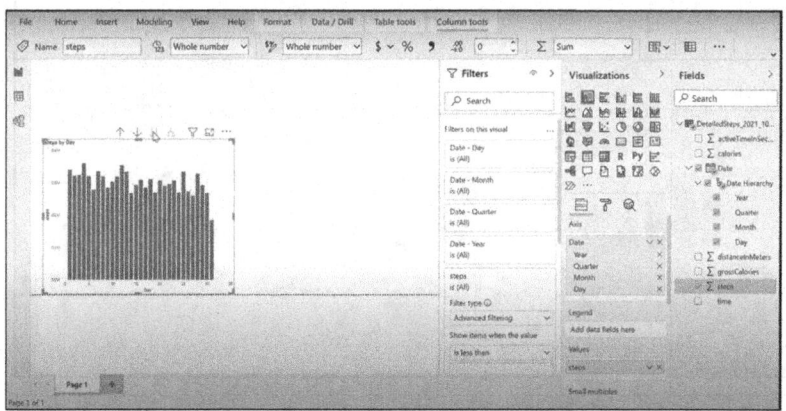

Figure 3-60. Data Broken Down According to the Day

One time-based question could be what is the busiest time of day? To answer this, we can add another histogram next to the first one to show the profile according to the time of day of activity (Figure 3-61).

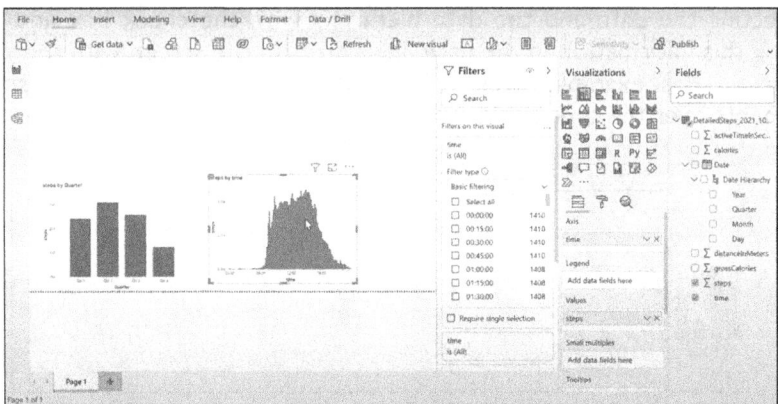

Figure 3-61. Sensor Activity According to Time of Day

Using the drag function with the cursor on the graph we can position the graph to build up our visual information set. By exploring the visualizations available, we can build up a visual report of the data. The visualizations field also has fields to select card icons to provide summary data like total sensor activity over the complete time period. Figures 3-62 and 3-63 show the process for selecting the visualization card.

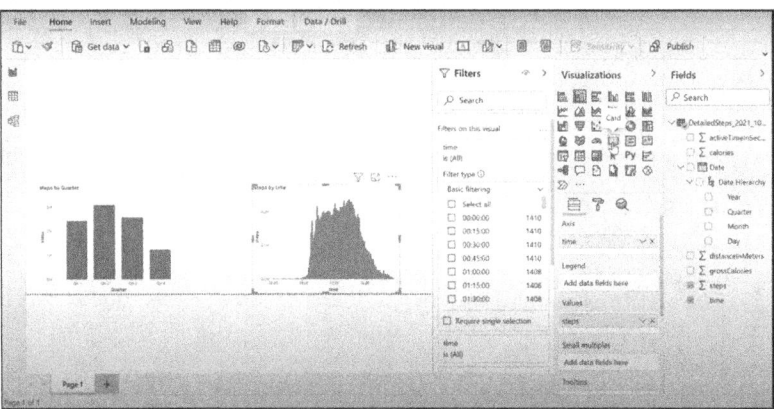

Figure 3-62. Card Icon Highlighted

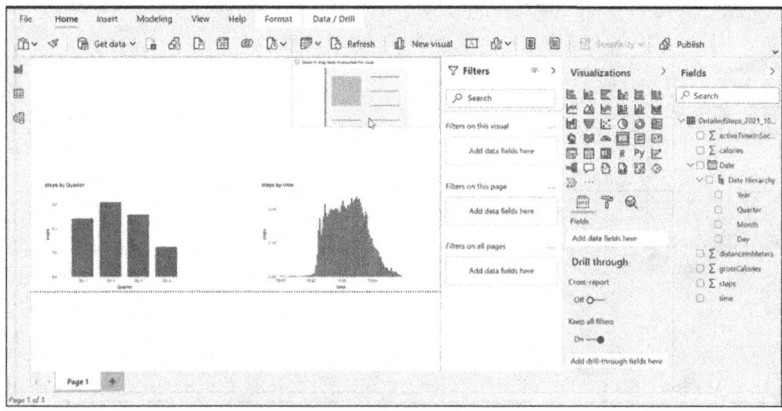

Figure 3-63. Selecting Information Cards from the Visualizations Field

We can then add in cards from the visualizations menu with titles and headline data.

For example, Figure 3-64 shows the total number of movements (9M) for the whole time period of the data set in the card.

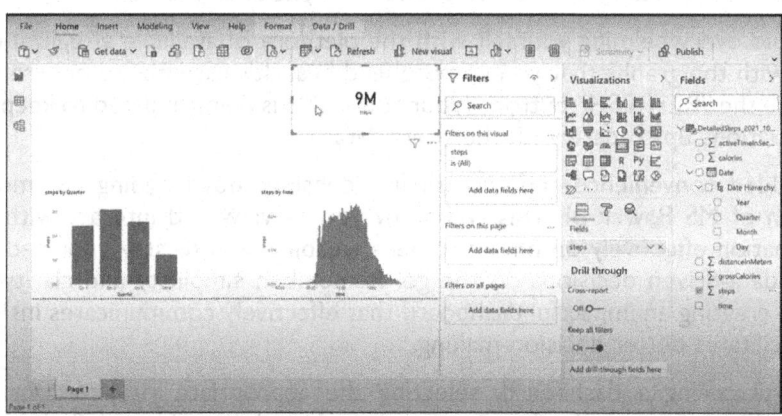

Figure 3-64. Add in Data Cards (Text Boxes) to Show Totals in Our Report

Figure 3-65 shows how we can add further text boxes to create dashboard headers as well as information from our data file.

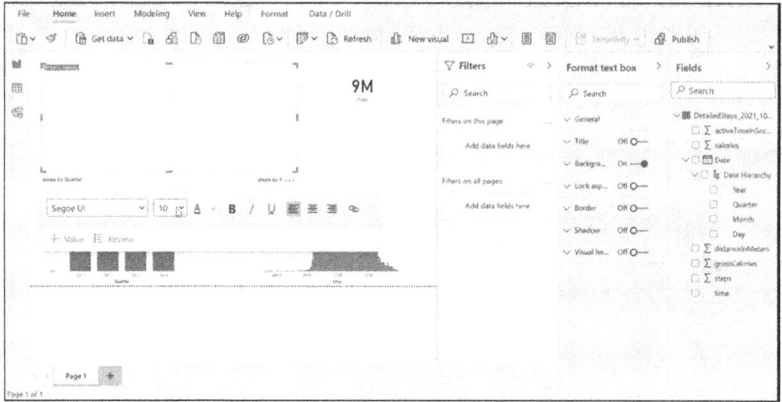

Figure 3-65. Creating Dashboard Headers

Selecting the "Card" label opens up a screen where you can add content, for example, images and the background and font can be edited (Figure 3-65).

By following these steps, you can swiftly produce a simple dashboard. Once you're satisfied with the dashboard's content, you can publish the data using the "publish" button icon located at the top right of the screen.

To avoid overwhelming yourself with the plethora of available visualizations, start with the graphs that you comprehend best. It's essential to ensure that you use the "REFRESH" button if your source file is being updated to keep the visualizations up-to-date with the latest data.

For added convenience and accessibility, consider downloading the mobile version of MS Power BI. This will allow you to view and interact with the information effectively on phone screens, enabling you to stay informed and make data-driven decisions on the go. Remember, simplicity and clarity are key to creating an impactful dashboard that effectively communicates insights and facilitates better decision-making.

After preparing a dashboard, selecting the appropriate visualizations can unlock insights not only about past events but also enable predictions for the future.

With the export feature in MS Power BI, you can seamlessly upload files into Lumen5 or MS PowerPoint. This capability allows you to create engaging presentations or videos that effectively communicate your findings.

As you further hone your skills, you will be capable of crafting more compelling dashboards, granting you immediate insights at a swift pace. Figure 3-66 showcases an advanced MS Power BI report, offering various views on a dataset. With real-time data updates, any changes in the source data will be promptly reflected in the report.

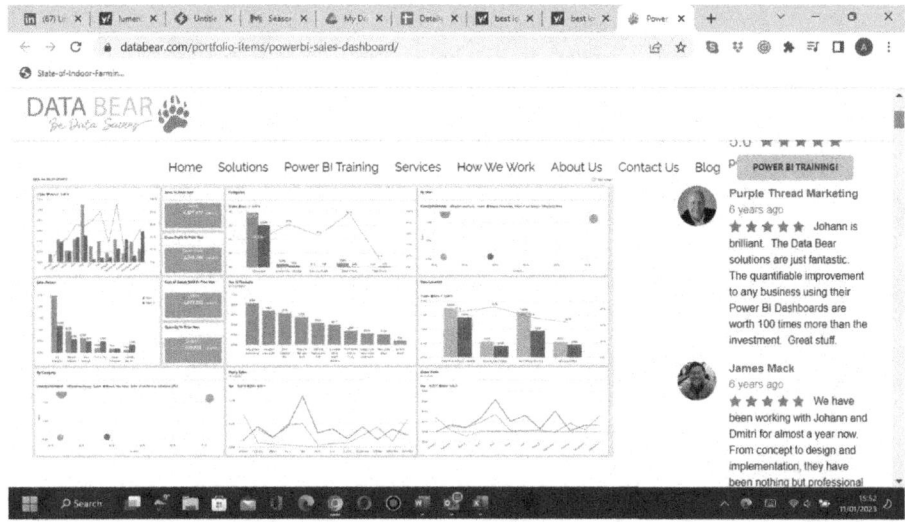

Figure 3-66. Advanced Power BI Dashboard. Source: `databear.com`

Conclusion

We've witnessed the transformative power of digital tool sets like Miro, Marvel, Lumen5, and Power BI in addressing some digital business challenges. These tools can empower us to overcome obstacles without the need for external data experts or consultancies, resulting in resource savings while ensuring alignment with our business needs.

By breaking free from the limitations of traditional digital office tools like MS PowerPoint, Excel, and Word, we can embrace a new era of exploration, practice, and perseverance with these basic tool sets. Gaining confidence in their capabilities allows us to actively participate in and successfully deliver on our business needs through digital transformation. This can only be achieved by continuous exploring and playing with new tools.

In the upcoming chapter, we will delve into how business owners can take greater ownership of the digital transformation process. By leveraging the potential of digital tools and strategies, they can drive their businesses forward and embrace the advantages of digitalization to stay competitive in today's dynamic business landscape.

We will then look at some low-code automation tools that use Artificial Intelligence.

Delivering Digital Transformation Through Business Outcomes

Introduction

We have defined digital transformation through some classic case examples from different verticals, carried out a deep dive into data and looked at some practical digital tools to empower business owners to become comfortable working with data.

© Attul Sehgal 2024
A. Sehgal, *Demystifying Digital Transformation*,
https://doi.org/10.1007/978-1-4842-9499-4_4

In this chapter, we will take a look at the issues with implementing digital transformation (DX) initiatives and how companies could do better. We'll present a way that digital transformation can be more driven by the business problem and how business owners can take the lead by being more insight driven. We'll also see how this approach can be applied in different verticals.

We'll focus on the following three key aspects:

1. What we can learn from digital natives.

2. How unclear business targets contribute to DX failure.

3. How to align DX projects to your business goals.

4. How to build a business case for your DX projects.

Digital transformation is a complex and challenging process, but it's one that can be incredibly rewarding.

So let's get started!

Can Buying a Car Be Considered a True Financial Investment?

Do people purchase cars as investments? Unless you happen to own a luxury vehicle such as an Aston Martin DB9, a Rolls Royce, or a Bentley, it's not very common for cars to be bought as financial investments. Over time, their internal combustion engines tend to degrade, and their exterior loses its luster. In fact, the unfortunate and harsh reality is that a new car experiences a depreciation in value of around 20% as soon as it is driven off the showroom floor. Figure 4-1 shows the depreciation of a typical car over ten years (www. webuyanycar.com/car-valuation/car-value-after-3-years/#:~:text=Our%20used%20car%20value%20calculator%20is%20based%20on,Year%204%20E2%80%93%20and%2060%25%20at%20Year%205).

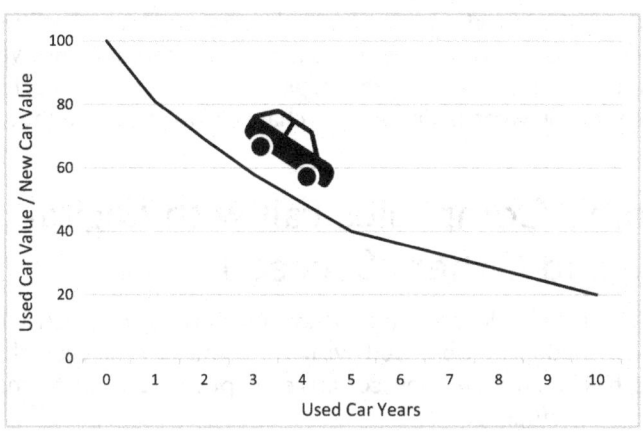

Figure 4-1. Average Car Depreciation over Time: Source WebuyAnyCar.com

While it is widely accepted that cars generally depreciate in value, there was a revolutionary statement made in 2019 that challenged this notion. A prominent digital entrepreneur declared that buying a car today could be an investment into the future. He said, "If you buy a car today, it's an investment into the future. [By] Buying a Tesla 3 [full self-driving option], I believe you are buying an appreciating asset, not a depreciating one."

This perspective was based on the belief that with the rise of digital innovation, cars could increase in value through the building of data intelligence. In this scenario, purchasing a car could be seen as an investment similar to buying stocks, shares, or real estate.

This statement carried significant weight, especially considering the history of entrepreneurs who attempted to introduce radical changes to the US car market, but ultimately failed. Examples include Avanti Motor Car with its unique fiberglass body and DeLorean with its stainless steel body and futuristic doors.

Elon Musk was, of course, the entrepreneur behind Tesla, with a strong personal brand who made this bold statement. Specifically, he stated that buying a Tesla Model 3 with the full self-driving option could be considered an appreciating asset rather than a depreciating one.

The underlying concept is that future software updates, combined with driving-based data, would enable more advanced self-driving features, thereby increasing the value of Tesla cars over time. This idea challenges the traditional understanding of car depreciation.

This raises the question of why it often takes an outsider, like Elon Musk, to describe and execute a visionary approach within the automotive sector. It prompts us to consider our own respective sectors or workplaces and contemplate who or what is driving the changes within those industries.

Why Some Companies Fail with Digital Projects and Others Succeed

Tesla doesn't just build electric cars – they build intelligent electric cars. In the United States, a country obsessed with cars, the key success challenge for electric cars has been how they compare to petrol cars in terms of range, cost, and ease of refueling.

Traditionally, buying a petrol car has meant accepting that the car will depreciate in value over time. However, Tesla CEO Elon Musk has challenged this status quo by boldly stating that the intelligent Tesla 3 model will actually appreciate in value. This statement, coupled with the growing interest in sustainability, Tesla's strong presence as a stylish and desirable brand, the company's direct sales to customers (avoiding dealerships), and government incentives, has made the Tesla 3 a very desirable proposition.

This is what we call a "game changer" for the overall value proposition of electric cars. It is a game changer that has been driven by Elon Musk's understanding of how digital technology and data can be used to radically transform a business.

According to McKinsey analysis (see Figure 4-2), AI and automation will drive up to 2/3rds of Europe's GDP growth by 2030. "Digital winners" typically employ hyper-scalable software-based business models that can rapidly scale up the number of users and revenue with only minimal changes to the underlying cost structure.

This is a tantalizing opportunity to explore, but it does raise questions about how digital transformation works best today and who is best positioned to drive this.

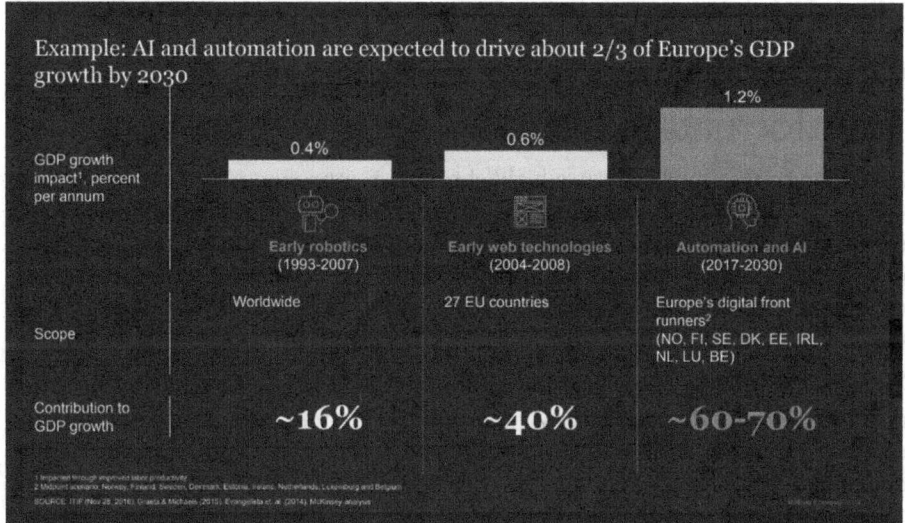

Figure 4-2. Source: McKinsey

The reality is, however, for most established Fortune 2000 companies that are investing into digital transformation projects, most are not realizing their potential. Studies show that up to 87% of digital transformation efforts fail to realize the full impact of their digital investments (www.accenture.com/_acnmedia/PDF-142/Accenture-What-Is-Industry-X.pdf). This is an appalling and extremely costly failure rate – both in terms of the project cost and in realizing business outcomes.

There is a paradox here: we know that digital transformation is fundamental to any business's wealth creation, yet investments lead to high chance of failure. We don't appear to know how to maximize on the opportunity presented. With such high costs, it can make you wonder whether undertaking a serious digital transformation investment makes any sense.

In recent years, I have come across various reasons why businesses embark on digital transformation efforts, such as following the trend, demonstrating organizational agility, or seeking cost-cutting opportunities through new toolsets. However, many of these initiatives fail due to unrealistic business expectations, poor planning, adopting inappropriate technology, and insufficient resources or skills to execute the projects effectively. I have personally witnessed how business owners, influenced by the hype surrounding digital tools, often hold lofty expectations of technology without having adequate exposure to them. Additionally, it is common for companies to rely heavily on outsourced systems integrators for the strategy and approach, thus delegating critical business thinking to third parties.

Is there anything that business owners can do directly to enhance the delivery of business outcomes through digital technology?

How Unclear Digital Transformation (DX) Outcomes Contribute to Digital Transformation Failure

In 2019, a report by Accenture highlighted that approximately 30% of Fortune Global 2000 companies allocated a minimum of 10% of their revenue toward digital transformation initiatives. These findings shed light on the significant investments being made in this area. Notably, the report identified customer experience, marketing, and sales as the most common domains for digital transformation projects.

To provide context, let's consider a hypothetical scenario where you are a major shareholder in a company generating $100 million in annual earnings. In this case, the company is allocating at least $10 million for digital transformation endeavors. However, instead of witnessing substantial returns in digital transformation efforts, the executive teams frequently report delays, unexpectedly high cloud licensing costs, and abandoned pilot projects. Meanwhile, the primary digital success seems to be on teams involved in website relaunches!

What is going on?

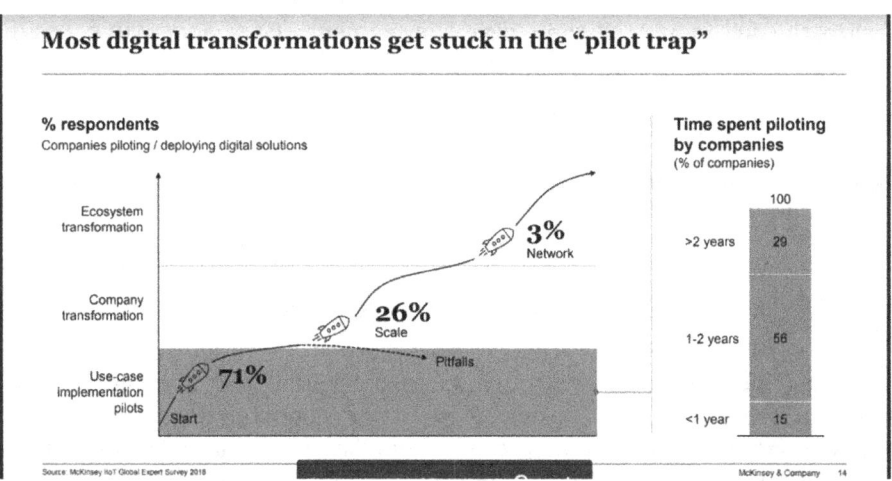

Figure 4-3. Most Pilots Get Stuck in the Pilot Trap Consuming Lots of Resources at the Same Time: Source: Mckinsey

A 2018 survey by McKinsey showed that despite intense implementation pilots by fortune 5000 companies, a high number of pilots fail to scale. Figure 4-3 shows a survey carried out by McKinsey showing the typical duration of digital transformation projects and the proportion that get to ecosystem transformation. They break digital transformation down into Ecosystem transformation and Company transformation.

Ecosystem transformation in a company involves altering the way the company engages with its customers, suppliers, partners, and other stakeholders. This process aims to adapt the company's external interactions to align with evolving market dynamics. On the other hand, company transformation focuses on internal changes within the company itself. These changes encompass various aspects, including the business model, products and services, marketing and sales strategies, and organizational structure. Company transformation is typically driven by factors originating from within the organization, such as new leadership, strategic shifts, or mergers and acquisitions. In contrast, ecosystem transformation is primarily motivated by external influences like advancements in technology, evolving customer preferences, and the need to address competitive forces.

Critically, there is a gap between the high-level strategic plan in the organization for business transformation and the execution of digital transformation projects. The preceding figure shows the proportion of projects that get to each stage.

Sadly, over 71% of digital transformation projects get stuck in the "pilot trap." Over the next five years, there has been little improvement. In 2023, McKinsey, in their publication, Rewired, stated that 89% of companies capture just a fraction of expected revenue and cost savings from digital and AI transformations.

If we consider the level of investment into digital transformation projects in light of the pilot trap, where is the money being spent?

- Is it going to expensive external consultants to produce strategy roadmaps and ideas?

- Is it going to the heads of IT departments to perform little pilot projects of no consequence?

- Is it going to upgrade existing operations? Essentially, upgrading an existing infrastructure element that is being digitized?

Are certain digitalization projects being promoted as digital transformation projects because they are relatively easy to implement? For example, a simple website redesign.

Before moving on, can you think of some digital transformation (DX) engagements going on in your business? Are these digital transformations side projects, step change improvements, company transformations, or something larger? Are the business outcomes clear and do they justify the costs?

Let's try and put these digital engagements into context and try and work out how transformational they are.

Assessing Digital Transformation (DX) Effectiveness

To assess the effectiveness of DX, it is important to be clear on the difference between "digital transformation" and "digitalization." While many firms mistakenly view digitalization as a part of their digital transformation and create KPI measures to show their digital transformation success, the two concepts are distinct. Digitalization simply involves converting human-driven processes into software-driven ones, representing a mere upgrade. This process, although relatively straightforward, often allows businesses to retain their existing underlying models and so there is no change to the business operating model.

Numerous frameworks exist for evaluating the progress of a digital transformation journey. However, when it comes down to it, a few key factors emerge:

- Customer: Are you meeting your customers' expectations? Digital transformation should focus on understanding and satisfying evolving customer needs and preferences. A bottleneck can occur with internal customers in your organization who are most comfortable with outdated structures and legacy systems.

- Innovation: Are you consistently introducing new and radical services? Successful digital transformation involves fostering a culture of innovation and leveraging digital capabilities to deliver unique and impactful offerings.

- Competition: Are you ahead of the competition? Digital transformation should enable companies to outperform competitors by embracing emerging technologies, keeping pace with industry trends, and proactively adapting to market dynamics.

- Data: Are you effectively utilizing and sharing data? The ability to collect, store, analyze, and leverage data is crucial for making informed business decisions in the digital age.

- Value: Are you developing new propositions to strengthen your brand? Digital transformation should drive the development of compelling value propositions that enhance the company's brand and attract customers.

It's important to note as well that simply acquiring digital tools such as sensors, e-commerce platforms, mobile apps, and a social media presence is not enough. The true challenge lies in harnessing the generated data to make well-informed decisions. To succeed in the digital age, business owners at all levels must excel at collecting, storing, and analyzing data effectively. This is also a people and culture issue.

Digital transformation has heightened customer expectations, necessitating companies to match those expectations. It requires a continuous focus on innovation, staying ahead of the competition, developing new propositions to strengthen the brand, and, most importantly, utilizing data effectively. While it may be easy to adopt digital tools, leveraging the generated data for informed decision-making is the key to success in the digital era.

Bill Schmarzo described in his book *Big Data MBA* a framework that describes how effective an organization is at leveraging data and analytics to power the business. It is called the Big Data Business Model Maturity Index (BDBMMI) and has five stages:

- Stage 1: Business monitoring: Organizations are using data and analytics to monitor the business. They are gathering data from internal and external sources, and they are using this data to create reports and dashboards.

- Stage 2: Business insights: Organizations are using data and analytics to gain insights into their business. They are using data to understand their customers, their products, and their operations.

- Stage 3: Business optimization: Organizations are using data and analytics to optimize their business processes. They are using data to identify opportunities for improvement, and they are implementing changes to improve their efficiency and effectiveness.

- Stage 4: Insights monetization: Organizations are using data and analytics to monetize their insights. They are using data to create new products and services, and they are using data to sell advertising and other marketing services.

- Stage 5: Metamorphosis: Organizations are using data and analytics to transform their business. They are using data to create new business models, and they are using data to change the way they operate.

If we try to apply the five parts to some of the companies we mentioned earlier, we can see where things can break down for most companies when doing DX.

Incredibly, 98% of businesses get stuck at the "Business Monitoring" phase of the digital journey. Essentially, this is where business have data projects and tools to help them understand what was happening in the past. In this context, the descriptive analytics tools we discussed in Chapter 2 are used. To illustrate, Figure 4-4 shows some of the case examples we discussed earlier and where they could be in the maturity index.

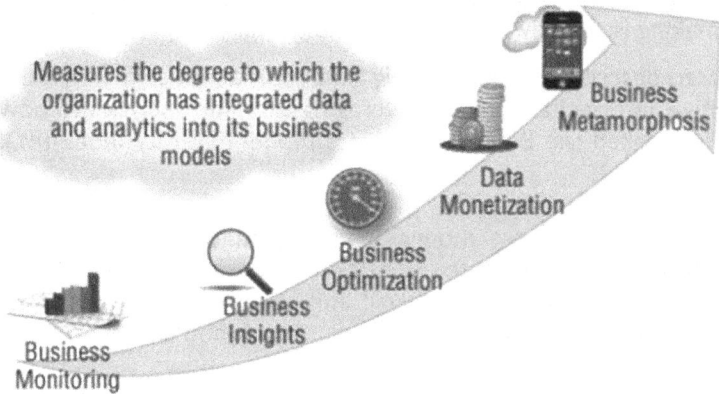

Figure 4-4. Big Data Business Model Maturity Index, Source: Big Data MBA, William Schmarzo

If we look at firms like Circuit city in the early 2000s, they were using their closely guarded data sources and market data to understand what was happening in the past, but not using the data to the extent to even predict what would happen in the future or fuel new propositions. At the business monitoring stage, they were very much asking individual members of teams to analyze the historical data to make decisions. Whereas the digital natives like Amazon were deriving insights from understanding how customers were behaving today, and using tools to predict how they could behave in the future, prescribe new insights and then use these insights to create new revenue streams, then transform the business like using recommendation engines to upsell other products and services. We will look at some of these methods and tools in Chapters 6 and 7 and in ways even a non-technical executive can get an understanding of them.

If we consider the Hilton Hotels, their challenge against Airbnb is to keep up with the deep data insights generated by digital natives while managing their existing processes. This slows down the progression from business monitoring to business insights. The challenge is whether you invest in making existing operations more streamlined or invest in building new data driven propositions.

If we reflect back to when Elon Musk made bold statements about radically transforming products, he is very much talking from the "business metamorphosis" stage, showing the advanced thinking about leveraging data and advanced algorithms to power business models. He is using data and analytics to transform the business model for automotive.

A case in point is shown in Figure 4-5 from VisualCapitalist.com in 2022.

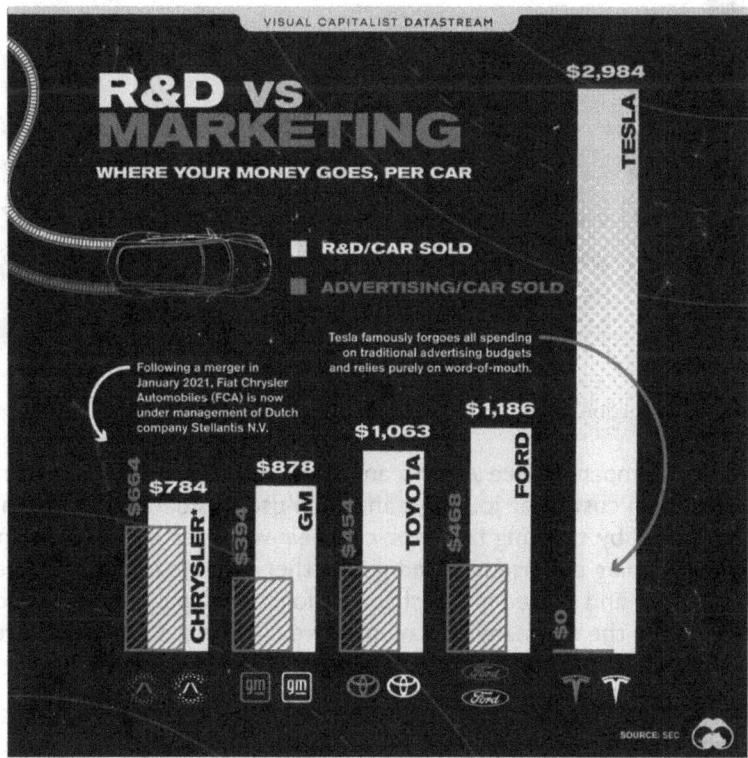

Figure 4-5. R&D and Advertising Per Car Sold; Source VisualCapitalist.com

VisualCapitalist.com produced in their data stream showed a comparison of R&D and advertising per car sold of Chrysler, GM, Toyota, and Ford against Tesla, and the comparison is quite remarkable. Tesla outspends its competitors on R&D twofold and uses its brand strength to undersell in direct advertising.

Looking at profitability, Tesla is way ahead of traditional car manufacturers. Typically car manufacturers have a gross margin between 10–20%, but despite the economic slowdown and the drop in the price of the Model 3, Tesla still report figures in the 20–30% range. Figure 4-6 shows the Gross Margin for Q2 2023 against other leading car manufacturers. It is researching heavily in driverless digital technology using sophisticated data acquisition, robotics, artificial intelligence, and semi-conductor chips. Another feature of its strong profit margin is in its direct sales rather than dealership experience. To buy a car, you simply go to the Tesla web page and click the model you want to buy, configure your vehicle, and make a deposit.

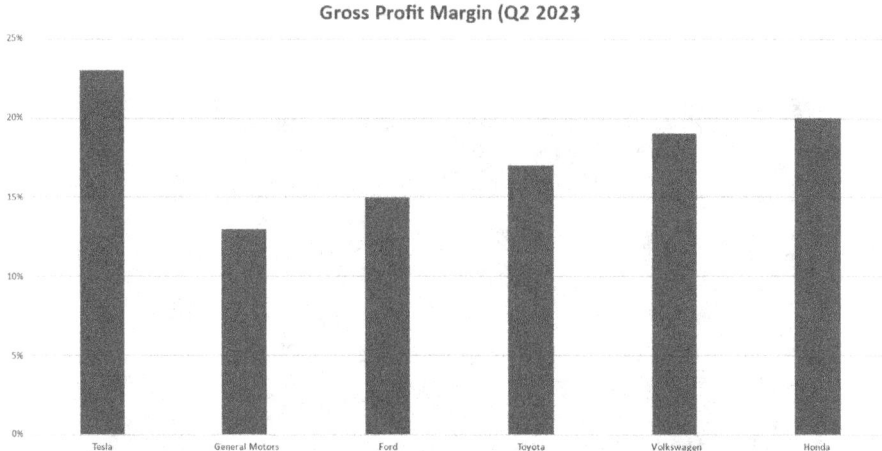

Gross Profit Margin (Q2 2023)

Figure 4-6. Comparison of Gross Margin for Leading Automotive Firms

Digital native companies, like Airbnb and Tesla, are inherently structured to acquire data from customer journeys and then use this data to derive insights of its customers, by tracking behavior on their websites to build insights on abandoned shopping experiences and get further insights from that. The data can be presented and shared in any shape or form to departments to produce new learnings for the company to, say, improve customer loyalty, explore new revenue streams, and move further ahead of the incumbents.

By being higher up the Big Data Maturity model index can improve their usage of data, exceed their KPIs and hence business performance.

It is imperative to master the power of data insight in this current innovation cycle.

There is no better example in seeing the power of data insight for business metamorphosis and success than looking at the story of Waze and how they revolutionized route planning through the power of data.

Waze provide driving directions, live traffic, and road updates via a mobile app. The traditional approach to traffic management tools involved starting with available maps and identifying the busiest roads, from major highways to minor streets. One would assume for a company providing traffic directions that the first thing needed would be to acquire content for a roadmap, but

Waze did something completely different. When they set up in 2008 (which coincidently was the year of Circuit City's downfall), and through an initial investment of $12M and recruitment of 100 employees, they built their map from global positioning system (GPS) data generated from test drivers who drove in their pilot cities and then crowdsourcing the information. From understanding the frequency of movement of the traffic they could identify the minor and major roads and forecast the traffic and the best routes for drivers more effectively than traditional methods. Crucially, Waze's effectiveness depends on user participation, and the company actively encourages people to share data. This approach fosters greater accuracy and reliability in the system. Moreover, Waze also collaborates with state agencies to access information on traffic events like road construction.

Waze's success in harnessing data and crowd wisdom has transformed the way people navigate roads, making their journey smoother and more efficient. It creates revenue through hyperlocal advertising. For more details, look up the publication *Fall in Love with the Problem and Not the Solution*, by Uri Levine.

Figure 4-7 shows how the map was made through data.

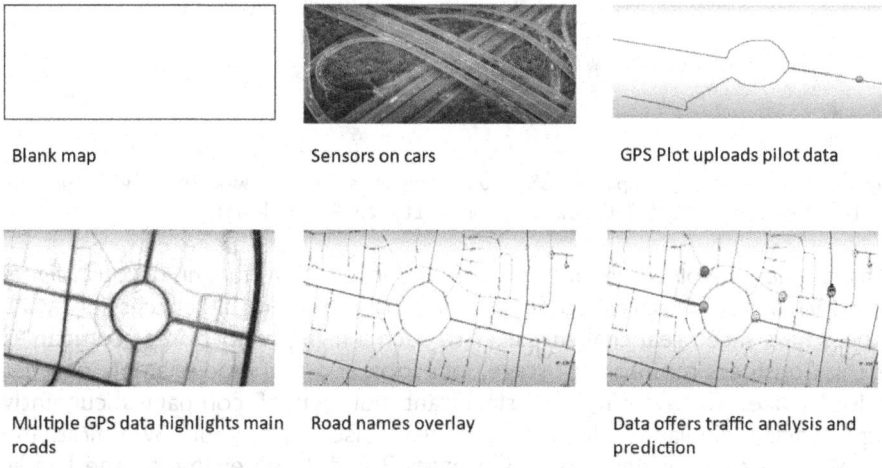

Blank map   Sensors on cars   GPS Plot uploads pilot data

Multiple GPS data highlights main roads   Road names overlay   Data offers traffic analysis and prediction

Figure 4-7. Design of the Waze Map

The app proved to be highly popular, and the company was sold to Google for $1.3Bn in 2013.

Despite the efforts of traditional firms to do digital transformation and emulate success, 98% of companies are still using digital techniques at the business monitoring stage. To show what is at stake, let's look at Figure 4-8. The S&P 500 index tracks the share prices of 500 of the largest public companies in the

United States. Innosight, a US consulting firm, produced a report in 2016 that looked at the turnover of the companies in the S&P 500 index (www.innosight.com/wp-content/uploads/2016/08/Corporate-Longevity-2016-Final.pdf). In 1965, the average tenure for a company in the S&P 500 was around 33 years; by 1990, it had shrunk to 20 years and is expected to reach 14 years by 2026, coinciding with the uptake onset of the fifth and sixth innovation waves.

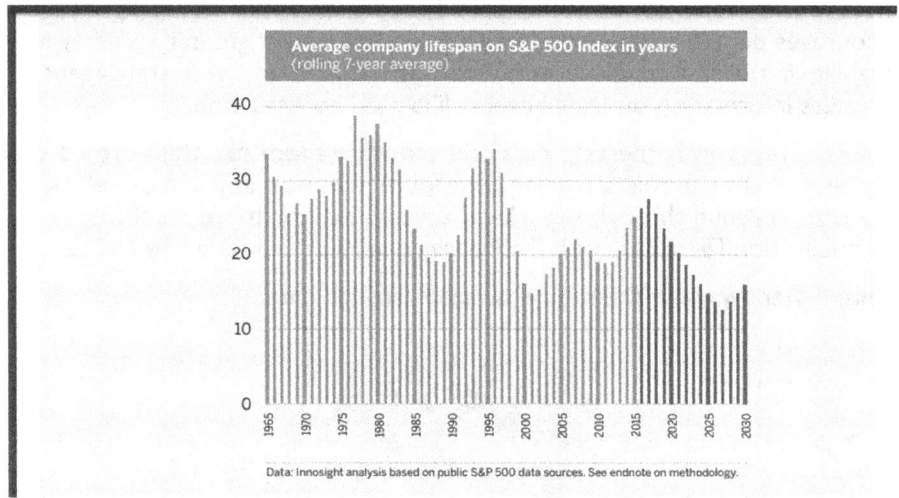

Figure 4-8. Average Lifespan of S&P 500 Companies. Source: www.innosight.com/wp-content/uploads/2016/08/Corporate-Longevity-2016-Final.pdf

I have been involved in and provided consultation for numerous digital transformation initiatives, some of which have been highly successful, while others have faced real challenges. With such a high proportion of companies at this "business monitoring" stage, let's look at a real case example of what it looks like. Considering the significant number of companies currently experiencing similar challenges, you may also have your own firsthand experiences to consider too. In Chapters 2 and 3, we examined the Landis Car Hire case study, which provided us with insights into various fundamental digital tools that could be utilized to enhance the front-end experience of their digital channels. Allow me to present a case example of a fictional utility company using data purely for business monitoring. This scenario offers valuable lessons on how to avoid pitfalls and achieve a successful digital transformation.

Case Example: Bigview Water Ltd

In 2017, Bigview Water embarked on a digital transformation effort to overhaul their IT, digital operations, digital marketing, as well as explore game-changing innovative propositions.

The operator was responsible for delivering clean water services to a vast customer base, including millions of residential customers and prominent businesses such as airports and breweries in the area. The primary function of this service was straightforward: whenever you turned on your tap, the water flowing out was supplied by this operator.

The presence of leaks and microleaks in the pipes posed significant efficiency challenges for all operators. However, this particular operator took pride in implementing a digital sensor rollout as an effective solution to promptly address these issues. The theory was that by deploying sensors across the network, the operator could detect flows and identify leaks, aiming to conserve water within the network while minimizing downtime and reducing costs associated with repairing burst pipes. These devices intelligently reported faults, including their precise location, to a centralized network management center. Additionally, the operator had the prestige of being an early adopter among UK water operators in investing in a cloud network and an extensive remote sensor network.

With an annual revenue of approximately £300 million, the operator allocated around 8% of its revenue toward IT-driven projects, most of which were focused on digitalization, digital marketing, and digital transformation initiatives. Since the operator held a license to provide services within a specific region, it enjoyed a monopoly over the service operations in that area. Consequently, customers relied entirely on the regulator, OFWAT, to ensure the provision of high-quality services. The concept of quality of service encompassed swift resolution of burst pipe incidents, effective management of customer service matters, and the overall efficiency of the operator's operations

The regulator carried out independent surveys with customers and issued a ranking of the operators in terms of performance. Despite the digital investment, time and again the operator was near the bottom of the ranking table. The consequence was that the operator was liable for fines to the regulator for bad service. Here is a headline showing the size of fines that operators can pay.

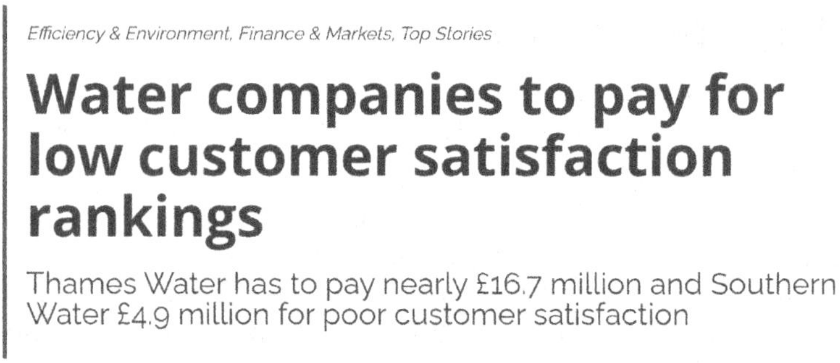

Efficiency & Environment, Finance & Markets, Top Stories

Water companies to pay for low customer satisfaction rankings

Thames Water has to pay nearly £16.7 million and Southern Water £4.9 million for poor customer satisfaction

Figure 4-9. Regulator Fines for Bad Customer Service. `www.standard.co.uk`

These fines impinged on the returns of the operator as well as overall customer perception. So, despite being pioneers in the cloud migration effort, having a widely deployed sensor network to proactively detect faults, why was the operator not showing delivering customer service ratings to customers? Why didn't digital transformation take them on the path to business optimization and beyond?

Let's look at some of the assets. Here is a snapshot of a customer bill from 2021 – four years after the digital transformation exercise took place. The bill consisted of a summary page, some ideas of water management, and ways to pay the bill.

between 30 April 2021 and 31 March 2022

Non-metered water charge (336 days) (363.00 x £0.7458 per year)	£249.22
Fixed Charge (30/04/21 - 31/03/22)	£43.17
Clean water total	£292.39

– your service provider for waste water between 30 April 2021 and 31 March 2022

Non-metered waste water charge (336 days) (363.00 x £0.5959 per year)	£199.12
Fixed Charge (30/04/21 - 31/03/22)	£57.80
Waste water total	£256.92

Your charges/refunds for this bill

Validation fee Includes 20% VAT	£47.88
Total	£47.88

The above charges are VAT exempt, unless specified otherwise

Combined clean water and waste water charges for this bill **£597.19**

Fixed Charge
This is the fee your supplier charges for providing their service to your property and goes towards the cost of maintaining their networks. You may be able to pay less if rainwater from your property drains into a stream, river or soakaway instead of into a sewer. To find out more go to: **thameswater.co.uk/swd** or call 0800 009 3673.

Validation fee
A one-off cost for confirming who's at the property (after no response to our recent letter).

Any questions, visit affinitywater.co.uk

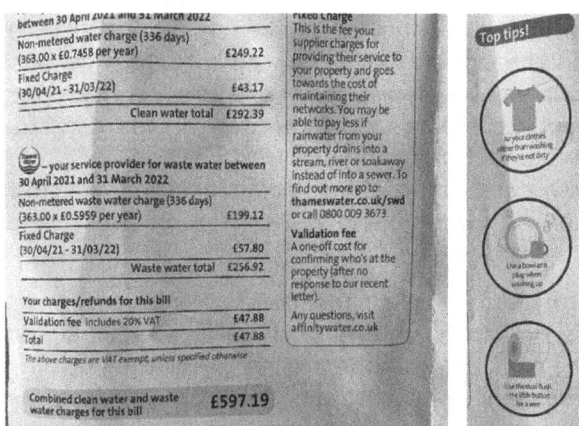

Figure 4-10. BigView Water Customer Bill Snapshot

At the time, there was an ongoing initiative to migrate customers to an online experience, but the bill contents were of the same format. The bill describes metered water charges, fixed charges, validation fees, and tips on washing clothes less often, using a plug when washing up. They basically invested in digitalising the paper experience!

At first glance, most customers who use digital experiences like a smartphone or the Internet would automatically have a much higher expectation of the billing experience. For example, if you use Amazon for buying books, music, and other products, you would get an online bill with a complete breakdown of the costs, possibly some background on overall spend in the previous months or years. There would also be personal recommendations on things that customers like you would be spending on. Such experiences raise the expectation levels when billed by other companies, even utilities. Sadly, these features were missing entirely.

Couldn't the operator have replicated at least some of these experiences?

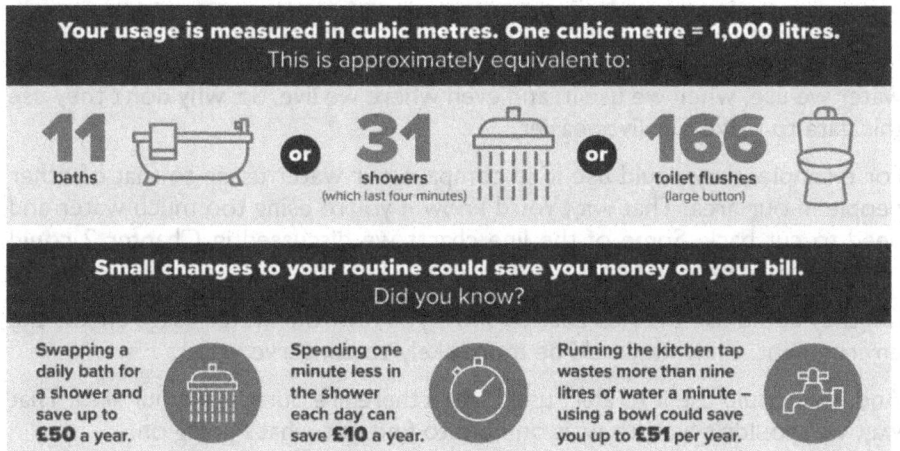

Figure 4-11. Snapshot of the Rich Information Available

There are ways for a utility company to provide a better experience. All customers appreciate advice regarding how to reduce bills, particularly if related to their own water consumption patterns. There is in fact a wealth of rich published data that the operator could use. Figure 4-11 shows some of the data management information available.

With the deployment of IoT sensors, they could provide more personalized and intelligent information to the local area. The data could directly answer questions that a customer could have:

- How does my bill compare with my neighbors?
- Is my consumption within the expected range for my home?
- Are there any leaks in my home that I should be aware of?

The operator could also use the data to provide personalized recommendations to customers on how to reduce their water consumption. For example, if a customer's water consumption is above the expected average range, the operator could send them a message with some tips on how to reduce their usage. Perhaps some of the visualizations we discussed in Chapter 2.

The operator could also use the data to identify areas where there is a high risk of leaks. This information could then be used to target these areas with leak detection and repair activities. These could be presented with some of the mapping tools shown in Chapter 2.

By using the data in this way, the operator could provide a better customer experience, reduce water consumption, save money, and also improve customer experience.

Water companies have a lot of data on our usage. They know how much water we use, when we use it, and even where we live. So, why don't they use this data to make our lives easier?

For example, they could use it to compare our water usage to that of other people in our area. That way, you'd know if you're using too much water and need to cut back. Some of the line charts we discussed in Chapter 2 could represent this information.

Or, they could use the rich data to show you how our water usage affects the environment. That way, we'd be more likely to conserve water.

And, they could use it to alert us to when there are outages in your area. That way, we wouldn't have to wait on hold to find out what's going on.

Water companies are regulated by the government, and there are rules about how they can use your data, but there are ways for customers to opt out or just offer more general guidance.

If the benefits of these features outweigh the costs, then most people would be happy to share their data if it meant they could get better service.

Are these features on a network with a wealth of sensors so complicated that only a digital pioneer can do them? Were there other priorities that supersede these?

Let's try and understand the priorities.

The first problem was trying to execute everything at once. That is to say, upgrading the IT function, conducting digital marketing, streamlining operations, and developing game-changing ideas.

KPIs were put in place for automating tasks, improved decision-making, improved service reliability, reduced environmental impact, as well as enhancing customer service. However, the KPIs were internal figures with no external benchmarking to deem whether they were really successful.

So to embark on a digital transformation journey, they sourced a consultancy to create the vision and implemented all sorts of new digital technologies. But guess what? Their customer service ratings stayed rock bottom!

So, what went wrong? Well, there were a few things. First, the company didn't really have a clear business vision for what they wanted to achieve with digital transformation. There were perceived cost savings and showing the regulator they were being innovative with technology.

Second, the engagement didn't fully involve the employees in the process. The end users of the systems were not seen "digitally" ready as the IT personnel and so their views were not as highly valued. The consultants came in, made all the decisions, and then implemented changes without early input from the people who would actually be using the new systems. They oversimplified the datasets in assuming that the data in the data warehouse was clearly defined and could be easily migrated to the cloud with the single sources of truth. They asked the business owners what they wanted when the systems were already being put in place. The remit was all under the control of the IT department who saw digital transformation as an opportunity to bring operations activities into their division, hence increasing company influence as part of OT/IT alignment strategy. The IT division had complete control over all the software and systems utilized by the organization. While this arrangement ensured strong security and support, it also limited the non-IT divisions from exploring, learning, and gaining confidence in using digital tools outside the IT umbrella.

Without any confidence in experimenting with digital tools, the employees' ideas thus lacked any forward thinking. For example, upgrading the website was seen as a major technological achievement.

Third, they didn't train the end users employees on how to configure the new systems. So, when the changes went live, everyone was lost and confused. For example, investing in business intelligence platforms that the operations staff were afraid to configure themselves.

Fourth, the source data being used to drive the systems was not checked and cleaned, and so it produced unreliable outputs when put into the system. It was assumed by the IT organization that the digitalized data was inherently correct and had no mistakes. For example, it was discovered that service gangs being sent out to fix a fault in the wrong location due to incorrect source information on the systems, thus taking longer to locate and fix faults! Service gangs then reverted to their old ways of speaking to their colleagues who knew about the fault locations from years of experience rather than referring to the digital tools.

Fifth, despite being lauded for having an infrastructure for the future, they had no idea if they were actually making progress on business outcomes or not as no reference point was established to agree on a point of success.

Finally, with regard to digital marketing to simply making customer bills more attractive for improved customer service, the other repair priorities took over leaving the retail teams with little support to execute.

So, there you have it. A few of the things that can go wrong with digital transformation. If you're thinking about embarking on a digital transformation journey, make sure you avoid these pitfalls. Otherwise, you might just end up like the Bigview Water: spending a lot of money and not really getting anywhere.

Digital transformation can be a great way to improve your business. But it's important to do it right and there will always be some constraints. So how can we do it better?

Aligning Digital Transformation to Business Goals

From the Bigview water case example in the last section, we can see the way that digital transformation was perceived as a technical driven initiative rather than a business initiative. This approach is not uncommon but is one of the main reasons of digital transformation failure.

The process primarily involves investing into hyped up technology and putting it into the architecture. We then look at the data generated by this technology to see what questions the technology could answer. Finally, we assess these questions in line with the organizational decisions to derive the business initiatives through the business stakeholders. This is summarized in Figure 4-12.

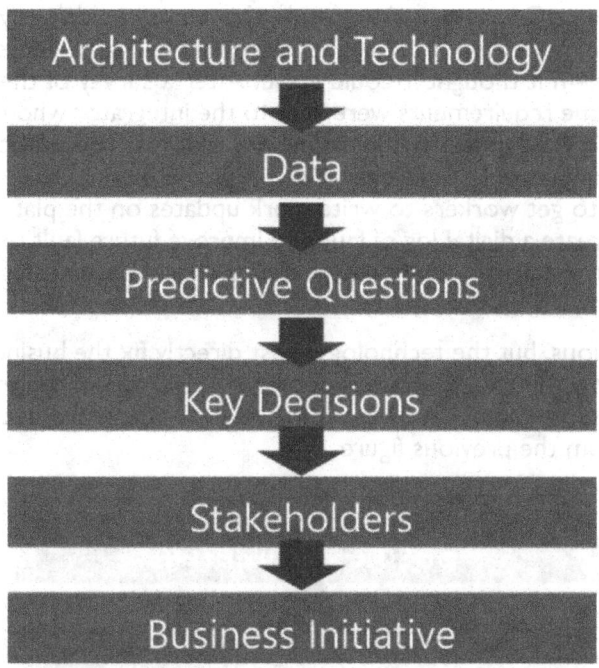

Figure 4-12. Today's Approach to Digital Transformation

This approach to digital transformation is a major factor in its failure. Relying solely on digital technology to solve multiple business issues without a clear understanding of the actual business objectives leads to misaligned investments. Consequently, product owners are driven to prioritize the technology itself, often shaping the end user story to fit the acquired technology. By the time the needs of the end users and the true business requirements are assessed, substantial resources have already been consumed and budgets have been allocated.

On many occasions, the business problem is clear, but the way a technology already purchased can solve the problem is not clear – but the priority is to use that new technology.

For instance, a few years ago, I had a client who purchased a cutting-edge work scheduling tool worth millions of dollars from a leading system integrator. This tool allowed maintenance teams to view, manage, and update their work orders without having to return to the service center after each job, thus saving time and resources. The work scheduling platform with its data management and prediction elements performed admirably and was an excellent software tool. However, it had a crucial dependency on consistent 4G mobile network coverage to function properly and update the job orders. Unfortunately, a significant portion of the maintenance work was conducted in areas without 4G coverage. As a result, the teams couldn't rely on the data in the tool and ended up not using it, ultimately failing to address the main business problem it thought it could solve. After a survey of the operational gangs' needs, the requirements were sent to the integrator who then charged a few million dollars more to implement the changes. The service was finally integrated many years later at over four times the original cost. The original problem was to get workers to write work updates on the platform on each occasion to create a digital log of faults to improve future fault resolution and diagnostics. It is unclear today whether the original business problem was ever solved.

It sounds obvious, but the technology must directly fix the business problem. The reason why this isn't the case is because of the hype of the technology to fix the business problem. Let's look at Figure 4-13 where the decision making is reversed from the previous figure.

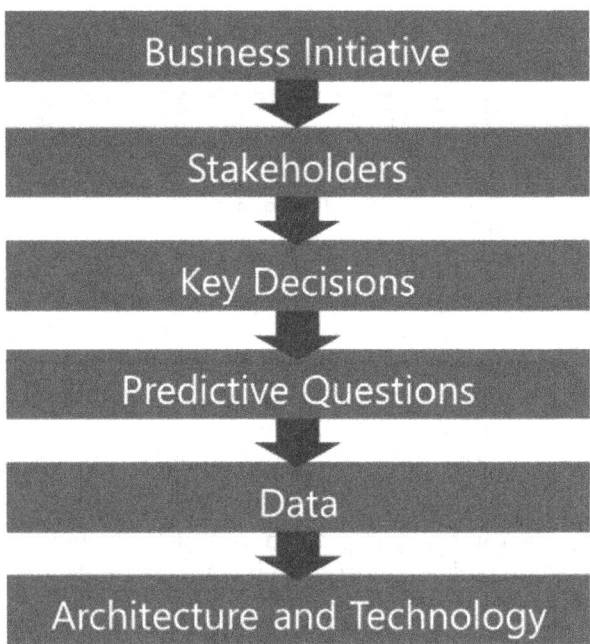

Figure 4-13. An Insight-driven Approach

The insight-driven approach starts from the business initiative itself. By looking at data points, a business can make the right decisions. Advanced analytics techniques, are then applied to uncover patterns, identify opportunities, and make informed predictions like future revenue.

By utilizing these insights, organizations can even make data-driven decisions regarding technology adoption, process optimization, and customer experience enhancement.

An insight-driven approach also fosters a culture of continuous learning and improvement. It encourages organizations to continuously monitor and measure their digital transformation efforts, allowing them to adapt and refine their strategies based on real-time feedback and insights gained from data analysis.

The classic example is one of Starbucks using their data set of 100,000 transactions per week and 30,000 stores globally to decide on the locations of their future stores, the products to sell, and the habits of their users to drive loyalty. They use this data in conjunction with external data too. For example, to decide on the location of a new store, they would source data on incomes, population density, and traffic to agree on a location to discuss with the stakeholders. By prioritizing and collecting relevant data from various sources, both internal and external, to gain a comprehensive understanding of their operations, customers, and market trends, they can make better decisions.

When we think about the earlier case example of Waze, why did it take a start-up and not the automobile associations to think of this solution? With the restrictions imposed on non-technical business owners, they do not have the freedom to explore, so tackling this task can be extremely challenging and often results in the data and technology teams driving the requirements through business owners' lack of understanding of data mining, visualization tools, and simple algorithms. As time moves on, business owners will struggle to keep up with the rapidly evolving technology and data science methods, leading to a further disconnect between their customer needs and the solutions being developed.

The process of gathering requirements for specific initiatives becomes even more difficult when business owners lack basic knowledge about the capabilities of data and analytics. To truly understand what data and analytics can accomplish, business owners need a higher level of proficiency with data and digital tools. Fortunately, there is a range of low-code/no-code tools available that do not require coding or systems engineering skills. These tools offer business owners the opportunity to explore machine learning and other relevant concepts without feeling the need to rely solely on the IT department or traditional Office365 tools. We already introduced some of digital tools in the previous chapter that can help and will look at some mining and analytics tools later on in Chapter 8.

By embracing these new tools and exploring others, business owners can break free from the constraints of familiar platforms and gain a deeper understanding of the potential of digital technologies. This empowers them to drive their own digital transformation initiatives and make informed decisions regarding the adoption of data-driven technologies.

If we go back to the Elon Musk statement of a vision of a car appreciating over time, we can see how this is an illustration how an insight-driven approach could make a radical change. It can be proven by using the power of data to radically transform the business offering. Figure 4-14 shows how the data can be generated.

The business insight is that we want the customer to consider a car getting better over time. The data generated by the car through sensors and other digital equipment, if managed correctly, can ensure the car can be driven more efficiently the more often it is used as it builds a data set of driver behaviors. Through a constant learning system, it would mean a safer, personal, and more energy-efficient car over time.

This could then be the proposition to the organization and to the data scientists. Putting the technical jargon to one side, we can use the analogy of the child being educated over time. By creating a learning engine into the car, the car will have new attributes that are better than when the car left the showroom.

For all the individual drivers of the Tesla sharing their data into the cloud creates a powerful data set for a more intelligent car. And that is the insight-driven thinking.

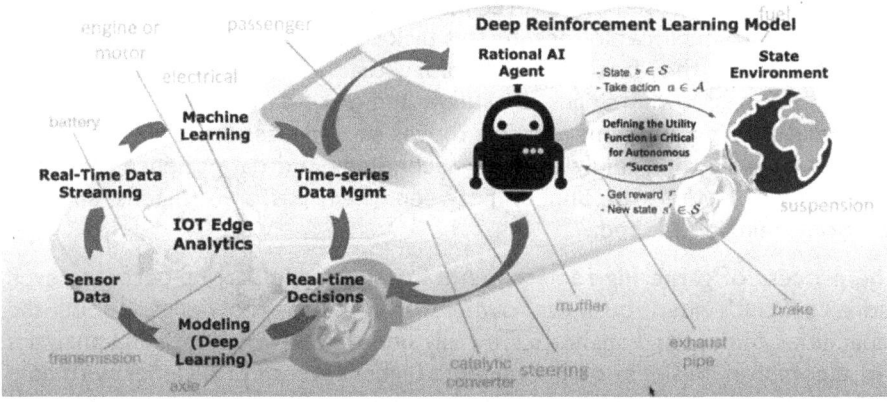

Figure 4-14. The Intelligent Car (Source: Economic of Data, Analytics and Digital Transformation, Bill Schmarzo)

Let me illustrate how this concept works by looking at Figure 4-14. Imagine starting with a basic car chassis equipped with essential components like the engine, battery, steering, and wheels. We then incorporate data from sensors and advanced analytics into the car, which continuously collect data while the car is in use. This data is fed into an AI-driven learning model, which constantly learns and improves based on the real-world experiences of the car.

Unlike traditional learning models that rely on website data, this car's learning model benefits from insights gathered each time the engine is turned on and the car is driven. As a result, it becomes an intelligent and valuable car, capable of providing unique intelligence about how it is driven.

Here are some direct business benefits of this approach:

- Enhanced safety: The car becomes a reliable companion for the driver, compensating for potential dangers on the road. It can identify and warn about hazards such as potholes, sharp curves, or high-accident areas, thereby ensuring a safer driving experience.

- Environmental intelligence: The car can gather and analyze data to provide valuable environmental insights. For instance, it can generate location reports, helping the driver navigate efficiently. It can also intelligently detect high-crime areas, enabling the driver to avoid them. By leveraging data, analytics, and AI-driven learning, this transformed car goes beyond its traditional capabilities, delivering tangible benefits that enhance safety, provide environmental intelligence, and improve the overall driving experience.

Through the engineers creating an AI-driven learning model inside the car, these benefits can be achieved creating an economic advantage. For example, the same technology used for its lane detection algorithm it uses for its humanoid robot, Optimus, to predict walking paths in factories and in homes.

The real challenge then lies for the business owners in the digital transformed environment is to be custodians on how the tools are used responsibly. Ethical issues to consider are: Whether privacy rules are being broken? Will the driver data be shared? Will the data affect any car insurance policy? Are there some services that should not be permitted?

Schmarzo Economic Digital Asset Valuation Theorem

The Schmarzo Economic Digital Asset Valuation Theorem is a valuable tool for organizations that are trying to maximize the value of their digital assets and we can apply it to the Tesla example. The theorem is described in his book, *The Economics of Data, Analytics and Digital Transformation*.

The Schmarzo Economic Digital Asset Valuation Theorem states that the value of digital assets increases over time as they are reused and shared. This is because the marginal cost of reusing a digital asset is very low, while the marginal benefit can be high.

In simple terms, this means that the more you use a digital asset, the more valuable it becomes. This is because you learn more about how to use it, and you can find new and innovative ways to use it. Additionally, as you share a digital asset with others, they can also learn from it and use it in new and innovative ways. This can lead to a virtuous cycle of increasing value, as the digital asset is reused and shared more and more.

There are a number of things you can do to maximize the value of your digital assets. First, you should focus on creating and collecting digital assets that can be reused and shared. Second, you should invest in tools and processes that make it easy to reuse and share digital assets. Third, you should measure the value of your digital assets and track how they are being used.

So Elon Musk, he may appear a bit crazy at times, but on this occasion in the current climate, he was absolutely right. What is remarkable is that this initiative is driven by a business need not a technically driven one and so creating new customer value.

We have looked at examples of missed opportunities in the established utility sector, and also for bold new innovation in the automotive space by using an insight driven approach that is driven by data insights.

For any business owner, there is still a dilemma about being comfortable in using data and gleaning insights. The visualizations tools described in the earlier chapters are quite helpful for this as they can provide a snapshot of insights quite easily. A data analyst can support in providing details on what is available, but in the meantime, don't be afraid to try out data sets at hand with external data sets to discover insights and opportunities. In the next section, we will be determining whether going on a digital exercise will bring about success.

Before moving on, can you think of any radical business outcomes you wish for in your area of focus that could use an insight-driven approach?

Can you map out where the new monetization opportunities could lie? Try using the Miro Whiteboard we discussed in Chapters 2 and 3 to map them out.

A Way to Build Insight-Driven Use Cases for DX Success

I collaborated with an agency that was working with a major US big tech organization to develop a tool for creating business-driven use cases for digital transformation in various industry sectors. The main objective of this exercise was to ensure that business owners prioritize their business objectives over simply adopting the latest technologies. Some of the methods used can assist a non-technical leader.

In any industry sector, key performance indicators (KPI) data are available that can be applied to a business strategy. In many cases, internal KPIs are used, but by measuring them against industry averages or the industry leaders, business owners can benchmark success. A standardized benchmark KPI dataset helps establish measurable targets for our digital engagement initiatives. The overall process followed a six-step approach, as shown in Figure 4-15, and described as follows:

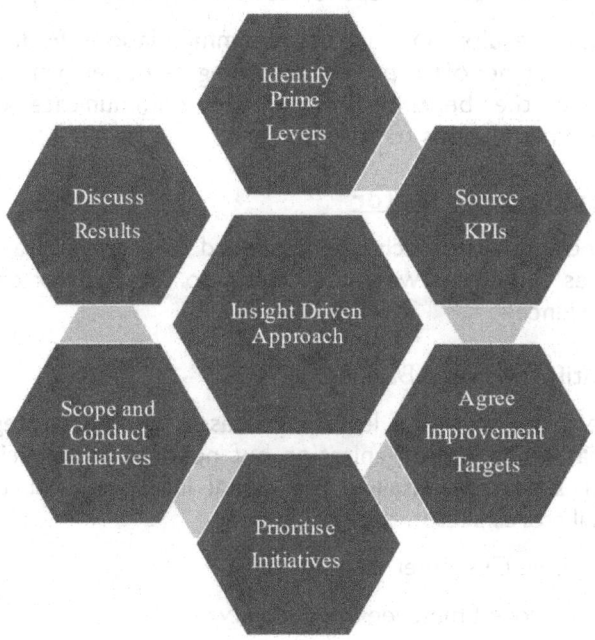

Figure 4-15. Building Insight-Driven Use Cases in Six Stages

The six stages are:

1. Identify the prime business levers: Determine the key drivers that have the most significant impact on the success of the business.

2. Source the KPIs and external benchmarks: Gather relevant key performance indicators that align with the identified business levers.

3. Agree on performance improvement targets: Set specific targets for performance improvement based on the selected KPIs.

4. Agree on priority initiatives: Determine the initiatives that are most crucial for achieving the performance improvement targets.

5. Scope out the initiatives and carry out the priority projects: Scope and identify parameters of the digital transformation project, taking into account the data needed working with the data analysts. In Chapter 6, we look at the specific steps for conducting a data project.

6. Discuss results and share the recommendations: Evaluate the outcomes of the project according to the performance against the benchmark KPIs and communicate the recommendations to stakeholders.

Example: Retail Stores Sector

Let's explore how this approach can be applied to derive digital initiatives in the retail stores sector, (as we can all relate to the goals of enhancing the shopping experience).

1. Identify the Prime Business Levers

   The prime business levers are based on the strategic initiatives of the organization but need to be explicitly expressed to crystallize the digital initiatives. For the retail stores sector, they could be:

   - Drive Customer Acquisition

   - Improve Employee Productivity

   - Reduce Shrink

   - Improve Operational Efficiency

   - Better Store Layout

   - Reduce Sales Friction

2. Derive KPIs for Drive Customer Acquisition Lever

   Each lever has a set of KPIs. If we focus on the first lever "Drive Customer Acquisition," we can identify some KPIs that fit into this lever.

   - Store Visit Frequency

   - Average Transaction Value

   - Average Foot Traffic

   - Customer Conversion

   - Average Customer Revenue

These targets would normally be defined by the business owners in the company. By sourcing industry averages and best in class figures from the sector, we can measure the performance of our company against others. These benchmarks can be found via Internet sources and company reports.

For example, if our retail outlet was for a grocery store in the United States, some of the KPI figures found (2019 figures) were:

- Best in class store visit frequency from the Walmart benchmark at 83 Visits per year. Average Foot traffic revenue as a proportion of overall revenue – 83%

- Average Customer Conversion – 20%

3. Identify the realistic performance improvement targets.

   By comparing against our own internal figures against the industry averages, we can identify the delta and define reasonable improvement targets. For example, if our customer conversion rate is 15%, then there is a delta of 5% to the benchmark. We can look at a plan to increase this by 5%.

   Once these targets are agreed by all business stakeholders, we can then share them with the data teams for an improvement plan identifying data sources, suitable digital technologies, and success criteria. If the business owners have a deeper awareness of the digital tools available, it will help in ensuring the digital technologies are used to their best business effect. In the next chapters, we will look further at some of the key data-enabling tools.

4. Agree on the priority initiatives

   So let's say we want to improve the store visits KPI by 5%. There are a number of questions we could ask for example. Some questions we could ask could be:

   - Can we improve the uptake of particular customer segments?

   - Can we improve the store layout?

   - Could we offer more attractive product upsell offers?

We can then look at what digital tools we can use to carry out the initiatives and target a KPI improvement for each.

Target customer segments	Identify less frequent shoppers	Data mining prediction tools
Improve store layout	Identify movements in stores	Sensors in test stores
Product upsell	Product categorization	Data mining
	Time of year deals	Algorithms

By following this approach, we will build up a suite of business-driven initiatives that can be prioritized according to business KPI delivery target with measures that are tangible and scalable post any pilot. The priorities can be sub-categorized according to cost, value to customer, impact on other systems, or resources needed.

5. Agree on the project scoping and then execute and monitor the progress.

    In order to drive results, it is essential for business owners to oversee the progress of the project. Subsequent chapters will delve into the techniques employed for data mining and the suitable classification algorithms for categorizing datasets in this case example. Additionally, we will explore AI-powered visual tools that aid in behavior identification. Throughout this process, we will explore strategies for business owners to enhance their collaboration with data teams and optimize their effectiveness.

6. Discuss the results and share recommendations.

    Once the results have been shared, the outputs should be assessed against any changing market behavior and needs in the organization to assess the KPI improvement.

    We have looked at using an insight-driven approach to improve footfall into retail stores. Let's now use the approach to look at stepwise improvement in the automotive sector using digital techniques.

Delivering Business Outcomes – Automotive Sector

The challenge is that car manufacturers used to stand out from each other based on the quality of their combustion engines. However, with the ongoing transformation of cars into "computers on wheels," automakers are now seeking to distinguish themselves through digital technologies, which has not been their main area of expertise. This does mean a change in the domain of expertise – away from car engine performance improvement toward automotive software improvement. By considering the business drivers, we can develop digital solutions with a focus on achieving tangible business outcomes.

To identify the prime business levers and the KPIs in this example, we need to appreciate the market is changing quite dramatically and new KPIs may need to be used.

Outside the rise of the electric car that we discussed, the business landscape in today's automotive world is about a shift from privately owned cars to using car sharing services, the rise of autonomous driving and low energy cars in smarter cities. These are all fueled by digital transformation. There are also knock-on effects to ancillary sectors too. With the wealth of car data now available, insurers can build products based on driving habits rather than the traditional one size fits all.

For the car manufacturer, maximizing client trust and loyalty, better channels to market through dealerships, improving the revenues through unit sales or lease models are vital in the world of the "connected car."

From the business outcomes, there are many KPIs we can measure like customer lifetime value, cost of sales, operational efficiency, net promoter score, and car safety. Most of the benchmark figures can be found from the annual reports of competitors or from industry reports. For example, the US government NHTSA publishing some useful benchmarks, data sets, and visualization on car safety, which can be a great reference point. Figure 4-16 shows a screen grab of some of the data available.

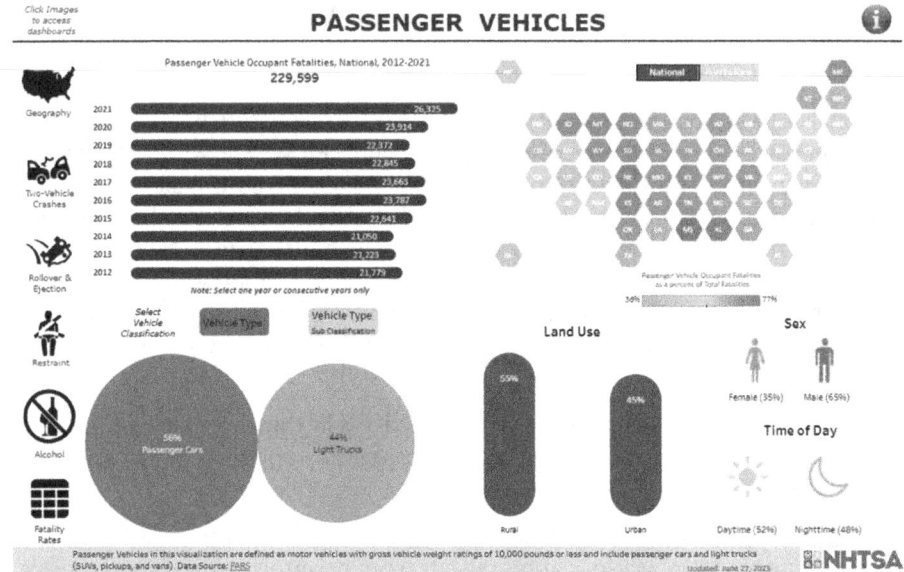

Figure 4-16. Screen Grab from the NHSA Website on Passenger Injuries in 2021

Some of the business levers could be around driving revenue from new business models, increasing customer loyalty with a better brand experience, accelerating innovation.

With these levers, and via expert discussions and desktop research, the KPIs could be

1. Driving revenue with new business models

    - Improve automotive safety

    - Subscription revenue and attach rates

    - Improve customer lifetime value

    - Reduce time to market

    - Reduce warranty and liability costs

    - Lower customer acquisition costs

    - Lower retention costs

    - Increase economic value add

    - Improve market share

2. Increasing customer loyalty and improve brand perception

   - Improve customer lifetime value

   - Improve customer satisfaction

   - Lower customer acquisition and retention costs

3. Improve market position by accelerating innovation

   - Improve customer lifetime value

   - Improve customer satisfaction

   - Lower warranty and liability costs

   - Lower customer acquisition costs

   - Lower customer retention costs

From this, we can see that some KPIs can be used to satisfy multiple business levers.

By simply drawing a table and sourcing industry leader and industry average data for each KPI, we can build up target benchmarks. By examining the primary key performance indicator (KPI) related to generating revenue through enhanced automotive safety and new business models, we have access to a wealth of information available on the Internet.

Notably, Visual Capitalist.com provides industry averages for car safety, as depicted in Figure 4-17. This data showcases the evolution of car safety from 1960 to 2019. Throughout this period, there has been remarkable innovation in improving car safety, starting with the introduction of the nine-point seatbelt in 1969 and culminating in the debut of the first backup cameras in 2019. Consequently, car safety has witnessed a significant improvement, with the number of fatalities per 100 million miles decreasing from 5.1 in 1960 to 1.1 in 2019. Innovation has played an important part in this improvement as well as safer roads and better road regulation.

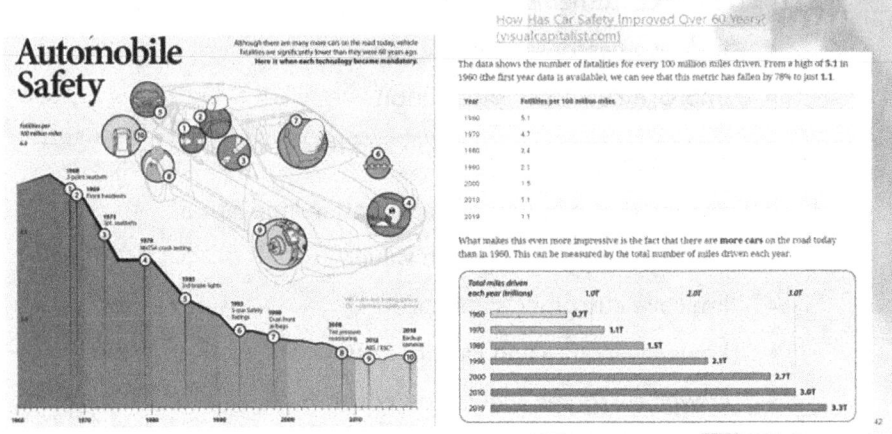

Figure 4-17. Evolution of Automobile Safety: Source VisualCapitalist.com

Similar to the previous example, from the target figures, we could possibly create a suite of digital initiatives to either reach the industry average of 1.1 or improve things even further to exceed the business target. The following table highlights some of the digital initiatives that could take place to improve car safety.

Improve overall visibility	Environment detection	Sensors
	Tire wear detectors	Machine learning algorithms
Driver performance profiles	Object detection systems	Data mining a data visualization system
	Driver sleep sensor	
Better equipment	In car – performance monitors through data visualization	Speech recognition
	Voice activation systems	

The next step would be to provide targets for each initiative, prioritize, execute, and report the findings. By applying this methodology to all the different factors at play, we can construct an extensive collection of initiatives. These initiatives can then be organized and prioritized to form a comprehensive business vision through digital transformation.

We have examined two instances of employing the business outcomes approach. In the appendix B, you will find KPI data that focuses on different verticals deriving digital initiatives for local government. The provided sample data sets are meant to assist you in attempting to formulate some these initiatives yourselves. Feel free to give it a try and explore the possibilities, otherwise, if you have data from your sector, feel free to use to approach to derive your own initiatives suite.

Conclusion

If you are thinking about digital transformation, you are not alone. In fact, many businesses are looking into it. But here's the thing: the vast majority of those businesses fail to reach business expectations.

Real life examples of failure are across many verticals and we looked at one in the utilities sector. On the other hand, we looked at how business ambition through the effective use of data can be a game changer in the automotive space and in route planning.

So what's the secret to digital transformation success? Well, it's not easy. But it does involve a few key things:

- Do not confuse digitalization with digital transformation.

- Data competence: You need to be able to define, collect, and analyze data in order to make informed decisions.

- Digital maturity: You need to be at a certain stage of digital maturity and thinking in order to successfully implement digital transformation. This involves business owners having some comfort with simple digital tools as well.

- Think of it as a staged process of IT upgrade, digital marketing investment, digitalizing operations, and investigating new business ventures.

- A business-driven outcomes approach: Focus on the business outcomes you want to achieve with digital transformation, rather than the technology itself.

Digital transformation is a vital undertaking in today's fast-paced and ever-changing world, despite its complexity and challenges. To remain competitive, business owners, regardless of their position in the company hierarchy, such as C-Suite executives, product owners, entrepreneurs, product managers, or company lawyers, must adapt and evolve alongside the digital revolution. While not all business roles necessarily require technical expertise, having a practical understanding of digital capabilities and the significance of data is crucial for the success of any business owner.

In the next chapters, we will try and unravel the hype around technology and algorithms and explore some more methods and practical tools for working more effectively with the data teams.

Exploring Data Mining and Algorithms

If I had an hour to solve a problem and my life depended on the solution, I would spend the first 55 minutes determining the proper question to ask, for once I know the proper question, I could solve the problem in less than five minutes.

—Albert Einstein

Introduction

We examined numerous case examples of digital transformation, delving into topics such as big data utilization and the integration of digital tools to enhance productivity. Subsequently, we adopted a business-driven outcomes strategy for digital transformation and focused on effectively managing the pace of innovation. We also emphasized the critical significance of preparing datasets to ensure the success of our digital transformation endeavors.

© Attul Sehgal 2024
A. Sehgal, *Demystifying Digital Transformation*,
https://doi.org/10.1007/978-1-4842-9499-4_5

In this chapter, we will discuss data mining and algorithms in detail. We will explore how business owners can understand these technologies and how they can use them to achieve successful business outcomes.

It is important to understand that data mining and algorithms are not silver bullets. They can be complex and expensive to implement, only be as good as the data they are trained on and the algorithms used must be chosen carefully. As the quote from Einstein says, it is vital to think about the problem first. It is important for business owners to wisely consider their business needs, and data available before embarking on a data mining or algorithm design project. There are many pitfalls. We will look at lessons from the classic case of IBM Watson from being billed as Watson was hyped as a "new kind of computer" that could "think for itself" to being one of the biggest digital transformation failures in recent times. It brings to life the Einstein quote about thinking about the problem before acting.

A Cure for Cancer Through Artificial Intelligence (AI)?

During its 114-year history, IBM has developed and brought to market new technology that has really transformed society – think of cash registers, floppy disks, Random Access Memory (RAM), Fortran, and mainframes to name just a few. In fact, IBM currently has over 9000 patents.

It is therefore unsurprising that IBM was an early developer of Machine Learning, the most public demonstration of this being the defeat of world chess champion Garry Kasparov by the computer Deep Blue, in 2011. Artificial Intelligence (AI) was the way for machines to make decisions on their own similar to how humans make decisions. Public excitement saw IBMs stock price grow by 3.6% on the day after the tournament.

Figure 5-1. IBM Watson. Source: analyticsinsight.net

As a result, IBM built a computer, named "Watson" after its founder Thomas John Watson (not Sherlock's sidekick), to develop natural language processing. Natural language processing essentially means programming computers to "recognize" words, syntax, and their context. When Watson triumphed at the US game show quiz "Jeopardy!" in Jan 2011, the public response was overwhelming. People were amazed how this "super brain" was able to deduce words from clues faster than humans. Watson rapidly became a household name and raised the awareness of AI. IBMs stock price at the time rose by 2.2% as executives saw AI as the next stage in innovation.

In Jan 2012, IBM announced that Watson would revolutionize cancer care by using its intelligence to diagnose patients. Given the heritage of IBM, this announcement was greeted with great fanfare – and hope. "I'm exceptionally optimistic about what the future holds in the potential treatment and eradication in these forms of cancer," Steve Gold, IBM's vice president of marketing for Watson Solutions, told VentureBeat in a 2013 interview. The stock price rose by 6.3% after this game-changing development was announced. IBM set up Watson Health partnering with the oncologists at Memorial Sloan Kettering Cancer Center in New York. They built a large clinical dataset to "feed" Watson with data. IBM spent more than $4 billion acquiring companies with medical data, billing records and diagnostic images on hundreds of millions of patients. To process all this data, Watson became a supercomputer with thousands of processors capable of running millions of lines of code.

According to Statnews, IBM claimed,

> *Watson for Oncology, through artificial intelligence, can sift through reams of data to generate new insights and identify, as an IBM sales rep put it, 'even new approaches' to cancer care.*

Source: www.statnews.com/2017/09/05/watson-ibm-cancer/

Watson's natural language processing allowed integration of physician and patient expressions of symptoms and preferences, allowing it to "see" patients as "individuals."

So you could say "Hi Watson, I have a pain in my stomach and my skin is a yellow color, and I have lost my appetite."

From that input, Watson would scan through large volumes of literature, in addition to the patient's electronic medical records, and then return output ideas and suggestions for the patient that would be individualized and supported by evidence.

In 2014, Watson, as part of a demonstration, took a collection of patient symptoms and presented a list of possible diagnoses, each annotated with Watson's confidence level and links to supporting medical literature.

However, it was discovered that Watson could not provide any clinical rationale for its recommendations. Its diagnostic process (Figure 5-2) was largely based on the generalized clinical opinion of doctors at Memorial Sloan Kettering Cancer Center rather than a complete assessment of the patient's history from the medical records. The process is summarized in Figure 5-2.

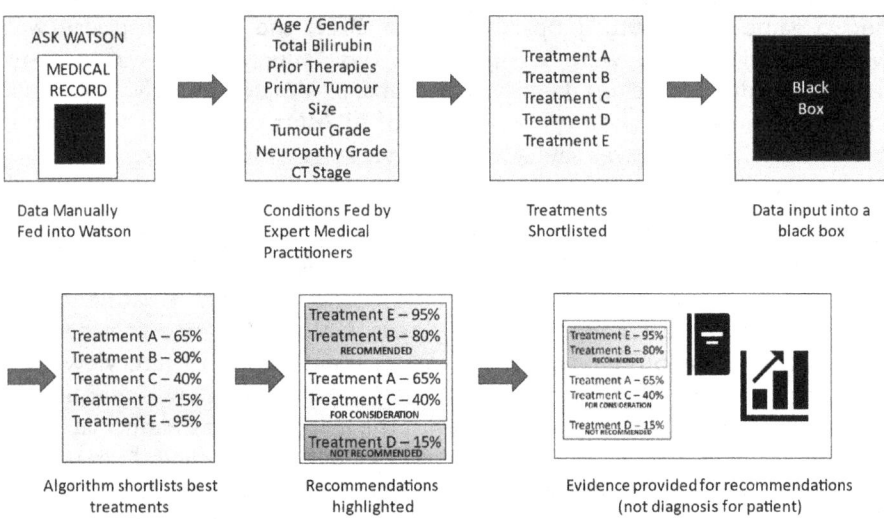

Figure 5-2. IBM Watson Diagnostic Process

Skepticism started to grow both from difficulties in automating clinical data entry into Watson, and medical experts highlighting erroneous, or even dangerous therapeutic suggestions not based on the full medical history. In 2017, Statnews, a media company focussing on news stories about health, medicine, and scientific discovery commented, "at its heart, Watson for Oncology uses the cloud-based supercomputer to digest massive amounts of data — from doctor's notes to medical studies to clinical guidelines. But its treatment recommendations are not based on its own insights from the data. Instead, they are based exclusively on training by human overseers, who laboriously feed Watson information about how patients with specific characteristics should be treated. Perhaps the most stunning overreach is in the IBM's claim that Watson for Oncology, through artificial intelligence, can sift through reams of data to generate new insights and identify, as an IBM sales rep put it, "even new approaches to cancer care." StatNews found that "the system doesn't create new knowledge and is artificially intelligent only in the most rudimentary sense of the term."

This started a wave of criticism and mass overhype leading to cancer centers pulling out of the Watson Health program. The loss of confidence was such that in 2022, The Watson Health platform was sold for just $1bn. A huge loss on the investment.

So given the heritage of IBM

- For such colossal investment, was the business owner leading the initiatives or the data scientists?

- Did the business owners know enough about the real issues with medical data to really come up with a solution or did they think that the AI solution would fix the data entry issues too?

In an attempt to uncover the answers to these questions, we will dive into the mining of data, the power of algorithms, and then review the technical challenges Watson Medical had from a business perspective.

Data Mining, Algorithms, and Digital Transformation

Whatever the reasons, such failures like the one with IBM represent mis-management on a colossal scale and incalculable lost opportunity.

However, as we have seen, it is not uncommon – over **87%** of digital transformations in 2021 (in 2018, it was reported as 70%) fail to reach expectations. In fact, a study by McKinsey in 2022 and published in 2023 surveyed 2500 executives in 25 countries and showed that only 16% of digital transformation projects were successful in meeting their objectives. According to Forbes in 2021, today, the global investment in digital transformation by large enterprises was over $2 trillion. (Source: www.forbes.com/sites/ forbestechcouncil/2018/03/13/why-digital-transformations-fail-closing-the-900-billion-hole-in-enterprise-strategy/?sh=55406 9507b8b;www.forbes.com/sites/forbestechcouncil/2021/07/21/digital-transformation-is-not-a-technology-problem/?sh=31893cd5735e)

These are staggering failure statistics. Are we just seduced to testing technology but cannot really bring the technology into the organization to address any business problems?

Whatever the reasons for the failure to achieve transformational results from digital transformation investment, we cannot ignore the power data in our business planning.

The volume of data continues to grow and digitally driven decisions are generally seen to be superior than those based on pure intuition and experience. More effective understanding of data mining by business owners is key.

In Chapter 2, we talked about data lakes and data warehouses as huge information repositories for volumes of data being generated by businesses and consumers. To get a real sense of the rate of data generated, DOMO, a media analytics company, produces an annual snapshot of the activity that occurs in an "Internet Minute" (Figure 5-3).

In their 2022 Internet Minute report, it reported Google conducts 5.9M searches, Instagram shares 66K photos, MS Teams connect 100K users, Twitter users post 575K tweets, 1.1M Tinder users swipe, and TikTok users watch 167M videos!

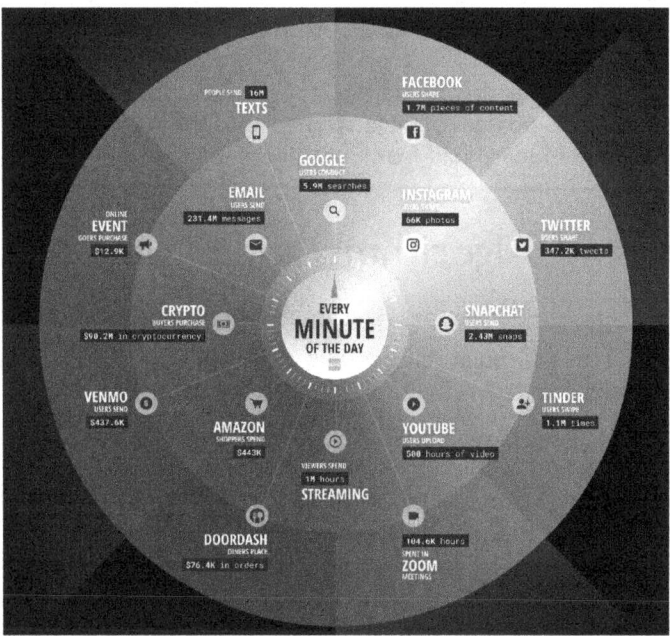

Figure 5-3. An Internet Minute. Source: DOMO

That is a huge amount of intelligence available. How can we best dive into this data ocean, extract real insights, manage expectations, apply learnings to our business, and avoid the risk of digital transformation failure? It is important for business owners to get closer to understanding what data can do.

Let's first try and understand data mining.

Data Mining

Data mining is the process of extracting knowledge from large data sets. Individuals and organizations often collect large amounts of data, perhaps out of a sense of security. However, unless this data is properly defined, sourced, coded, tagged, and cataloged, its value is limited or even worthless.

Data can be invaluable if it is stored in a way that allows it to be mined. The growth of big data has led to a rapid increase in the use of data mining techniques over the past few decades. Data mining is now used to classify, recognize patterns, associate, and predict outcomes.

The four-step process of data mining is as follows:

1. Set business objectives: What do you want to achieve by using data mining?

2. Source and prepare data: Collect the data you need and clean it so that it is accurate and consistent.

3. Perform analysis: Use data mining algorithms to identify patterns and relationships in the data.

4. Interpret results: Communicate the technical findings of your analysis and business recommendations to stakeholders

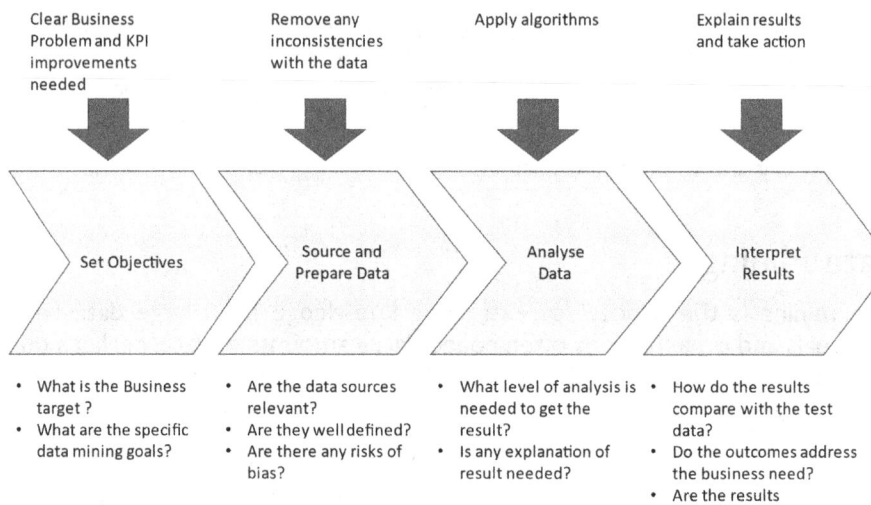

Figure 5-4. Data Mining Process

Let's look at each stage in more detail.

I. Set the business objectives: The process of establishing clear business objectives might seem straightforward at first, but it is, in fact, the most arduous phase in the data mining process. Unfortunately, many organizations tend to neglect this crucial step and dedicate insufficient time to it.

    Business leaders often oversimplify this stage, underestimating the impact of unreliable data and data that might not directly align with the business problem they are trying to address. Instead of properly defining the problem and assessing the relevance, completeness, and potential insights of the available data, they agree on a dataset with the data team and expect the data team to figure out its value for the business.

    To ensure successful data mining projects, it is vital for management, data scientists, and other stakeholders to collaborate closely and comprehend the business problem(s). They must collectively agree on the data-related questions and parameters for the project. Here are some initial questions to consider:

What specific business problem or goal will the model aim to solve? Is it focused on driving customer acquisition or retention? Or is it geared toward reducing maintenance or operational costs?

How do these chosen business problems or goals translate into well-defined data mining project goals? The answers to this question will dictate the data required to potentially address them and identify the datasets that may be necessary.

What existing knowledge, targets, or datasets are already available? It's essential to assess the business purpose and be aware of any potential data bias before finalizing the project.

Once these criteria have been fulfilled, the next step is to gather or acquire the data relevant to the identified questions. This data will be sourced from various places, including structured data like tables and unstructured data like images. Later in this chapter, we will explore some ways in which business owners can assist data scientists in creating their models effectively. To understand the business problem, business owners may want to apply a business canvas approach. www.strategyzer.com has some great templates to use.

2. Data preparation: After defining the business problem and its scope, the identification of relevant datasets to potentially address the business challenge becomes much more straightforward. Nevertheless, this process hinges on a comprehensive understanding of the data itself.
To determine whether the data is suitable, it is essential to answer crucial questions. Are the data sources clearly defined, relevant, up-to-date, and timely? Do we understand all the attributes present in the data to build a customer picture? Additionally, it is vital to assess the original purpose of data collection and recognize any potential risks of bias that could affect the new model.

Conducting a visual inspection of the data, along with spot checks performed by a data scientist, ensures a thorough understanding of all components within the dataset.

Once the raw data is collected, a crucial step is to "clean" it. This involves the data team removing erroneous entries, duplicates, missing values, outliers, and any other noisy or biased data points that could interfere with the analysis.

In some cases, depending on the dataset, an additional step might be taken to reduce the number of dimensions or data categories. Having too many dimensions can slow down subsequent computations and may lead to inaccurate or biased insights. Data scientists play a pivotal role in ensuring that the models are accurate and optimized, addressing these challenges appropriately.

3. Data analysis: Various analytical methods can be used to derive insights depending on the raw data – and the question being asked. This stage is led by the data team, but the management team should remain active players and maintain an understanding of the approach. In many instances in the past, business owners have taken a back seat and let the data team make key decisions that affect the outcome of the project. Some of the most common analytical methods are described in the next section to help business owners get a clearer understanding of the different analytical approaches.

4. Evaluation of results and implementation: After aggregating the data, the next crucial step involves evaluating and interpreting the output results. When finalizing and presenting these results, it is imperative to ensure that they are valid, free from bias (or any bias is explicitly reported), and directly address the business needs in a simple and accessible manner.

By presenting insights in such a clear and understandable form, the data gains the power to be optimally comprehended. This facilitates the assessment of the original (and potentially supplementary) questions, leading to appropriate operational implementation and, ultimately, business transformation.

Now that we have covered the four steps of data mining to produce results, let's explore the various analytics approaches that are available.

Analytics Approaches

Data analysis encompasses a variety of techniques employed to uncover patterns, identify relationships, and predict trends within datasets. From basic descriptive analytics to advanced prescriptive analytics (Figure 5-5), data can be analyzed at various levels. Unfortunately, most organizations limit their data analysis efforts to the descriptive analytics level as part of their digital transformation. This approach restricts their understanding of "what" is happening and "why" it is happening. To determine the next steps, they rely on internal analysis through meetings and advice from subject matter experts.

However, businesses can greatly benefit by incorporating slightly more sophisticated analysis, allowing them to explore "what could happen" and, as a result, drive the determination of optimized business strategies that offer significantly higher business value.

Reaching this stage of more advanced analytics can be challenging for traditional companies due to operational reasons. Now, let's delve into these different stages in detail.

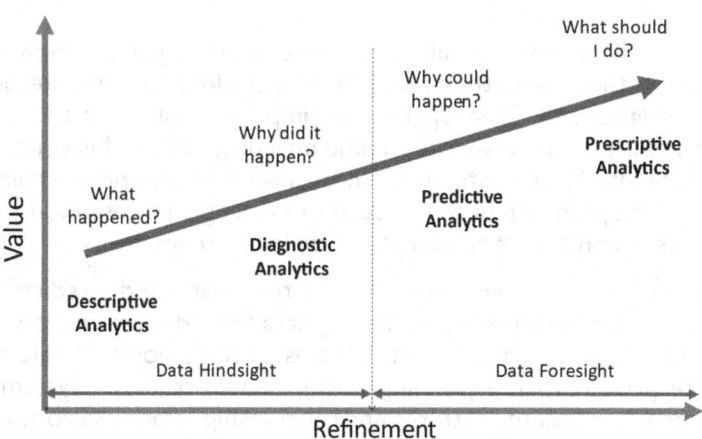

Figure 5-5. Data Analytics Methods Measured Against Business Value

Descriptive analytics describes what happened in the past, using the basics of distributions and descriptive statistics covered in Chapter 2. As we discussed in Chapter 4, approximately 90% of organizations use descriptive analytics, the most basic form of analytics. (Source: www.projectpro.io/article/types-of-analytics-descriptive-predictive-prescriptive-analytics/209) Thus, the vast majority of big data analytics spent on digital transformation projects is on descriptive analytics. A limitation can be that as it uses information from past events, it then leaves it to the organization to discuss why certain events occurred and the course of action, and so letting the intelligence be within experts in the organization.

Most reporting data uses descriptive analytics. For example, social media analytics data we may encounter today are descriptive analytics. For instance, they summarize groupings based on simple data sets such as "number of followers," "likes," "posts," "fans" over time which are simple counters – but can provide significant insights. More sophisticated "relative" metrics can also be used to characterize social media impact such as "average response time," "the average number of replies per post," "number of page views.

Diagnostic analytics represents a more sophisticated level of analysis, offering insights into why specific events occurred. It builds upon descriptive analytics, going beyond "what" happened to uncover the underlying "why" by identifying trends, patterns, and associations in the data.

For instance, major eCommerce companies like Walmart can investigate why they missed their profit targets by delving into detailed sales and inventory data to glean valuable insights.

The production of scatter charts and calculation of correlations can be highly effective in understanding past events and exploring potential relationships. While correlation doesn't imply causation, careful analysis can reveal significant insights.

Descriptive and diagnostic analyses provide a retrospective view of past events, but on their own, they may not be sufficient to generate powerful actionable insights and drive operational improvements. For this purpose, predictive and prescriptive analytics come into play, utilizing historical data to offer foresight into future outcomes. These advanced analytics techniques are instrumental in optimizing business decision-making and operations, and the most successful companies are adept at employing them.

Predictive analytics involves forecasting future data and predicting likely outcomes. This process involves gathering data from diverse sources, such as customer relationship management systems (CRM), point of sale systems (POS), enterprise resource planning (ERP), human resource systems (HR), and the Internet, to identify patterns and relationships among various variables in the dataset.

To derive valuable business intelligence (BI) from predictive analytics, the data used must be sufficient and appropriate, which varies depending on the industry, business, audience, and most importantly, the specific problem being addressed.

Predictive analytics can be applied in various ways, including

- Predictive modelling: Forecasting future outcomes based on certain occurrences

- Root cause analysis: Determining the reasons behind particular events

- Sentiment analysis: Evaluating whether feedback is positive, negative, or neutral

- Identifying correlated data: Discovering similarities among datasets

- Forecasting: Predicting potential future trends if existing patterns continue

- Monte-Carlo simulation: Exploring various possible scenarios and outcomes

- Pattern identification and alerts: Recognizing when corrective actions should be taken to improve a process

- Retailers often use predictive analytics to understand customer buying patterns, forecast stock levels, and estimate sales revenue within specific periods, such as quarterly or annually

Sentiment analysis is another prevalent area of predictive analytics used by organizations to assess customer feedback. Machine learning and natural language processing are combined in a learning model to analyze plain text inputs, scoring words, and providing a sentiment score that indicates whether the sentiment is positive, negative, or neutral.

If you've used Grammarly to enhance your writing style, you've experienced predictive analytics in action without realizing it. The algorithm used by Grammarly to achieve its goals incorporates predictive analytics principles. If you haven't tried it yet, you can do so at www.grammarly.com.

Prescriptive analytics uses simulation and optimization to predict what should happen, not just what could happen, helping address, "What should a business do?"

Millions of us benefit from prescriptive analytics every day when we use navigation tools like Waze. Very quickly, the software gathers and analyzes gigabytes of real-time traffic data, to calculate probabilities and then recommends a route based on traffic, time of day, road conditions, for fast transit.

In the retail example, prescriptive analytics can help address how category managers cold adjust pricing, promotions and assortment in every aisle of every store this week to boost revenue, profit and loyalty? Through advanced analytics methods, it can uncover hidden patterns and links in behavior not easily seen.

Similar to Waze, can you think of some automated tools you use every day that use these analytics techniques? These tools could be apps on your smartphone, hobbies outside work. Would you consider them using descriptive or more predictive analytics?

Let's now look deeper into the data at the types algorithms available that make these analytics happen.

Introducing Algorithms

Figure 5-6. "Many a Truer Word Said in Jest." Source: XKCD.COM

I have conducted digital transformation in many different organizations over the years, and one thing I've noticed is that there's often a disconnect between business owners and data teams. In some cases, the data team is tucked away in a "data lab" and only comes out to share their findings with the business owners when they have something new to show. This can be frustrating for business owners, who may not have the time or expertise to understand the data team's jargon and findings. The business owners resort to a role of turning the findings into "digital playbooks" for the sales teams to sell onto clients. A playbook is a set of guidelines, best practices, and standard operating procedures that employees follow in specific situations. It can cover various aspects of a business, such as sales, marketing, customer service, and crisis management.

On the other hand, data scientists can sometimes feel like they're working in a vacuum – in many instances they are siloed away from the organization. They may have great ideas, but they don't always have the opportunity to share them with the business owners. This can lead to models that aren't aligned with business goals, aren't accurate or reliable, and aren't scalable. So how can we bridge the gap between business owners and data teams?

In this section, we will look at ways to

- Provide data scientists with clear and concise instructions. Don't just give them a big pile of data and say "go figure it out." Help them understand what you're looking for and what questions you need answered.

- Review data models and results. No longer taking the data scientists' word that their models are accurate and have their explanations go over your head but rather having the time to review their work and ask questions.

- Using the knowledge set to provide feedback on data models and results.

- Work with data scientists to develop a plan for implementing and monitoring models. Once you've agreed on a model, it's important to have a plan for how it will be implemented and monitored. This will help ensure that the model is used effectively and that it continues to be accurate and reliable.

These small tips can help to bridge the gap between business owners and data teams and ensure that the data and analytics is used effectively to achieve the business goals and a successful digital transformation.

So let's begin!

The success of many data-driven firms is based on the intelligence gained from data and the algorithms they use. This intelligence can be used to optimize business costs, or sales, and thus profit. However, with the invention of the Internet, a number of companies now actively mine data and sell it with key insights to other businesses including advertisers. This data is highly valuable as it can be used to deliver more relevant content and upsell new service offerings to existing and new customers.

For instance, in 2022, Amazon made over $955,517, Apple $848, 090, and Microsoft around $330,000 in revenue in every minute due to the way they use data and algorithms. But what exactly is an algorithm?

You're probably familiar with algorithms without even realizing it. Every time we sort a column in a spreadsheet, algorithms are in the background,. Algorithms help gadgets respond to voice commands, recognize faces, sort photos, and build and drive cars. Most financial transactions take place through algorithms. Our lived experience is driven by algorithms.

They help us analyze the data generated for business intelligence and information monetization. They can perform simple calculations, help program robots and manage platforms. The Internet runs on algorithms and all Internet/ app searching is based on them. Emails get sent thanks to algorithms. Computer video games and mobile apps use algorithmic storytelling. Surfing Tinder, Skyscanner, and other search websites rely on algorithms. GPS mapping systems direct people to their destinations via algorithms. However, there are down sides – hacking, cyberattacks, and cryptographic code-breaking exploit algorithms.

As you can see, algorithms are all around us and they're only becoming more important. Think of algorithms as essentially procedures used to solve a problem or to perform a series of computations producing an output based on data inputted. They are created using computer code that are fast to process, as in Figure 5-7.

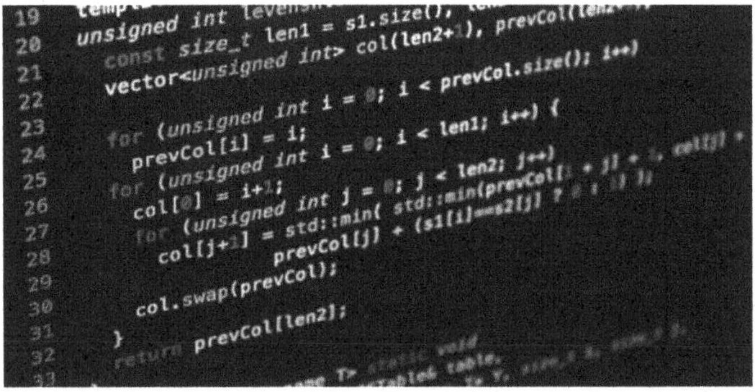

Figure 5-7. Computers and Robots Driven by Algorithms. Source: Unsplash

Algorithms process data using a series of steps – akin to an "instruction set" or data "recipe." To make sense of the raw data, algorithms use features, dimensions, and parameters to make decisions. Features are the input data that the algorithm uses to make a decision. Dimensions are the different ways that the features can be measured. Parameters are the settings that the algorithm uses to control how it makes decisions.

If we use the analogy of making the perfect cake machine using an algorithm, the features used would be the type of cake, ingredients, techniques used, and decorations; the dimensions would be the size and shape of the cake; the parameters would be the time to bake, temperature, and cooling period.

Usually, there are three basic building blocks (constructs) to be employed when designing algorithms:

- Sequencing (the order in which instructions are performed)

- Selection (where decisions are made)

- Iteration (where steps are repeated)

For the "perfect" cake recipe, things may vary depending on the features, dimensions, and parameters. Thus, the algorithm can describe how to make the cake, but through assessment based on repeat testing and varying the amounts, the cake can be optimized to be the perfect cake.

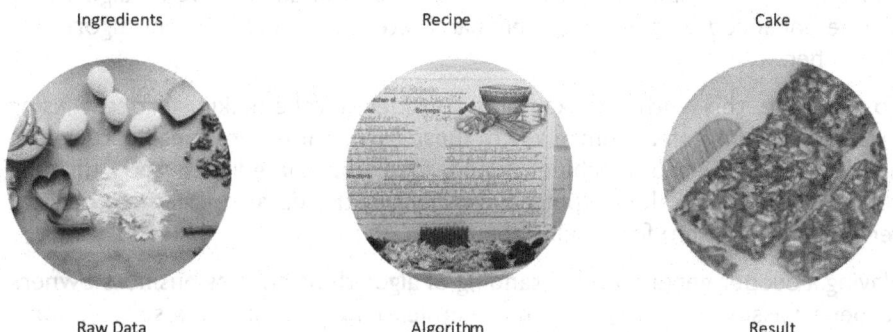

Ingredients   Recipe   Cake

Raw Data   Algorithm   Result

Figure 5-8. How to Make a Cake

This process is the foundation of search engine movie recommendations and even used by LinkedIn to run algorithms to suggest connections or targeted adverts and then based on the success of the output accept (and reuse) or refine the algorithm.

Computer algorithms can be powerful, but their real key is speed. An analogy would be to compare a complex calculation performed with a pen and a piece of paper compared to doing the same on a calculator.

Algorithms initially allowed automation and repetition of computations that were dependent on processor power. Managing the number of features (columns of data) and the amount of data (rows of information) is thus key when using algorithms.

Before going to the next section, think about any repetitive chores either at work or at home that you do. Can you think of ways they could be automated with simple instructions?

Machine Learning Algorithms

When delving into machine learning (ML) algorithms, we discover a deeper level of data analysis. ML algorithms are computer programs that learn patterns from a given dataset and can then apply this knowledge to make decisions on new datasets. They continually learn from past decisions, incorporating new insights into their original algorithm to provide outputs for new data situations.

To train an ML algorithm, the first step is to collect a representative training dataset that resembles the real-world data the algorithm will encounter. The algorithm is then trained using this dataset, which involves providing examples of how to perform the desired task. Once trained, the algorithm is tested on a fresh dataset to evaluate its performance. If the algorithm underperforms, it may require retraining on a larger or more diverse dataset. Some algorithms can be enhanced by adjusting their parameters or using different algorithms altogether.

To illustrate this with an example, consider a cake-making process using machine learning algorithms. With these algorithms, no specific recipe is needed. Instead, the machine would take the ingredients and, through generating various cake outputs, "learn" about the data to create an optimal recipe (or algorithm) for making the cake.

Having a deeper general understanding of algorithms enables business owners to better assess which type of machine learning application is suitable for a given business situation. This understanding facilitates improved communication with data teams, cost management, and effective project timelines for data-related endeavors.

Now, let's explore the different ways in which machine learning algorithms deliver outputs. These algorithms can be categorized into four main types:

- Supervised Machine Learning
- Unsupervised Machine Learning
- Semi-supervised Machine Learning
- Reinforcement Machine Learning

Each of these methods serves distinct purposes and applications. Before delving into more detailed explanations of each approach, the key uses of supervised, unsupervised, and reinforcement learning are summarized in Figure 5-9.

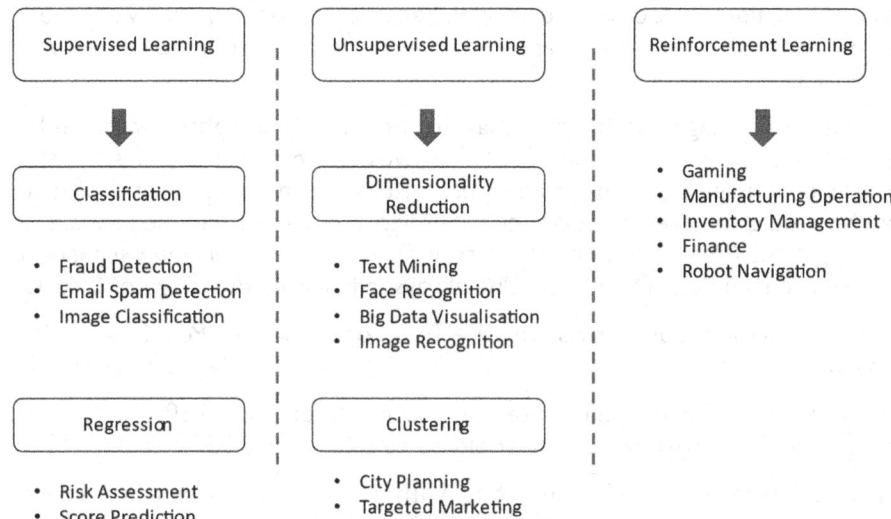

Figure 5-9. Machine Learning Categories, Algorithm Types, and Applications

Supervised Machine Learning

Supervised machine learning represents the most straightforward type of machine learning algorithm. It functions by mapping an input variable "X" to an output variable "Y" based on known input–output relationships from past data. In this approach, a labeled dataset is utilized, where each input variable is paired with a corresponding output variable or "Label." The term "Supervised" stems from the fact that an expert supervises the algorithm and provides labels for the data.

There are two sub-categories of supervised learning: classification and regression.

Classification: This involves training the model using historical data to predict binary outcomes, such as yes/no, true/false, or 0/1. It enables the classification of datasets or objects based on their attributes. For instance, it can predict whether a customer will churn within the next 9 months or not.

Let's explore how supervised learning can be applied in image classification through the example described in Figure 5-10:

In this demonstration, we utilize supervised learning to classify images, specifically focusing on differentiating between cockroaches and houseflies. The process involves providing the machine learning model with a set of labeled images, containing examples of both cockroaches and houseflies. By presenting the model with labeled data, it learns to identify patterns and distinct characteristics associated with each insect.

After the training process, the model becomes capable of analyzing new images and accurately determining whether they depict a housefly or a cockroach.

In some cases, image classification may not be entirely straightforward, and a performance metric known as "Recall" proves to be useful in assessing the model's effectiveness on the training data. Recall quantifies the ratio of true positive results (images correctly classified) to the sum of true positives and false negatives (images incorrectly classified). A higher recall value signifies a more efficient model. The recall value always falls within the range of 0 to 1.

The Recall formula is as follows: Recall = True Positives/(True Positives + False Negatives)

For example, if the housefly detector accurately predicts 950 images and misclassifies 50 images, the recall would be calculated as 0.95.

If you're interested in experimenting with supervised learning for image classification yourself, you can explore Google Quick Draw, a platform available at https://experiments.withgoogle.com/quick-draw

Regression: involves predicting numerical values based on historical data trends. Imagine connecting dots on a straight-line graph, and by extrapolating the line, you can map an x value on the x-axis to a corresponding y value on the y-axis by finding where it intersects the line.

Regression can be applied to predict sales for a product or service. By using historical sales data to train a model, it can forecast future sales based on a linear relationship between time and sales volume.

Unsupervised Machine Learning

Unsupervised machine learning tries to make sense of data that hasn't been classified or labeled. In this case, the algorithm only receives the input data and it has to act on the information without any guidance or output data to produce the labels.

Therefore, the algorithm must find patterns and similarities within the input data. Unsupervised learning is used for clustering and association problems in any data, including image, video, audio (e.g., messages), and emails.

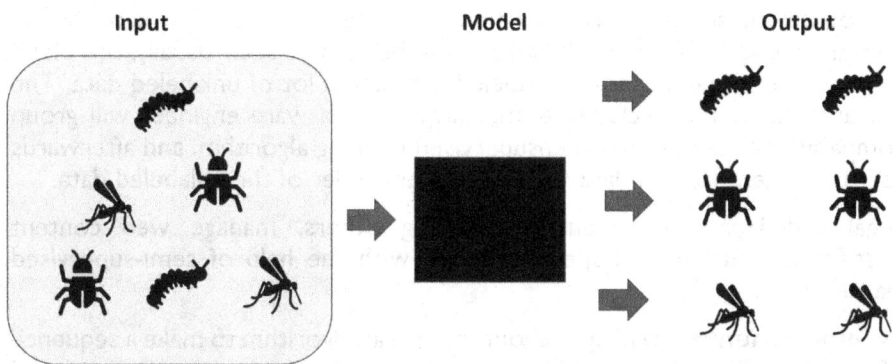

Figure 5-10. Classifying Insects with Unlabeled Input

Unsupervised machine learning employs two key techniques to describe data:

- Clustering: This technique explores data patterns and groups the data into meaningful clusters without any prior knowledge of group attributes. The primary goal is to identify similarities among data points and group them accordingly. Clustering can also be used to exclude specific attributes or detect anomalies in the data.

- Dimensionality reduction: When dealing with a large number of inputs or factors, the performance of the algorithm may suffer. Some factors might overlap with others or lack real relevance to the output required, leading to increased training time and storage space. Dimensionality reduction is employed by machine learning algorithms to eliminate irrelevant or noisy data (referred to as "data noise") while extracting essential information, thereby improving algorithm speed and efficiency. This process ensures that the algorithm focuses on the most relevant features and reduces computational complexity.

Semi-supervised Machine Learning as the name implies is a middle-ground between supervised and unsupervised machine learning. To understand its benefit let's look at the drawbacks of supervised and unsupervised machine learning.

The most essential drawback of any type of supervised learning algorithm is that the data set must be labeled by humans – which is time-consuming and can have human error. Whereas, the biggest challenge with unsupervised learning is that its application range is restricted.

To counter these problems, semi-supervised learning allows an algorithm to be trained upon a blend of labeled and unlabeled data sets. Usually, this blend will contain a small quantity of labeled data and a lot of unlabeled data. The fundamental system included is that first, the software engineer will group comparative data utilizing an unsupervised learning algorithm, and afterwards use the current labeled data to label the remainder of the unlabeled data.

Legal and Healthcare industries, among others, manage web content classification, image, and speech analysis with the help of semi-supervised learning.

Reinforcement Learning is about training an algorithm to make a sequence of decisions. The algorithm faces a game-like situation where, by trial and error, it comes up with a solution to a problem. To get the machine to do what the programmer wants, the algorithm gets either rewards or penalties for the actions it performs. Its goal is to maximize the total reward. It does this by amending its algorithm each time.

Think of the process in training a dog to think of food and start jumping when a whistle is blown (Figure 5-11).

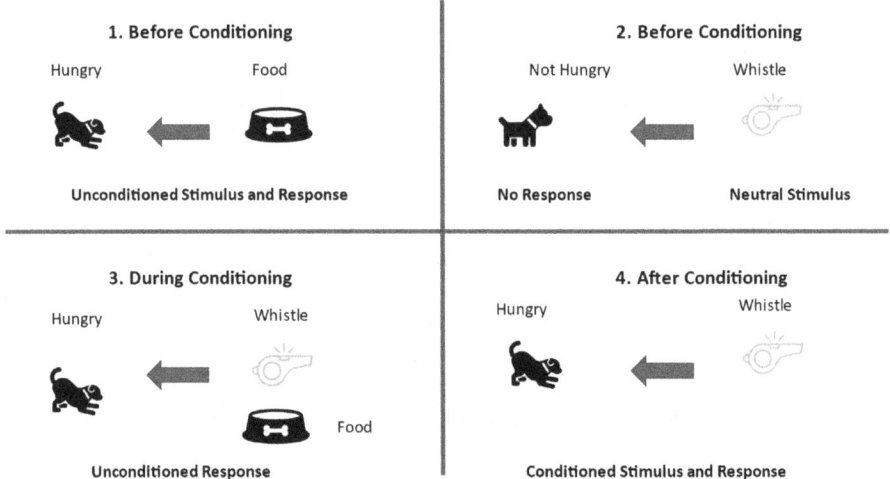

Figure 5-11. Reinforcement Learning. Source: www.edureka.co/blog/machine-learning-tutorial/

Owner wants to train his dog to recognize the whistle. He trains his dog in four stages.

> Stage 1 – Owner shows food to the dog and in response to the food, the dog starts jumping.
>
> Stage 2 – Owner blows a whistle, but the dog does not respond.
>
> Stage 3 – Owner tries to train his dog by blowing the whistle and then showing food. The dog starts jumping when he sees the food. He then repeats the actions.
>
> Stage 4 – Eventually the dogs starts jumping just after hearing the whistle, by seeing whistle before seeing the food as the dog becomes "conditioned" to associating the owner blowing the whistle with subsequently getting the food.

These algorithms are also termed "Artificial Intelligence Algorithms." As we have seen, in general terms, an algorithm takes some input and uses mathematics and logic to produce an output. In contrast, an Artificial Intelligence Algorithm takes a combination of both – inputs and outputs – simultaneously in order to "learn" the data and based on this produce outputs when given new inputs.

Common Machine Learning Algorithms

Machine learning algorithms broadly fit into the categories described previously. The most common methods used in these categories are in Figure 5-12

Algorithm	Description	How it works	Examples of use	Limitations
Linear regression	Predicts a continuous value based on a set of input features.	It finds a line that best fits the data points.	Predicting house prices, predicting sales, predicting stock prices.	Sensitive to outliers.
Logistic regression	Predicts a binary value based on a set of input features.	It finds a line that best separates the data points into two classes.	Predicting whether an email is spam or not, predicting whether a patient has cancer or not.	Sensitive to outliers.
Decision tree	Predicts a value based on a set of input features by breaking the data down into smaller and smaller groups.	It creates a tree-like structure where each node represents a decision and each leaf represents a possible outcome.	Classifying text, predicting customer churn, fraud detection.	Difficult to interpret.
Support vector machine (SVM)	Finds the best hyperplane to separate the data points into two classes.	It finds the hyperplane that maximizes the margin between the two classes.	Image classification, spam filtering, text classification.	Computationally expensive.
Naïve Bayes	Predicts a value based on a set of input features by assuming that the features are independent of each other.	It uses Bayes' theorem to calculate the probability of a class given the features.	Spam filtering, text classification, medical diagnosis.	Inaccurate if the features are not independent.
K-nearest neighbors (KNN)	Predicts the value of a new data point based on the values of its k nearest neighbors.	It finds the k data points that are most similar to the new data point and then averages their values to predict the value of the new data point.	Recommender systems, fraud detection, image classification.	Slow for large datasets.
Random forest	Combines multiple decision trees to make predictions.	It creates multiple decision trees and then averages their predictions to make a final prediction.	Image classification, spam filtering, text classification.	Computationally expensive.
K-means clustering	Groups data points into clusters based on their similarity.	It finds the k clusters that minimize the within-cluster sum of squares.	Customer segmentation, image segmentation, text clustering.	Sensitive to outliers.
Neural network	A type of machine learning algorithm that are inspired by the human brain. They are made up of layers of interconnected nodes, each of which performs a simple calculation.	The network learns by adjusting the weights of the connections between the nodes, so that it can make accurate predictions.	Used to solve a wide variety of problems, including image classification, speech recognition, and natural language processing. Particularly well-suited for problems that involve complex relationships between the input and output data.	One of the limitations of neural networks is that they can be difficult to train. This is because they require a large amount of data to learn from. Additionally, neural networks can be computationally expensive to train.

Figure 5-12. Most Common Algorithmic Methods

A very broad understanding of the main algorithmic methods will enable us to keep pace with the approaches the data engineers use in addressing business problems.

There is also an approach that you may come across called *Ensemble learning* that combines the approach of different methods and then finding a combined prediction from each of the methods. We will discuss this in the classic case example in Chapter 9.

Let's have a deeper look at each of the algorithmic methods:

1. Linear regression

   Linear regression is a powerful algorithm employed for predicting numerical values from a given dataset by identifying a linear relationship between two sets of values.

   In Chapter 2, we explored statistical methods and defined mean, mode, and median. While these calculations can be used to predict numerical values for a dataset, incorporating additional information allows us to achieve more accurate predictions.

   You might recall from your school days the equation of a straight line: $y = mx + c$ (where m represents the slope or gradient, and c denotes the intercept – the value of y when $x = 0$).

   Imagine a scatter plot of data as depicted in Figure 5-13 – Line of Best Fit. A linear regression model endeavors to find the line of best fit that minimizes the distance (difference) from each data point to the line. Subsequently, this line can be used to predict other data points based on its equation. It's important to note that data points often do not lie exactly on the line of best fit; instead, they disperse around it. Nevertheless, various methods can assess the strength of the linear relationship.

   One common way to evaluate how well a linear regression model fits a dataset is by calculating the root mean square error (RMSE). The RMSE measures the average distance between the predicted values from the model and the actual values in the dataset. A lower RMSE indicates a better fit of the linear model to the dataset.

Linear models can be constructed based on more than two dimensions, although interpreting them becomes more challenging.

Linear regression finds extensive use in advertising to discover correlations between advertising expenditure and sales revenue.

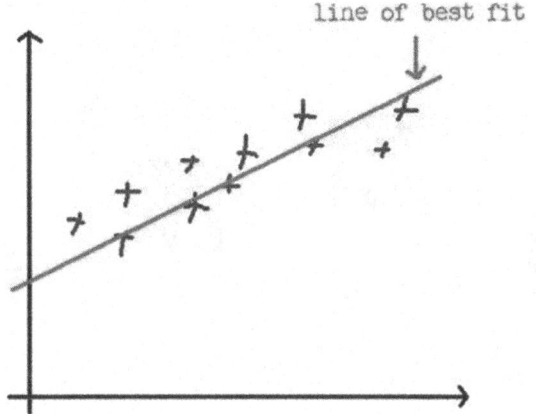

Figure 5-13. Line of Best Fit

Application Example: Building a simple predictive model with a simple well-structured dataset to Predict Crop Yields

Let's consider an application where a farmer aims to assess the impact of water on crop yields. To achieve this, the farmer decides to conduct an experiment by applying different amounts of water to various areas of a field and then observing how it affects the yield. For this task, a linear regression model seems appropriate, as it can handle multiple factors and provide a straightforward explanation of the contributing factors to the yield prediction. Moreover, linear regression is computationally efficient and can even be executed using tools like MS Excel. In the following tutorial, we will demonstrate how to build and utilize this model.

Before moving to the next algorithmic method. Can you think of any area where a regression model could work to predict a future outcome? Would you be able to make a set of observations and then check whether a future `observation would work?

2.   Decision tree algorithms

A decision tree is a way to separate observations and place them into sub-groups according to a decision process. It is very useful in data mining to a target variable. A simple example of a decision tree could be whether to eat dinner or have a snack (Figure 5-14).

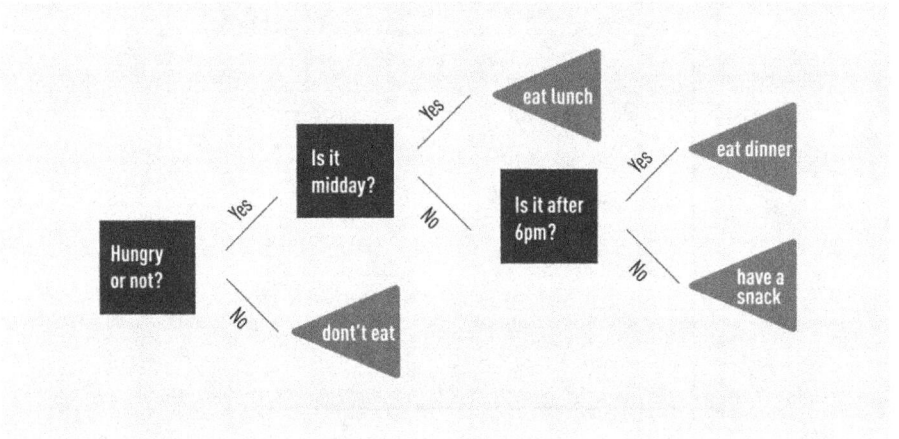

Figure 5-14. Decision for Having a Snack

A decision tree follows a set of if-else (Yes/No) conditions. It's like a flow chart pointing to different outcomes and destinations. Each tree has a root, branch, and leaf to break down a data set. Decision trees can be used for both and classifying data into categories and predicting numerical values (regression). One of the key values of decision trees is the representation permits easy retracing (auditing) of the decision path.

Application Example: Classifying result points that come out of a well-defined structured process – like job interview rounds to predict the number of hires – by understanding the probability of success at each stage.

A decision tree algorithm could work in this scenario as it would clearly explain what the split points are between classifying something into one decision group or another.

Can you logically break down any routine everyday decisions you make? Could you describe this in a decision tree?

3. Random forest

    While decision trees are simple and flexible, they can over-simplify a decision process, leading to inaccuracies. In a random forest algorithm, the machine learning algorithm predicts a value or category by combining the results from several decision trees. It is from a family of Ensemble Algorithms. Ensemble algorithms are techniques that combine individual models to create a more accurate and predictive model. This is a type of "Ensemble algorithm" as it combines several decision tree algorithms to produce a single predictive model improving generalization and reducing bias. The model predicts by taking the mode or mean of the output from various trees; generally increasing the number of trees increases the precision of the outcome.

    For example, if you worked in a bank and wanted to predict how much a bank's customer will use a specific service a bank provides with a **single decision tree**, you would collate how often they've used the bank in the past, and what services they utilized during their visits. You would add some features that describe that customer's "decisions." Thus, the decision tree will generate rules to help predict whether the customer will use a particular bank service. But this is liable for bias.

    If you inputted that same dataset into a **Random Forest**, the algorithm would build multiple trees out of randomly selected customer visits and service usage. Then it would output the average results of each of those trees. By averaging the results of randomly selected customers, you would get a better prediction.

    While random forest algorithms are powerful, a clear disadvantage is, unlike with decision trees, you cannot trace how the model came to its final result.

4. Logistic regression

    Logistic regression is a classification algorithm.
    It is used to predict an outcome based on a set of independent variables when there are only two possible scenarios – either the event happens (1), or it does not happen (0).

Independent variables are those variables or factors which may influence the outcome (or dependent variable). Independent variables are either continuous variables (e.g., temperature or weight) in intervals, ordinal data (such as customer feedback from 1–5), or discrete data that can only be of certain finite values – usually whole numbers or integers (e.g., different colors).

Logistic regression also requires a number of assumptions that the data must fulfill. For instance, data must fit into one of the two distinct categories, the independent variables must not correlate, and the independent variables should be linearly related to the log odds (think of if you play ten card games with a friend and win four of them, your log odds are 4/6).

In addition, the sample size should be sufficiently "large" to be valid.

Logistic regression is used to calculate the probability of a binary event occurring, or to facilitate classification.

Application Example: Classifying data that's already been labeled into two or more sharply distinct types of labels (e.g., trying to determine if a customer will default or not default on a credit card) in a supervised setting.

Expect a logistic regression model to be applied. A credit card company requires a method or model to predict, whether or not a given customer is likely to default on their payments. Thus, there are two possible outcomes, "will default" or "will not default" over a given period of time, which means that it is binary data. Thus logistic regression is optimal. Based on defining characteristics of the customer, the credit card company can model the data that determines whether the person falls into one of the two different categories, allowing you to make an informed business decision of whether to issue the card. The logistic regression model can also be easily generalized to working with multiple target and result classes if that's what your problem demands.

5. Clustering

Clustering is a technique that involves the grouping of data points. Thus, a clustering algorithm, when provided with a set of data points, attempts to classify each data point placing it into a group or "cluster."

In theory, data points that are in the same group should have similar properties and/or features, while data points in different groups should have highly dissimilar properties and/or features. Using unsupervised learning, clustering algorithms can identify patterns in data so they can be grouped based on one or many parameters.

Clustering algorithms are the basis for online shopping recommendations and of course Netflix. Essentially, you watch something on your account, and movies with similar characteristics, watched by accounts with similar viewing histories generate "personalized lists."

There are several clustering methods, but perhaps the most common is a supervised learning algorithm called K-nearest neighbors (k-NN).

Let's say we got two categories A and B (Figure 5-15) and we add in a new data point – highlighted in Green. To understand where the data point would reside we would look at the nearest data points to allocate the categorization. The number of data points to be assessed is assigned by the "k" number. In general, the k number is assigned generally by the Sqrt (of the number of samples in the data set). Source: https://towardsdatascience.com/a-simple-introduction-to-k-nearest-neighbors-algorithm-b3519ed98e. k-NN is based on assigning each data point a probability of belonging to each defined cluster. It uses an approach of dividing into subsets according to the "k" number and aggregating to highest density. For example, if we define k=3, then the algorithm would look at the three nearest data points to categorize our new data point. In the example, it would end up in Category B. k-NN clustering is powerful and can be used on even small datasets.

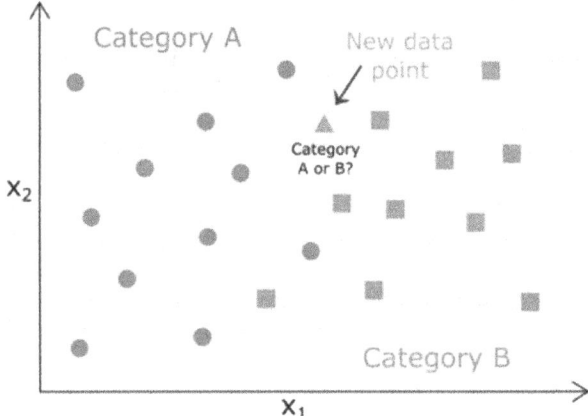

Figure 5-15. k-NN Clustering

k-NN clustering is used widely in areas such as market research and pattern recognition, in addition to data and image processing.

There is also an unsupervised clustering algorithm called "k-means clustering" that requires only a set of unlabeled points and a threshold: the algorithm will take unlabeled points and gradually learn how to cluster them into groups by computing the mean of the distance between different points.

Application Example: Assessing customers in a queue with certain recorded traits and trying to discover the categories/groups they could reside

The data is from a continuous data set and unlabeled and needs to be categorized. In this case, a K-Means clustering algorithm could be a natural fit as it will group and cluster the customer data according to the distance between each data point.

6. Support Vector Machines (SVM)

    Support Vector Machine (SVM) is a supervised machine learning algorithm that also can be used for classification and regression tasks. The core principle of SVM is to find the best boundary (or hyperplane) that separates the data into different classes.

The boundary is chosen in such a way that it maximizes the gap, the distance between the boundary and the nearest data points from each class called support vectors (Figure 5-16). SVMs have several advantages, such as the ability to handle high-dimensional data and the ability to perform well, even with small datasets.

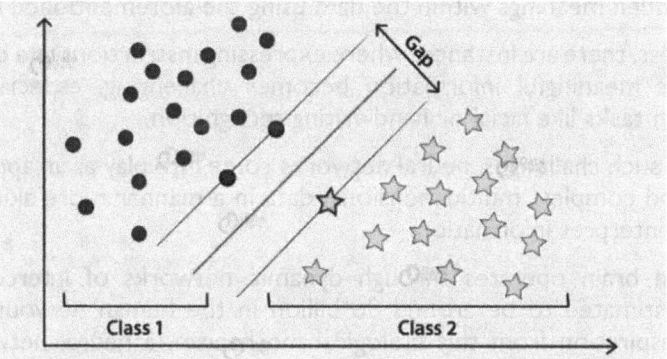

Figure 5-16. Support Vector Machines

SVM has been used in many contexts, including in medicine to look at historical data from patients diagnosed with cancer, to enable the doctors to differentiate malignant and benign cases based on attributes.

7. Naïve Bayes classification

Naïve Bayes Algorithm is a form of supervised learning and is mainly used to solve classification problems. A probability is based on the likelihood of an event occurring which is calculated using Bayes' theorem. We can also apply the theorem to classification. For example, most common birds cannot be easily identified based on simple features and color as there are many birds with similar attributes. However, naïve Bayes algorithms generate a probability (probabilistic) prediction of likelihood of being in a particular class. It is naïve because it assumes there are no relationships between the features, which may not always be the case.

Naïve Bayes algorithms are used in text analysis. Imagine you are looking to predict a sequence of words. The algorithm can be used to predict if a "u" would follow "q" as in "quick," or "quiet."

Neural Networks

The methods described earlier are generally sufficient for analyzing, predicting, and prescribing actions in various business scenarios with a reasonable level of accuracy. By employing these techniques, business owners can gain valuable insights from their data by collaborating closely with their data teams. This mutual understanding between business owners and data experts helps uncover hidden meanings within the data using the aforementioned methods.

Nevertheless, there are instances where expressing instructions to a computer to uncover meaningful information becomes challenging, especially when dealing with tasks like facial or handwriting recognition.

To address such challenges, neural networks come into play as an approach to comprehend complex, multidimensional data in a manner more akin to how our brains interpret information.

The human brain operates through dynamic networks of interconnected neurons, estimated to be around 86 billion in the human nervous system. Drawing inspiration from this biological mechanism, a neural network is a type of machine learning model designed to mimic the brain's functioning.

Neural networks consist of multiple layers of interconnected nodes, where each node performs a simple calculation. These layers are organized hierarchically, with the input layer at the bottom and the output layer at the top. The input layer receives the data that the network aims to learn, while the hidden layers lie between the input and output layers. These hidden layers are responsible for learning the essential features of the data. The number of layers in a neural network can vary based on the complexity of the task at hand. For simpler tasks, like classification, one or two hidden layers may be sufficient. However, for more intricate tasks, such as image recognition, multiple hidden layers may be necessary (Figure 5-17). When a neural network has multiple hidden layers, it is referred to as "Deep Learning."

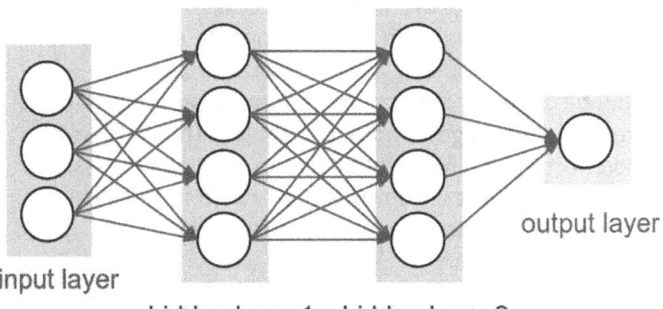

Figure 5-17. Neural Network

Neural networks represent a type of machine learning algorithm that mimics human learning by understanding from examples. When faced with tasks like recognizing handwriting or facial features, our brains quickly interpret information and discern its meaning. Neural networks aim to emulate this process by processing data and uncovering its representations. Visualize the brain as an information scanner, trying to establish associations and understand the received data.

In a neural network, connections between neurons possess weights that determine the significance of input values. Data is fed through the network's layers, and the output is produced by the output layer. These weights initially have random values in the neural network algorithm.

Throughout the training of the neural network, these weights are adjusted based on input data and the desired output. This essential process is known as backpropagation, which aims to minimize the error between the predicted output and the expected output.

As training progresses, the neural network's weights are iteratively fine-tuned, enabling it to make more accurate predictions. This iterative process may take some time, but eventually, the neural network becomes proficient at making precise predictions (see Figure 5-18).

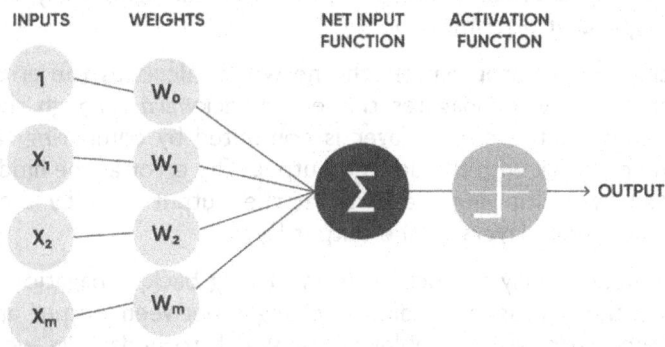

Figure 5-18. Neuron Structure Diagram

Neural algorithmic networks consist of neurons, each equipped with an Activation Function. The primary purpose of these activation functions is to introduce non-linearity into the neuron's output. This non-linearity is essential because, without it, the network would only be capable of learning linear relationships and fitting straight lines to data. However, real-world relationships are often not linear, making non-linear activation crucial for capturing complex patterns.

The choice of activation function is problem-specific, and there is no universal solution. The best activation function depends on the characteristics of the data and the desired outcome of the neural network. Several commonly used activation functions include:

Sigmoid function: This function is often employed in classification problems, where it can output values between 0 and 1, representing probabilities. For instance, a sigmoid function could be used to classify images of cats and dogs.

Tanh function: Similar to the sigmoid function, the tanh function has a range from -1 to 1. It is suitable for regression problems, as it can output real numbers. For example, a tanh function might be utilized to predict the price of a house.

ReLU function: The Rectified Linear Unit (ReLU) is a popular non-linear function in deep learning. It is computationally simple and highly effective for training neural networks. For instance, a ReLU function could be applied to classify text documents.

The activation function decides whether a neuron should be activated or not based on the input it receives. For instance, if an animal is described as striped, fluffy, and meows, we instinctively associate it with a cat, placing the maximum weight on the "meow" parameter as a key distinguishing feature. Even if the animal is not striped or fluffy, but it meows, it is still highly likely to be a cat due to this significant discriminator.

In the process of backpropagation, the network calculates the error at the output layer and then propagates this error backward through the hidden layers. The error at the output layer is computed by comparing the actual output of the network with the desired output. The error at the hidden layers is determined by multiplying the error at the output layer by the weights connecting the hidden layers to the output layer.

Activation functions play a crucial role in making backpropagation possible. They provide the necessary gradients (changes between output and input) along with the error, which enables the network to update its weights and biases during training, ultimately improving its performance and ability to learn from data.

In the cat detection scenario, during the backward propagation process, if the combined weights of the "striped" and "fluffy" neurons exceed the weight of the "meow" neuron, the gradient-based backpropagation function should be able to detect this error and adjust the network accordingly.

Training is a critical step in this process, but it comes with challenges. Neural networks demand substantial and diverse datasets to be effective and produce accurate results. Additionally, the training process requires significant computational power for processing the vast amount of data and optimizing the network's parameters.

For a practical example, let's consider filtering of spam emails using a neural network.

Figure 5-19. Spam Emails

A spam filter is a machine learning model designed to detect and filter out spam emails. It employs a neural network, which learns the characteristics of spam emails and uses them to identify potential spam among new emails. The neural network consists of input layers, where email messages are received as input, and hidden layers, which learn the features of spam through a process called feature extraction. For spam filtering, this involves extracting crucial words and phrases commonly found in spam emails.

The hidden layers utilize various techniques, one being word embeddings, which represent words as vectors, capturing their meanings. This helps the neural network learn relationships between words associated with spam. Once the hidden layers have grasped these spam features, they can assess new emails for spam likelihood. The output layer of the neural network produces a score, indicating the probability that an email is spam. High scores suggest spam, while low scores imply non-spam.

To train the neural network, a dataset containing both spam and non-spam emails is used. The training data updates the neural network's weights and biases, enabling it to make accurate classifications. Once trained, the neural network becomes an effective tool for spam filtering.

While neural networks are powerful, they can be computationally expensive and require substantial training data to produce reliable results. Other practical alternatives for spam filtering include Naive Bayes, which assigns probabilities to each word in an email and calculates the probability of it being spam, and Support Vector Machines (SVMs), which find a hyperplane to separate spam from non-spam emails.

In conclusion, neural networks offer enhanced accuracy for spam filtering, but one must carefully consider the trade-offs before choosing an approach. Different algorithms, such as Naive Bayes and SVMs, also provide viable options for effective spam detection, depending on specific requirements and available resources.

Generative AI Algorithms – As Explained by ChatGPT

An emerging algorithm is Generative AI. Generative AI algorithms are a type of machine learning algorithm that can create content, such as images, text, or music. They are trained on a large dataset of existing data of approximately 175 billion parameters, and they learn to identify the patterns and relationships in that data. Imagine being able to query a chatbot and produce new content, like computer code, essays, emails, social media captions, images, poems, excel formulas, and more within seconds. It is drawing a lot of attention due to the results produced (see Figure 5-20). It uses two neural networks where one is the discriminator of the other that verifies if the answer is right or wrong.

The definition of Generative AI produced by ChatGPT 3.5 is:

"Generative AI refers to a category of artificial intelligence (AI) algorithms that generate new outputs based on the data they have been trained on. Unlike traditional AI systems that are designed to recognize patterns and make predictions, generative AI creates new content in the form of images, text, audio, and more."

Generative AI uses a type of neural network called generative adversarial networks (GANs) to create new content. A GAN consists of two neural networks: a generator that creates new data and a discriminator that evaluates the data. The generator and discriminator work together, with the generator improving its outputs based on the feedback it receives from the discriminator until it generates content that is indistinguishable from real data.

Generative AI has a wide range of emerging applications, including

> Images: Generative AI can create new images based on existing ones, such as creating a new portrait based on a person's face or a new landscape based on existing scenery.

> Text: Generative AI can be used to write news articles, poetry, and even scripts. It can also be used to translate text from one language to another.

> Audio: Generative AI can generate new music tracks, sound effects, and even voice acting.

To understand the accuracy of the algorithms, in March 2023, Open AI produced a technical report (https://cdn.openai.com/papers/gpt-4.pdf) that benchmarks the capabilities of ChatGPT. OpenAI simulated test runs of various professional and academic exams. This includes SATs, the bar examination, and various advanced placement (AP) finals. Figure 5-20 shows the percentile gradings of Chat GPT 4. A 99% percentile grading means that only 1% of humans performed better than Chat GPT4.

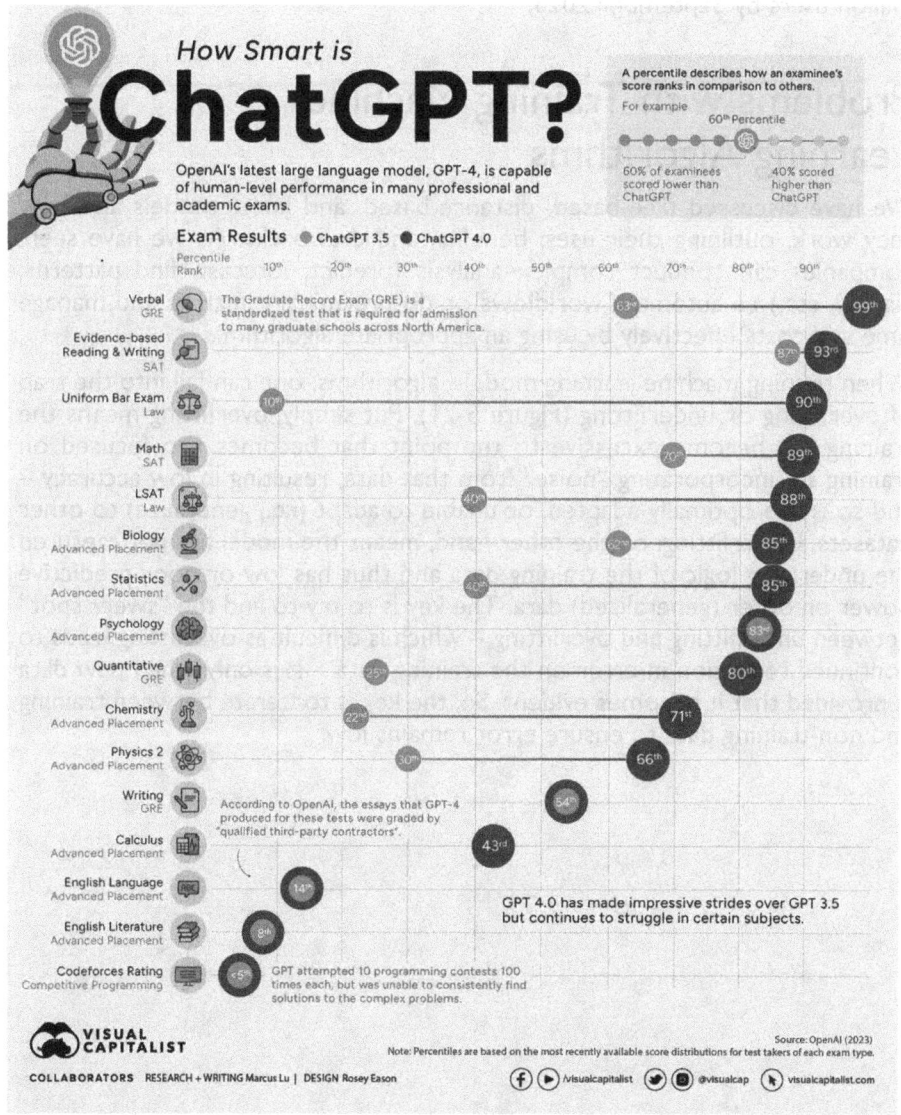

Figure 5-20. Chat GPT 4 Benchmarked: Source Visual Capitalist

In many instances and for many subjects, the GPT neural network performed higher for these traditional exams than the typical human. This demonstrates the disruptive effect of artificial intelligence and how our society needs to evolve to take into account artificial intelligence. Although there is only a beta version available, the excitement around the technology had generated 280 million users by September 2023.

Problems with Training Machine Learning Algorithms

We have discussed tree-based, distance-based, and linear models and how they work, outlining their uses, benefits, and drawbacks. As we have seen, companies can conduct complex analysis (predict, forecast, find patterns, classify, etc.) to automate workflows or do preliminary analysis and manage time and costs effectively by using an appropriate algorithm.

When training machine learning models' algorithms, one can fall into the trap of overfitting or underfitting (Figure 5-21). Put simply, overfitting means the training has become excessive to the point that becomes too focused on training set incorporating "noise" from that data, resulting in low accuracy – and so is sub-optimally adapted, or unable to adapt (i.e., generalize) to other datasets. Underfitting, on the other hand, means the model has not captured the underlying logic of the training data and thus has low or poor predictive power on other (generalized) data. The key is to try to find the "sweet spot" between underfitting and overfitting – which is difficult as overfitting leads to continued reduction in error on the training data – it is only when new data is provided that it becomes evident. So, the key is to iterate between training and non-training data to ensure error remains low.

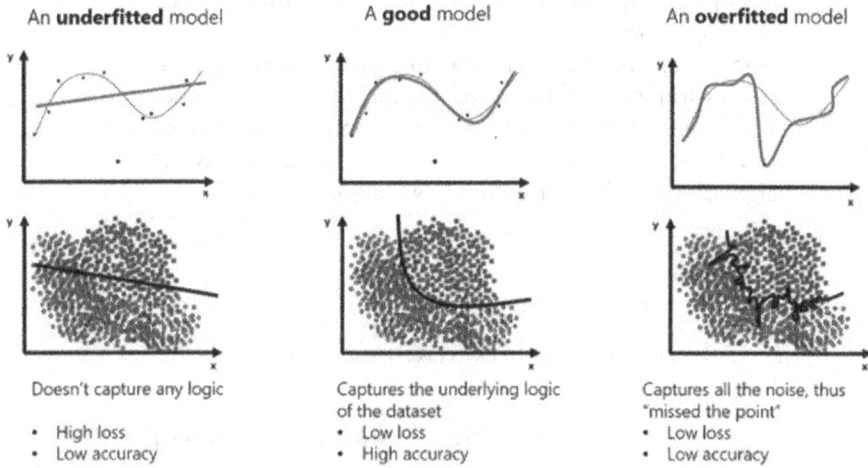

An **underfitted** model   A **good** model   An **overfitted** model

Doesn't capture any logic
- High loss
- Low accuracy

Captures the underlying logic of the dataset
- Low loss
- High accuracy

Captures all the noise, thus "missed the point"
- Low loss
- Low accuracy

Figure 5-21. Overfitting and Underfitting. Source: 365datascience.com

While it may seem that Neural networks can generate insights to anything through self-learning – they have their challenges. Here are a few.

1. **Lack of Explain-ability:**

   In simple terms, the Neural network "Black Box" does not explain how the model generated a particular output, or what features were emphasized or deemphasized in the process. For humans to understand, trust, and respect the output insights, there are three key areas where transparency is required (or at least desirable):

   - Model transparency: The ability to describe how a model is trained on a step-by-step basis.

   - Design transparency: Having the ability to provide an explanation for decisions such as the model architecture and parameters used such as the scale of the training data or the type of information it contains/represents.

   - Algorithmic transparency: The capability of explaining how automated optimizations work.

   Being able to articulate these factors are crucial when a business refuses a loan or blocks a customer from a social media interaction. We will discuss the ethical issues later on.

Where transparency is key for customer interactions, or regulatory accountability, it may be that more transparent methods such as decision tree or logistic regression should be used rather than neural networks even though to do so may come at the cost of model accuracy. Figure 5-22 shows an overview of algorithm prediction accuracy vs. explain-ability.

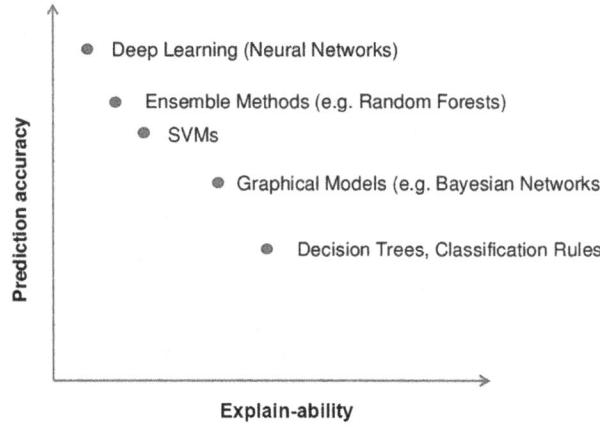

Figure 5-22. Prediction Accuracy Trade-off vs. Explain-ability

During the last few years, the first few explainable AI models have emerged. Some of the most successful ones are: Reversed Time Attention Model (RETAIN), Local Interpretable Model-Agnostic Explanations (LIME) and Layer-wise Relevance Propagation (LRP) [5]. However, these methods used for producing explainable models are still not able to produce very detailed results, therefore research in this area is still needed.

2. **Long Development Time**:

It takes time to train a neural network – which can be months, or even years. As we discussed earlier, you can overtrain a model, but even before that, it is important to define what is acceptable performance to end the training phase.

If the training period will be longer than you anticipated, you may have the option of adjusting the parameters of the algorithm or choosing an alternative algorithm to implement in order to shorten the amount of time required to train the model.

3. **Computationally Expensive:**

   As the data volume increases, patterns can become more difficult to find, particularly if there are strong inter-relationships between parameters, which increase the computational cost – and thus the neural network costs.

   Remember the cost of the algorithm must be less than the business benefit – which means the return-on-investment horizon is an important consideration.

How Can the Business Owner Size a Data Project?

Thus, the first step must be to clearly define and set the objectives for business problem. Some things to consider when doing this are:

1. Understand the business goals and use the business outcomes approach. We discussed an approach in Chapter 4.

   - What are the company's overall goals?

   - What are the specific goals for the department or team that is sponsoring the data science project?

   - Are the goals realistic or too easy? Are there external benchmarks that can be applied?

2. Identify the specific business problem.

   - Can the business goals be broken down into discrete projects?

   - What are the specific problems the data science projects can try to solve?

   - What are the symptoms and root causes of the problem?

3. Quantify the business impact of the problem.

   - How much money is the problem costing the company?

   - How much time is it costing the company?

   - How is the problem affecting customer satisfaction?

   - Are there any other KPIs affected?

4. Gather data.

- What data is available that can be used to solve the problem?

- What further data needs to be collected?

- How reliable is the data?

In short, it depends upon the problem statement, the desired business outcome, the available data, and assessment of cost-benefit.

If the business outcomes are unclear, then any analytic exercise is likely to fail to provide satisfactory business outcomes (or objectives that underpin them). Too often, business owners leave to the data scientists to "play with the data" and identify a problem. This, as we have seen, is the path to failure.

Algorithms must be used in a pragmatic way – what is the real value from the process? What is the cost-benefit of acquiring the data required to employ the "correct" algorithm? The business owner must play a role once the objectives are defined. The key questions to address are:

- Is the algorithm being employed appropriate for the task?

- Is the solution path being over-engineered?

- Is the data available sufficient to feed the algorithm and to inform it with respect to the defined outcomes?

- Will the algorithm be too broad and be capable of defining all outcomes into the solution?

To plan the model, it is almost always best to start simple and then build up toward more complex models as approach limitations are identified. A broad understanding of the dataset(s) is key for any problem definition. As a recap, here is a table that summarizes the differences between features, dimensions, parameters, but also hyperparameters:

Feature	Dimension	Parameter	Hyperparameter
Individual pieces of data for a data point (customer name, age, address)	Number of unique values that a feature can take on (number of records)	Values used to predict a target variable (values used to predict house prices)	Values that are set by the data scientist before the model is trained (e.g., number of trees in a decision tree)

Some of the factors for the business owner to consider when specifying requirements to data scientists are:

- Linearity
- Size of the training set
- Accuracy required
- Training time
- Number of parameters
- Number of features
- How explainable must the solution be

Let's look at each of these.

- **Linearity**

  A key factor that should be taken into account is whether the data observes linear relationships rendering machine learning algorithms based on linearity (or constant bias) such as linear regression, logistic regression, and even Support Vector Machines. The key benefits of linear approaches are they are relatively easy to perform, are simple to understand and interpret, and do not require much training time, but can have good predictive accuracy and hence can simplify the whole modeling process.

- **Size of the training set**

  We looked at some of the issues in training algorithms. If the training data set is not sufficiently large, it always results in poor accuracy. An over-constrained model with insufficient training data set will result in underfitting. On the other hand, an under-constrained model is likely to result in overfitting of the data set (as described earlier). In either cases, the outcome will be sub-optimal. For a small training data set, as the low bias/high variance classifiers (random forest) are likely to overfit the training data set, the high bias/ low variance classifiers (such as Naive Bayes) are better.

- **Accuracy required**

  We use machine learning algorithms to make valid decisions, and stronger (better trained) model results lead to less error but come at the risk of overfitting the training data set. The accuracy needed will be dependent on the business requirements, budget, and time available.

- **Training time**

  Time taken to train the model varies for each algorithm. This running time also correlates with the size of the data set and depends on the desired accuracy.

- **Number of parameters**

  The number of parameters is one of the most important factors affecting model performance. Models with more parameters can be more versatile and accurate, but they can also be more prone to overfitting and underfitting. Approaches that minimize the number of parameters are often desirable for real-time operations. There is a trade-off between the number of parameters and model performance. Models with more parameters can be more accurate, but they can also be more complex and require more data to train. Models with fewer parameters can be less accurate, but they can be faster and easier to train. The ideal number of parameters for a model depends on the specific application. For real-time operations, it is often desirable to use models with fewer parameters so that they can be executed quickly. For tasks that require high accuracy, it may be necessary to use models with more parameters.

- **Number of features**

  Compared with the number of data points, the number of features for certain mined datasets may be large. Algorithms such as Support Vector Machines (SVM) are particularly useful in this situation as they can group features to simplify the algorithms used.

  In some situations, there could be more than one algorithm that could be suitable. The optimal algorithm depends on the question you are trying to answer, the variables you consider to be important, and the amount of relevant data at your disposal and the time needed to process and consider this data. Consider doing an ensemble of different methods and testing all of these methods against one another, depending on the dataset in question.

Application example: Assessing whether a customer review is positive or negative.

When looking to predict whether a string of characters or a grouping of traits falls into one category of data or another (supervised text classification), there are a few options:

- **Näive Bayes**, as we have seen, can be used for text classification. With some text pre-processing and cleaning (being especially careful to remove filler stop words such as "and" that might add noise to the dataset), you can get a remarkable set of results with a very simple model.

- **Logistic regression** could be another strong alternative which is a simpler model to grasp and explain, and has not got some of the drawbacks of Naive Bayes (which will often assign probabilities word by word rather than holistically labeling a text snippet as being part of one group or another).

- **Support Vector Machine** algorithm will likely help improve the performance

- **Neural networks** are generally optimal where accuracy is critical, whereas where computational efficiency (data, computational, cost, or explain-ability are critical, then traditional algorithms such as Linear Regression and SVMs are likely to be more suitable).

It is not the role for the business owner to perform the analysis, but by having a clear insight of the desired outcomes, a broad view of the landscape to *ask the right questions* will help to ensure the analyst team are on the track they need to be on.

It is from this position we can define the expected outputs in terms of whether to categorize data, find a number, or perform a mixture of the two and how to get to that point through description, pattern recognition, prediction, or automation.

Having the right organizational training of the business aspects of data in place will address the technology gap between the business and technology parts of the organization.

Before moving on, can you think of ways that a business problem could be redefined to incorporate a better understanding of the algorithm that could be produced?

We discussed at the beginning of this chapter the story of IBM Watson. Are there some lessons we could apply from our understanding of data and algorithms to avoid the outcome?

Analysis of Watson Health Failure

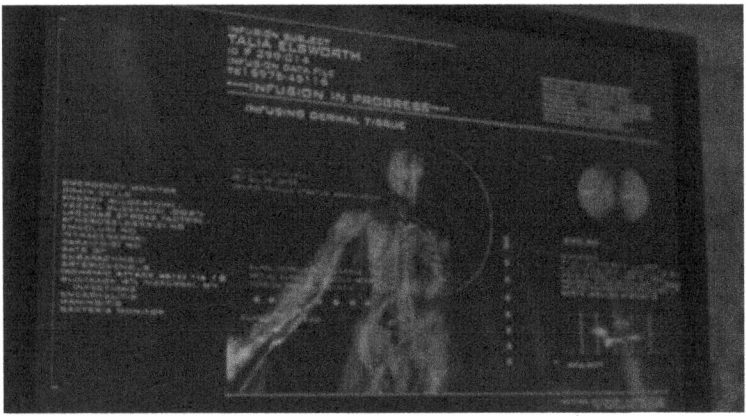

Figure 5-23. IBM Watson Oncology, Source: mpo-mag.com

Watson Health, a division of IBM, was a multibillion dollar investment that ultimately failed.

There were a number of factors that contributed to its failure, including

- Unclear business outcomes: IBM was not clear about what it hoped to achieve with Watson Health. Improve cancer treatment? Create new drugs? Or something else? This lack of clarity made it difficult to measure the success of the project. Were the business owners themselves just "misty eyed" about AI and lost focus on the business objectives?

- Oversimplification of data input: Watson Health was designed to analyze medical data. However, medical notes are often complex and unstructured. Watson Health was not able to effectively analyze this data, which limited its usefulness. With an understanding of simple data mining, a business owner should have raised this.

- Inflated expectations: IBM and its partners made some overly ambitious claims about Watson Health on the back of the success of "Jeopardy." For example, they claimed that Watson could "revolutionize" cancer care. These claims were not supported by hard evidence.

- Technology hype: The hype surrounding AI in general, the threat from Big Data firms, may have led IBM to overinvest in the project. AI is a powerful tool, but it is not a magic bullet. Watson Health was not able to live up to the hype, which ultimately led to its failure.

Despite its failure, Watson Health did have some successes. For example, it was able to identify previously unidentified mutations that proved important to support novel therapeutic recommendations. These successes suggest that AI has the potential to be a valuable tool in health care in the future. Whether AI will be a replacement for human doctors seems a long way off. AI can be a valuable tool, but it is important to use it wisely.

For more commentary on Watson, check out the following references:

1. `www.technologynetworks.com/informatics/articles/the-hype-of-watson-why-hasnt-ai-taken-over-oncology-333571#:~:text=Since%20many%20lab%20results%20are%20quantitatively%20analyzed%20and,it%20dealt%20with%20clear%2C%20defined%20tasks%20like%20diagnosis`

2. UNC researchers find Watson for Genomics tech useful for identifying potential therapies (beckershospitalreview.com).

3. *Your Future Doctor May Not be Human. This Is the Rise of AI in Medicine. (futurism.com)*

Conclusion

Bridging the knowledge gap between business owners and data scientists is not easy but essential for the success of any digital transformation project. By working more closely together, we can use data and algorithms to make better decisions and solve the problems that matter most. Hopefully the information contained in this chapter is a start. Try and consider how you use some of these tools in your day-to-day. There will be another practical chapter were we will apply to the Landis Car Hire example some of the data mining and machine learning techniques covered.

We know that data and algorithms are all the rage these days. People are talking about how they can solve all of our problems, from doing puzzles to curing cancer. And while there's no doubt that data and algorithms have the potential to do a lot of great things, it's important to remember that they're not magic. They can't solve every problem, and they certainly cannot solve any problem on their own. Despite all the hype, the failure statistics in digital transformation are quite staggering. The case study of Watson Health shows that AI is not a silver bullet. It is a powerful tool, but it is important to use it wisely. AI should be used to complement human expertise, not replace it. This is where business owners need to step up.

The real power of data and algorithms lies in their ability to help us make better decisions. But in order to make the most of them, we need to bridge the knowledge gap between business owners and data scientists. Business owners need a deeper understanding of the basics of data mining and algorithms so that they can effectively work in a more effective and agile way with data scientists and be able to articulate their business goals and objectives clearly and be able to understand the data scientists' recommendations. We looked at a high level at some of the data mining and algorithm families that can help business owners and realities of these processes delivering the right results. At the same time, they need to manage the hype and expectations of technology within the wider organization and not let the technologists get carried away.

The broad knowledge sets covered will help in understanding some of the game-changing algorithms and technologies that have made digital so transformational. We will also look at ways to manage the technology hype and also some of the ethical challenges of working with data.

Groundbreaking Digital Innovations

Introduction

We have defined digital transformation through various classic case studies, studied innovation cycles, dived into the role of data, looked at a business outcomes approach to successful digital transformation as well as some practical digital tools to enable use to work more effectively in the digital age. We also did a review of some of the data mining and machine learning techniques that are used currently. What are the huge digital innovations that made digital transformation have such a profound effect and make non-technical business owners feel so out of step? As consumers, we probably take most of these innovations for granted without realizing how they have permeated into our day-to-day.

In this chapter, we'll dig deeper into the journey of the digital pioneers and uncover the key disruptive innovations that sparked the era of digital

© Attul Sehgal 2024
A. Sehgal, *Demystifying Digital Transformation*,
https://doi.org/10.1007/978-1-4842-9499-4_6

transformation. We'll examine how the pioneers' innovative skills have evolved over time as they ventured into new territories, pushing the boundaries of what's possible.

We will start by scoping what makes an innovation so transformative and then delving into the algorithms that have emerged from this digital revolution. We will also explore how these innovations are reshaping the business manufacturing landscape allowing us to be more operationally efficient.

We will then look at other emerging transformative technologies that could redefine our relationship with money, how we will potentially use the Web in the future and also how we use digital to solve our most fundamental problems.

So let's start…

What Makes a Digital Innovation So Groundbreaking?

An innovation becomes groundbreaking when it changes things in a big and fundamental way, shaking up how we used to do stuff and making a huge impact on the environment, society, industries, or people. Some of the key factors are highlighted in Figure 6-1.

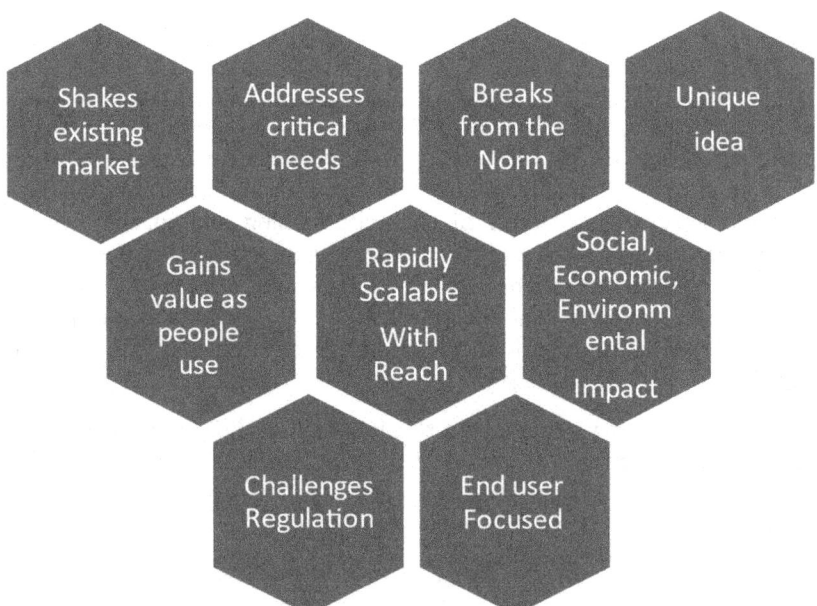

Figure 6-1. Aspects That Make an Innovation So Transformative

As Figure 6-1 shows, groundbreaking innovations often originate from unique ideas that disrupt the established norms by harnessing previously unknown or underused technology.

- Tackle problems for which existing solutions were ineffective or inefficient.

- Dare to challenge prevailing attitudes and beliefs.

- Through network effects, their value escalates with increasing popularity through a scalable solution.

- Transcend geographical boundaries, swiftly reaching a wide audience.

- Have a profound focus placed on addressing customer needs.

- Have a high environmental or social effect.

- Boldly challenge regulatory norms.

Look around yourself. Can you think of any innovations and how they measure up to the criteria in Figure 6-1?

We have seen how the FAANG companies (Facebook, Apple, Amazon, Netflix, and Google) have revolutionized the digital landscape with their ground-breaking ideas. These tech giants have not only amassed incredible resources but have also mastered the art of understanding data, enabling them to create innovative products and services that redefine our digital experiences. Let's now look at a few of the groundbreaking innovations that have created the digital transformation effect we see today. If you do not use any of these products yet they are innovations to consider in any future landscape thinking for a business owner.

We will look at digital devices, groundbreaking algorithms, and then the potential of decentralized databases and quantum computers to digitally transform us even further in the coming years.

Emergence of the Smartphone

Smartphones are a prime example of a groundbreaking innovation. When smartphones as we see them today launched in 2007 with the launch of the iPhone, they caused a disruption to multiple pre-existing technologies and industries. They shook the existing market, simplifying how we interact with technology, were very user centric, they scaled up quickly with a global reach, gaining value as people used them, and at the same time improving people's day-to-day lives.

With their platform architecture, they allowed app developers to connect to users and by consequence disrupt many existing technologies at the time, including photocopiers, scanners, navigation systems, personal digital assistants (PDAs), digital cameras, and portable music and video players and also, to some effect, the appeal of laptop and desktop computers. The unique high user-centric design, user touch screen technology, and platform-driven apps enabled the iPhone to have an enduring sustained effect in the market place in the eyes of customers. Further, it wasn't just a one off as they sustained innovation through various new versions of the model despite the high price point. The more recent versions of the smartphone enable payment devices, channels to financial service products, health monitoring features, and fitness devices. Quickly Google and Samsung released Android OS for their smartphones which had similar iPhone features to compete in this marketplace (`www.the-waves.org/2020/10/05/wave-theory-of-innovation-diffusion/`; `www.the-waves.org/2020/07/26/evolution-of-iphone-as-seasonal-crop-why-does-apple-keep-releasing-better-versions/`).

Can you think of any features that you could expect on the iPhone or any smartphone in the future?

From the introduction of the smartphone, another disruptive step took place in the form of intelligent algorithms.

Game-Changing Algorithms

A key behind the success of many big data firms has been the way they have effectively deployed key algorithms to drive engagement to their platforms. These unique algorithms have allowed them to address critical customer needs globally by helping them to simplify people's lives by managing the mundane and enabling faster decisions, and the data insight accumulated has allowed them to create further value as more people used them. From slowly emerging into our lives, we now take them for granted as a mainstay and many companies as part of the digital transformation efforts are implementing them into their operations.

What are these pioneering algorithms and who pioneered them? Figure 6-2 shows some of the leading digital companies and the algorithms they pioneered.

Figure 6-2. Game Changing Digital Deployments of Leading Data Firms

We will go through each and then review how relevant these algorithms are in our day to day to lives:[1]

1. **Page Ranking Algorithms**

   A page ranking algorithm is a method used by search engines to determine the relevance and importance of web pages in response to a user's search query. In 2022, Google's parent company, Alphabet, generated $257.6 billion in revenue. Of that, $207.3 billion came from advertising, which is primarily driven by the page ranking engine. The page ranking engine, also known as the "Google algorithm," is the core of Google's business model and still drives over 80% of Alphabets revenue. It is what allows Google to deliver relevant search results to users, which in turn attracts advertisers.

---

[1] Note: Large Language Models (LLMs) is an emerging AI innovation pioneered by OpenAi. They are covered in the next chapter. Consensus Algorithms are also emerging with the growth of cryptocurrencies pioneered by Bitcoin. We will look at the most ground-breaking ones at the end of this chapter.

2. **Behavioral Targeting Algorithms**

    Behavioral targeting algorithm is a type of algorithm used in online advertising and marketing to deliver targeted content or ads to individual users based on their online behavior and preferences. The majority of Google's advertising revenue comes from online display ads, which are the ads that are displayed on websites and in apps. This behavioral targeting algorithm is a key part of Google's online display advertising business and contributes significantly to the revenues. Google acquired the algorithm from DoubleClick in 2008. It works by tracking the websites that users visit and the pages that they view. The algorithm then uses this information to create a profile of the user's interests. The behavioral targeting engine works by tracking the websites that users visit and the pages that they view. This information is then used to create a profile of each user's interests. Advertisers can then target their ads to users who are likely to be interested in their products or services.

3. **Social Media Ad Serving and News Feed Algorithms**

    A social media algorithm is a set of rules and signals that automatically ranks content on a social platform based on how likely each individual social media user is to like it and interact with it. Social media ad serving algorithms are used by social media platforms to determine which advertisements to display to users on their feeds and other parts of the platform. The ad serving and news feed engine is a complex system that delivers ads to users on Facebook, Instagram, and other social media sites. The system takes into account a variety of factors to determine which ads to show to users, including the user's interests, the content they are viewing, and the time of day. In 2022, Meta generated $117.9 billion in revenue. Of that, $107.3 billion came from advertising, which is primarily driven by the ad serving and news feed engine. This engine still drives 90% of Meta's revenue.

4. **Recommendation and Rationalized Ordering Algorithms**

A recommendation and rationalized ordering system is an algorithm used by various platforms and services to provide personalized recommendations to users. For example, Amazon's pioneering platform allows customers to simply and quickly find, buy, and receive what they want (one-click ordering system) while also being shown (upsold) "related" items based on your behavior. The revenue made for Amazon is not clear however, but Netflix's recommendation algorithm generated $29.7 billion in revenue in 2021. Netflix believes that these algorithms contribute to around $1 billion in yearly revenue by providing value to customers and keeping them subscribed. Although the exact figure is not available, a significant portion of this revenue was generated by users who were retained or acquired due to the company's recommendation engine.

5. **Surge Pricing Algorithm**

A surge pricing algorithm, also known as dynamic pricing or demand-based pricing, is an algorithmic method used by businesses to adjust the prices of their products or services based on fluctuations in demand or other relevant factors. Uber's algorithm determines the price of rides based on demand. It takes into account a number of factors, including the number of riders in the area, the time of day, and the weather conditions. It doesn't report its revenue on algorithms, but in 2017, Uber reported that surge pricing accounted for 15% of its revenue. This means that surge pricing generated $1.5 billion in revenue for Uber that year.

6. **Fraud Detection Algorithm**

A fraud detection algorithm is a type of algorithm used to identify and prevent fraudulent activities or transactions in various systems, such as financial transactions, online platforms, insurance claims, and more. The primary objective of fraud detection algorithms is to analyze patterns and anomalies in data to distinguish legitimate transactions from fraudulent ones. The first use of fraud detection algorithms is generally credited to American Express in the early 1960s. American Express was facing a growing problem with credit card fraud, and the company was looking for a way to identify fraudulent transactions.

American Express developed a statistical algorithm that used historical data to identify patterns that were associated with fraud. One of their tools – the enhanced authorization tool – has enabled them to reduce fraudulent transactions by 60% (https://d3.harvard.edu/platform-digit/ submission/american-express-using-big-data-to-prevent-fraud/#:~:text=By%20leveraging%20EA% 2C%20American%20Express%20has%20reduced%20 fraudulent,and%20is%20offered%20free%20of%20 charge%20to%20merchants).

Let's look at how these algorithms have permeated into our everyday and changed the way we behave and make decisions.

Page Ranking Algorithms

When we do a web search, the output is presented according to a ranking criteria to ensure that the most relevant result is at the top.

Google is by some margin the most popular website in the world and has been for many years. According to SimilarWeb.com in Figure 6-3, over 91% of all web searches are conducted over Google with an average duration of 10n 39s per session. Its captive audience dwarfs the other leading websites – the top 15 used sites as of April 2023 are shown in Figure 6-3 – showing its importance to advertisers.

Rank	Website	Monthly Traffic (billions)	Category
1	google.com	83.9	Search Engines
2	youtube.com	32.7	Streaming & Online TV
3	facebook.com	16.8	Social Media Networks
4	twitter.com	6.4	Social Media Networks
5	instagram.com	6.3	Social Media Networks
6	baidu.com	4.7	Search Engines
7	wikipedia.org	4.5	Dictionaries and Encyclopedias
8	yandex.ru	3.3	Search Engines
9	yahoo.com	3.2	News & Media Publishers
10	xvideos.com	2.9	Adult
11	whatsapp.com	2.8	Social Media Networks
12	pornhub.com	2.6	Adult
13	xnxx.com	2.3	Adult
14	amazon.com	2.2	Marketplace
15	tiktok.com	2	Social Media Networks

Figure 6-3. Top 15 Websites, April 2023, Source: SimilarWeb

Google carries out up to 6 billion searches a day and many-thousands of searches per second. Its search index contains hundreds of billions of web pages and is well over 100,000,000 gigabytes in size.

PageRank, launched in 1998, is the web search algorithm that is used for highly efficient web searching. Its efficient method of search allowed Google to overtake the market and become the giant that it is today.

When we do a search, the responses we receive are carefully curated by the algorithm. It uses the network of links between web pages to determine their value and, famously, judges a page to be important if it is linked to by other important pages. According to Google:

> PageRank works by counting the number and quality of links to a page to determine a rough estimate of how important the website is. The underlying assumption is that more important websites are likely to receive more links from other websites.

One crucial feature of this idea is that it requires an iterative approach to constantly re-evaluate the value of a page as the importance of others varies. The algorithm has consistently evolved over the years and some of the key development ranking factors are highlighted in Figure 6-4.

Year	Ranking Factor
Pre 2011	Any Content and Inbound Links
2011	Relevant Content
2012	Local Relevance and quality links
2013	Social mentions
2104	FAQs
2015	Responsive Websites
2016	Mobile First and Local results
2017	Secure server and mobile speed
2018	User behaviour
2019	Neural matching of words and phrases
2019	Mobile Friendliness
2019	Ranking on Higher Quality Sites

Figure 6-4. Google Ranking Evolution to 2019: Source Google

Today, there are many other companies and platforms that utilize similar algorithms to curate our search results, including Microsoft's search engine, Bing, which uses its own ranking algorithm called RankNet; Baidu, the dominant search engine in China, uses an algorithm called BaiduRank; Yandex, a leading search engine in Russia, employs an algorithm called MatrixNet.

Behavioral Targeting Algorithms

Google tracks us and every search we make and uses the data to monetize through advertising. In 2007, it purchased Doubleclick who created digital advertising technology platform that helps publishers and advertisers manage their online advertising through an Ad serving, Ad targeting, Ad measurement, and Ad fraud prevention. For all the searches we make, there are adverts that are sent related to our search history. The purchase enabled Google to become the dominant player in the online advertising market. The Doubleclick purchase case $3.1 Bn, but as Figure 6-5 shows, that seems to be money well spent.

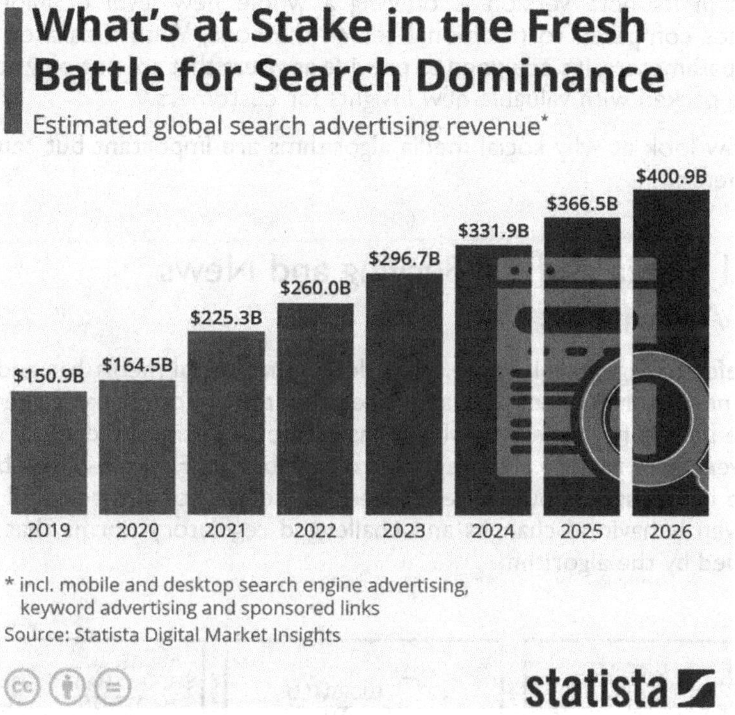

What's at Stake in the Fresh Battle for Search Dominance

Estimated global search advertising revenue*

* incl. mobile and desktop search engine advertising, keyword advertising and sponsored links
Source: Statista Digital Market Insights

statista

Figure 6-5. Global Search Revenue Predictions: www.statista.com/chart/29272/global-search-advertising-revenue/

According to estimates from Statista (Figure 6-5), global search advertising revenue reached $260 billion in 2022 and could reach $400 billion by 2026.

In 2019, Google generated $135 billion in advertising profits through the search data it generates. In 2022, Google's share of the global digital advertising market was estimated to be 28.6%. This means that Google is responsible for more than one-quarter of all digital advertising revenue generated worldwide. But there are ongoing challenges, in particular customer privacy issues. As consumers, we seem to forego the privacy invasion for the convenience the search brings. With the growth of in-home devices that connect to the Internet like Google Home and Nest, the privacy invasion is only increasing. Google uses the data generated for advertising.

Also, as online advertising evolves, Google appears closer and closer to having paid search engine results resemble organic search engine results, further clouding the ethical space between ads and organic content and how each appears to users. Paid results are more lucrative than organic content. While regulation is light in this area, there are now emerging technologies to compete with search – in particular, ChatGPT from OpenAI. This large language model chatbot in its beta version is offering a whole new level of informative responses compared to traditional search methods. With a dataset of 100 million parameters, it's equipped to provide answers that are not only accurate but also packed with valuable new insights for customers.

Let's now look at why social media algorithms are important but can be so controversial.

Social Media and Ad Serving and News Feed Algorithms

If we refer to Figure 6-1, there is no doubt that social media has addressed human needs for connection, has broken traditional norms, has gained value as more people have used it globally, has created a positive and social impact, and is very user friendly. The caption from Dilbert in Figure 6-6 may be seen as quite harmless fun, but there is a serious side to social media and how it has driven behavioral changes and challenged regulatory norms that are all controlled by the algorithm.

Figure 6-6. Does social media drive behavioural changes? Source: Dilbert

On Figure 6-2, we can see that social media sites like Facebook, Instagram, WhatsApp, and Twitter are among the most visited sites in the world. Nearly 60% of the population use free social media with revenue made through advertising. In 2022, Postbeyond, shared a snapshot of the revenue and revenue per user of various social media platforms and the figures are astounding (Figure 6-7).

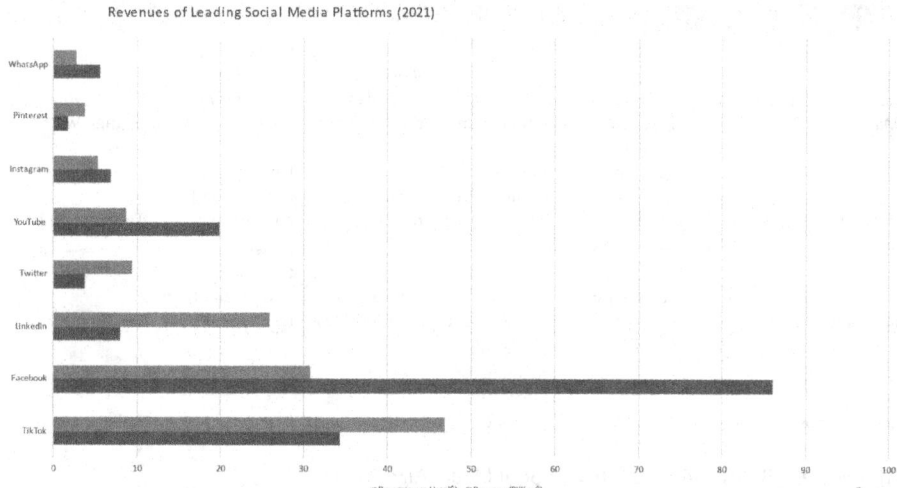

Figure 6-7. Social Media Users Numbers and Revenue

For any social media algorithm, engagement is key. The more eyeballs, the more revenue. To drive engagement, factors or user behavior are ranked and they include

- How much time a user spends on the post?

- Is the user likely to like the post?

- Would they possibly comment on the post?

- Would they want to save the post?

- How likely are they to tap through to the profile after viewing the content?

- Would the content result in direct messages (DMs) to the poster?

- Are they likely to click a link?

These triggers rank differently for different social media companies according to the brand missions. Figure 6-8 summarizes some of the key ranking factors of different organizations.

Instagram	TikTok	Facebook	YouTube	LinkedIn	Twitter
Connections/Followers Matter	Previous Interactions	Connections	Video click rate, likes, duration	Post Quality according to Spam, Low and high quality	Tweets you engage with
Interests	Content with special effects- Captions, sounds	Prefered Content Type - videos, photos	Similar watch history	Early Engagement before broadcast content	Trending topic
Relevant and Timely	Locaton and language	Popular posts	Topically related videos	LinkedIn Connections Priority and then hashtags	Location
Speed of post interaction	Trending topics	authentic meaningful, informative content			Relevance

Figure 6-8. Rules and Signals from Social Media Algorithms

Also the social media algorithm adapts according to the traffic during the day. For advertisers to maximize on eyeballs on social media, timeliness is everything. The American Marketing Association posted details of the best times to post on social media. For example, if we look at global engagement of LinkedIn posts (Figure 6-9).

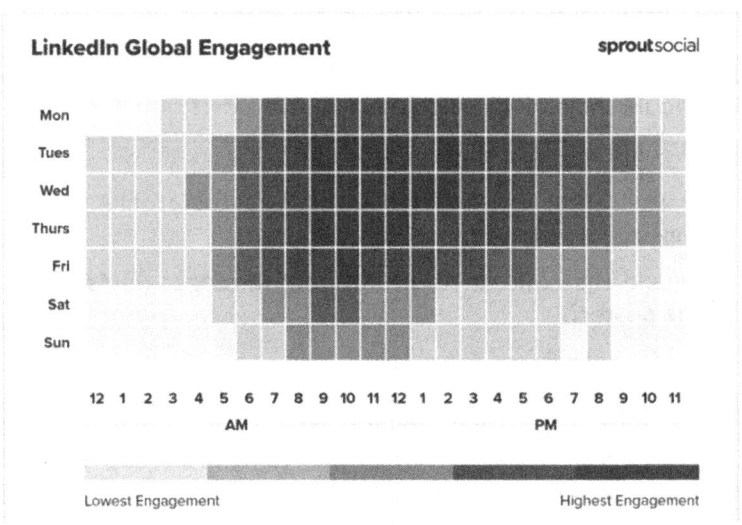

Figure 6-9. Best Times to Post Content on LinkedIn (www.ama.org/marketing-news/the-best-times-to-post-on-social-media/)

For every time segment, there is a different engagement rate. In each case, the advertisers and influencers are playing with the algorithm to maximize audience and revenue.

Although it may seem to be simply about higher customer engagement to allow advertisers to create revenue, the way that different social media sites drive customer attention with their algorithm is designed is causing major concern.

In Chapter 9, we will look at the rise of digital ethics as a result of algorithms driving human behaviors.

Recommendation and Rationalized Ordering Algorithms

Recommendation systems have quietly become a big part of our daily lives since the early 2000s. They started with search engines and now they help us find things we like on platforms like Amazon, Netflix, and YouTube. These systems use special methods (called Collaborative filtering) to figure out what we might be interested in, based on what other people like. By suggesting products and content we might enjoy, companies can make more sales and build a better relationship with us. The more we interact with the system by giving likes or ratings, the better it becomes at recommending things we'll like to see.

To give an idea of the amount of data used to feed an algorithm, let's look at Netflix. As of the end of 2022, Netflix had over 222 million subscribers globally. The key to their growth has been their focus on correctly recommending movie content to users. Eighty percent of Netflix viewer activity is a direct result of recommendations. Their main goal is to personalize the Netflix experience for each user, and this recommendation feature is integrated into every aspect of their platform. The engine is made up of several algorithms that filter content according to a user's profile, preferences, and characteristics. The platform has about 90 seconds to grab a viewer's attention, so it focuses on promoting content that is likely to be viewed and enjoyed quickly. The algorithms are always analyzing user choices and habits. Every time a user opens Netflix, the recommendation system calculates the probability of a specific title being selected using various data points.

Figure 6-10 shows the various collection points that they feed into their algorithm. This includes data on viewing history, ratings given to titles, the type and genre of shows watched, and the nature of the content. Additionally, Netflix collects data on when users watch, the devices they use to watch, how long they watch, and whether they watch the same content on multiple occasions. They have around 800 Software Engineers at their headquarters dedicated to maintaining and improving these personalized experiences (Vanderbilt, 2018).

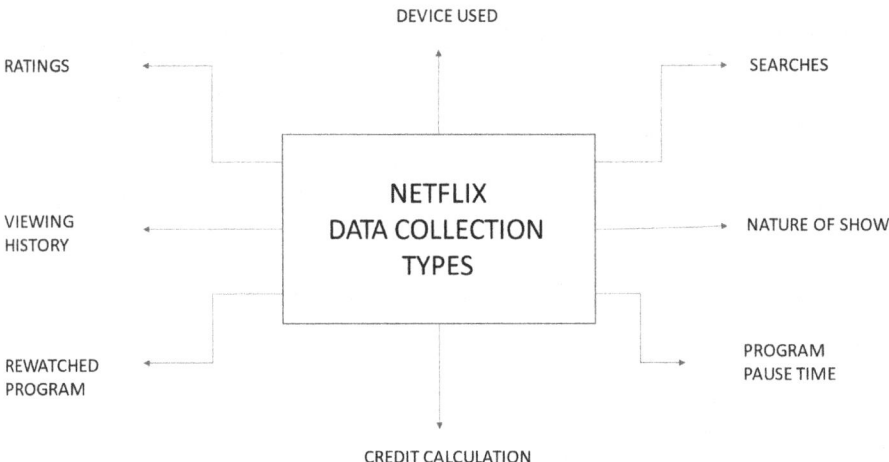

Figure 6-10. Netflix Data Collection Types

The specific user viewing history in the data collection is huge and includes

- Time duration of a viewer watching particular content
- Content viewing history
- How titles were rated by the user
- Other users who may have similar content selections
- Information about titles such as genre, actors, and release year
- The time of day you watch content
- When the user watches a scene more than once
- If the content was paused, re-wound, or fast-forwarded
- If the viewer resumed watching content after pausing
- The device you are watching content on
- The number of searches and what is searched for
- Screen shots when the content was paused
- When the user left the content

As of February 2023, Netflix has around 13,612 titles with their US library alone consisting of 5087 titles. According to (Netflix Technology Blog, 2017b), the data library for the engine includes

- Billions of ratings from its members. More than a million new ratings are being added every day.

- A popularity metric. For example, they compute it hourly, daily, or weekly. They also examine clusters constituting members either geographically or by using other similarity metrics. These are some of the different dimensions over which popularity is computed.

- The pattern and the titles that their subscribers add to their queues each day which number in the millions.

- All the metadata related to a title in their catalog such as director, actor, genre, rating, and reviews from different platforms.

- The search-related text information by Netflix subscribers or members.

- Film box office information, performance, and critic reviews.

The size of the data store for this information to feed the recommendation algorithm is vast.

In 2016, it was calculated that Netflix stores approximately 105TB of video data alone (https://cordcutting.com/blog/how-many-titles-are-available-on-netflix-in-your-country/#:~:text=Worldwide%2C%20Netflix%20has%20the%20rights%20to%2013%2C612%20titles,and%20some%20of%20them%20are%20very%20tiny%20indeed).

All this data then shows that, on average, each Netflix subscriber watches about two hours of video content daily, resulting in a total of around 2 million hours of content streamed every day (Clark, 2019).

The biggest challenge for Netflix is in rising churn (3.3% in 2021) and how the recommendation can help address this. Other new streaming services like Disney+, HBO Max, and Amazon Prime also use effective recommendation systems as well as original content.

Surge Pricing Algorithms

Uber offer a ride-sharing service where an algorithm matches drivers to passengers via an app. In the first quarter of 2023, Uber's ridership worldwide totaled 2.1 billion trips, a 24.1% increase year on year. Uber generated around

US$31.88 billion in net revenue in 2022 with around 130 million users globally. In 2014, Uber began experimenting with surge pricing in Boston. The company found that surge pricing was an effective way to manage the number of drivers available during peak times, and it soon began using surge pricing in other cities. The best evidence for the effectiveness of Uber's surge algorithm is the remarkable consistency of the expected wait time for a ride. Regardless of demand conditions, the surge algorithm filters demand and encourage supply such that a ride is almost always fewer than five minutes away, thus improving customer wait times. (Source: http://andrewchen.com/wp-`content/uploads/2016/01/effects_of_ubers_surge_pricing.pdf)

The algorithm uses a method called linear regression. The linear relationship between the input variables and the output value is the relationship between the current demand for rides, the number of available drivers, the time of day, the weather, and the surge price factor. Here's how the surge pricing algorithm works:

1. Uber collects data on the current demand for rides in different areas. This data is collected from a variety of sources, including historical data, real-time rider requests, and the number of available drivers.

2. Uber uses this data to calculate a surge multiplier. The surge multiplier is a number that is used to increase the price of rides. The higher the surge multiplier, the more expensive the ride will be.

3. Uber displays the surge multiplier to riders before they request a ride. This gives riders the opportunity to decide whether or not they want to pay the higher price.

4. If a rider requests a ride during a surge, Uber will charge them the higher price. The surge price is calculated based on the surge multiplier and the distance of the ride.

We will cover linear regression in the chapter on algorithms. Surge pricing is now used by other ride hailing companies, as well as Airbnb, hotels, airlines, event ticketing, and vehicle charging stations.

We have looked at some of the more generic algorithms that can be applied to everyday consumer applications. Before moving on to the more business-orientated innovations, can you think of any applications you use and how any of these algorithms could help improve the offering?

Game-Changing Business Intelligence and Operational Tools

The term "Business transformation" refers to a fundamental and significant change in the way a company operates, strategizes, and delivers value to its customers and stakeholders. The goal is to enhance efficiency, competitiveness, and overall performance to meet evolving customer demands and stay relevant in the market. There are specific tools that have improved business intelligences and operational tools that have been very transformational in this regard. Here are a few of the leading ones in Figure 6-11 that we will review. Collectively, these business intelligence and operational tools give rise to a new phrase called "Industry 4.0," which we will describe at the end of the section.

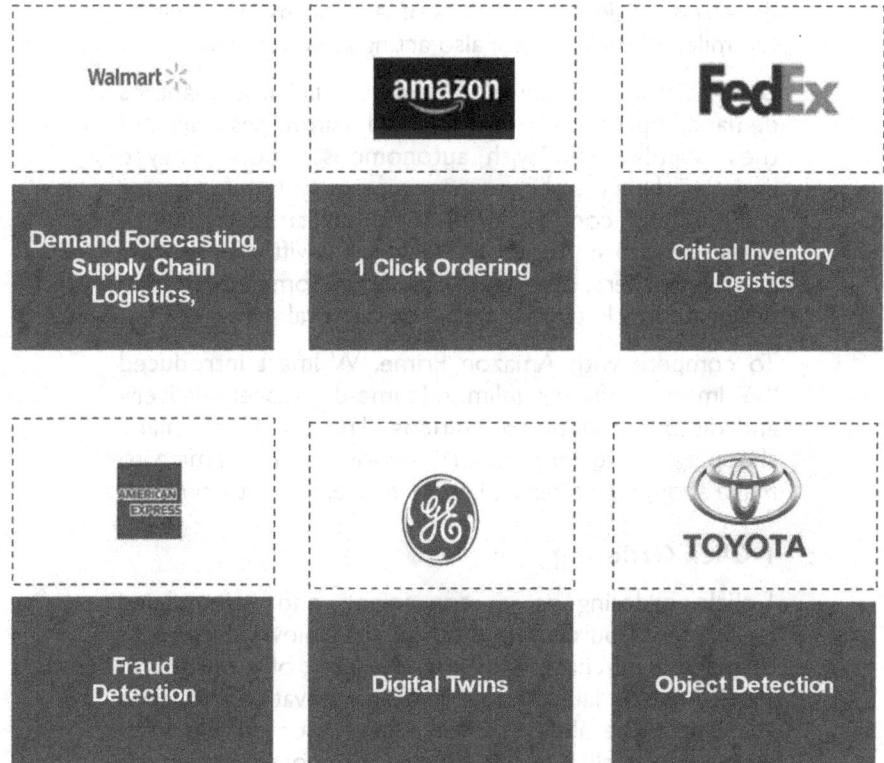

Figure 6-11. Game-Changing Productivity Deployments

1. **Demand Forecasting and Supply Chain Logistics**

   Demand forecasting and supply chain logistics are vital in operations and supply chain management. Demand forecasting predicts future product or service demand using historical data, market trends, and relevant factors. Supply chain logistics involves efficiently planning, implementing, and controlling the movement and storage of goods, services, and information from origin to consumption.

   In 1983, Walmart pioneered demand forecasting and supply chain logistics by being the first to use barcodes on all products. They adopted advanced technology and innovative strategies, like RFID, which replenish products three times faster and reduced out-of-stocks by 16%. Walmart's online storefronts offer millions of items, delivered quickly due to 90% of Americans living within ten miles of their stores, also acting as warehouses.

   Using digital techniques, Walmart efficiently manages demand, optimizes inventory, and automates parts of their supply chain with autonomous robots. They're updating their warehouse management system for better planning and control. With these investments and an extensive store network, Walmart swiftly picks and prepares orders, often within an hour. Some stores have designated pickup areas for quick retrieval.

   To compete with Amazon Prime, Walmart introduced "Walmart+," offering unlimited same-day grocery delivery and discounts at petrol stations. This combines online shopping convenience with in-store options, aiming to make shopping easier and more efficient for customers.

2. **1-Click Ordering**

   1-click ordering is a convenient and streamlined e-commerce purchasing method that allows customers to make a purchase with just one click of a button. In 1997, Amazon launched 1-Click, an innovation that gives customers the ability to make purchases on the Web with just one click of the mouse – no more entering the same information over and over again for each purchase. 1-Click was a first-of-its-kind approach to retail. Before, customers had to re-enter their payment information – even on sites they regularly used – to complete a purchase. 1-Click eliminated this redundancy, making customers' shopping experiences easier and more seamless. According to Amazon, 1-Click accounts for over 15% of all orders placed on the site.

3. **Critical Inventory Logistics**

   Critical inventory logistics refers to the management and transportation of essential or high-priority inventory items that are crucial for a company's operations. This type of inventory can include items such as spare parts, raw materials, and finished goods. Critical inventory logistics is important because it can help businesses to ensure that they have the right amount of inventory on hand to meet demand. This can help to prevent stockouts, which can lead to lost sales and revenue. Fedex was a pioneer in this as it uses its distribution centers as central locations, delivering efficiently according to customers need. The system uses a number of technologies, including RFID: Radio frequency identification (RFID) tags are used to track and trace inventory and GPS: Global positioning system (GPS) tracking to track the location of vehicles and shipments. This helps to improve visibility and ensure that shipments arrive on time as well as provide analytics to analyze data on inventory levels, demand, and transportation costs and machine learning algorithms to identify patterns in data and make predictions about future demand to improve inventory management decisions.

4. **Fraud Detection Algorithms**

   Fraud detection algorithms are widely used by financial institutions to identify fraudulent transactions. They do this by analyzing data about the transaction, such as the amount of money being transferred, the IP address of the sender, and the type of account being used.

   There are two main types of fraud detection algorithms:

   - Statistical algorithms: These algorithms use historical data to identify patterns that are associated with fraud. For example, a statistical algorithm might look for transactions that are unusually large or that are made from IP addresses that have been associated with fraud in the past.

- Machine learning algorithms: These algorithms learn to identify fraud by analyzing data about transactions that have already been labeled as fraudulent or non-fraudulent. For example, a machine learning algorithm might be trained on a dataset of transactions that have been labeled as fraudulent and non-fraudulent. The algorithm would then learn to identify patterns that are associated with fraud.

Today Fraud detection algorithms are used to detect a wide variety of fraudulent activity, including credit card fraud, identity theft, phishing, insurance fraud, healthcare fraud, telecommunications fraud, and utilities fraud.

5. **Digital Twins**

A digital twin is "a virtual representation of a physical asset that is synchronized with the asset in real time." The first commercial digital twin was created by General Electric in 2002. GE used a digital twin to improve `the performance of its jet engines. In 2019, GE reported that it had saved $1 billion through the use of digital twins.

Digital twins can be used to improve the performance, reliability, and safety of physical assets through providing a semi-conductor chip inside the physical asset. They can also be used to reduce costs and to improve efficiency. Digital twins use a mixture of algorithms to make predictions, simulate physical systems, and optimize the operations. As the cost of sensors and computing power decreases, digital twins are becoming increasingly popular and are being used by a wide range of companies in many verticals. A challenge lies in the availability of semi-conductor chips to service the demands for assets with sim cards.

The demand for these assets can be seen in the demand for chips in connected cars. As cars become more autonomous, they need to classify different objects present in an image, and know the precise locations of these objects.

Figure 6-12. Some Sensors in Today's Connected Cars (Source: freepic)

Let's look at how object detection works in connected cars.

6 Object Detection

Object detection in connected cars refers to the technology and system that enables vehicles to identify and recognize various objects in their surroundings using sensors, cameras, and advanced algorithms. Object detection was pioneered by researchers from academia but has found great use in industry.

In 2004, Toyota showcased its early efforts in autonomous driving with the launch of the Toyota Advanced Active Safety Research Vehicle (AASRV). The AASRV featured an array of sensors, including cameras and LIDAR, to detect obstacles and navigate through complex environments. This was a significant step in bringing object detection and autonomous capabilities to traditional vehicles.

According to a McKinsey estimate, connected cars through sensors create up to 25 gigabytes of data per hour – equivalent of nearly 30 hours of HD video playback and more than a month's worth of 24-hour music streaming. The intelligent assets are used crucially in the deployment of object detection algorithms to detect hazards.

To understand how object detection works, look at the following image (Figure 6-13). It may be easy to distinguish with the human eye the cyclist, cars, trunk, and salient features such as traffic lights but for an algorithm to determine accurately each time what the image components are, it needs to assess millions of images. This is even more challenging if you are behind the wheel of a car and trying to distinguish objects.

Figure 6-13. Object Detection Example. Source: `https://www.kaggle.com/datasets/` `sshikamaru/car-object-detection`

Machine learning is essential in connected cars because it continuously renders the surrounding environment and makes predictions of possible changes to those surroundings. Machine learning tasks in a self-driving car are mainly divided into four sub-tasks: object detection, object identification or recognition, object classification, and object localization and prediction of movement.

A range of algorithms are used including

- **Regression Algorithms**

    Images (radar or camera) play a very important role in localization and actuation regression algorithms to predict future images while the car is in motion.

- **Classification Algorithms**

    These algorithms help in reducing the data set by detecting object edges and fitting line segments (polylines) and circular arcs to the edges. Line segments are aligned to edges up to a corner, then a new line segment is started. Circular arcs are fit to sequences of line segments that approximate an arc. The image features (line segments and circular arcs) are combined in various ways to form the features that are used for recognizing an object. The support vector machines (SVM), Bayes decision rule and K nearest neighbor (KNN) are the algorithms used.

- **Clustering Algorithms**

    Sometimes the images obtained by the system are not clear and it is difficult to detect and locate objects. It is also possible that the classification algorithms may miss the object and fail to classify and report it to the system. The reason could be low-resolution images, very few data points or discontinuous data. These types of algorithm are good at discovering structure from data points. The most commonly used type of algorithm is K-means, or a Neural network.

Industry 4.0 Applications

In 2015, a new term was coined to conceptualize the change in data, interconnectivity, smart automation, cloud computing, machine learning, and Internet of Things or "IoT." It was termed "Fourth Industrial Revolution" or "Industry 4.0." By merging the technologies together, a production environment could be made in which production facilities and logistics systems are organized without human intervention. In this "smart factory," environment sensors, 3D printers, and predictive maintenance tools would be used to ensure the factor is cost-effective and efficient. Two further applications on top of the tools already mentioned are in robotics and process mining:

1. **Robotics**

    Robots are machines capable of performing tasks autonomously or with some human assistance. They use sensors and actuators to interact with their environment. They can be programmed for specific functions and controlled by humans or intelligent algorithms. Robotics is becoming increasingly prevalent in industries, with the global market for industrial robots valued at $46.8 billion in 2021 and expected to reach $61.4 billion by 2026.

    There are two main types of robots: traditional robots that handle repetitive tasks in industries and intelligent robots that can gather information from their surroundings to make decisions, similar to behavior-based robots. Machine Learning plays a significant role in enhancing industrial robots' capabilities in areas like vision, object grasping, and motion control by using data to identify patterns for optimal actions.

    In Machine Learning, multilayer neural networks show great promise for Robotics Systems, excelling at tasks like image recognition, which is crucial for robotic vision.

2. **Process Mining**

Process mining is a data-driven technique that analyzes and visualizes an organization's actual processes using event logs and operational system data. In the context of Industry 4.0, process mining is a powerful tool that helps organizations enhance their business processes by identifying areas for improvement, such as reducing bottlenecks and eliminating unnecessary steps.

When combined with robotic process automation (RPA), process mining further enhances efficiency. RPA employs software robots to automate tasks currently performed by humans, freeing up employees to focus on more strategic work.

In the context of digital transformation, process mining has proven beneficial in various ways:

- A bank utilized process mining to pinpoint a bottleneck in its loan approval process. By automating the problematic steps, the bank reduced the loan approval time by 50%.

- A telecommunications company employed process mining to identify customers at risk of churn. Implementing targeted special offers for these customers led to a 10% reduction in churn rate.

- A manufacturing company harnessed process mining to identify areas of improvement in its production process. By making necessary changes, the company increased its output by 15%.

We have seen that some digital tools and key algorithms have had groundbreaking effects on how we search, buy, interact, but also how we get things delivered efficiently. We have seen how incumbents have used these tools to effectively compete against the digital natives. Let's now look at some other digital innovations that will transform the way we work in the near future – e-commerce, blockchain, and the evolution of the Web.

Emerging Disruptive Innovations

Through the use of fast data processing, there are some innovations that are emerging outside the consumer and business algorithms we mentioned earlier and disrupting particular industries. In this section, we will look at how new technologies like blockchain and new consensus algorithms are rethinking how we carry out e-commerce transactions and could use the Web and how quantum computing can help revolutionize how we could work with data in the future.

Blockchain is a revolutionary technology that has the potential to change the way we work together by creating better payment methods to reduce fraud and improve efficiency in supply chains. Blockchain can also be used to improve content privacy, which can help to create a more open and transparent Web.

However, many people still don't understand how blockchain works, and they are skeptical of its potential. This is due in part to the hype that surrounded blockchain in its early days. Many people jumped on the bandwagon without fully understanding the technology, and this led to a number of scams and high profile failures.

Let's take a look at its game-changing potential and then we will move to an overview of quantum computing.

E-Commerce, Blockchain, and the Evolution of the Web

Bitcoin Pizza Day!

Figure 6-14. Bitcoin Pizza Day Poster, Source: bitcoincryptoadvice.com

On May 22, 2010, a transaction occurred which was very disruptive to how we traditionally do business. The day is known as Bitcoin Pizza Day? Here's why. A bitcoin is a digital currency which operates independently of a central bank – a physical bitcoin does not exist. New units of bitcoin currency are generated by the computational solution of mathematical problems. On May 18, 2010, Forum member Laszlo offered the following trade on the BitcoinTalk forum:

> I'll pay 10,000 bitcoins for a couple of pizzas.. like maybe 2 large ones so I have some left over for the next day. I like having left over pizza to nibble on later. You can make the pizza yourself and bring it to my house or order it for me from a delivery place, but what I'm aiming for is getting food delivered in exchange for bitcoins where I don't have to order or prepare it myself, kind of like ordering a 'breakfast platter' at a hotel or something, they just bring you something to eat and you're happy!
>
> I like things like onions, peppers, sausage, mushrooms, tomatoes, pepperoni, etc.. just standard stuff no weird fish topping or anything like that. I also like regular cheese pizzas which may be cheaper to prepare or otherwise acquire. If you're interested please let me know and we can work out a deal.
>
> Thanks,
>
> Laszlo

After four days, a fellow crypto enthusiast, Jeremy Sturdivant (aka jercos), took him up on his offer and carried out the first bitcoin trade.

The actual cost of two pizzas at the time was around $25. Given, that Laszlo paid over 10,000 bitcoins, it seems a bad deal when compared to the price it reached in 2022, as shown in Figure 6-15. This transaction proved that Bitcoin had a real-world use case and could be used instead of fiat currency like the US dollar to purchase physical products. A fiat currency is a government-issued currency that is not backed by a physical commodity, such as gold or silver, but rather by the government that issued it.

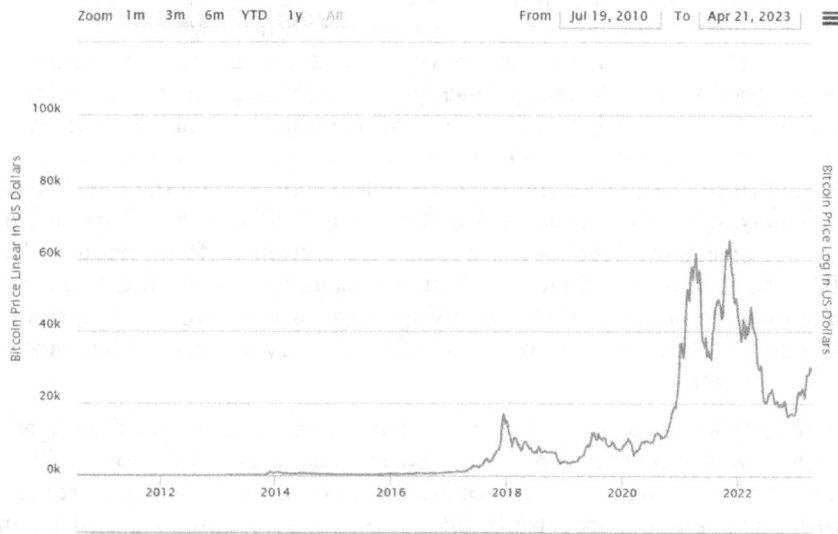

Figure 6-15. Bitcoin Price 2010–2022

By looking at the price of Bitcoin in Figure 6-15, you can see how those coins would have fared. Laszlo paid 10,000 Bitcoins for the two Papa John's pizzas. Ten thousand bitcoins were worth a staggering $170 million by January 2023 or roughly $17,000 bitcoins. [Source: Bitcoin Talk Forum]

In 1984, economist, Friedrich Hayek stated

> I don't believe we shall ever have a good money again before we have the money out of the hands of government – all we can do is by sly roundabout way introduce something they can't stop

It seems that Bitcoin may have answered Hayek's call. Looking at Figure 6-15, how did digital innovation lead to 10,000 bitcoin transaction carried out over the Internet in 2010 get to be worth the equivalent of around $170,000,000 in just 13 years?

We will look further into Bitcoin and how it works, but let's first understand how the digital economy has grown.

Growth of the Digital Economy

To understand, let's look at the growth of the digital economy which happened in parallel with the development of digital tools. We discussed earlier the failure of bricks and mortar stores to address the phenomenal growth of the Internet. Even by the late 1990s, it was practically impossible to buy anything online.

At this time, the Internet was mostly used for reading information from static websites with very little interactivity, let alone secure payments. This was the first iteration of the Web – called Web 1.0. But then, new technologies like secure socket layers(SSL) and encryption certification that allowed data to be transmitted securely and later on new technologies enabled websites to be interactive and user-generated content became possible like social media. This also led to the rise of e-commerce, or online shopping. By the mid-1990s saw the emergence of marketplaces like Amazon and eBay. As businesses did more business online, the need for more secure transaction platforms became clear. In 2004, the Payment Card Industry Security Standards Council (PCI) was formed to ensure businesses were complying with various security requirements. (Source : `https://blog.miva.com/the-history-of-ecommerce-how-did-it-all-begin`)

For businesses, e-commerce tools help to increase sales, brand engagement, reach new customers, and reduce costs over bricks and mortar. Many of these online brands became popular without even having any stores. For consumers, e-commerce tools offer a wider selection of products, more convenient shopping experiences, and lower prices. This new iteration of the Web – called Web 2.0 – also allowed users to create different accounts for various applications, allowing them to create unique personal identities on the Internet. Think of your Facebook or Twitter account. As a result, e-commerce and social media platforms started exploring new product tools for reaching a wider audience like news feeds and reels. The rise of Web 2.0 also fostered the development of many revolutionary web technologies such as Hypertext Markup Language 5 (HTML5), and JavaScript that enabled the interactivity to happen.

The Development of e-Commerce

E-commerce has been steadily growing, and it is now a major part of our global economy. According to an e-Marketer's report, titled "Global E-Commerce Forecast, 2023 to 2027," in 2023, global e-commerce sales are expected to reach $4.9 trillion, up from $4.94 trillion in 2022. This represents a compound annual growth rate (CAGR) of 14.6% from 2022 to 2023.

Traditional commerce, on the other hand, is growing more slowly. In 2023, global traditional commerce sales are expected to reach $23.1 trillion, up from $22.5 trillion in 2022. This represents a CAGR of 3.4% from 2022 to 2023.

The growth in e-commerce is being driven by a number of factors, including

- Improved technology: The development of new technologies, such as faster Internet speeds, more powerful computers, and mobile devices, makes it easier and more convenient for people to shop online.

- Increased access to the Internet: The number of people with access to the Internet has grown exponentially in recent years. This has made it possible for more people to shop online, regardless of their location.

- Brand focus on engagement: Retailers endeavor to drive engagement, and Internet shopping is a great way to do this.

- Better security: The security of online transactions has improved significantly in recent years. This has made people more comfortable shopping online.

- Pure convenience: Online shopping is often more convenient than traditional brick-and-mortar shopping. People can shop online 24/7, from the comfort of their own homes.

However the growth rate is slowing compared to the earlier years. There are a number of reasons why. Markets are becoming more saturated making it more difficult for new retailers to enter the market. Another reason is that consumers are becoming more price-conscious. They are looking for the best deals, and they are not willing to pay a premium for convenience that online shopping brings. Finally, the growth of e-commerce is being hampered by logistical challenges. It can be difficult and expensive to ship goods to consumers, and this can lead to delays and frustration for customers.

A new way of conducting transactions is through digital currencies – like Bitcoin – which have the potential to take e-commerce to a new level. Although they are still in their early stages, they can potentially allow

- Faster and cheaper transactions: Digital currency transactions are typically much faster and cheaper than traditional payment methods, such as credit cards and bank transfers. This is because there is no need for a third party to process the transaction.

- More secure transactions: They are also more secure than traditional payment methods because they are encrypted and robust through efficient consensus algorithms. This means that the data cannot be intercepted or tampered with.

- More transparent transactions: Crypto transactions are more transparent than traditional payment methods because they are recorded on a public ledger. This means that anyone can view a transaction history.

Let's take a deeper look at Bitcoin.

Arrival of Digital Currencies

When it was launched, a Bitcoin was worth 0.0008 of a US Dollar. We have seen in Figure 6-15 how its value has grown.

Bitcoin is a decentralized currency, which means that it is not subject to a single government or financial institution control. Bitcoin transactions are verified by network nodes through cryptography and recorded in a public distributed ledger called a blockchain.

Although the market for digital currencies is small, the market size of digital currencies in relation to e-commerce transactions is expected to grow significantly in the coming years. A report from Statista anticipates the global market for digital currencies is expected to reach $2.8 trillion by 2025. Of this, the e-commerce segment is expected to account for a significant portion, with a market size of $1.5 trillion.

How Digital Currencies Could Change the World

As we discussed, literally every aspect of our day-to-day is now dependent on the way we can store and retrieve data and e-commerce is no exception. To understand how we can actually carry out trusted transactions without the need for a central authority, we will start with how we retrieve data through databases.

Databases

A database is a collection of data that is organized so that it can be easily accessed, managed, and updated. In the simplest form, it could be data on a spreadsheet. However, real databases need to handle larger information sets, be able to retrieve the data more quickly, have a higher security, and allow many users to access the information at the same time.

Relational Databases takes things a step further by providing a structured way to store data in table form with rows and columns. This makes it easier to find patterns and relationships. Relational databases are also efficient at storing and retrieving data, which is important for the data mining algorithms that need to process large amounts of data.

Relational databases are typically centralized, meaning that they are stored on a single server or cluster of servers. This makes them easy to manage and secure, but it also makes them a single point of failure. If the central server goes down, the entire database is unavailable.

A decentralized database means that it is stored on a network of computers and not in a central server. It stores data in blocks and is called a Blockchain. Each block contains a set of transactions, and each transaction is linked to the previous block. The data in a blockchain is then stored in a public ledger, and it can be verified by anyone. As the data it not stored in a central place it is more secure and resistant to attack.

Because the blockchain is decentralized, it is secure without the need of a central control authority.

So prior to Bitcoin's creation in 2009, one could argue that Hayek's appeal to decentralized competition, quoted earlier, was irrelevant. Money had to be centrally planned. In 2009, a group of people under the name Satoshi Nakamoto released an open source software called "Bitcoin" to carry out decentralized transactions using a blockchain. Bitcoin is a global currency, and it can be used to buy goods and services from anywhere in the world. Bitcoin is unique in that there are a finite number of bitcoin tokens: 21 million in fact. This means that Bitcoin is not subject to inflation, as the supply of new Bitcoins is limited. Bitcoin is also secure, as all transactions are verified by network nodes through cryptography. This makes it difficult to counterfeit or double-spend Bitcoins.

To understand its benefit in today's world, we make online payments through our bank as a trusted authority, but we have to pay a commission to do this. If we could record transactions on a ledger that cannot be tampered with then we can send money anywhere without having to worry about any bank commissions and even currency conversion. We can do this by using a digital currency – or virtual currency – like Bitcoin. A broker would then do the transaction through an exchange similar to Lazlo using Bitcoin Talk to do his pizza transaction. This is the principle of a digital currency. It is also called a "cryptocurrency."

Carrying out transactions using Bitcoin carries some other benefits over a traditional bank transaction:

- In places where there is little trust for formal central institutions, making payments through a cryptocurrency that are recorded on a secure public ledger ensures that the transaction is safe.

- The transparency of the public ledger makes things auditable.

- The process can be used for payments to anyone in the world where you could be worried about restrictions on international payments.

- You can store your money on a digital wallet instead of a bank account, making it accessible from anywhere in the world. It means if you are a frequent traveler, you don't need to carry so much foreign currency on you.

On the other hand, there are concerns on how crypto is used today, with transactions being anonymized and just seeing a public key, it can be used to traffic illicit goods. Also the threat of government crackdown on illicit traffic and the difficulties to convert to normal money without the value dropping does cause the value of crypto currencies to fluctuate, allowing traders to make a quick profit from the trade.

Because Bitcoin is open source, so people could make their own versions of the currency with different features. These versions of the Bitcoin are called alt coins. Since 2009, other cryptocurrencies have emerged that are faster, more energy efficient, which can allow them to be used in different applications. Here are some of the most popular blockchain currencies: Bitcoin (BTC), Ethereum (ETH), Tether (USDT), Solana (SOL), Cardano (ADA).

Blockchain has all attributes to accelerate e-commerce growth by making it more affordable, secure, transparent, and efficient, but it still needs get a wider acceptance and demonstrate a positive social impact against the traditional payment systems.

With the perceived robustness, lower transaction cost and higher convenience many central banks around the world are piloting digital versions of their currency called Central Backed Digital Currency (CBDC).

Blockchain Applied Outside Payments

Blockchain is a powerful new technology that has the potential to revolutionize many industries. As blockchain technology continues to develop and gets more accepted, it will play an increasingly important role in the e-commerce industry, especially in the way that it redefines how we work with untrusted parties. Outside of purely digital payment transactions, it has the potential to be used in many other areas to accelerate digital transformation outcomes. The following are some examples.

Real Estate

When you buy a house, you need to register the sale with a trusted authority to confirm that you now own the house – in the UK, this is called the Land Registry. This is typically carried out by a conveyancing lawyer, who will check the earlier records of ownership, make sure that everything is in order, and then make the request to update the ledger.

However, in some countries, you cannot rely on the approved registrar to keep the correct records. Perhaps these institutions are not stable and the register is not reliable, or because it is simply inefficient. In these cases, blockchain could be used to create a more efficient and secure system.

With blockchain, the information about who owns a house would be stored on a decentralized database. This means that it would not be controlled by any one person or organization. Instead, it would be maintained by a network of computers.

This would make it much more difficult for the information to be tampered with. It would also make it much easier to transfer ownership of a house.

Supply Chain

Another area where blockchain could be used is in supply chain management. When you buy goods from abroad, they need to be shipped to you. Every time the goods get shipped, they need to be recorded at destination points by an authority. This can be a time-consuming and expensive process.

SALES JOURNAL

Date	Account debited	Invoice number	PR	Accounts receivable-Dr.	Sales taxes payable-Cr.	Sales-Cr.	Cost of goods sold-Dr. Inventory-Cr.
2018							
Mar. 05	Besco Co.	113		2,040	40	2,000	1,600
Mar. 12	Rivo Co.	114		5,100	100	5,000	4,000
Mar. 18	John & Co.	115		3,060	60	3,000	2,400
Mar. 25	Hasan Bro.	116		1,020	20	1,000	800
Mar. 31	Fesco Co.	117		8,160	160	8,000	6,400

Figure 6-16. What a Traditional Ledger Looks like. Source: www.excelstemplates.com

Blockchain could be used to automate these processes. With blockchain, the information would be stored on a decentralized database. This would make it possible to track the goods as they move through the supply chain.

This would make it much easier to ensure that the goods are delivered on time and in good condition. It would also make it much more difficult for the goods to be lost or stolen.

Health Care

Think of Healthcare records; using a blockchain, we can ensure that records do not get tampered with, ensuring better health care by better communication between hospitals and doctors.

How Does Blockchain Work?

To recap, a Blockchain is a decentralized database that can be used to store and track information. The decentralized approach is a seismic shift in how we use parties to carry out our transactions when we don't know them.

Blockchain has solved something known as the "Byzantine General's Problem," of how to get multiple parties to agree on something to avoid failure, when some of the parties can't be trusted. The bitcoin consensus algorithm addresses the problem through the following:

Deriving consensus through computationally difficult puzzles

- Miners solve difficult computational puzzles to add a new block to the chain and win a reward.

- The puzzles are time-consuming and consume a lot of power.

The special process of consensus agreement

- Once a miner solves the puzzle, the solution is broadcast across the network along with a new block for the network.

- The other nodes then quickly check that the solution is correct.

- Once a majority agree the block is valid, consensus is formed and the block is added to the chain.

- The chain with the longest computational work is added if there are competing blocks.

Expended resources from miners is a sign of good faith in the system

- The difficulty of solving the puzzles shows investment into real-world resources like electricity and hardware.

Malicious actions are costly to miners

- The cost of performing a malicious action, like rewriting a blockchain history, is prohibitively high.

In simple terms, imagine you have a community of people offering charity donations to a cause. To keep track of the donations, you can ask everyone to give the details to a responsible person. There are problems of trust here – maybe the responsible person runs off with the money. Each member could keep their own records and compare the details, but this would also be very inefficient. Another way is to create a ledger that is shared that everyone can access and see the latest updates. Each time someone donates something, a new entry to the ledger would be produced for everyone to see. The person who successfully adds to the ledger gets a reward, but to add something takes a lot of effort, making the effort of creating false records inefficient. This would be a more secure and efficient way to keep track of ownership. This is the essence of how the bitcoin blockchain works.

To produce a blockchain in the real world, there are various parties involved. Let's say, like Laslo, you want to send some bitcoins to a friend to buy a Pizza. The steps are shown in Figure 6-17.

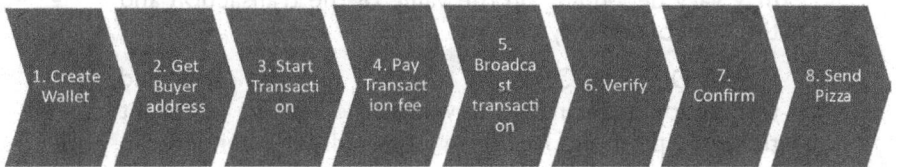

Figure 6-17. Bitcoin Transaction Steps

1. Create a bitcoin wallet: A Bitcoin wallet is a software application or an online service that allows users to send, receive, and store Bitcoins securely.

2. Obtain the recipient's Bitcoin address: A Bitcoin address is a unique string of alphanumeric characters that serves as the destination for the Bitcoins. It is similar to a bank account number.

3. Initiate a transaction: This would typically include elements of the amount of bitcoin to send, the address of your friend's wallet.

4. Pay transaction fee: To incentivize miners to include the transaction in a block and verify it, a small transaction fee is usually added to the payment. Miners are computers

that are constantly scanning the network for new transactions to verify and add new blocks to a blockchain.

5. Broadcast the transaction: Once the sender confirms the transaction details and includes the appropriate transaction fee, the transaction is broadcast to the miners on the Bitcoin network.

6. Verification: Bitcoin miners on the network collect and validate transactions into blocks. They confirm the sender's ownership of the Bitcoins and ensure that the transaction adheres to the network rules. Miners use the PoW consensus algorithm to solve complex mathematical puzzles, and the first miner to solve the puzzle adds the block to the blockchain. Once the transaction is verified, it is included in a new block on the Bitcoin blockchain. The first miner to verify it and add it to a block gets rewarded with cryptocurrency for their work.

7. Confirmation: Once a block is full of transactions, it is added to the blockchain. For the transaction to be considered confirmed, it should be buried under several subsequent blocks. The number of confirmations required may vary depending on the value of the transaction and the level of security needed

8. Goods Delivery: Once the recipient sees the confirmed transaction in their Bitcoin wallet, they can be confident that the payment has been received. The sender can proceed with delivering the goods or services to the recipient.

How Blocks Are Securely Added to the Blockchain

Blocks are groups of transactions that are added to a blockchain in chronological order. Blocks are added when a miner finds a number that when added to the block header produces a hash that meets specific criteria. The hash number is unpredictable, and so for a miner to find a number that meets the criteria is very difficult. Miners typically use a trial-and-error method to do this. This number is called the "nonce." The hash function or "hash" takes a block of data, including the transactions and the previous block's hash, and produces a unique string of characters of 32 bytes. Each block contains a "hash" of the previous block, which links them together in a chain.

To explain hash, let's say we have a hash function from a block that takes some text as input and produces a 16-character hash value as output. If we input the string "Hello, Pizza!", the hash function will produce the hash value "5eb63bbbe01eeed093cb22bb8f5acdc329711781".

If we change the string to "Hello, Pasta!", the hash function will produce a different hash value but with the same number of bytes, namely, "9f86d081884c7d7111b738cbaf1c177b16568d11".

This is because even a small change in the input will result in a different hash value which gives the indication of the integrity of the data. To see a practical demonstration of a blockchain in action, check out Anders Brownworth's site, www.andersbrownworth.com, on blockchain 101, where he provides a detailed explanation of blockchains, hash functions, and public and private keys with a useful no-code demonstration tool.

Depending on the type of blockchain, there are different rules on how a block can be added to the chain. These are called Consensus Mechanisms. The two most common methods are proof of work (PoW) and proof of stake (PoS).

Proof of Work (PoW)

Miners compete for a crypto reward by finding a random number, called the nonce, that when added to the block produces a hash number below a certain value. The speed at which miners can perform computations is called the "'hash rate." The higher the hash rate, the more likely a miner is to solve a block and earn a reward. The deciphering of the hash function is what all miners compete to achieve to win cryptocurrency. Imagine when many miners are trying to solve the block, they will consume high amounts of electricity.

The high energy costs can limit applications for blockchain, which is why some cryptocurrencies are moving to alternative consensus mechanisms, such as proof of stake (PoS).

Proof of Stake (PoS)

Proof-of-stake (PoS) is a consensus mechanism in which miners are chosen to add new blocks to the chain based on the amount of cryptocurrency they stake. PoS blockchains use Validators instead of Miners. Validators are chosen based on the amount of cryptocurrency they "stake" or lock up as collateral. To become a validator, a user needs to deposit a certain amount of the blockchain's native cryptocurrency into a special wallet within the network. Validators take turns proposing new blocks of transactions. The probability of being chosen to propose a block is directly proportional to the amount of cryptocurrency they have staked. Once a validator proposes a new block, other validators on the network need to validate it. They check the transactions within the block to ensure they are valid and follow the network's rules. Validators look for things like double-spending attempts or invalid transactions. Validators communicate with each other to reach consensus on the validity of the proposed block. If the majority of validators agree that the block is valid, it is added to the blockchain. As a reward for their efforts, the validator who successfully proposed a valid block (the "block proposer") and the validators who validated it receive rewards in the form of the blockchain's native cryptocurrency. Validators are also subject to penalties if they behave maliciously or try to cheat the system. Validators are typically rewarded with a portion of the transaction fees for their work. The typical validator transaction fee varies depending on the blockchain network. Ethereum is the most common blockchain that uses this mechanism. For example, the Ethereum network uses the Ether (ETH) currency. The typical validator transaction fee is 0.00001 ETH, or about $0.02. The mechanism can achieve around 3–5k transactions per second, far higher than the transaction volume using proof of work.

With this higher efficiency, there has been a rise in applications leveraging the cryptocurrency as a foundation for fundraising through issuing tokens. This fundraising method is commonly known as an Initial Coin Offering (ICO). In this approach, the application provider generates a token whose value is tied to the base cryptocurrency, either to secure funding or offer services. The token's valuation against the base currency is influenced by factors such as the appeal of the application, prevailing market conditions, specific token attributes, and investor confidence. An example is CryptoKitties (www. cryptokitties.co), a blockchain-based game where users can collect, breed, and trade virtual cats. It gained significant attention as one of the first major use cases of tokens called CryptoKitties, to represent unique digital assets on the blockchain. The game's popularity in December 2017 congested the Ethereum network, causing it to reach an all-time high in the number of transactions and slowing the network down significantly.

As Figure 6-1 shows that if blockchain is to succeed in the future, it needs to be sustainable by minimizing potential environmental harm.

We have discussed that some blockchains, such as Bitcoin, use a lot of energy to verify transactions and add new blocks to the chain. In 2021, Bitcoin mining was estimated to consume as much energy as the entire country of Argentina!

PoS is much more energy-efficient in this regard than PoW. This is because validators do not need to use powerful computers to solve mathematical problems. They simply need to stake their cryptocurrency.

Please be aware that there exist alternative consensus mechanisms such as Proof of Authority (PoA) and Proof of Burn (PoB). However, these are beyond the focus of this book.

To address the power consumption issues of blockchain, there are a number of things that can be done. These include

- Developing more energy-efficient consensus mechanisms. PoS is one example of a more energy-efficient consensus mechanism.

- Using renewable energy sources to power blockchain networks. This would help to reduce the environmental impact of blockchain technology.

- Educating the public about the energy consumption of blockchain technology. This would help to raise awareness of the issue and encourage people to use more energy-efficient blockchains.

Blockchain and Electronic Wallets

While Bitcoin is inherently secure, there are vulnerabilities surrounding its use that hackers exploit to steal users' private keys. In Figure 6-17 we highlighted the process for buying a crypto asset. Electronic wallets, the most common method of storing private keys due to their convenience, represent a primary weakness. The prevalence of crypto-based scams and hacks is likely to persist as cybercriminals become more adept at their methods and platforms with inadequate security, and inexperienced investors remain easy targets. In 2023 alone, several high-profile hacks have occurred, including the $100 million theft from 5,000 user accounts on Atomic Wallet, the $200 million crypto hack of Mixin, and the $4.4 million crypto hack of Lastpass, a crypto password manager.

Wallets kept by a third party on a crypto exchange have seen some high-profile failures. Despite offering easy ways to manage private keys and a convenient way to access funds, they do mean a loss of control on private keys and less ease of use. The collapse of the FTX exchange and the use of FTX's custodial wallet became a major point of contention when the exchange filed for bankruptcy in November 2023. Billions of dollars' worth of customer funds were missing, leading to accusations of mismanagement and lack of transparency for users. This incident highlighted the inherent risks associated with custodial wallets, as users do not have direct control over their assets and rely on the custodian for security and safekeeping. However, according to *The New York Times*, 20% of bitcoin has been lost by users who lost their private key, and so these process issues really need to be made simpler for users (www.nytimes.com/2021/01/13/business/tens-of-billions-worth-of-bitcoin-have-been-locked-by-people-who-forgot-their-key.html).

Blockchain and the Evolution of the Web

It is not only financial systems that use a centralized system for validation. The Internet itself is subject to centralized storage and management through servers of specific trusted institutions. Firewalls are essential for safeguarding data on these servers and system administrators have to address the concerns of server and firewall management. In such cases, the power and control accumulate within centralized entities.

On the other hand, the setbacks associated with centralized power have been clearly evident with prominent examples in the past. If we think about Web 2.0 platforms, Google, Facebook, and Twitter are great examples with their social interaction, news, and community features where their central platform gets all the advertising benefits and the user gets nothing.

The evolution to a new type of Web – called Web 3.0 – where the Web is decentralized. It allows users to store and access data directly from other users without the need for a central server. This also makes it more resistant to censorship and data loss, as the data is not stored in a single location. It can resolve the issues emerging from centralized power and control and thus enables higher user trust, transparency, and privacy as users would have more control over their data and online experiences. Web3 pioneers see Web 3.0 as an evolution from Web 2.0 in terms of data control, commercial applications, data security, and other features. It allows users to create decentralized apps (dApps) that are controlled by the users of computers on a distributed network. These dApps create their own tokens but with different features on top of an existing blockchain infrastructure and on the native token of the blockchain. For example, Ethereum provides ERC-20 tokens to dApps to provide their own special features. Decentraland, for example, uses an ERC-20 token called MANA for users to buy virtual land and goods within the Decentraland virtual world. MANA token holders can access exclusive in-game benefits, such as access to VIP areas, discounts on goods and services, and unique in-game items. MANA tokens have the potential to appreciate in value as Decentraland grows in popularity and the demand for virtual land and goods and services increases. As of October 1, 2023, MANA was approximately 0.00022195 ETH.

Through blockchain, Web 3.0 platforms, and dApps can also allow the user to earn cryptocurrency from their own consumption and content creation. Users can be rewarded directly for viewing ads and can be compensated directly for producing original content. Figure 6-18 summarizes some of the differences of Web 1.0, Web 2.0, and Web 3.0.

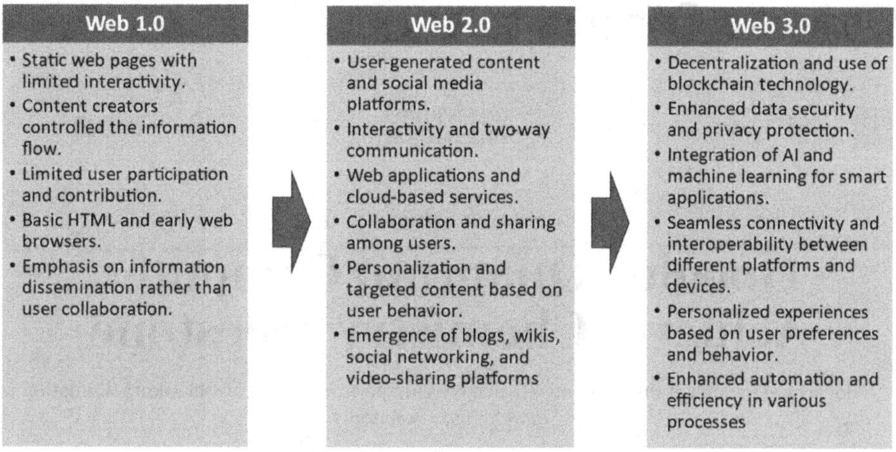

Web 1.0	Web 2.0	Web 3.0
• Static web pages with limited interactivity. • Content creators controlled the information flow. • Limited user participation and contribution. • Basic HTML and early web browsers. • Emphasis on information dissemination rather than user collaboration.	• User-generated content and social media platforms. • Interactivity and two-way communication. • Web applications and cloud-based services. • Collaboration and sharing among users. • Personalization and targeted content based on user behavior. • Emergence of blogs, wikis, social networking, and video-sharing platforms	• Decentralization and use of blockchain technology. • Enhanced data security and privacy protection. • Integration of AI and machine learning for smart applications. • Seamless connectivity and interoperability between different platforms and devices. • Personalized experiences based on user preferences and behavior. • Enhanced automation and efficiency in various processes

Figure 6-18. Differences Between Web 1.0, 2.0, and 3.0

If you want to try Web 3.0 and explore its benefits, download the brave.com browser at www.brave.com. Brave Browser is a free and open-source web browser that puts a strong emphasis on privacy, security, and an improved browsing experience. By default, Brave blocks unwanted ads, third-party trackers, and other web nuisances that compromise user privacy and slow down page loading. This not only enhances browsing speed but also reduces the amount of data that websites collect about users. Moreover, Brave offers a unique approach to advertising through its opt-in Brave Ads program. Users can choose to participate and receive privacy-respecting ads that reward them with Basic Attention Tokens (BAT), a cryptocurrency native to the Brave ecosystem. These tokens can be used to support content creators or be converted into traditional currencies.

The security of blockchain relies on cryptography, which is the science of using complex mathematical problems to secure data. There is an emerging technology that could solve the mathematical problems faster than a traditional computer and break the encryption used in blockchain – Quantum Computing. Let's take a look at this technology and its uses.

Quantum Computing

SCIENTIFIC
AMERICAN.

QUANTUM COMPUTING

Google's Quantum Computer Achieves Chemistry Milestone

A downsized version of the company's Sycamore chip performed a record-breaking simulation of a chemical reaction

By Neil Savage on September 4, 2020

Figure 6-19. Google Quantum Milestone, Source: Scientific American

In 2020, using a quantum computer, Google simulated a chemical reaction in three minutes that normally takes three weeks to simulate.

Quantum computers are superfast machines that can solve problems by looking at really tiny particles. They have many practical uses that can make a big impact.

For example, by being able to analyze the 42 million atoms in a protein molecule, we can find cures for cancer and other diseases. To look deep inside batteries to see how they react can create better power sources that are more efficient and environmentally friendly.

In addition, quantum computers can study how different chemicals interact, which can help us create fertilizers that are better for the environment. They can even help us understand how the universe works and make sense of really large databases of information.

And if that wasn't enough, quantum computers are also really good at solving really hard math problems that even smart mathematicians struggle with.

Up until a few years ago, scientists could not get quantum bits to be stable enough to do these tasks, but now, with better control technology, lasers, measurement systems, and effective noise mitigation techniques, this is achievable. To understand how it works, let's understand the components involved.

Quantum computing is all about how qubits, or quantum bits, behave. These are the basic units of information used by quantum computers. Unlike regular bits that can only be at a state "1" or a "0," these qubits are the ultimate multitaskers. They can be at both 1 and 0 state at the same time.

The magic of qubits lies in their ability to exponentially expand the amount of information we can process. Figure 6-20 shows a qubit chip. With two qubits, they can take on not just two, but four possible states. And if two qubits can take on four states, think about what happens when we bring three of them onto the stage. They can be in eight different states! Opening up a range of possibilities.

Figure 6-20. A Quantum Bit Chip Is the Size of a Thumbnail

Imagine for 300 qubits. These entities can embody more states than there are atoms in the entire Universe!

So, with qubits leading the charge, quantum computing defies the limits of traditional computation. It's a mind-expanding ride that opens up a whole new world of information processing.

Back in 2017, D-Wave made waves in the tech world by unveiling their mammoth creation: a quantum computing chip that boasted a mind-boggling 2000 qubits all packed into one powerful piece of silicon.

However, the cost to create it was $15,000,000. According to the quantum pioneers at Google, to truly unlock the full potential of this technology in our day-to-day lives, we will need to build a 1-million-qubit machine.

With this type of investment needed, it leaves it to only a handful of corporations who can make this technology and it is still a technology to be explored in the future. Some of the key reasons are

- **Temperature.** Quantum chips are sensitive and require freezing them down to 15 millikelvins, which is −459.6 degrees Fahrenheit through a liquid helium cooling system.

- The qubits are **delicate**. They need to stay in their quantum state to perform their computations effectively. They're easily swayed by disturbances in temperature, frequency, and motion. So, any slight changes can throw off their accuracy and potentially sabotage the entire calculation.

- Quantum machines are quite **prone to errors** at the moment. There are inherent computational errors that are part and parcel of quantum systems. Huge investment and talent is being poured into quantum error detection to minimize and mitigate those errors.

Experts predict that by the end of 2023, we'll have around 5000 quantum computers in existence.

Classical computers are all about precise outputs, giving you definite answers to questions. But when it comes to the quantum computers, they offer you a likelihood of a range of different answers.

Where do quantum computers truly shine? Well, imagine a scenario where you're juggling complex algorithms or testing a wide range of inputs. That's when quantum really shines. They're masters of handling multiple variables and crunching mind-boggling calculations that would leave your regular computer scratching its head.

While a classical computer with "N" bits can perform a maximum of "N" calculations simultaneously, quantum computers blow the lid off the possibilities. They can manage up to a staggering 2 raised to the power of "N" calculations! So, if a classical processor can handle 10 calculations, a quantum processor would effortlessly handle 2 raised to the power of 10, which is 1024 calculations.

In certain industries, even if a quantum computer solves a problem "only" 1000 times faster than a classical computer, it could still make economic sense to hop onto the quantum train. It's all about finding that sweet spot where the advantages of quantum computing outweigh the costs.

The key areas where Quantum is predicted to flourish are in

- Drug development: We discussed earlier the immense costs and time involved in developing new medications. By performing computational simulations of drug molecules, quantum computers significantly slash those costs and time frames.

- Optimization problems: Think about puzzles like figuring out the most efficient placement of equipment in a factory or devising the best strategy to optimize a transportation network. These mind-boggling challenges require sifting through countless possibilities. But with the power of quantum computing, we can narrow down those options dramatically, opening the door for classical computers to provide straightforward answers.

- Autonomous vehicles: The race is on to create autonomous vehicles that can navigate busy roads anywhere on our planet. Billions of dollars are being poured into this cutting-edge technology, aiming to make these vehicles the epitome of smartness. Quantum computing plays a crucial role, infusing intelligence and efficiency into the fabric of these futuristic vehicles.

- Cryptography. As quantum computers grow exponentially powerful, they have the potential to crack any password. That's why it's absolutely imperative for researchers to invest in new, quantum-safe cryptography. Blockchain developers are starting to use quantum-resistant cryptography, which is designed to be secure against quantum computers. They can also start using quantum-safe blockchain protocols, which are designed to be resistant to quantum attacks. To mitigate against the risks, there are a number of quantum-resistant cryptographic algorithms available, such as the post-quantum cryptographic standard (PQC) that developers can use.

Conclusion

Game-changing innovations like the smartphone and disruptive algorithms have transformed how we live today, giving huge revenues to the pioneers and radically transforming our lives.

Established companies that are navigating the digital age are actively looking at these technologies and finding ways to apply them directly to their business outcomes. Many customers use these solutions to their great success.

Today, Domino's Pizza uses a variety of these to redefine their operations:

- Marketing: Domino's Pizza uses algorithms to target its marketing campaigns to its customers. This helps Domino's Pizza to reach its target audience and to increase sales.

- Delivery route optimization: This algorithm is used to find the most efficient routes for delivery drivers. This helps Domino's Pizza to reduce the time it takes to deliver pizzas and improve customer satisfaction.

- Inventory management: This algorithm is used to track the inventory of ingredients and supplies. This helps Domino's Pizza to ensure that it has the necessary ingredients to make pizzas and to avoid running out of supplies.

- Fraud detection: This algorithm is used to identify and prevent fraudulent transactions. This helps Domino's Pizza to protect its customers and its revenue.

We saw as well how blockchain and quantum technology are future disruptors that can rewrite the rules of digital transformation.

Navigating the Technology Deluge

Introduction

Up to this point, through classic case examples, we have established the concept of DX, delved into the fundamentals of big data and analytics, explored various productivity tools, overviewed the basics of data mining and algorithms, and examined strategies for making more business-oriented decisions in our DX endeavors.

With the flood of new digital innovation, have you ever wondered how big tech giants seem to effortlessly stay ahead of the innovation curve, while many Fortune 500 companies struggle to make their digital dreams a reality? It's a fascinating question, and we try and explore that in this chapter.

We will first take a look at a classic example of how data science techniques are being used today and where it might take us in the future.

© Attul Sehgal 2024
A. Sehgal, *Demystifying Digital Transformation*,
https://doi.org/10.1007/978-1-4842-9499-4_7

We will address whether there is a "secret sauce" that big tech firms possess, giving them a competitive edge in digital transformation that traditional companies just can't replicate? Are Fortune 500 companies forever destined to play catch-up in the innovation race? We will address the question on whether computers are cleverer than humans.

To uncover these answers, we'll not only try to debunk the hype surrounding digital transformation, look at some successful AI-driven applications, but also chart a course for how businesses can prepare for game-changing innovations in the future.

So let's go!

Overcoming the Fear – Even Digital Natives Are Fallible

Let's examine a rapidly expanding multinational digital company that excels in automation, content management, streaming, and supply chain operations. This company is renowned for its industry-leading practices in utilizing data to enhance business operations. For the purpose of this discussion, we'll refer to them as Company X, as shown in Figure 7-1.

Figure 7-1. Fast Growing Company: Source: Unsplash Jason Goodman

Company X experienced steady growth over several years, expanding its workforce to employ over 200,000 individuals worldwide. In 2015, with expectations of significant future growth, the company's board directed the Human Resources (HR) Director to initiate a recruitment campaign aiming to hire approximately 150,000 additional employees by 2017. This ambitious effort was intended to achieve a total headcount of approximately 350,000 employees.

This represents a huge undertaking for any HR Department and the major questions to address at this point are

- How can we efficiently hire a large number of individuals within a limited time frame?

- How can we effectively manage the high volume of resumes and applications?

- How can we streamline our decision-making process for recruitment?

The conventional method would involve engaging a recruitment agency to design and execute a comprehensive recruitment campaign, conducting searches and handling the subsequent influx of CVs. This process typically spans several months. Additionally, considering an estimated success rate of 5% for identifying suitable candidates, we would need to process approximately 3 million CVs.

To address this challenge, the internal data team proposed a solution: utilizing an intelligent decision making tool to streamline the candidate shortlisting process. This tool would be a computer program consisting of various decision-making models tailored to specific job functions and locations. Its purpose would be to assist the HR team in identifying top candidates by scanning the CVs and pinpointing relevant keywords related to job functions and location information and shortlisting them.

The data engineers at Company X explained to the HR department that they could train their model using intelligent AI algorithms called Neural Networks. By analyzing patterns in the CVs of successful candidates from the past decade, the model would be able to identify key elements, words, or phrases that differentiate these successful candidates from the less successful ones to make the recommendation.

The model even identified terms used by unsuccessful candidates and then used this to reduce the "grading" of these CVs. If there were common words that everyone was using, these words would then be discounted.

Indeed, it initially seemed like a sensible approach – leveraging the descriptors of successful past candidates to identify promising future candidates. By comparing historical data from the previous ten years of successful CVs with the ones submitted, the model could efficiently shortlist candidates for interviews, saving valuable time and resources for the HR department.

However, a problem arose during the pilot phase in 2016. The HR team noticed a significant bias in the candidates being shortlisted – predominantly men. It turned out that the tool penalized applicants who mentioned words like "women," "female," or "girl" in their descriptions. Even candidates who attended all-women's colleges, joined women's chess clubs, or mentioned having daughters were unfairly disadvantaged.

The issue stemmed from the fact that the model learned from historical data that contained unchecked biases, and these biases were inadvertently perpetuated by the machine learning process. Everyone, assumed the data used would be accurate and fair, but no one in the data team verified this. As a result, the system was discontinued after the pilot and eventually disbanded in 2018.

This overreliance on outdated data and the perpetuation of biases may resonate with experiences you have encountered.

Before proceeding further, let's reveal the name of the company that developed this AI-driven CV scanning tool: It was Amazon.

Even digital giants like Amazon, who are at the forefront of the data-driven revolution, are not exempt from making errors when it comes to handling data. While AI-driven resume screening tools offer significant advantages in expediting the hiring process, it is important to recognize that even the most advanced data models are only as intelligent as the information they are provided. If flawed or biased data is fed into the system, it will incorporate and perpetuate those flaws and biases.

Despite Amazon's experience, it is worth noting that the company never solely relied on AI tools for recruitment and eventually dissolved the unit responsible for their creation. On the other hand, it has been successful in selling AI scanning tools to other companies who then found their own problems (see Chapter 9).

Considering the significance of data in driving transformative change, it raises the question of why even digital leaders make these fundamental mistakes?

In Chapter 4, we highlighted the significant investment and failure rate associated with digital transformation initiatives undertaken by leading Fortune 500 companies. It is evident from this example that even highly successful digital companies are susceptible to making fundamental mistakes. It may raise concerns about the feasibility of achieving successful outcomes if even the digital leaders make fundamental mistakes. This realization implies that traditional companies are treading on fragile ground. If digital natives cannot get it right, what hope do non-digital natives have?

To answer this, let's take a step back and reflect on how Amazon could have done things differently.

Was the Amazon HR team just too "data driven"?

Data driven is a common phrase used for companies living the "digital culture." Harvard Business Review defines the term as "A business condition that embraces and successfully manages data in all its forms to achieve digital transformation, compete on analytics or become AI-first."

There are other definitions of "data driven"

- According to Gartner, a data-driven organization is where "Data is organized and examined with the goal of better serving one organization's customers and consumers." (Gartner)

- According to Open AI, "Data driven means using data as the primary source of information to make decisions or guide actions. It generally refers to using data and analytics to inform business or organizational strategies, rather than relying solely on intuition or past experience. It's an approach that emphasizes the collection, analysis, and interpretation of data in order to make informed decisions."

Sadly, none of the definitions really highlight that fundamentally, data biases must be managed effectively to be used in any data-driven organization.

If we return to the AI-driven CV scanning example and "examine the wreckage after the car crash," there are some process questions we could ask to test the correct use of data.

- Who was responsible for the source data? Did they know how it would be used in the platform? Was there a data governance process in place?

- Should the data teams have worked more closely with the HR team during the exercise to check on data sources and how the data would be manipulated?

- Could a bias analysis have been carried out first on the historical data by the data team?

- Further, did anyone verify consent rules on re-using people's personal data for the scanning tool?

- Was any diversity or any other selection criterion provided by HR, or was everything just left to the data team to decide?

- Or, on the other hand, could the argument be that the process used was absolutely correct. The historical data doesn't lie and the path to success is to follow its conclusions?

The link https://nshcs.hee.nhs.uk/about/equality-diversity-and-inclusion/conscious-inclusion/understanding-different-types-of-bias/ describes some of the inherent biases when doing recruitment, namely, gender bias, beauty bias, ageism, affinity, attribution, conformity, confirmation, halo effect, and name bias. Perhaps these biases could have been analyzed before any scanning took place.

Imagining the Process

Let's try and picture the scenario as it may be instructive in highlighting ways to apply data-driven techniques in a better way. Figure 7-2 summarizes what could have taken place.

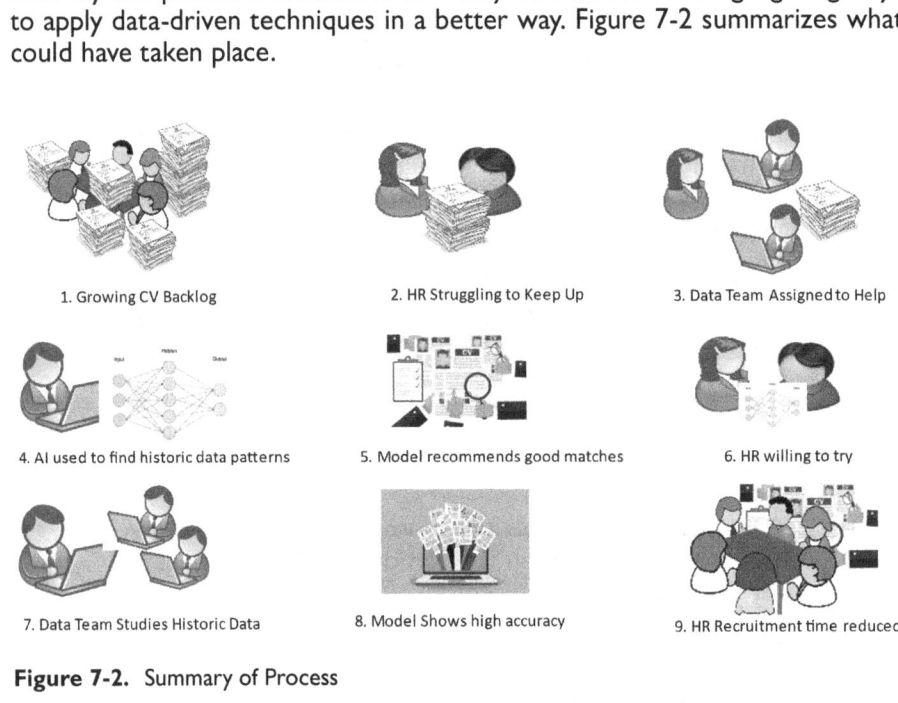

1. Growing CV Backlog   2. HR Struggling to Keep Up   3. Data Team Assigned to Help

4. AI used to find historic data patterns   5. Model recommends good matches   6. HR willing to try

7. Data Team Studies Historic Data   8. Model Shows high accuracy   9. HR Recruitment time reduced

Figure 7-2. Summary of Process

The HR team was confronted with a data volume issue at its core. They had accumulated a substantial backlog of resumes for review, struggling to manage the workload effectively. To address this challenge, the data team stepped in and proposed a data-driven solution. Their plan involved utilizing an algorithmic model to analyze and categorize approximately 50,000 words within the historical dataset. By leveraging these keywords, the model would generate recommendations regarding the most suitable CVs for the available positions. Although the HR team was more accustomed to traditional recruitment methods rather than data-driven approaches, the proposed logic resonated with them, prompting them to give it a chance. They entrusted the data team with a decade's worth of historical resume data and provided minimal oversight as the team proceeded with modeling. The HR team was astounded by the swiftness and efficiency of the new CV scanning tool, as it significantly reduced the time and resources previously dedicated to resume reviews. They trusted the output of the scanner to speed up CV shortlisting, but also iron out any potential discrepancies in the data. It seems that there was an implicit view that the original data could be trusted.

This type of improved efficiency scenario is not uncommon and can be applied to many other business problems too. The outcome of the CV scanning tool project and its consequences was that the data team who built it were disbanded. Thus, the finger of responsibility was pointed in their direction. Was this fair or even appropriate that they should be seen as the custodians of the source data?

If we look back at the "dirty data", we can understand what could have happened. As part of a digitalization process in the organization. Old data that was in paper form would have been made digital through the use of transfer onto digital media like CDs possibly through optical character recognition technology (OCR). This may have been carried out by an IT department who were versed in digital equipment and it did not occur to anyone to check the validity of the data or whether any authorization was needed by the candidates at the time.

However, irrespective of the way the media is stored, the data retains a level of subjective "bias." As a result, a host of biases, conscious and unconscious, some intended, some not ,will have been present in the data The amount of skew and outcry depends on the values of the company and social and political climate at the time. In Chapter 9, we will look at data and the regulatory situation with regards to data bias.

So how do we work with non-technical business specialists in a digitally transforming data-driven environment?

Prior to digitalization, when the corporate pace was somewhat slower, if a decision-maker was perceived to be biased, that person could be identified and their decisions challenged. Once data at volume is digitalized, it takes a whole new definition of trust – we assume that it is trustworthy. The speed of innovation is clashing with traditional ways of working and companies find it hard to keep up.

What is clear is that the "effectiveness" of any data-driven initiative is based on the quality of data, the inherent assumptions and the appropriateness of the questions asked of it. If you put biased, or poor quality data into a system, then you run the risk of acquiring poor (or misleading) insights. The term used is "garbage in, garbage out." There are no exceptions to this. Irrespective of the algorithm, nothing can "fix the data."

The responsibility for the source data must lie with the business owners even if they are non-technical. Therefore, data preparation and curation of its sources are critical steps for any business, and where the business owner, despite not being fully versant with managing data, needs to be leading in order to support identification of bias and risk. An element of understanding key tools to do this by a non-technical business owner is absolutely key to doing this. In Chapter 9, we will look at a case example where the non-technical business owners were held to account for their algorithms decisions.

Figure 7-3 highlights some question to ask of any data source. These questions are not too technical and can ensure the source data is fit for purpose. Some particular areas where these are particularly important are the identification of missing data as this, particularly if there is a systematic reason (i.e., departmental failure), can significantly skew the output.

- Completeness: Is there any missing information?
- **Quality: Are the records correct or are there** any obvious mistakes?
- Quantity: Is the data provided enough? Accessibility: Is all the data accessible?
- Connectivity: Can any data sources be joined together?
- Validity: Does the data contain information that should be discarded?

Figure 7-3. *Some Business Questions to Ask of Any Data Set*

They are also questions that can be asked by any business owner not necessarily the product owner or product manager.

Data size can be an important consideration too when testing certain types of algorithms, which we will discuss later on. Also supplementing a data integration effort with external meta datasets could also be considered to give a more up-to-date response (i.e., some recent legislation).

But the central lesson here is that the design and preparation of data requires real engagement and leadership from business. This is an important step to digital transformation success. It is critical to exercise that institutional knowledge at the start because once the models begin to provide new insights, there is the human tendency to trust such data as unbiased (non-human). Outsourcing this to a business analyst outside the function or a data analyst in the data team does not help the business function become closer to working with data. The reality is that business divisions cannot avoid data! It can also be difficult to track back and find the incorrect data entry or assumption once the model is in place and so it is important that the business owners have some practical tools to be active stakeholders from the start. This is a challenge for non-technical business owners, but a culture of learning and exploring new low-code toolsets will help in building up the skills.

Without addressing these points, the process could become even more onerous as algorithms are now trained to establish end goals and even adapt themselves automatically to reach predetermined outcomes. They might be considered more reliable than humans; however, it would be impossible to question any discrepancy in their outputs. As we saw in Chapter 5, these do exist in algorithms in machine learning and are called "Artificial Intelligence" or "AI."

If things do go unchecked, should we just accept that computers will be cleverer than humans?

Let's start by looking at where AI performs better than humans with some practical examples, but before moving to the next section, if you have worked with digital teams, have a look at Figure 7-2.

What processes have you encountered in your data engagements? Are there any similarities? How are things like data bias managed? Are there questions you would like to ask your data counterparts but hesitate because of the technical response you receive?

Can AI Perform Better Tasks Than Humans?

In this section, we will explore AI's role in

- Strategy based board games
- Drawing images from a text description
- Generating human-like texts
- Creating music

And then we will explore how AI can pervade our day-to-day interactions in human society.

Strategy-Based Board Games

Figure 7-4. Strategy Games Checkers, AlphaGo, and Chess

Figure 7-4 Approximate Number of Moves and Game Configurations for Checkers, Chess, and Go. Source: University of Heidelberg.de

Some of the most pioneering work began with strategy-based board games.

In 2019, Frank Gabel, published a paper on the suitability of certain board games for using a computer. Essentially games with a low number of game options and legal moves for a given position are easier to configure and require less computing power than the more complex games. Figure 7-4 shows the differences between Checkers, Chess, and AlphaGo. (Source: https://hci. iwr.uni-heidelberg.de/systen/files/private/downloads/636026949/ report_frank_gabel.pdf)

Checkers has 10^{31} possible games and AlphaGo has an 10^{350} possible games. To be able to configure the next best move meant studying all these options. It was in this approach that algorithms were used to beat the best players.

In 1946, Arthur Lee Samuel, a pioneer in computer games and artificial intelligence (AI), became a Professor of Electrical Engineering at the University of Illinois. He participated in a project to design one of the earliest electronic computers. Samuel believed that teaching computers to play games could effectively address decision-making problems using electronic means. To develop this concept, he chose the board game checkers, because of its relative simplicity combined with deep layers of strategic gameplay.

During the process of teaching his computer how to play checkers, Samuel popularized the term "Machine Learning" in 1959. He ran the first checkers program on IBM's inaugural commercial computer, the IBM 701. Samuel's Checkers-playing Program stood as one of the world's earliest successful self-learning programs, demonstrating a fundamental concept of artificial intelligence.

By the 1970s, Samuel's program had reached a respectable level, comparable to that of an amateur checkers player. This pioneering work laid the groundwork for further advancements in decision-based games.

In 2014, Deepmind, a UK start-up that created algorithms to play games in a similar way to humans was acquired by Google. In late 2017, DeepMind introduced AlphaZero, a system capable of independently mastering games like Chess, Shogi (Japanese chess), and Go from scratch. AlphaZero surpassed world-champion programs in each respective game, marking a significant milestone in the development of AI.

It was chess that really took Artificial Intelligence into the public stratosphere of super human intelligence. Chess has approximately 10^{123} games over 9M variations after just three moves on each side, 288 billion different positions after 4 moves on each side, and 318,000,000,000 ways to play just the first 4 moves. AlphaZero algorithm learnt the rules of chess in four hours to the level of a grandmaster. (Sources: https://chessjournal.com/shannon-number/; https://chess24.com/en/read/news/deepmind-s-alphazero-crushes-chess)

According to Garry Kasparov, Chess Grandmaster and former World Champion in 2017, "I can't disguise my satisfaction that it plays (Chess) with a very dynamic style, much like my own!"

In December 2018, DeepMind published a full evaluation of AlphaZero. It described how AlphaZero rapidly learns each game to become the strongest player in history for each, despite starting it's training through from random play, with no in-built domain knowledge except the basic rules of the game.

The key aspect of AlphaZero is that rather than using a rules-based strategy to predict eventualities, it employed a deep neural network with only general-purpose algorithms. To learn each game, the untrained neural network plays millions of games against itself and through a process of trial and error generates the best move through reinforcement learning. At first, it plays completely randomly, but over time the system learns from wins, losses, and draws to adjust the parameters of the neural network, making it more likely to choose advantageous moves in the future. The trained network uses a search algorithm – known as **Monte-Carlo Tree Search (MCTS)** – to select the most optimal move in a game. Thus, the volume of training the network requires depends on the variations and complexity of the game. For each move, AlphaZero searches only a small fraction of the possible positions considered by traditional Chess engines.

Even the quotes at the time from leading players give the impression of a superhuman chess player. The first thing that players notice is AlphaZero's style, says Grandmaster Matthew Sadler – "the way its pieces swarm around the opponent's King with purpose and power." Underpinning this, he says, is AlphaZero's highly dynamic game play that maximizes the activity and mobility of its own pieces while minimizing the activity and mobility of its opponent's pieces. Counterintuitively, AlphaZero also seems to place less value on "material," an idea that underpins the modern game where each piece has a value and if one player has a greater value of pieces on the board than the other, then they have a material advantage. Instead, AlphaZero is willing to sacrifice material early in a game for gains that will only be recouped in the long-term. "Impressively, it manages to impose its style of play across a very wide range of positions and openings," says Matthew, who also observes that it plays in a very deliberate style from its first move with a "very human sense of consistent purpose". (Source: www.deepmind.com/blog/alphazero-shedding-new-light-on-chess-shogi-and-go)

With the praise from Grandmasters even stretching beyond chess.

"The implications go far beyond my beloved chessboard... Not only do these self-taught expert machines perform incredibly well, but we can actually learn from the new knowledge they produce."Garry Kasparov, Chess Grandmaster and former World Champion (2017)

AlphaZero successfully demonstrates that a single generalized algorithm can learn how to discover new knowledge in a range of settings.

When looking at the achievements of algorithms to beat the best professionals at strategy-based games, it is clear that computers perform far better mathematically than humans. Does this really mean they are better? How does our emotion set influence our decisions ? Does the computer really play on a level playing field without the emotions or pressure from the media when playing in these competitions? Can AlphaZero get on the same emotional situation as humans?

However, machine learning applications' impact now extends beyond strategy games like Checkers, Chess, and Go and is permeating all aspects of society, including the creative industries.

Exploring the effects of AI in the creative sector unveils its potential to generate novel ideas, but also sheds light on wider ethical considerations, ways collaboration between humans and machines could work, and provides insights into how AI aligns with our cultural and societal values in the digital era.

Drawing an Image from a Text Description

Imagine a scenario where you can provide a description of an image, and a computer can create a corresponding visual representation. Stable Diffusion is one of the AI models in the realm of text-to-image diffusion that possesses the capability to generate photo-realistic images based on any text input. You can try it for yourself at https://stablediffusionweb.com/. There are a number of other sites like Midjourney, where you can experience a similar thing. Undoubtedly, this represents a significant advancement in the field of AI.

As an example, here are some images in Figure 7-5 I created using the Stable Diffusion platform. This is of the Picasso painting Guernica in the style of Kandinsky.

Stable Diffusion 2.1 Demo

Stable Diffusion 2.1 is the latest text-to-image model from StabilityAI. Access Stable Diffusion 1 Space here

For faster generation and API access you can try DreamStudio Beta.

guernica painting by picasso in Kandinsky style

Enter a negative prompt

Generate image

Figure 7-5. Text to Image Example: Source stablediffusion.eu

As we see, it opens the door to new ideas, but at the same time, there is an ethical dimension of how the information is used. In this case, the images are sourced from the public Internet, raising concerns about the ownership and copyright of the data. While the ability to generate images quickly is impressive, the question of data ownership and usage rights remains unclear. In Chapter 9, we will look at digital ethics and the copyright issue of public data.

Generating Human-Like Texts

Oh, digital realm, where transformation lies, Where customers seek value with longing eyes. Competition fierce, a battle to be won, Innovation's cry echoes, it can't be undone.

Amidst this tempest, data takes its throne, A treasure trove of insights yet unknown. In bits and bytes, the secrets lie concealed, Waiting to be harnessed, their worth revealed.

—Extract from an output "Digital Transformation" in the
Style of William Shakespeare using ChatGPT
(see Appendix C for the complete sonnet)

Picture a scenario where you're attempting to put your thoughts into words but struggling to find the perfect expressions. In the pre-digital era, you might resort to sketching your ideas, crafting a preliminary version, sharing it with a colleague for feedback, and then refining the draft. This process could span several hours or even days. Now, envision having a well-informed assistant right beside you, capable of offering conversational suggestions drawn from its extensive knowledge repository.

Enter Chat Generative Pretrained Transformer, or ChatGPT for short. It's a computational system employing machine learning algorithms to comprehend and produce text that closely resembles human language. The term "Chat" pertains to the bot, while "Generative Pre-Training" signifies that it has undergone extensive training on a large language model (LLM) consisting of 175 billion parameters. It demonstrates the power of unsupervised learning algorithms to predict the next word in a sentence.

OpenAI introduced ChatGPT in November 2022 as a pilot project, and it has swiftly captured the public's imagination. Within the first two months of the free pilot release, it attracted more than 100 million users, marking it as the most successful software application launch in history. (Source: www.reuters. com/technology/chatgpt-sets-record-fastest-growing-user-base-analyst-note-2023-02-01/#:~:text=It%20took%20TikTok%20about%20 nine,to%20data%20from%20Sensor%20Tower) It is a highly articulate artificial intelligence application that can write computer code as well as different types of text (in any language) faster than humans. It can generate effective, corporate emails, business plans, and school essays and even generate poems, speech, and prose in the style of famous writers, such as Chaucer, Shakespeare, and Dickens. The current version allows users to input images like contents of a fridge for food suggestions and a recipe is recommended. Chat GPT is provided by OpenAI (owned by Microsoft). There are other platforms available that work in a similar way. For example, Google BARD (https://bard. google.com/) is similar to ChatGPT, Copyai (www. copy.ai) is good for summarizing text, Bloom is a multilingual language model (https://hugging-face.co/blog/bloom), NoowAI (https://noowai.com/) is great for quick answers. In December 2023, Amazon launched their own generative AI chatbot called Amazon Q and Google launched an updated version of their platform to compete with ChatGPt 4.0 called 'Gemini'.

For example, when I asked ChatGPT to write a song about digital transformation in the form of a RAP song with the terms customer, innovation, competition, data, and value, in a matter of seconds it produced the lyrics as follows: I will let the reader decide if this lyric hits the right note, but there is no doubt ChatGPT does inspire new levels of inspiration:

Yo, listen up, let me tell you a tale,

'Bout digital transformation, it'll never fail. In a world of bytes and algorithms we reside, Where businesses thrive, and they reach new heights.

(Customer) The customer's the king, the centre of it all, Their satisfaction's the mission, hear their call. Gotta understand their needs, their pain points too, Give 'em what they want, make their dreams come true.

(Competition) Competition's fierce, it's a battlefield, Gotta stay ahead, be quick and yield. In this digital race, you can't stand still, Gotta innovate, bring that unique skill.

(Chorus) Digital transformation, it's the name of the game, Revolutionizing businesses, it's not the same. Unlocking new possibilities, breaking through the mould, Harnessing the power, turning iron into gold.

(Verse 2) Innovation's the key, let your ideas flow, Rethink your strategies, let your business grow. Embrace the technology, the digital age, Create a buzz, set the world ablaze.

(Data) Data's the gold mine, it holds the treasure, Analyse, visualize, to find new measures. Insights and patterns, hidden gems untold, Harnessing its potential, you'll never fold.

(Value) Value is the goal, it's what we strive for, Deliver more than expected, open every door. Give 'em something unique, something they can't resist, Creating loyalty, you'll make their list.

(Bridge) Digital transformation, it's a journey we're on, Embracing the future, a phenomenon. Innovation, data, value, and the customer's delight, Together they'll guide us, in this digital fight.

(Chorus) Digital transformation, it's the name of the game, Revolutionizing businesses, it's not the same. Unlocking new possibilities, breaking through the mould, Harnessing the power, turning iron into gold.

(Outro) So, let's rap it up, let's make this clear, Digital transformation's here, it's near. Embrace the change, the digital sensation, And witness your business's true transformation.

If you wish to try using LLM to write a song with other themes, check out `https://beta.character.ai/`, which allows different character versions.

Text prediction models are like superfast autocomplete engines. They predict the next word in a sentence based on the words that have come before it. They can also remember previous conversations and refine their output based on the user's feedback. However, these models do not understand what they are saying. They simply learn to generate text that is similar to the text they have been trained on. As they get more training, their output becomes more fluent and less error-prone, but it is still not possible to understand how they generate their output. There is no algorithm to provide an explanation. Figure 7-6 may illustrate the issue. The program can identify the dog, but not understand the reason why it is a dog.

Icon Source: Technology vector created by upklyak — www.freepik.com

Figure 7-6. The Explain-ability Challenge. Source: Freepik.com

It makes it difficult to trust the output of these models and to use them in safety-critical applications. Many organizations have banned their use.

Soon after the pilot launch of Chat GPT in Nov 2022, New York City public schools, blocked ChatGPT access on school computers and networks, citing "concerns about negative impacts on student learning, and concerns regarding the safety and accuracy of content." Without any established rules in place for its deployment, students are allegedly using it to do their homework submissions.

Before moving to the next section, in your opinion, who should be the custodian of the correct deployment of technology?

In Chapter 9, we will look at the moves in place to regulate AI.

Creating Music

The autocreation of music has the tones of the futuristic society thought about before the onset of digital. In George Orwell's book "1984," society is characterized by pervasive surveillance, constant propaganda, and the manipulation of historical facts to maintain the Party's power. The government seeks to eradicate independent thought and enforce conformity among the citizens. Published in 1948, it talks about an instrument called the "Versificator."

> *The tune had been haunting London for weeks past. It was one of countless similar songs published for the benefit of the proles by a sub-section of the Music Department. The words of these songs were composed without any human intervention whatever on an instrument known as a* **versificator**.

> —1984, George Orwell

Today this is no longer just an extract from a work of fiction but reality through AI although the social aspects have not been realized as yet. Here is an example of how it is being used.

The Beatles are widely regarded as one of the most successful pop music groups in history. Over the years, many artists, producers, and songwriters, driven by record companies and now music streaming services, have attempted to recreate the same level of "magic" that the Beatles achieved. Artificial intelligence has become the latest method to pursue their greatness. In 2015, scientists at Sony's CSL Labs decided to take on the challenge of creating their own Beatles-style tune. They utilized an AI system called FlowMachines, (www. sony.com/en/SonyInfo/design/stories/flow-machines/) which was fed a collection of Lennon–McCartney songs. Using these songs as inspiration, the AI generated a psychedelic composition called "Daddy's Car." The song's lyrics were suggested by Beatles song titles.

With the current rate of innovation, it is only a matter of time when we will be listening to the new album from the Beatles, having our latest versions of Picasso painting in our living room, and reading Dickens novels created by computers.

Will we think that in 100 years' time, human creativity was just an early stage in our evolution? Will hearing original works become old fashioned?

An ethical question raised is, if an AI system generates a song using historical music or famous classic literature as initial inputs, how is the copyright affected? We will look at this in Chapter 9.

Should artists have a bigger say in their copyright? On the other hand, can the technology make us better human creators?

Let's now look at how computers are permeating into our day-to-day activities.

Slaves to the Algorithm – The Computer Says "No"

Can you recall the times you applied for something and you got a decision from a computer without any explanation?

Figure 7-7. "Computer Says No," Carol Beer. Source: Little Britain, 2004

"Computer says no" originated from the lighthearted British comedy TV show Little Britain in 2004. The character in Little Britain, Carol Beer, represents a customer frontline representative, always responds to customer inquiries by inputting their query into her computer keyboard and replying with the phrase "Computer says no." Even when faced with reasonable and logical requests, the computer's response takes precedence over any common-sense answer.

Are we just laughing at ourselves? As we all interact with customer representatives in clinics, banks, ticket offices, we often accept the computer program's "NO" decision without questioning or challenging the underlying decision. We can see that from the CV scanning tool example that the prototype went to pilot without being questioned. Similar to Orwell and

Turing quotes from the 1940s and 1950s, we seem to anticipate a future without doing much about it.

As we delve deeper into the realm of data-driven innovation and encounter more complex models, it becomes increasingly challenging for programs to explain their reasoning. This even means to create more efficient service, technology will not merely assist in service offerings but actually drive the entire service, with human staff serving as support to the system in communicating results to end users where no human can explain the decision made.

Could this really happen? For the sake of speed and convenience, should we go down this path of using more complex AI systems forcing the customer to trust the outputs?

Let's put Carol Beer to one side and look at Amica – an artificial general intelligence robot.

Introducing AMICA

I believe that at the end of the century the use of words and general educated opinion will have altered so much that one will be able to speak of machines thinking without expecting to be contradicted

–Alan Turing in 1950

Around the same time of the publication of George Orwell's 1984, Alan Turing in his quote came up with his view of the future which could be played out with AI today. It is interesting that while we try and react to the technology deluge, a lot of the social consequences were played out by thinkers in another era. Even with the Carol Beer sketch example, it shows that society what is going on, but is impassive to react.

Amica is a research platform for artificial general intelligence (AGI) to possess the ability to understand, learn, and perform any intellectual task that a human being can do. By developing human-level intelligence, such as problem-solving, decision-making, creativity, and social interaction, it could effectively perform the role of the customer frontline representative.

It could even play a role in CV scanning that we discussed earlier. By scanning CVs, selecting candidates, and even conducting the subsequent interviews using a ChatGPT type application.

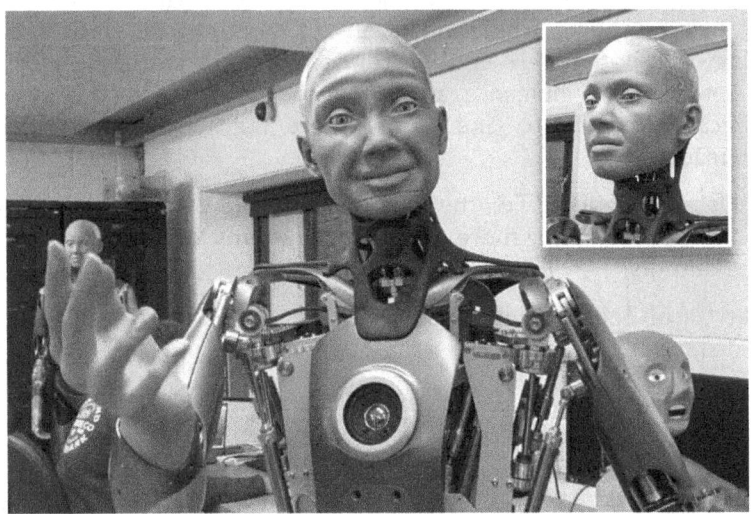

Figure 7-8. Introducing Amica. Source: nypost.com

Amica, shown in Figure 7-8, is a humanoid robot with human-like movements, including the maintenance of eye contact. Can you see a world where on top of the creative vision produced by ChatGPTs, humanoid robots like Amica derived from a neural network could advise or make decisions delivered with a calm but engaging voice.

How could that affect our ability to challenge? Will we move to a place where we place more trust in algorithms than over human intuition? What would be the social implications of such a change? Who is putting the guard rails in this?

With the earlier example of dirty data feeding algorithms to support the CV scanning tool, we seem to be on a dangerous technological path. Are business owners taking too much of a back seat?

Let's look at the data driving some of these algorithms. Is there sufficient data governance on companies that provide metadata that drive these algorithms that feed our systems?

There are organizations globally that democratize datasets for machine learning algorithms for the general public consumption. There is now an industry of data providers including: Kaggle Datasets, Amazon Datasets, UCI Machine Learning Repository, Google's Datasets Search Engine, 5- Microsoft Datasets, Government Datasets, Visual Data, and Lionbridge AI Datasets who provide data to feed algorithms created by data engineers.

Figure 7-9 outlines the principles of one of the organizations, LAION. who looks to provide datasets for large scale machine learning models. Many of the ethical questions raised about outcomes from algorithms are really about the data being used to produce the results. What are the rules for public data? Are entities allowed to use and share these?

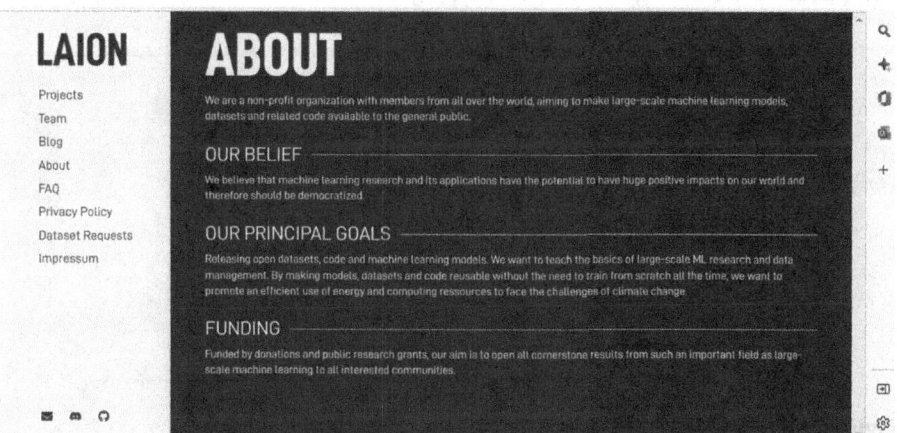

Figure 7-9. Well-Meaning Not-for-Profit Organization Providing Datasets. Source: LAION.AI

Thus, we must consider somehow the combination of the data sources, as well as the algorithmic processes that process the data that provide us decisions while being ever-mindful that the next big innovation is "just around the corner." It seems everything is taking place in a data engineering environment where there is little oversight from business owners. With looming regulation on data, business owners need to take stock of their responsibility (see Chapter 9).

In parallel, with such huge investments available, digital technology is moving ever faster, it is difficult to keep up.

Consider, ChatGPT-3 was relatively unheard of until December 2022, and after six months is considered the hot tool for search engines, potentially challenging the dominance of Google search. Only a matter of months previously, it was Augmented reality, and prior to that it was Crypto. How do we keep pace with innovation and how should we react to each hype?

How Do We Know What Is Really Coming Next?

Nothing captures our imagination quite like new digital technology. In a short amount of time, technological innovations such as wireless Internet and social networking have become a ubiquitous part of our everyday lives, quietly transforming the way we live, work, and communicate. However, some promising technologies appear destined to shine, or even achieve market penetration, but then fade into obscurity.

What will happen to Generative AI based technologies like CHATGPT? It was piloted by the OpenAI corporation on Dec 1, 2022. It reached 1 million users in just five days. To fuel the hype, a comparison was taken to show the uptake compared to other digital innovations. Figure 7-10 shows the comparison.

Netflix	3.5 years
Airbnb	2.5 years
Facebook	10 months
Spotify	5 months
Instagram	2.5 months
iPhone	74 days
ChatGPT	5 days

Figure 7-10. Time Taken for Digital Innovations to Reach 1 Million Users

Indeed, by September 2023, it had over 280 million signed up users. ChatGPT is not just revolutionary technology, it is proving valuable in a range of domains to save on time and resources. Does this mean we should prepare for our lives to be changed forever, including the loss of swathes of jobs. Should we all drop everything and look at this technology for applications and plan call center staff redundancies? Or, is this a false dawn and in the cold light of day the hype will fade away with a more limited user base or even obsolescence? Or will regulation kick in and agree that it is stopping children from doing their homework, and through the query system gathering too much data from businesses? In Chapter 9, we will look at legislation with regards to artificial intelligence that may help answer some of these points.

Above all, what makes us take notice of this technology above all others? We have, in the recent past, seen technologies such as Google Glasses, Crypto, 3D TV, 3D Printing, and Web 3.0, all grabbing headlines, but then fading away to serve specific niche areas. How can we manage expectations and plan more rational innovation roadmaps?

To any non-technical person struggling to keep up, you may think with the sheer number of digital technologies and buzzwords emerging over recent years and looking for a commercial conduit they must be produced from a faceless set and techno nerds with easy access to money. Don't worry, there is, in fact an evolutionary path.

Leading technology and research companies have mapped out the evolution stages of technology as a barometer of expectation to allow us to manage their introduction in the commercial space.

- One of the ways to understand the technology horizon is with the Gartner Hype curve. According to Gartner, major new technologies go through a "hype cycle." Since 1995, Gartner consultancy has produced more than 100 Hype Cycles in various domains to enable clients to track innovation maturity and future potential. Figure 7-11 shows the typical hype curve and what the stages of the hype curve mean. The curve is broken into five phases.

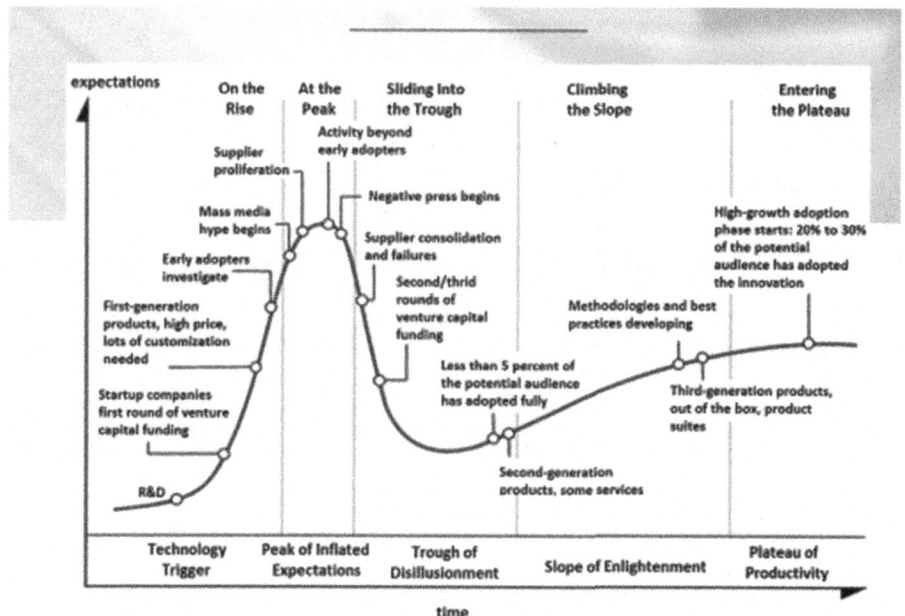

Figure 7-11. Gartner Technology Hype Cycle: Source Gartner

The horizontal axis of the Hype Cycle represents **time**, as a single innovation progresses through a series of stages. The vertical axis is labeled **expectations**, and the distinctive shape of the Hype Cycle curve shows how expectations surge and contract over time. This is based on the marketplace's assessment of the innovation's future expected value.

When an innovation is new and relatively unknown, expectations are extremely high. However, the innovation fails to live up to expectations, expectations plummet. Eventually, the innovation plateaus around more limited but relatively stable adoption, as its value becomes more rationally attributed. Visual capitalist produced a summary of the Gartner technology hype cycles from 2000–2018, as shown in Figure 7-12. We can now see whether the technology actually lived up to the hype. Do you recall any technologies that you may have been excited about a few years back, but still seek the path to mass adoption? For example, e-book readers definitely saw the path to adoption with the Kindle.

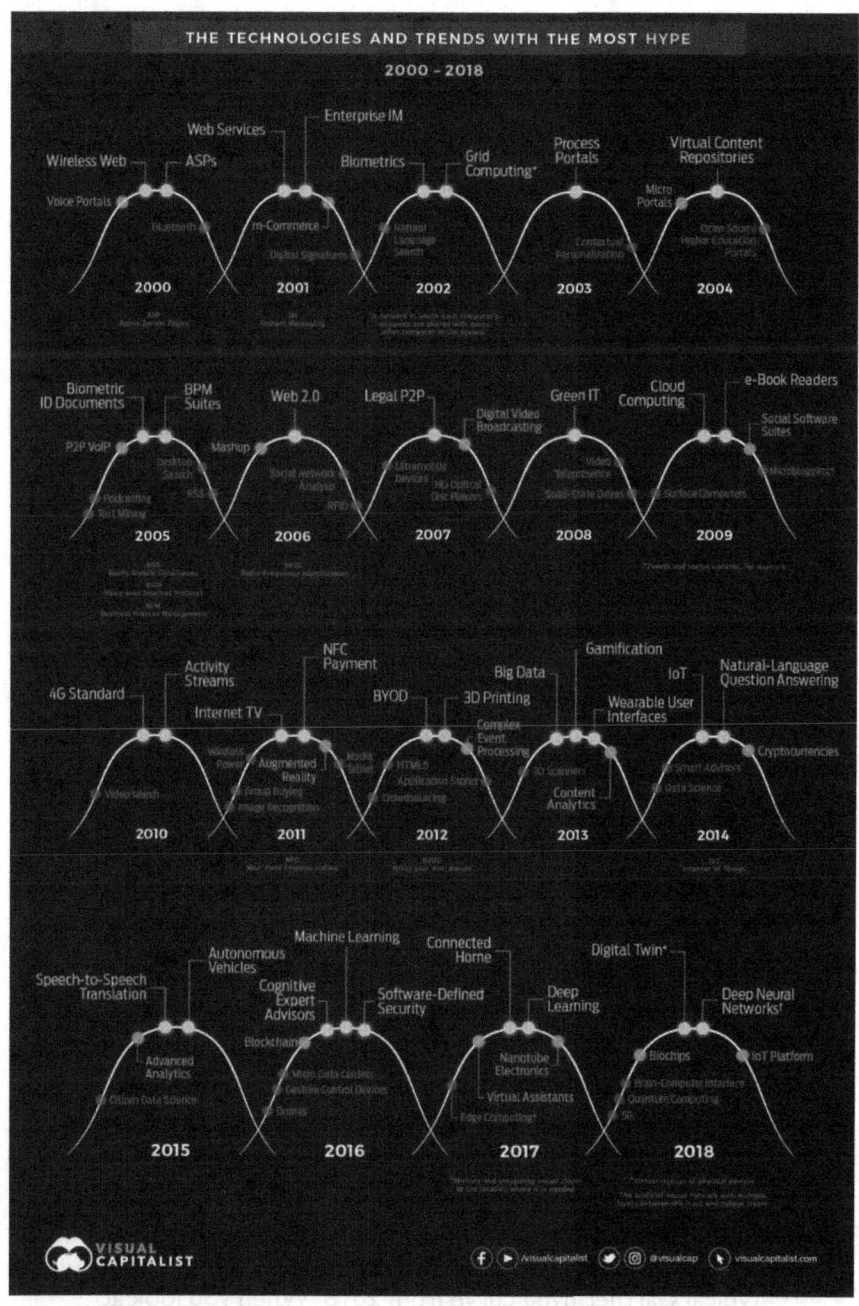

Figure 7-12. Technologies and Trends with the Most Hype. Source: Visual Capitalist.com

Let's now look at each of the five phases to understand how technology hype evolves.

- **Phase I: Innovation (technology) trigger**

  The Hype Cycle starts when a breakthrough, public demonstration, product launch, or other event generates press and industry interest in a technology innovation and starts the hype. At this stage, it is not something that should be on the business owners' radar unless they are an entrepreneur accepting the risk.

- **Phase II: Peak of inflated expectations**

  In Phase II, investors and media realize that the technology cannot do everything we believed it could, or the market was not as ready to employ the idea and so the hype reaches a peak.

- **Phase III: Enter the trough of disillusionment**

  In Phase III, negative hype begins, and those struggling technologies' sales go down a slope where at least some investors become disillusioned and/or the potential use cases appear far more limited.

- **Phase IV: Slope of enlightenment**

  Some of these use cases may be applicable for certain situations and if that is the case then the technology emerges into a new steady growth phase based on market acceptance. It is at this stage where business owners need to have a view on these as potential technologies to be deployed to improve business outcomes. If business owners do not keep an eye then they risk being swept away by the technology effect.

- **Phase V: The plateau of productivity**

  Once a technology has a pragmatic set of user cases with a positive business outcome, it is something which has achieved a uniqueness and should be something to consider.

  To understand how it all works, Figure 7-13 shows a typical Gartner hype curve from 2018. When you look at it, try and think of the number of innovations that made it to the present day and the ones that faded into obscurity. At the innovation trigger stage at the time, there was a prediction of autonomous flying vehicles, smart dust, exoskeleton quantum computing. On the other hand, we see autonomous vehicles and chatbots in the slope of enlightenment.

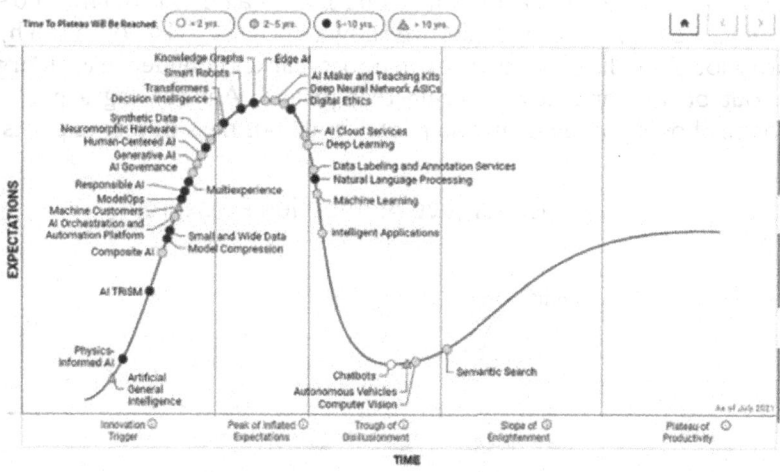

Figure 7-13. Gartner Hype Cycle 2018 Source: Gartner

While the hype cycle is a useful tool, it is not an exact science. Michael Mullany, a partner from ICON ventures, conducted a study of hype cycles in 2016 and showed that out of the more than 200 unique technologies that have appeared on a Gartner Hype Cycle for Emerging Technology, just a handful of technologies – Cloud Computing, 3D Printing, Natural Language Search, Electronic Ink – have been identified early and navigated through the Hype Cycle, as defined by Gartner from start to finish.

For instance, just over 50 individual technologies appear for just a single year on the Hype Cycle – never to reappear again such as Social TV (2011), Truth Verification (2004), Folksonomies (2006), and Expertise Location (2007). (Source: www.linkedin.com/pulse/8-lessons-from-20-years-hype-cycles-michael-mullany/)

Readers will come across it, but its most helpful aspect is that it gives a steer to where skills could be deployed in future digital services. From Figure 7-13, we see the various AI services being discussed, namely, Composite AI. AI Orchestration and automation Generative AI, Human Centered AI, Governance AI, and Responsible AI means a focus on building AI skills for the future is pretty important. The curves are very widely used and can result in pressure to adopt a technology coming from other areas. IBM conducted a survey in 2023 about where pressures arose to adopt Generative AI technology. (Source: `https://voicebot.ai/2023/08/15/two-charts-reveal-why-so-many-enterprises-are-rushing-to-adopt-generative-ai/`) The results are shown in Figure 7-14. With the hype, there are a lot of media benefits that can boost market confidence in an organization about being "innovative" during that period. Announcing a pilot is one of them. Should there be "media pilots" and "business outcome pilots"?

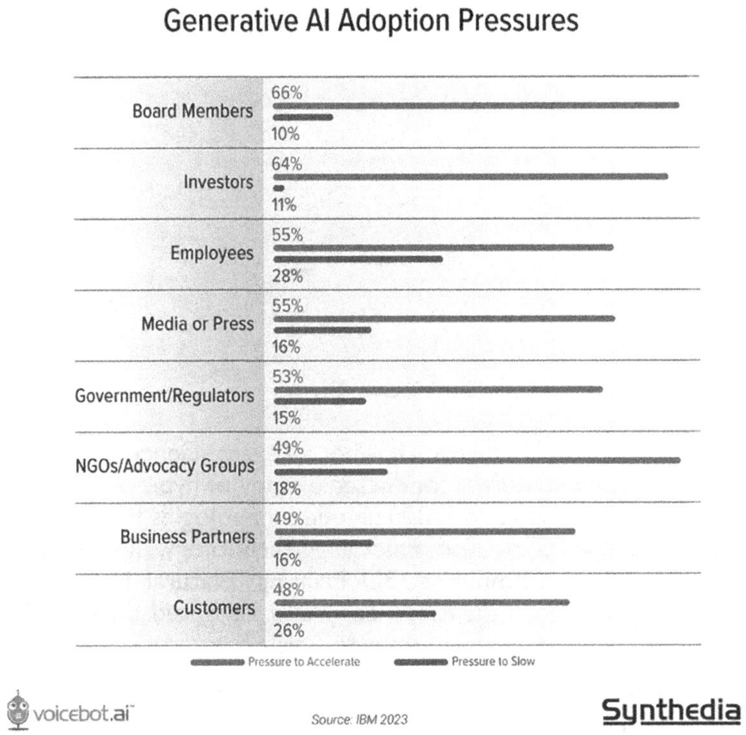

Generative AI Adoption Pressures

	Pressure to Accelerate	Pressure to Slow
Board Members	66%	10%
Investors	64%	11%
Employees	55%	28%
Media or Press	55%	16%
Government/Regulators	53%	15%
NGOs/Advocacy Groups	49%	18%
Business Partners	49%	16%
Customers	48%	26%

voicebot.ai   Source: IBM 2023   Synthedia

Figure 7-14. Generative AI Adoption Pressures

There are other tools that you may come across. We touched on the Schumpeter innovation curves in Chapter 2, which give a very broad view of the main innovation drivers. Related to the Gartner Curve discussed is the "Innovation S-Curve." It represents the typical pattern of innovation adoption and improvement over time. The curve typically starts slowly as the innovation is developed, accelerates as it gains traction, and improves and eventually levels off as it reaches its limits or maturity.

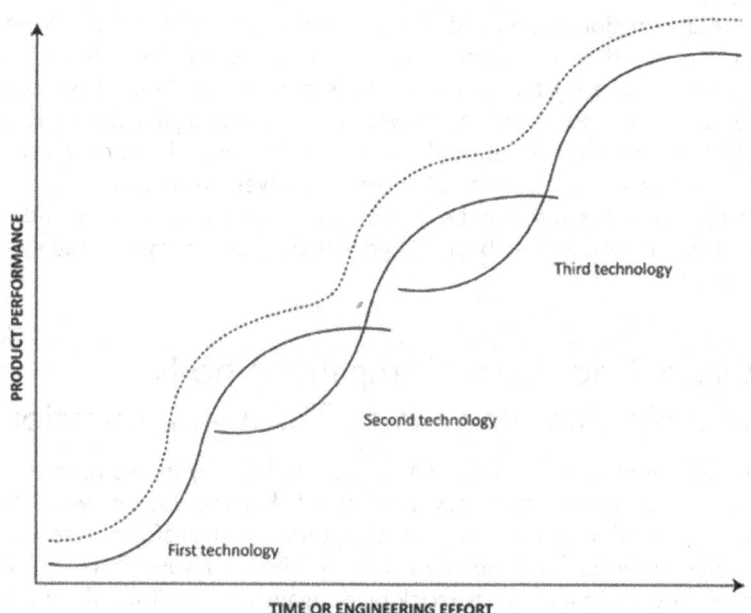

Figure 7-15. Innovation S-Curves. Source: www.futurebusinesstech.com/blog/the-s-curve-pattern-of-innovation-a-full-analysis

The Innovation S-Curve illustrates the evolutionary trajectory of products or technologies as they develop over time (see Figure 7-15). When a company accurately identifies the maturity level of a technology or product, it can strategically prepare for future improvements. As a product approaches maturity, new competitors enter the market and customer needs move on, profit growth may plateau, prompting the company to proactively introduce new offerings to improve revenue prospects. In chapter I, we discussed how companies, like Apple, increase value over time through new propositions. We can use the s-curve to see how they introduced their new products in a timely manner.

There is the Rogers Adoption Curve, which can help you understand how new products or technology might be accepted. (https://medium.com/the-political-informer/the-rogers-adoption-curve-how-you-spread-new-ideas-throughout-culture-d848462fcd24)

Bain & Co present four different forecasting tools, when used together, can predict the next disruptive technology – they call them the "E-Curves." The overall cost to provide the service, knowing what customers value, the adoption curve of the product, and then external barriers and accelerators (regulation, technology, economics, and consumer behavior). (Source: www.bain.com/insights/tipping-points-when-to-bet-on-new-technologies/)

When digital transformation is driven by technology, a reality check needs to be made on whether the technology invested would really reach business expectations. Too early an adoption can lead to wasted effort, whereas too late adoption can mean missed opportunities. Once again, the rationale for any technology investment should be on the delivery of business outcomes. We discussed earlier the volume of pilots that never make it to full commercial deployment. Pilot activity may be perceived internally as exciting and moving forward, but without a clear business goal at the start, they are mainly fruitive efforts.

Is There a Traditional Company Who Is Successfully Managing a Path Through Innovation?

To look at a company who successfully managed the hype, we have to look at Domino's Pizza under the stewardship of Patrick Doyle who led the transformation of the company at the time to transform itself into an "*e-commerce business that happens to sell pizza.*" Figure 7-16 shows the phenomenal performance of its stock price against its traditional competitors.

Domino's change in stock price compared to its competitors

During CEO Patrick Doyle's tenure

Source: FactSet • Created with Datawrapper

Figure 7-16. *Dominos Change in Stock Price. Source: Factset*

When the CEO became the leader of Domino's, their share price was trading below $8 a share. And then just under ten years later, each share was trading at $206 per share. This turnaround happened by focussing on their prime business targets and using digital to deliver on them. The targets were improving the profitability, operational efficiency, and the overall brand perception. In 2016, Domino's created an estimated $5.6 billion in global digital revenue, an improvement from 2015 of 19%. By 2018, over 60% of sales were through the digital channel.

Here are some of their digital initiatives:

- Customer ordering through any digital device and through any channel
- Crowdsourcing Customer Feedback via the "Think Oven" Campaign
- Emoji ordering
- No click ordering – push a button in your smart watch to order your saved pizza
- Regular Customer A/B feedback testing through digital media
- A fun pizza tracker for live status updates of the pizza order
- Introduction of an automated POS (Point of Sale) system to reduce the amount of order errors and improve training hours
- Vertically integrated dough processing system for better supply chain and consistent product
- Deliver to your car service during the pandemic

They didn't just deploy technology due to the level of hype but very much looked at technology and how it could support their business outcomes. A phenomenal growth despite all of the threats of digital start-ups and the existing fast-food climate. Domino's stock price has grown more than 1300%, surpassing even Google, Facebook, Apple, or Amazon's performance. Only Netflix's stock amongst big tech increased faster over this period.

This embracing of digital technology to find operational is an ongoing mission. In December 2023, I attended a hackathon where they invited participants from many walks of life to provide operational improvements to their food delivery service. The delegates were give real data and could consult with senior managers to discuss problems.

Conclusion

Even the largest big tech companies are not immune to mistakes in their digital solutions. The current excitement surrounding AI serves as a prime example of this. If business owners fail to be involved in the innovation process, especially concerning issues like data quality, bias and input integrity, there can be adverse consequences for end users, regardless of the advanced machine learning techniques employed. Business owners must get closer to their data teams, gaining a deeper understanding of what their counterparts are doing with the data. It is vital to pose fundamental questions about the data sets when they are being utilized, ensuring that the algorithms employed align closely with the desired outcomes. Specifically, they should grasp which raw data sets are used for training and check the explain-ability of algorithmic outcomes. Moreover, they should stay informed about critical technology use cases to chart effective roadmaps. In doing so, businesses can take charge of innovation rather than being driven by the technology.

For those who lack technical expertise, engaging closely with digital experts in this realm can seem intimidating. By comprehending various innovation methodologies, we can demystify the technological hype. Until a technology possesses a well-defined use case that contributes to achieving business objectives, it remains challenging to gauge its widespread adoption apart from being a way to ride a media wave of excitement. Several compelling success stories exist where companies have steadfastly pursued their digital transformation goals through strategic technology investments.

In the upcoming chapters, we will explore practical, no-code tools for data mining and performance prediction to assist further in building the competencies to be comfortable with digital technologies.

Introducing No-Code/ Low-Code AI Toolsets

Introduction

In Chapter 3, we examined digital toolsets that empower business owners to enhance their effectiveness in their roles. In the subsequent chapters, we delved deeper into game-changing algorithms, data mining, and machine learning methods. We will now look at AI tools to help you stay ahead. Figure 8-1 shows a summary of 120 AI tools that can help in improving productivity. If you get time, try to take a look and play with the apps and see how they can help you.

© Attul Sehgal 2024
A. Sehgal, *Demystifying Digital Transformation*,
https://doi.org/10.1007/978-1-4842-9499-4_8

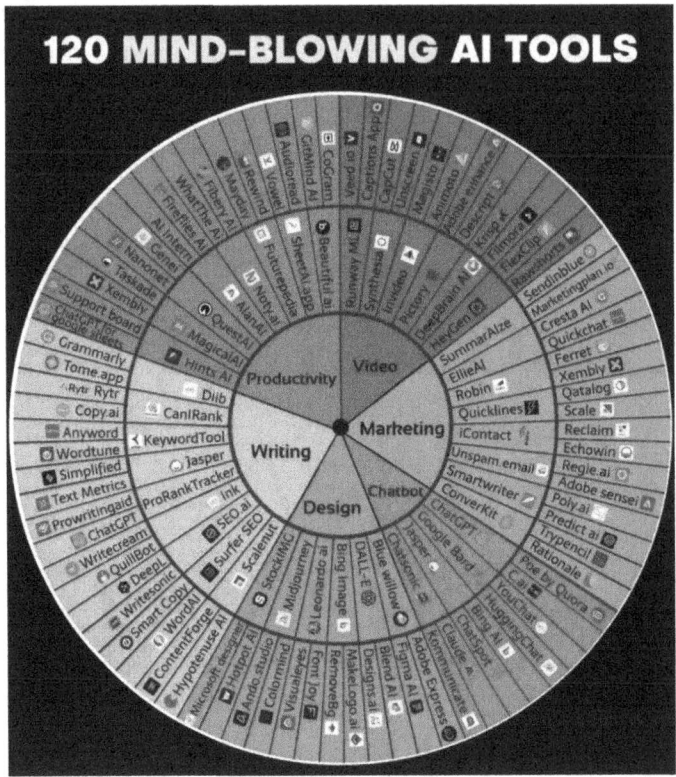

Figure 8-1. 120 AI Tools. Source: Cool Guides: www.reddit.com/r/coolguides/

In this chapter, we will apply some of these no-code/low-code AI tools into our case example for Landis Car Hire. Our exploration commences by tracing the evolution of apps and subsequently utilizing our Landis Car Hire case example to investigate the following topics:

- Predictive tools using Power BI
- Linear regression employing Excel
- Web scraping and image extraction
- Object detection through Google Teachable Machine
- Generative AI with OpenAI
- Sentiment analysis via Power Automate

Following this, we will provide an overview of some of the programming languages commonly employed in machine learning applications.

So let's begin!

"There's an App for That"

Apple, in 2010, trademarked the phrase "There's an app for that." It was used in TV ads to show off the multitude of apps available for iOS devices through its popular App Store, which opened July 2008. By 2022, according to App Annie's report, apps globally were downloaded 230 billion times in 2021, while $170bn (£125bn) was spent. TikTok was the most downloaded app worldwide, with users spending 90% more time there compared to 2020.

Figure 8-2. "There's an App for That". Source: http://www.presbymusings.com/2011/01/theres-app-for-that-intro.html

The use of no-code apps can be traced in the 1990s from the emergence of Word, Excel, and Powerpoint. Wordpress then simplified Web page development for non-coders. In the 2010s, no-code platforms, like Webflow, Figma, Notion, and Airtable, emerged to help, then today, it allows businesses to develop the most complicated models through point and click. In 2014, Forrester came up with the definition of low code as "Low-code platforms enable rapid delivery of business applications with a minimum of hand-coding and minimal upfront investment in setup, training, and deployment." The APP culture today has now spread to the most complex of operations; using Machine learning algorithms can be carried out with the click of a button.

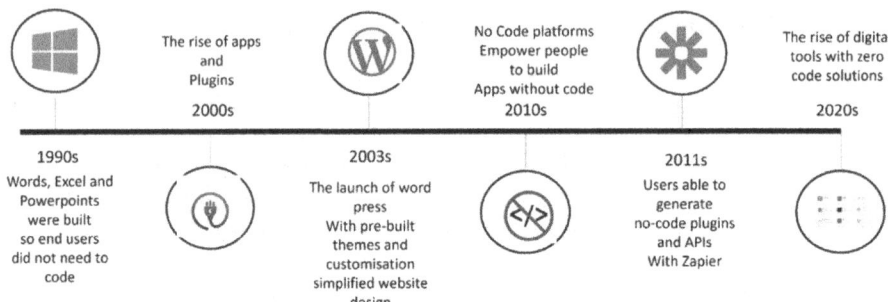

Figure 8-3. Evolution of Low-Code Apps

With this huge demand to automate everything, even the most simple of tasks, enterprises are struggling to respond because of the limited availability of developer talent. Low-code/no-code tools came about to address this shortage and allow a wider audience to make these tools. The benefits are that they can empower non-IT specialists to do these tasks, workers productivity improves, development costs are reduced, time to deployment shortens, and even allowing business users to participate in development, potentially providing a better understanding between the IT and business worlds.

With low-code platforms, a developer will need at least a basic understanding of programming, while no-code platforms that use a select then drag-and-drop approach don't require any coding knowledge at all. Today even non-technical people could use them to build applications using visual drag and drop components.

In Chapter 6, we discussed some of the concepts that we can use to accelerate our understanding of digital and working with data. From this foundation we can build the right expectations for our business outcomes before investing in a fully fledged AI project with the data teams.

In this chapter, we will introduce some no-code tools that can improve your expertise with data mining, algorithms, and AI, helping you to frame more clearly business problems that will require data scientist support. By trying these tools yourselves and understanding how the algorithms work, you will be empowered to have a clearer understanding of the business problem and the data challenges before embarking on deploying data scientists for a detailed solution. We will discover how carrying out some simple preliminary tests on the data and the planned approach can ensure that we can direct a data team more effectively.

We will use these AI toolsets to identify trends, predict behaviors, build data sets from the web, do object classification and sentiment analysis for the Landis Car Hire Case Study.

Deploying the Power of AI to Build Our Understanding of Landis Car Hire Performance

Understanding Behavior from the Landis Car Hire Data Set

Let us revisit the Landis Car Hire sensor data to understand how the staff use the showroom and forecourt facility over time. In the appendix, you will find some of the source files in the github account if you want to try this yourselves.

If you recall, we uploaded sensor data as a .csv file into Power BI to create a simple visualization of the performance of the sensor over time. Through using Power BI, we produced some simple visual forecasts of future performance.

Creating Trendlines Using Power BI

Trend lines (or line of best fit) is a powerful tool for visualizing overall changes and trends. Linear regression tools establish the linear relationship between two variables based on a line of best fit. It is usually graphically depicted using a straight line with the slope defining how the change in one variable impacts a change in the other – either as a positive or negative slope. An overall trendline can help us quickly navigate and find our way when reading charts. If the trend line is extended, it can be used to predict instances in the future with a level of confidence.

If we open up our saved Sensor Profile sheet, we have the .csv file data saved as histograms on the visualization. The graphs show the distance travelled in meters by the showroom sensor each year and for each day.

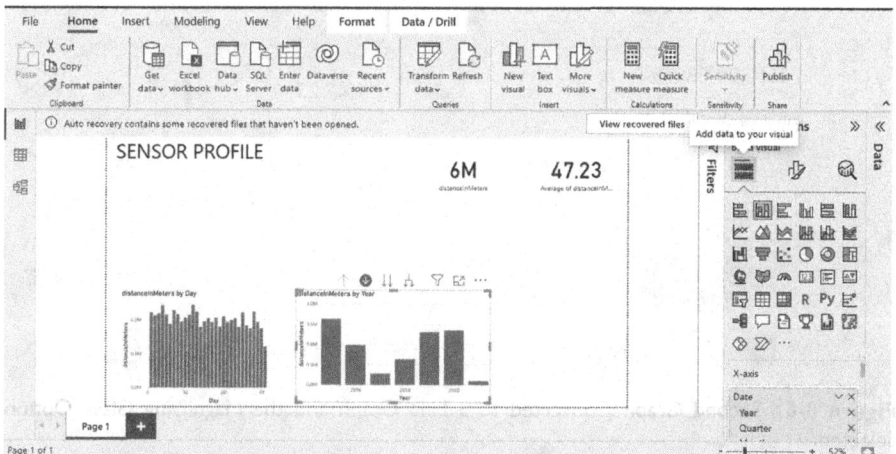

Figure 8-4. Sensor Profile in Power BI – Second Graph Selected

To place a trendline using Power BI, let's start by changing the visualization. We can select either a line graph by selecting the line chart icons or we could select a scatter graph. Once we highlight the graph, we move our cursor to the visualizations menu.

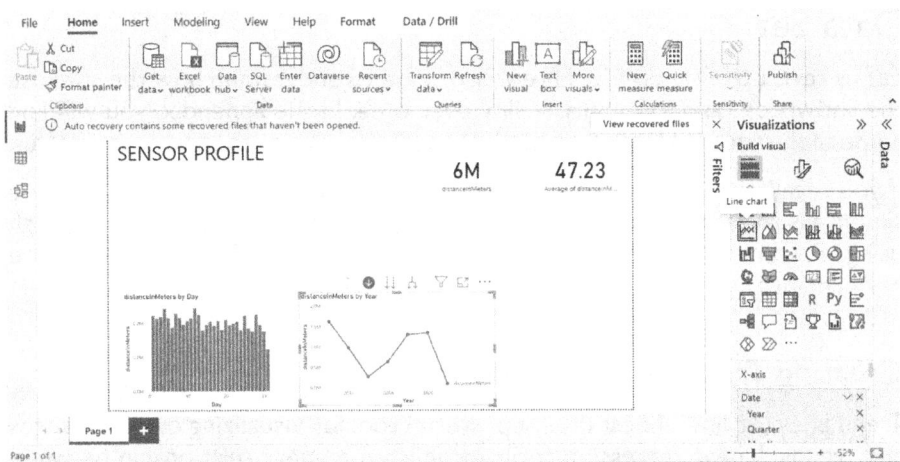

Figure 8-5. Using the Visualization from Histogram to Line Chart

This is on the right side of the screen under the tab called "visualizations." If we click the mouse onto the line graph visualization the graph will immediately change into a line graph. You will see the change on the main screen. Now we can add in a Trendline.

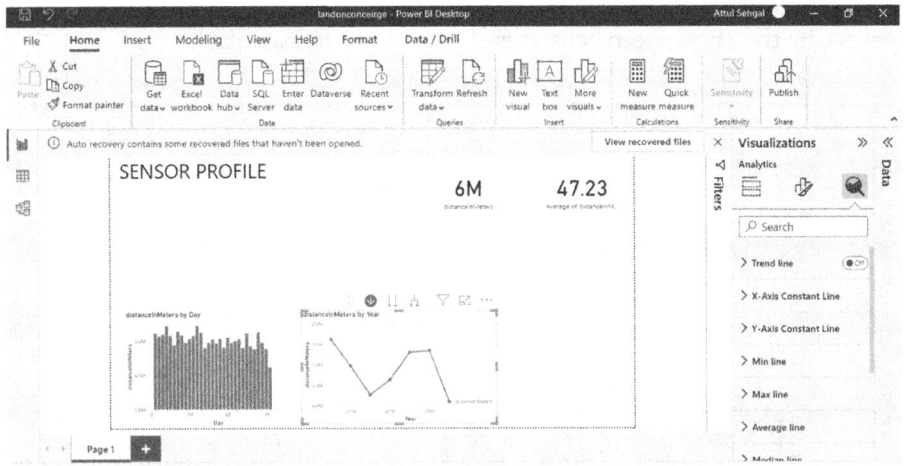

Figure 8-6. Second Graph Converted to a Line Graph and the Magnifying Glass Option Selected

Below the visualization field name in the analytics field, there is a "Magnifying glass" icon. If we select that icon we will be presented with a suite of options to analyze our data. The first option is called "Trendline." If we select this icon, a dotted line will appear on the line showing a linear regression for the sensor data.

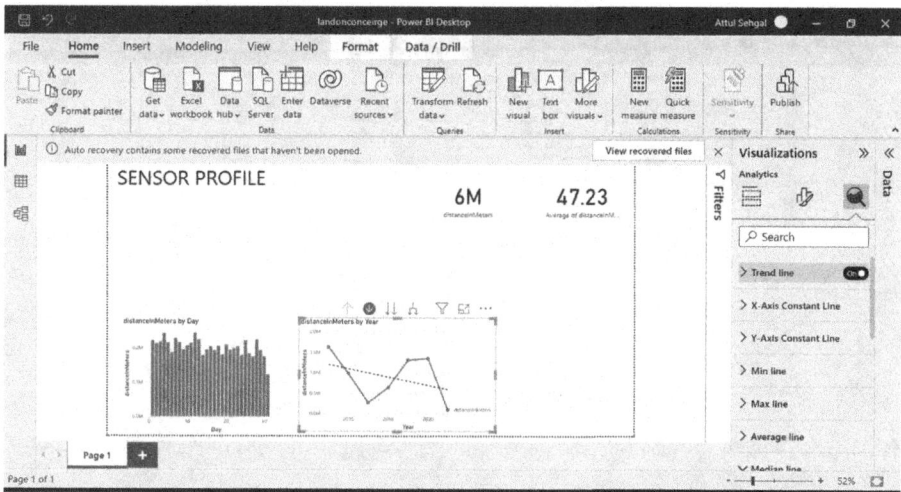

Figure 8-7. *Sensor Profile with Trendline Added*

We will see a downward dotted line on our line graph. If we scroll down further on this menu, there are also options to create an average or median line onto the graph. Let's select these lines as a comparison.

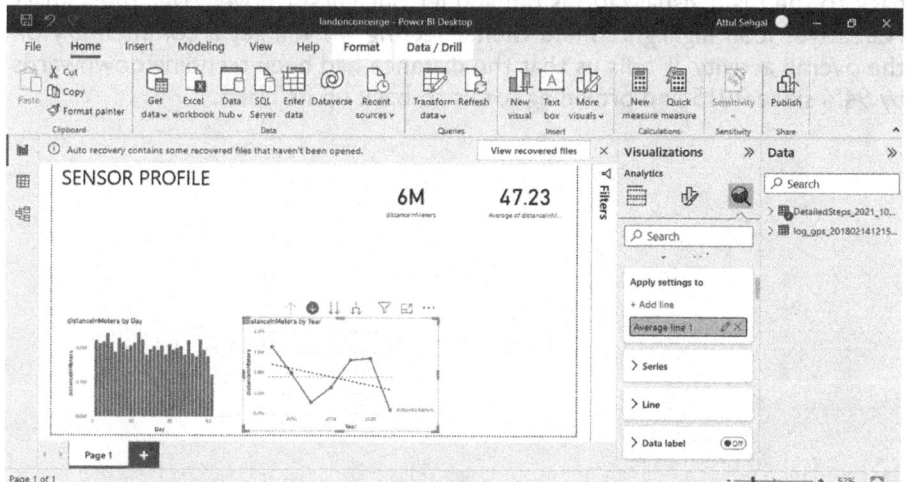

Figure 8-8. *Sensor Profile with Average and Median Line Added*

If you select the magnifying glass icon and scroll down further, you will come to a "forecast" tab which provides performance visualizations at various confidence levels in the future. The prediction of activity is shown in Figure 8-9. The extended line is the forecast figure and the shaded area is the 99% confidence interval. The tabs allow you to extend the forecast period to predict the output.

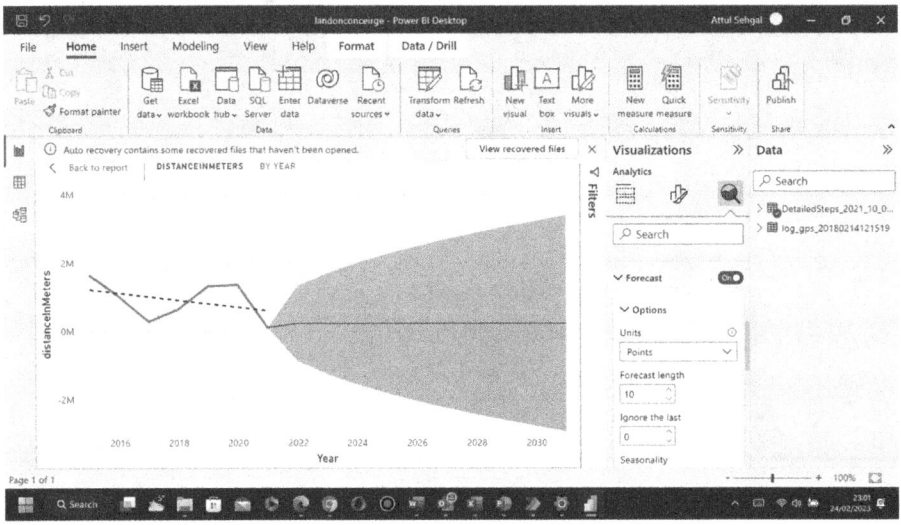

Figure 8-9. Ten-Year Forecast on Sensor Data

Power BI also has intelligence to read graphs and provide commentary on key trends as a text file in the dashboard. Let's try this for our line graph. If we go back to the main visualizations tab and let our cursor hover over the "Smart Narrative" icon highlighted and then selecting we will get a commentary on the overall activity. It tells us that the distance had been trending downwards by 94% since 2015 and providing totals to back up its claim.

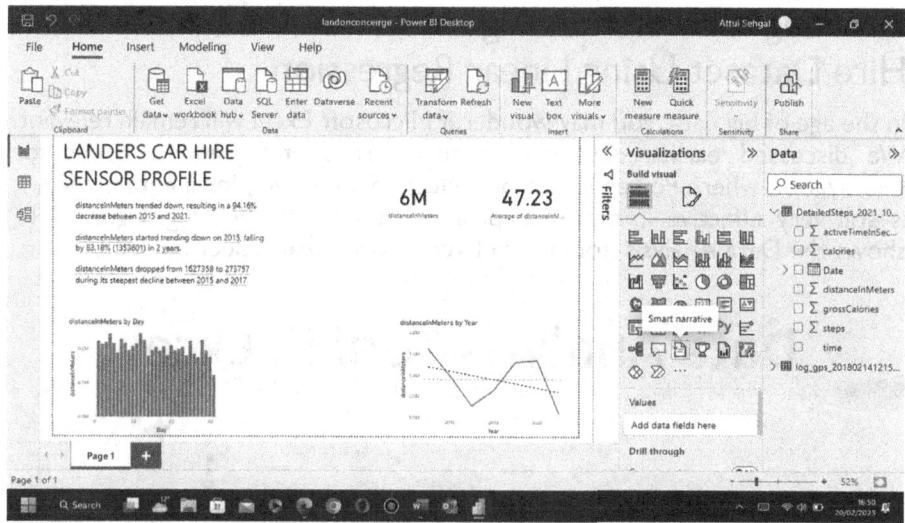

Figure 8-10. Sensor Profile

This is a very simple way of uploading a .csv file and getting a visual summary, forecast, and commentary for the dataset. Once you select the "Publish" button, you can share these insights with your team to get their feedback. This may be a good time to enlist the support of your data colleagues to discuss assumptions used in deriving the output.

The best way to see the benefits of these tools is by trying them yourself. There are some data sets in the appendix, but feel free to upload your own file, create the line graphs and derive your own data predictions. Once you do this, ask yourselves the questions:

- "Are the insights what I expected?"
- "Are there new things I learned from this forecast?"
- "What questions can I ask a data analyst to build on my understanding?"

Before moving on

- Can you think of the machine learning methods used to create the forecast?

Purely visualizing a trendline can seem a bit crude when trying to carry out a prediction. There are ways of using Power BI code – called DAX – to get the equation for the linear regression as well as other insights from the data. Your data team may be able to help you with this. We will not cover low-code tools in this chapter. Fortunately there are other established no-code tools that allow us to get this information as well as other statistics without any coding.

Creating a Prediction Algorithm for the Landis Car Hire Dataset Using Linear Regression

In the age of big data, you may wonder if Microsoft Excel will remain relevant. We discussed earlier data performance issues and graphics issues for visualization where Power BI is more effective. However, for a data novice, it is still very effective in data manipulation and sense checking. Figure 8-11 shows the Data Analysis Tool in MS Excel and you can select it.

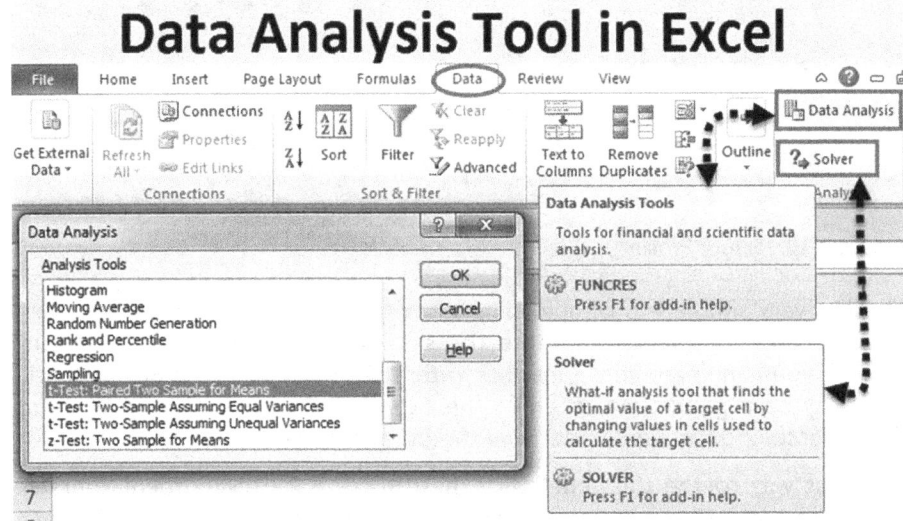

Figure 8-11. Excel Data Analysis ToolPack. Source: `https://cdn.educba.com/academy/wp-content/uploads/2019/01/Data-Analysis-Tool-in-Excel-1.png`

It can still help in sense understanding data for a training set to help on deciding whether a particular machine learning approach is the one. These analytics and data fixing tools don't need any coding and, in many ways, this data preparation by the business owner is crucial to save considerable time, effort, and resources down the line.

In addition to the Power Query tool to check data files, MS Excel has been introducing no code data forecasting features that enable you to create regression models from tabular data without any coding. There are two ways to do analysis:

- We can use the "Analyze Data" function in the "Home Screen" menu.

- Analysis ToolPak in Excel will not be found in an Excel workbook by default. It must be added and viewed under the Data tab menu.

Analyze Data is a very simple no-code intuitive tool. It helps us to understand data through natural language queries that allow you to ask questions about the data without having to write complicated formulas. In addition, Analyze Data provides high-level visual summaries, trends, and patterns. It can create automatic regression models and be set to one of several regression algorithms, including linear, polynomial, logarithmic, and exponential regression. It also automatically produces the equation of the regression line to enable prediction as well as other statistics information.

Predicting Performance of the Landis Car Hire Sensor

Let's now see how it can produce a linear regression algorithm for the Landis Car Hire Data Set so we can predict future performance.

If you recall from Chapter II, I presented some data from a CSV file that I uploaded from the movement sensor. The data file consisted of around 133,000 rows of data information in six columns. The data contains details of the power consumed by the sensor and the distance covered over six years. Let's see if we can find any correlation between the power consumed and distance covered and whether we can predict the future performance from the data.

To begin, you may need to make sure you are online to access the functions. From the top menu, we can select the Data tab to upload the .csv file using the Get Data command.

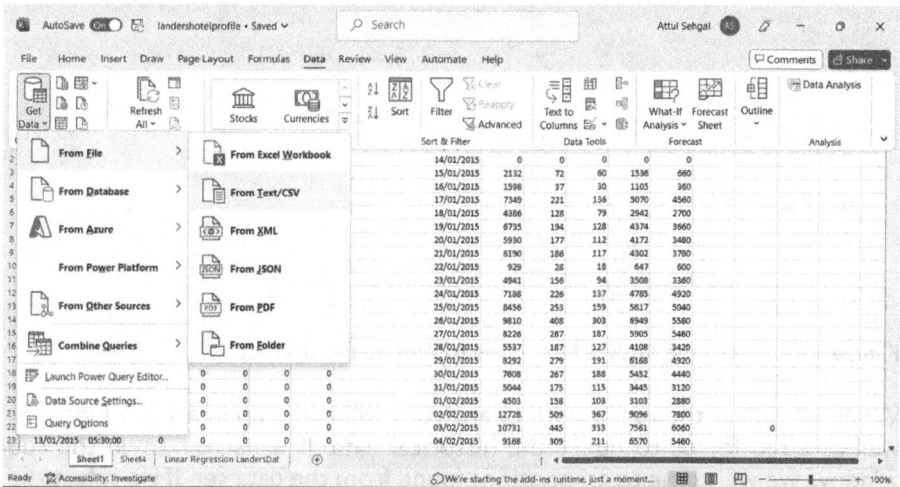

Figure 8-12. Uploading the .csv File Using the Get Data Command in Excel

From the "HOME" screen, we select the "Analyze Data" icon on the right side of the ribbon.

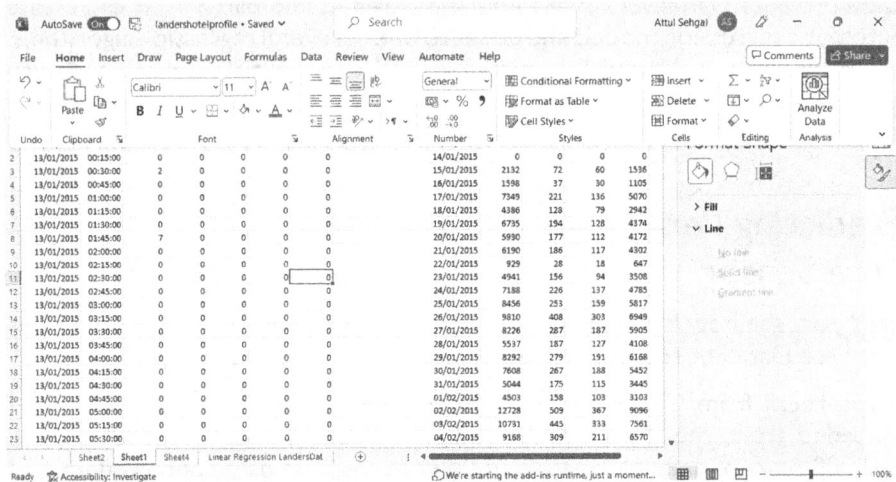

Figure 8-13. Analyze Data Icon on the Top Right

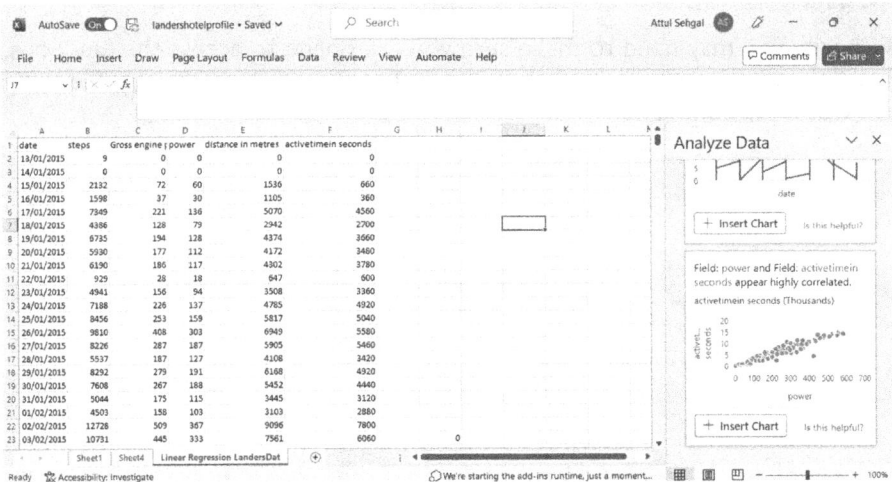

Figure 8-14. Using the Analyze Data Menu to Analyze the Data set

When we select the tab, a suite of analytics will come up in a sub window as well as a tab for us to query the historical data. If we scroll down the sub window, we will come to associations found from the data set. If we select the chart of power vs. active time in seconds, we immediately get the data profile with the trendline.

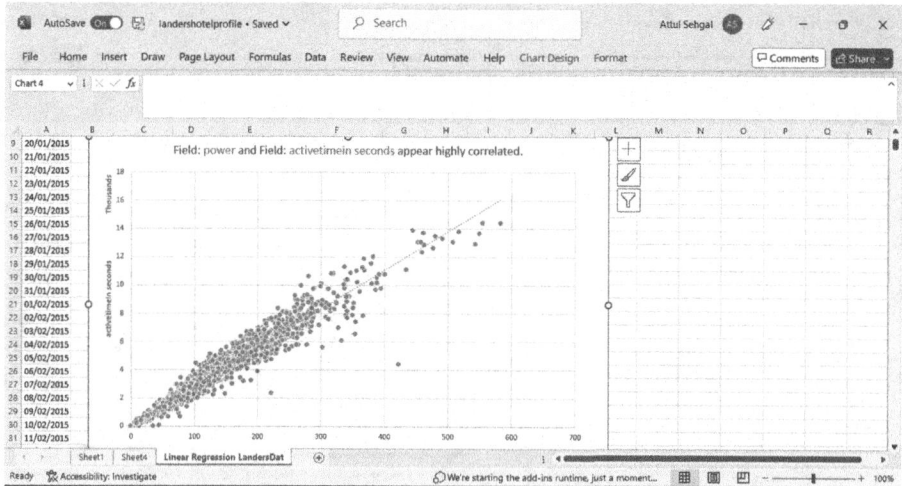

Figure 8-15. Selecting the Power vs. Active Time Correlation

If we click our mouse on the trendline, Excel presents us with a further sub-menu to format the trendline.

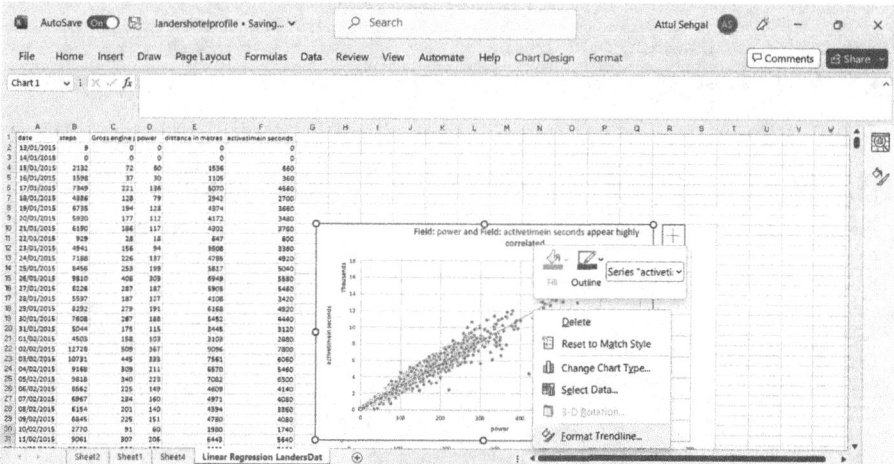

Figure 8-16. Selecting the Trendline Sub-menu

When we select the option to format the trendline, the tool provides option to change the regression model. There are other trendlines available depending on the scatter like Logarithmic, Polynomial, and Moving Average. If we just select between these options, the trendline will change automatically.

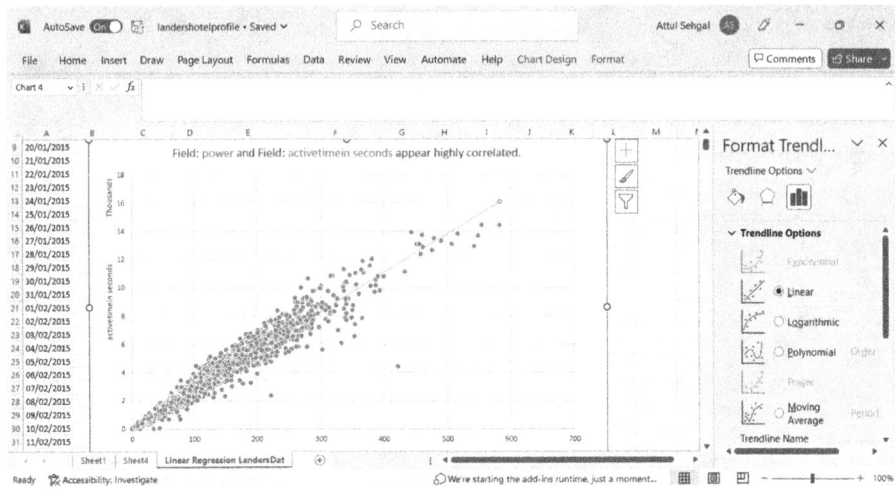

Figure 8-17. Selecting the Linear Regresson Option for the Trendline

If we scroll further down this menu, we will see the option "Display the Equation on the chart." If we select this, we will automatically get the equation for the trendline line. This is the line of regression.

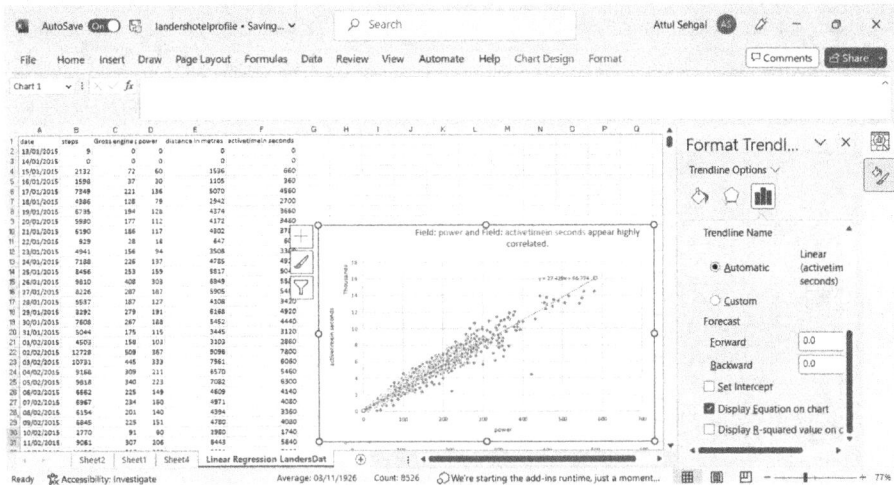

Figure 8-18. Adding the Equation for the Line of Best Fit

This is then highlighted on the screen as: $Y=27.429x+96.774$.

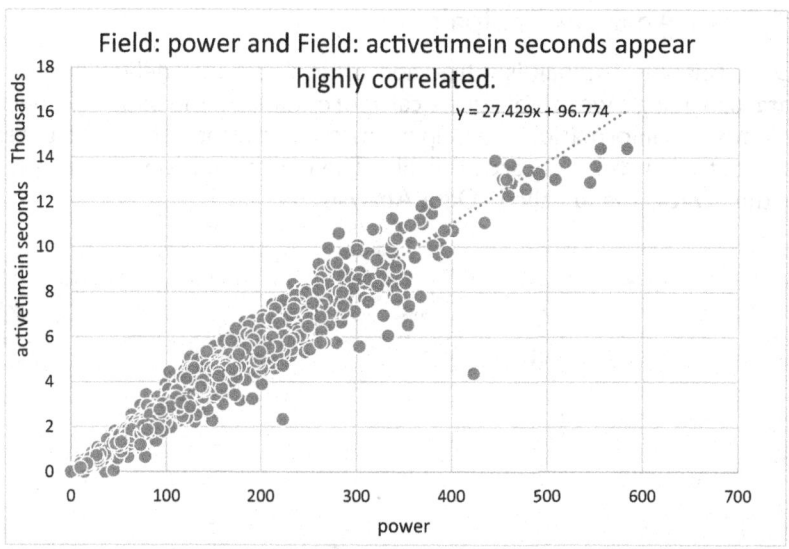

Figure 8-19. Linear Regression with Equation

There is also an option to select the R Squared Value on the Chart. R-Squared is a statistical measure of fit that indicates how much variation of a dependent variable is explained by the independent variable(s) in a regression model. R-squared values range from 0 to 1 and are commonly stated as percentages from 0% to 100%. An R-squared of 100% means that all movements of a security (or another dependent variable) are completely explained by movements in the index (or the independent variable(s) you are interested in). This figure lies between 1 and 0. The R figure for our graph is 0.93 and so there is a high correlation. What qualifies as a "good" R-Squared value will depend on the context. In some fields, such as the social sciences, even a relatively low R-Squared such as 0.5 could be considered relatively strong. In other fields, the standards for a good R-Squared reading can be much higher, such as 0.9 or above. In finance, an R-Squared above 0.7 would generally be seen as showing a high level of correlation, whereas a measure below 0.4 would show a low correlation. Once again this depends on the business owners view of the problem at hand.

The equation allows us to predict future outcomes once we test the equation outside the sample set. If there are too many outliers, then we may need to use another machine learning method to do the prediction.

Excel Data Analysis Toolpak

The Data Analysis Toolpak is a free add-on in Excel that delves deeper into the data, providing a wealth of statistical information on the data. A knowledge of the statistical information can help in any conversation with the data teams. Let's look at what data sets are available. The tool pack is on the main screen under the "Data" menu called "Data Analysis."

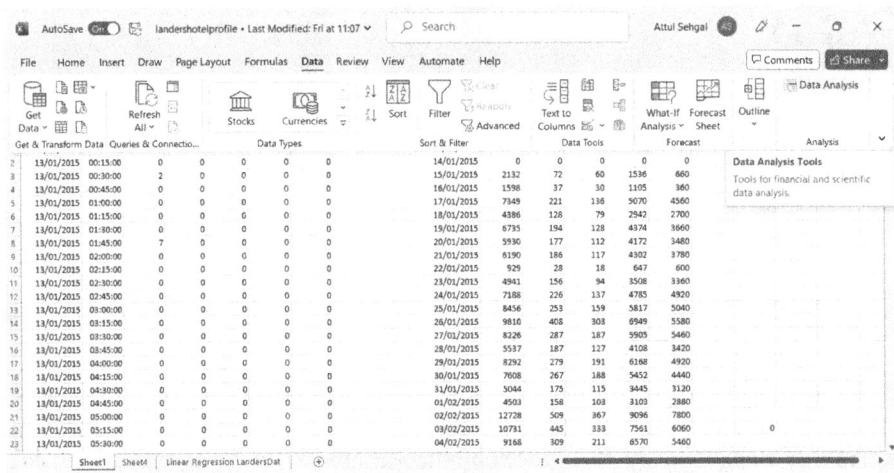

Figure 8-20. Accessing the Data Analysis Tool

Once we select this option a sub window will appear showing various data tools. There are 19 tools in this pack and they are summarized in the "Data Mining Methods" table at the end of this chapter.

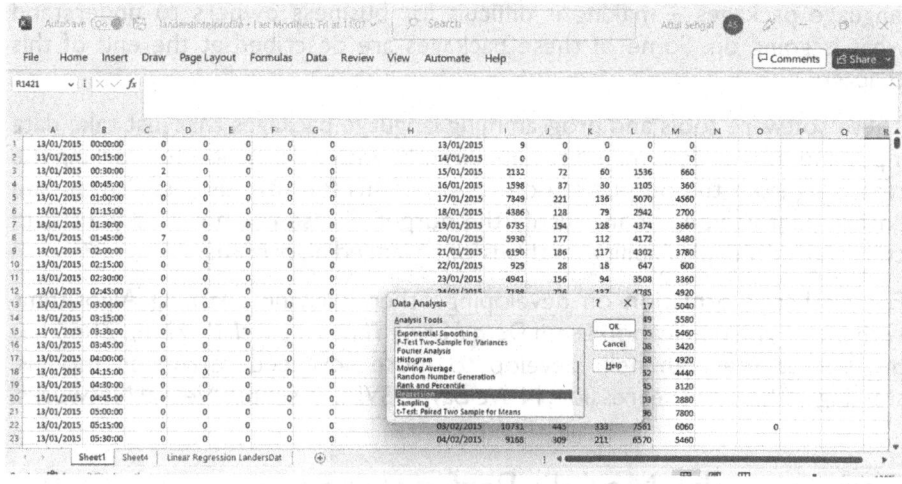

Figure 8-21. Selecting the Regression Analysis Tools

When we select the regression option, a summary table pops up that summarizes the measures in Figure 8-22. By selecting the rows from particular columns, you can get a further statistical summary highlighted as follows.

Regression Statistics	
Multiple R	0.990365833
R Square	0.980824483
Adjusted R Square	0.98078884
Standard Error	13.68691123
Observations	540

ANOVA					
	df	SS	MS	F	Significance F
Regression	1	5155103.447	5155103.447	27518.60937	0
Residual	538	100784.368	187.3315391		
Total	539	5255887.815			

	Coefficients	Standard Error	t Stat	P-value	Lower 95%	Upper 95%	Lower 95.0%	Upper 95.0%
Intercept	-0.379642523	1.225949864	-0.309672144	0.756930193	-2.787877814	2.028592768	-2.787877814	2.028592768
X Variable 1	0.034422841	0.000207507	165.8873394	0	0.034015217	0.034830465	0.034015217	0.034830465

Figure 8-22. Sample Regression Report from the Analysis Toolpack

While it is not imperative to be a statistical expert, being able to mine the data and understand changes is vital leading data teams. MS Excel has another benefit as it is easy to track back and explain how results occurred. This allows us to work with data in a very clear and transparent way. For example, when you open an Excel file, data is immediately visible and you can work with it directly. Results can be examined while you are conducting your mining task, offering a deeper understanding of how data is being manipulated and the results obtained. These critical transparent aspects of model construction processes are often hidden in advanced software tools and programming language packages — making it difficult for business owners to understand what is going on. Some of these packages are described at the end of this chapter.

These software tools and programming language packages that just take data input and deliver data mined results directly, with no insight into working the reasoning from the output can create problems for any business-driven data engagement as you try and justify the output. Please reach out to your data colleagues on explainability methods of advanced algorithms.

For further information on developing other Machine Learning Algorithms with Excel, the publication *Learn Data Mining Through Excel*, by Hong Zhou has procedures that can help develop to more advanced regression models, starting with Linear Regression, Naïve Bayes, SVM, to simple Neural Networks.

Evaluating the Model's Performance

By finding the difference between the actual values and the predicted values, we can evaluate the accuracy of the model. If the difference is too large, we can then investigate other methods with our data science counterparts. The equation of the line, the R value, and R squared value can help identify whether the correlation works. With a clear definition of the data set and the single source of truth, this simple analysis can already be powerful in predicting new outcomes.

If we wish to improve the prediction significantly from the linear regression, the data team can provide the recommendations of which approach to use with the potential outcomes, thus keeping the business owner in control and everyone serving the needs of the business objective.

A useful site to visit is www.medium.com. Here is one based on a scenario of IKEA products. (https://medium.com/@amalia.wulandiari/ikea-product-analysis-and-price-prediction-using-linear-regression-644e52542f35)

Before moving on, if you have a data set, then try and see if you can produce a linear regression and predict future outcomes. Otherwise look at some of the free datasets from the following sites and see what insights you can mine from the data.

www.kaggle.com/datasets

Kaggle: Daily Temperature of World Cities

BFI: Film Industry Statistics: Weekend Box Office Figures 2001 to Present www.bfi.org.uk/industry-data-insights/weekend-box-office-figures

Automatic Extracting of Large Datasets from the Web

As the amount of data in our lives grows exponentially, there is no doubt the biggest data repository is on the web. The ability to easily extract publicly available data is vital to build up data intelligence. The ability to extract high amounts of data from the web as quickly as possible is called "Web Scraping." Think of it simply as a large scale "CUT" and "PASTE" process.

Google regularly uses web scraping to analyze, rank, and index search content. Many companies also carry out contact scraping, which is when they scrape the web for contact information to be used for marketing purposes. If you've ever granted a company access to your contacts in exchange for using their services, then you've given them permission to do just this. When web scraping process is automated, the term Robotic Process Automation (RPA) is used. Web scraping with Robotic Process Automation (RPA) utilizes bots to automate the process of web data extraction from selected websites and store it for use. RPA delivers faster results by eliminating the need for manual data entry and reducing human errors.

There are free web scraping tools available like Parsehub or Extract.pics. You may want to experiment to see how they work. Let's look at one of these and see how we can apply it to our case example Landis Car Hire.

The website www.extract.pics is a free site that lets you extract unstructured data, like images, through a simple "point and click" method by simply entering the URL for the web page.

Figure 8-23. www.extract.pics site

This seems like a pretty simple thing to do, but the process used is key to extracting data from the large Internet depository. We can use software robots to record ourselves doing manual and tedious activities through many digital systems to create "BOTs." The BOTs, when activated, then mimic the recorded information. The five areas where RPA is used are for high volume, repetitive, labor-intensive, rules based, and low variance (routine) tasks.

There are many low-code tools to enable this, including UI path, Blue Prism, Automation Anywhere, and MS Power Automate.

Figure 8-24. Tasks to Automate with RPA

- Extracting data for competitor analysis
- Pulling stock prices for investment decisions
- Extracting information for brand and company monitoring
- Gathering social media data to understand customers' views and mindsets
- Build up sales contact details

Let's now try to extract multiple images. We we can then use them in a database for object detection. Let's apply this web scraping technique to extract image data.

Building Up a Luggage Detector for Landis Car Hire

We want to apply digital tools to help Landis Hire Customer Care and Sales Teams identify large packages from smaller packages. The opportunity to identify packages can help to upsell larger cars to customers to fit their luggage. It can also help to sort out the luggage left in cars to support customers.

The first thing they need to do is to train an algorithm to classify image data so that it can recognize luggage bags from anything else. Let's use the website www.extract.pics to do this.

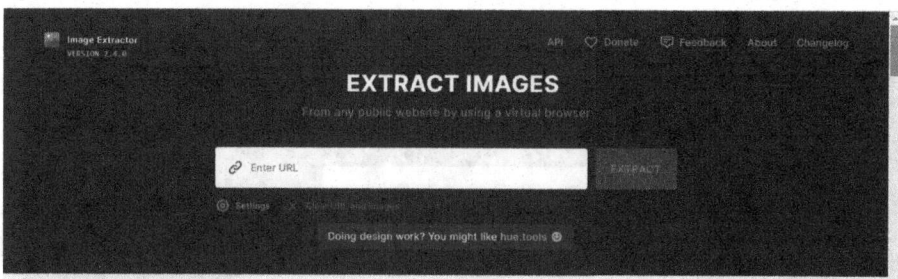

Figure 8-25. `www.extract.pics` Site

By building up a large volume set of image data, Landis can then train a Neural network to detect the object by recognizing the shape. By simply entering the website into the field, the BOT will start the image extraction process in five stages. For this example, we can go to Amazon and enter a search for the images. In this example, I have extracted hundreds of images from an Amazon search on the term "luggage." When we do the search, there are a lots of unnecessary words around the images. Using a select, cut, and paste approach will take hours to do, but by using the web scraping digital tool, we can do this in a matter of seconds.

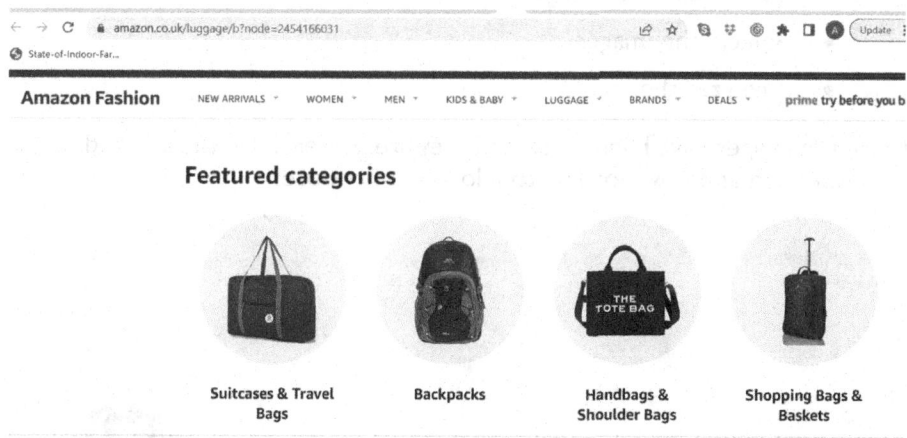

Figure 8-26. Amazon Site on Luggage Products

The first thing to do is paste the Amazon URL for the images into the data field.

Figure 8-27. Extracting Images

When we select the green button next to the URL field, the extraction process begins.

The 5-stage image extraction algorithm follows the process as follows:

- Creates a virtual browser
- Loads the URL
- Scrolls down the page
- Selects the images
- Analyzes the Images

Once the images have been extracted they are presented in the site and ready for inspection and downloading to a location I choose.

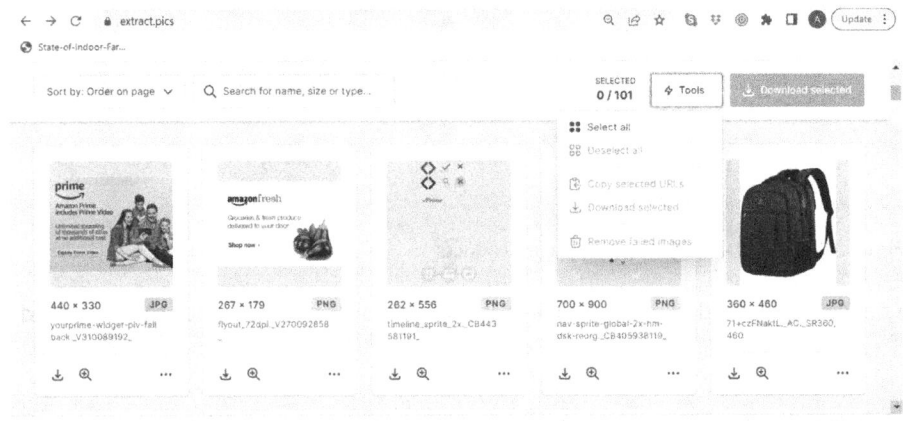

Figure 8-28. Initial Extraction with Anomalies

An important stage is to check the data and remove anything that looks inconsistent with the brief. A data analyst can assist with refining the request if there are too many anomalies. Once we are ready, we can download the data to a file.

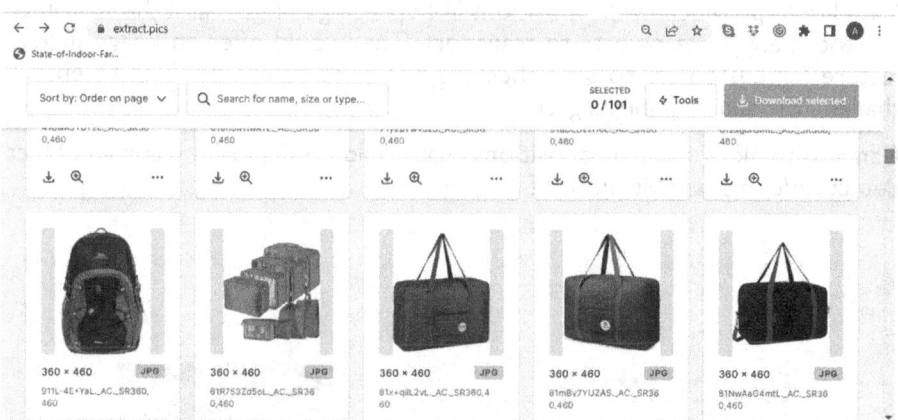

Figure 8-29. Image Data with Anomalies Removed

By selecting on the "Tools" option, I can select/deselect images to download. Once ready, by clicking the "Download" button at the top of the screen a ZIP file of the selected images as JPEGs is created. This image data is used to train the algorithm. With a sufficiently high volume of images, the algorithm should be able to provide a likelihood of the image being scanned as being a large item on not. It does this by providing a probability. The greater the images extracted the greater confidence the algorithm will have.

This simple process of building data sets through data mining by data extraction is how web scraping works. Once we automate processes like this, we enter the world of process mining. Many industry processes are being automated using process mining systems. Let us now see how we can use our image set to carry out object detection.

Landis Car Hire Luggage Detection

A simple way to understand object detection is by using Google Teachable Machine (www.teachablemachine.withgoogle.com). It is a web-based tool that makes creating and understanding machine learning models easy, and accessible to anyone. We can train a computer to recognize images, sounds, and poses without writing any machine learning code. We can then export the model and host it on Teachable Machine, so you can call it into any website or app. The location is www.teachablemachine.withgoogle.com. Try and have a go at experimenting with the tool. It is also excellent in computer vision, using the camera on your device. By playing with these toolsets, they allow us to explore new ideas without relying on other internal resources. For the Landis Car Hire, I have uploaded image files to train the machine on what is a large object and what is a small object. It could potentially allow Landis Car Hire to provide new propositions like upselling a larger car if the customer has too many large objects to transport. They could offer an image upload feature for customers to scan their luggage sizes before booking to ensure that the car can fit their luggage.

Can you think of other propositions that could be deployed using an object detection/computer vision tool?

Figure 8-30. Google Teachable Machine

Created by Google for internal company use, it uses a script called "TensorFlow."

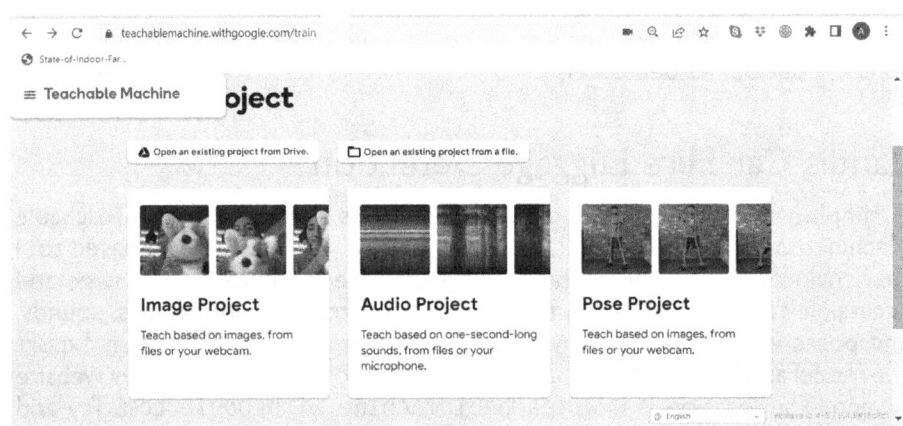

Figure 8-31. Three Detection Features Available

The models you make with Teachable Machine are real TensorFlow.js models that you see automatically produced while you do the training and object detection, but fortunately the machine requires no coding experience to do the object detection as it automatically creates the code. TensorFlow is fully capable of doing other things like recognizing places in images, offering on-point translations, providing accurate search results, and accurately identifying voices. Your data scientist associates may be using it for these purposes. The Teachable machine works in three steps: Gather, Train, and Export.

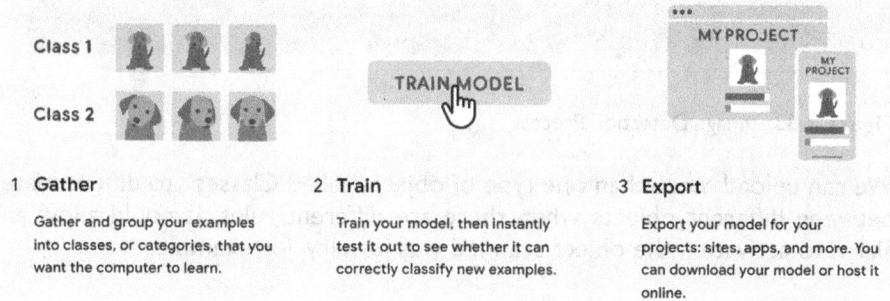

Figure 8-32. Google Teachable Machine 3-Stage Process

This three stage process is the process used to build the neural network. The greater the training images, the more effective will be the neural network.

The platform allows you train the model using images from a file or from a camera. In the previous section, we scraped images using www.extract.pics. Let us now upload these images to the Teachable machine and see if it can detect luggage from other smaller objects.

When we start the Gather stage, select "image project." We then select "standard image project" and the machine will open up a menu for us to upload our image files.

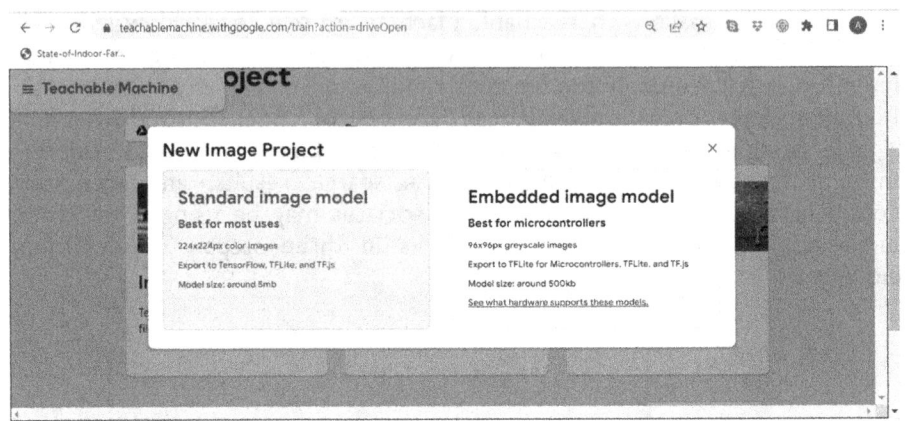

Figure 8-33. Image Detection Process

We can upload more than one type of object "called Classes" to differentiate between different objects when there are different rules. It could allow an alarm to activate if the object scanned was jewelry, for example.

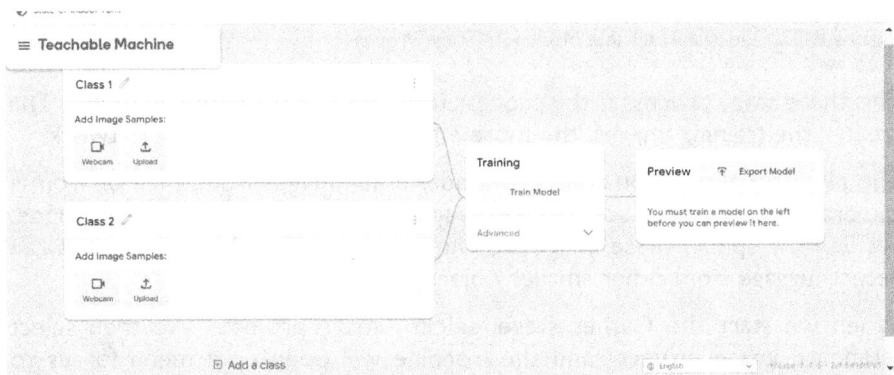

Figure 8-34. File Upload Screen into Class I

To gather the information, we simply upload the image samples to the Class. In this scenario, we are using luggage images in the Class named "large objects" and all other images in the class named "small objects." We can easily rename the class fields as "small" and "large" objects in the edit field.

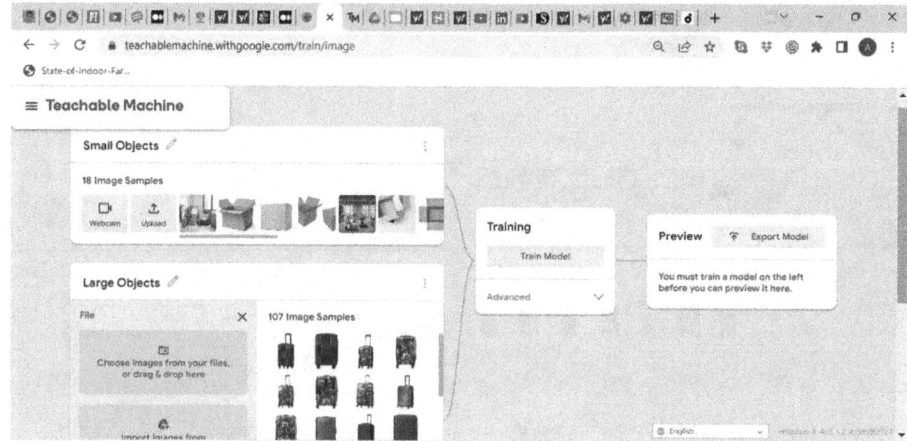

Figure 8-35. Upload of Image Files

When we upload the file into the machine, it processes the unstructured content to identify the images and uploads them as image samples. I then scan another URL of objects that I named small objects into the machine.

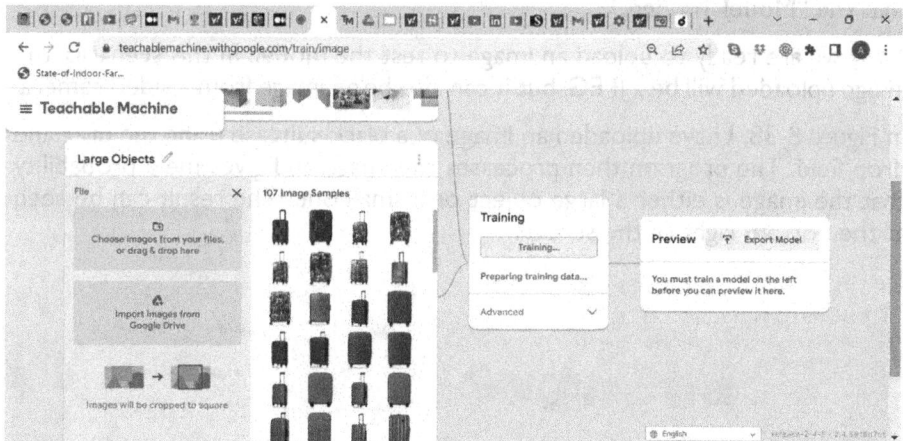

Figure 8-36. Upload of Web scraped Luggage Images

When the "Training" icon is selected the machine starts to classify the information and derives learnings about the images using artificial intelligence algorithms.

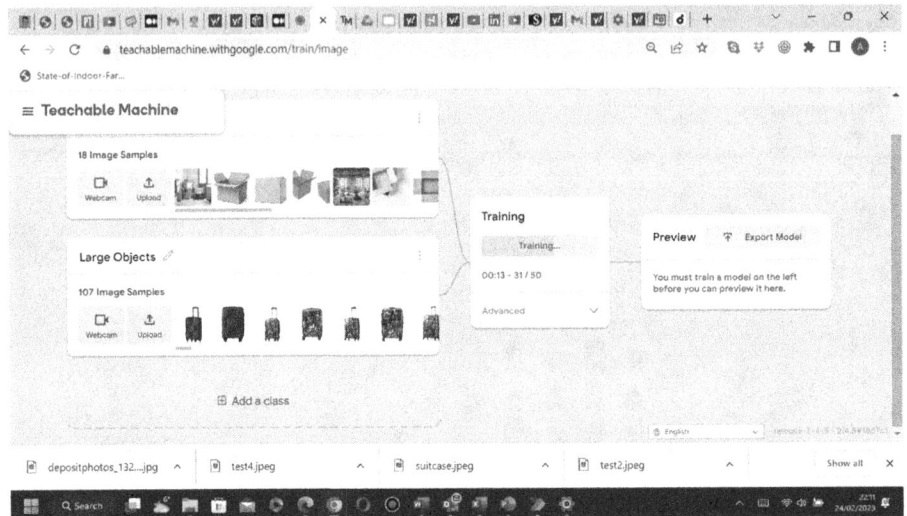

Figure 8-37. Training Process

This may take some time, depending on the data volume and the complexity of the images. Once the training is complete, the machine updates and states that the "Model Trained."

Now we are ready to upload an image to test the model. In this scenario, the image uploaded will be a JPEG, but it can also be an image from a video camera.

In Figure 8-38, I have uploaded an image of a black suitcase using the drag and drop field. The program then processes the image and gives me a probability that the image is either a large object or a small one. The result can be seen at the bottom right of the screen.

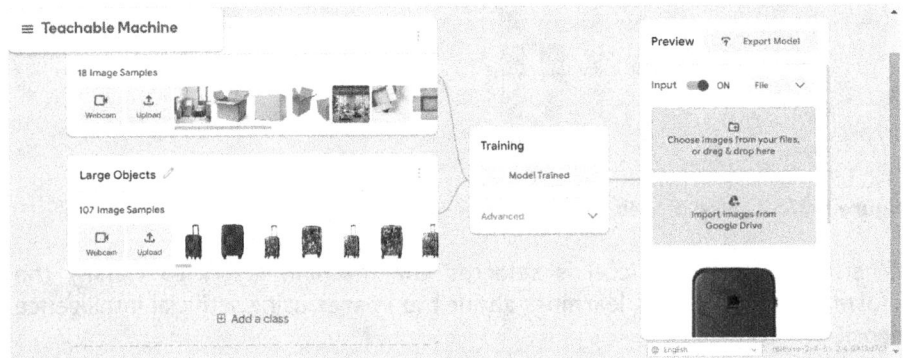

Figure 8-38. Testing of Object Detection with a Sample Image

Figure 8-39. Outcome of Detection

When I change the object under test to a parcel, the machine provides a prediction in the output. In this case, it has predicted it is a small object.

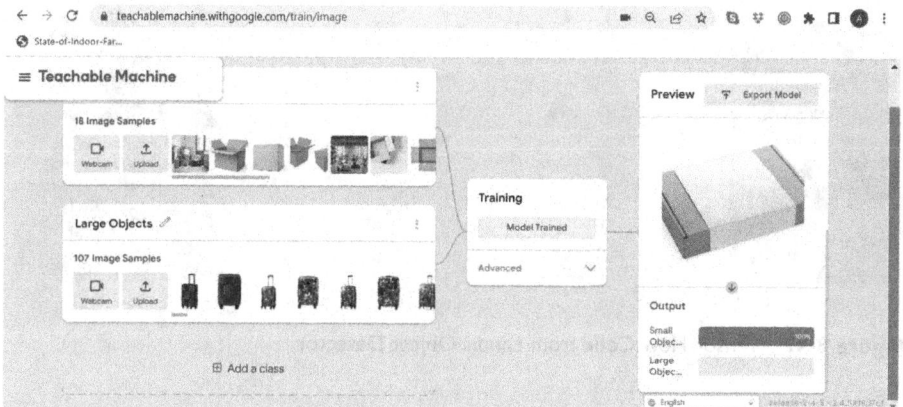

Figure 8-40. Testing for a Small Object

Once we are happy with the tests, we can publish the machine and use it for object detection.

Figure 8-41. Model Ready for Export

Through the upload and point and click approach, we have automatically created the code to do the object detection.

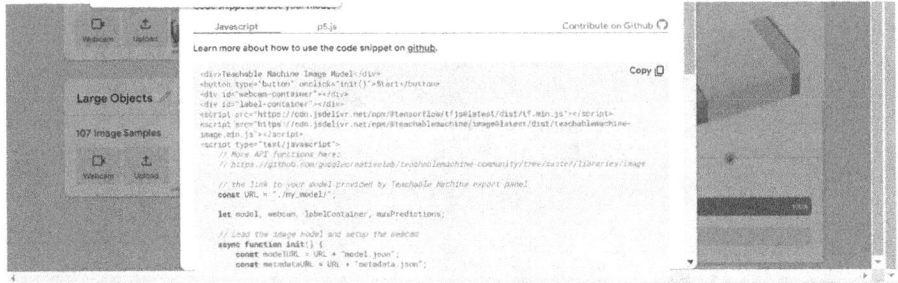

Figure 8-42. Tensor Flow Code from Landis Object Detector

Processing Automatically Customer Feedback Through AI-Driven Automation

We discussed earlier how web scraping and RPA can help automate some of the mundane processes we may need to do to mine web data. The types of algorithms can also help to simplify our everyday processes. If you recall, we used Power BI to create data visualizations. From the same "Power Suite" is Power Automate. Power Automate has a very rich (may be too rich!) feature set for automation, but uses the same screen and menu style as Power BI. Within Power Automate is AI Builder which is a one-stop point that provides many ready-made AI models which are designed to optimize business processes. With AI Builder, you don't need any coding or data science skills to try some of the machine learning methods we discussed. Some of the things you can do using ready-made machine learning algorithms are extract information from invoices, classify feedback, predict performance, and also understand positive or negative sentiment from text.

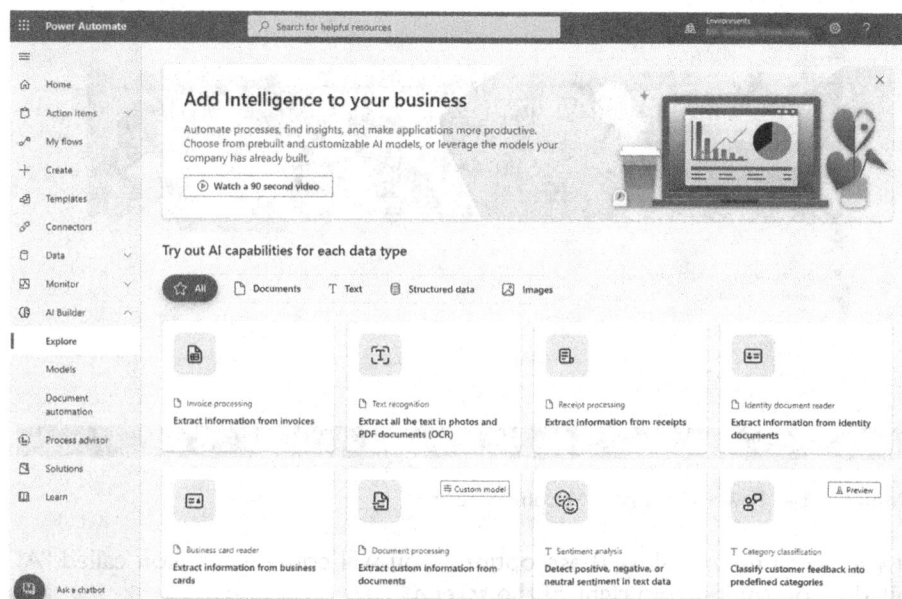

Figure 8-43. Ready-Made AI Tools in Power Automate

By visiting this site, you can try many of these to see the power of these AI tools. Any user can get a free 30-day trial of the services of the Power Apps. It may also be available as part of a subscription with Office 365. Power Automate itself is an automation tool that allows users to automate repetitive tasks. It calls these automations – "Flows." The creation of these flows is out of the scope of this book.

Let's now try these templates to read and assess text.

Analyzing Customer Feedback from Landis Car Hire Online Feedback Service

Let's take a scenario where Landis Car Hire have received feedback from their helpdesk and want to analyze the sentiment. The AI builder will allow us to do this using no-code techniques. If you delve into Power Automate, you will discover it also has the capabilities to automate a standard reply letter or sort the responses into a data base for client management, which can really save on time and resources.

Once you select the Power Automate icon, you are presented with a number of options.

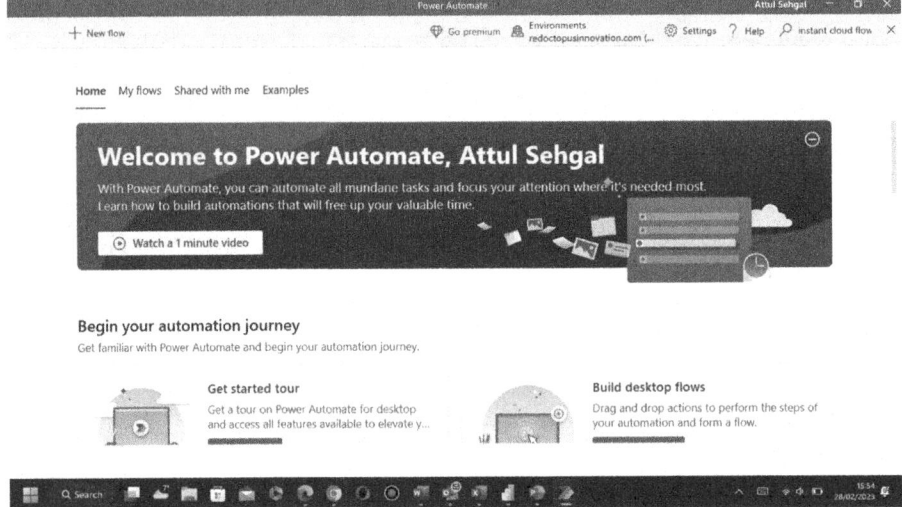

Figure 8-44. Power Automate Welcome Screen

If you scroll down below these options, you will come to an icon called "AI builder" on the bottom right of the screen.

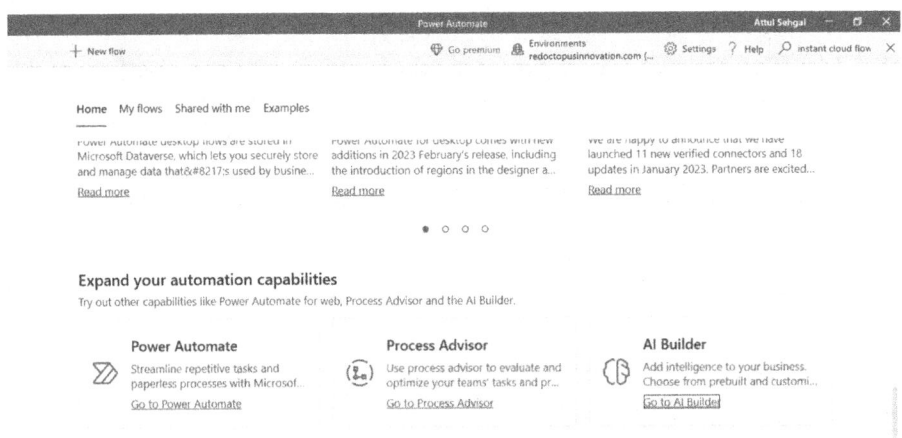

Figure 8-45. AI Builder

When you select this icon, it opens up a new menu with "AI Builder" in the list and a sub-menu.

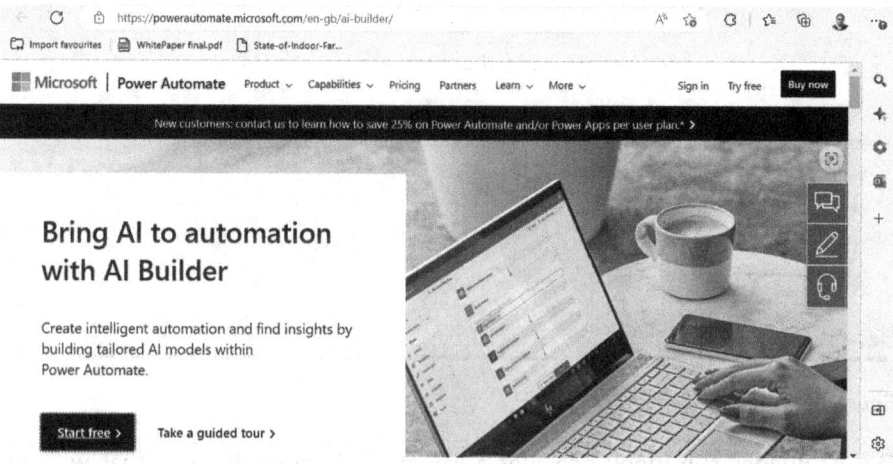

Figure 8-46. AI Builder Front Page

When you scroll, you will see some of the AI tools that the builder has available and scrolling further down you will come to the free trial for AI builder.

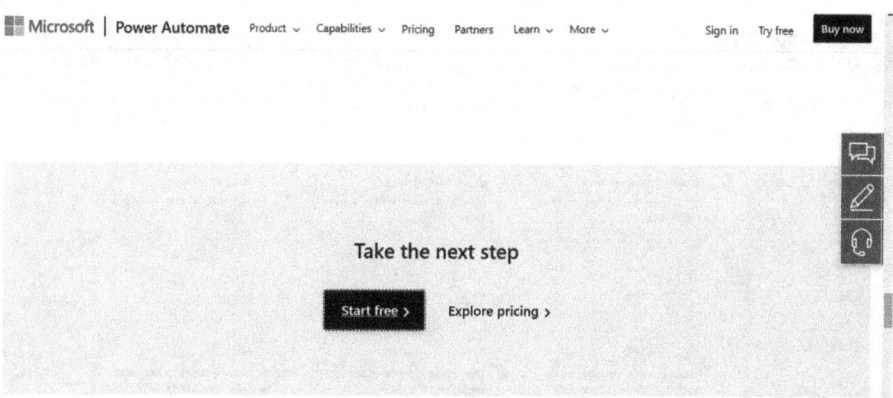

Figure 8-47. Entry into AI Builder

Once you select this, a new screen will open up. On the left side of the menu is an icon called AI builder with a sub-menu. The main screen is the Power Automate screen.

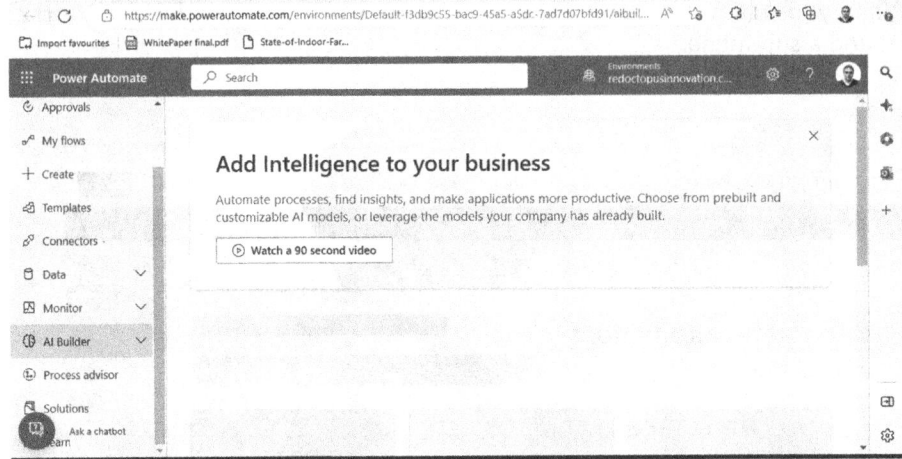

Figure 8-48. Home Screen

The AI Builder sub-menu provides a list of 15 AI prebuilt tools that we can use. Each module has a tutorial that explains how the feature works so feel free to explore. If we now select the AI template for *"Detect positive and negative sentiment in text data"* and apply it to our Landis Car Hire Example, let's see what happens.

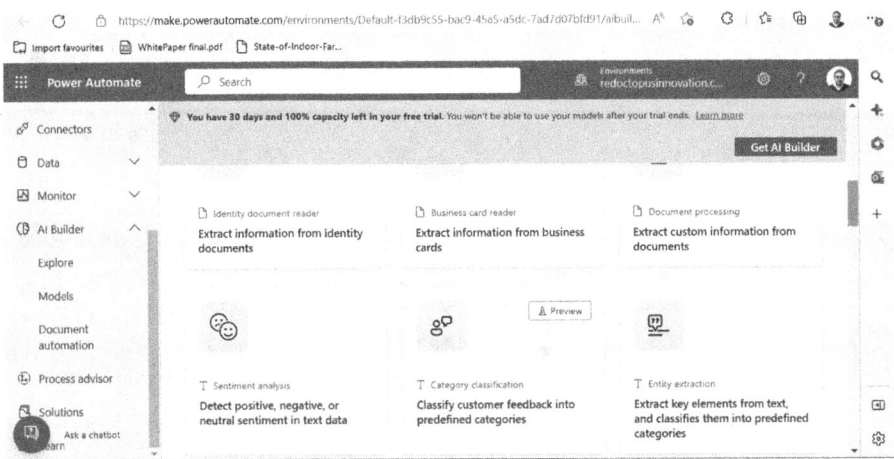

Figure 8-49. AI Builder Options

The screen will open up a new template for us to post our text data. We can upload customer feedback and the sentiment analysis tool will analyze the words to detect a positive, negative, or neutral sentiment in the text.

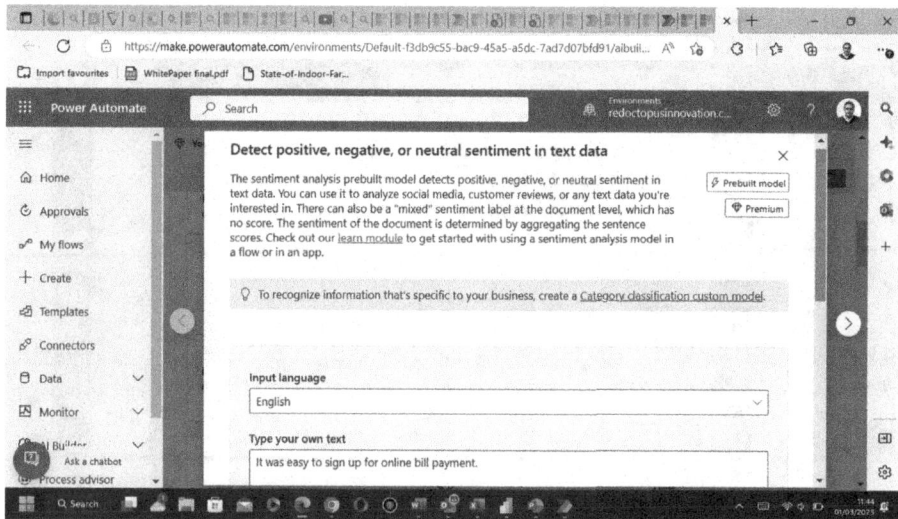

Figure 8-50. *Sentiment Analysis 1*

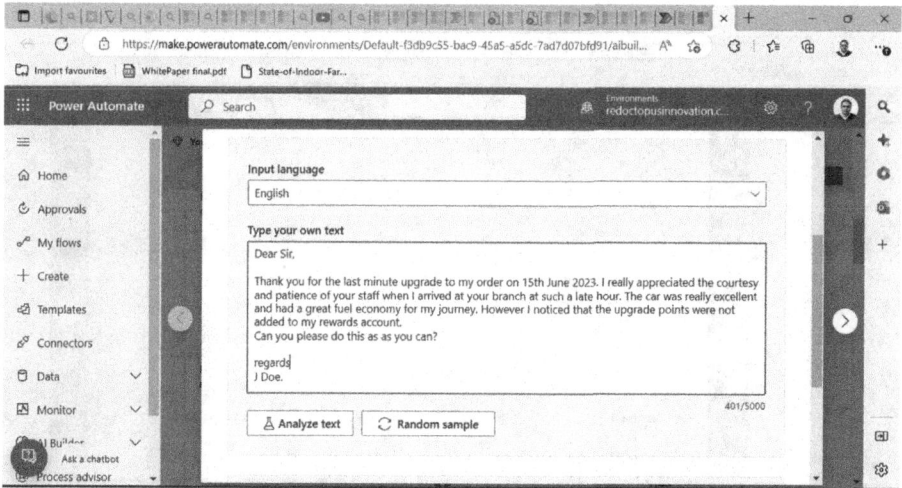

Figure 8-51. *Sentiment Analyzer in Action*

If we now upload or paste our letter into the template and then select the Analyze text icon, the algorithm will present a confidence score of the sentiment. In the following example, the score is 100% positive.

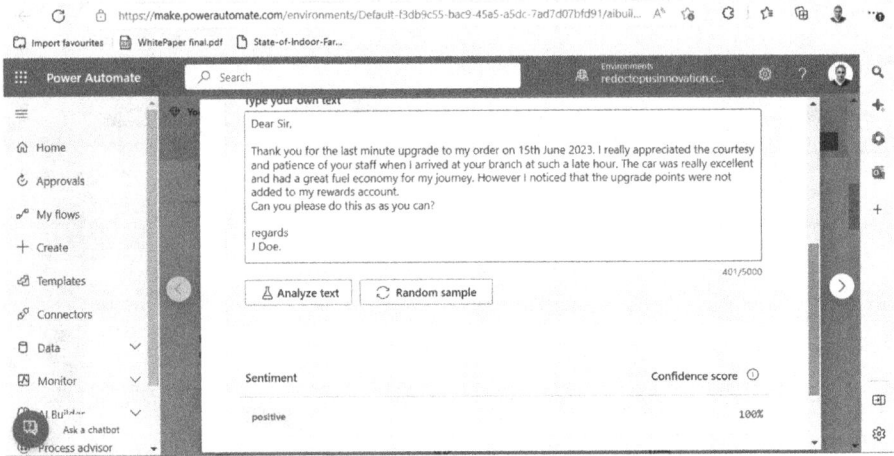

Figure 8-52. Sentiment Analysis Step 1

If we enter another feedback, we can see that the confidence score changes to a negative sentiment.

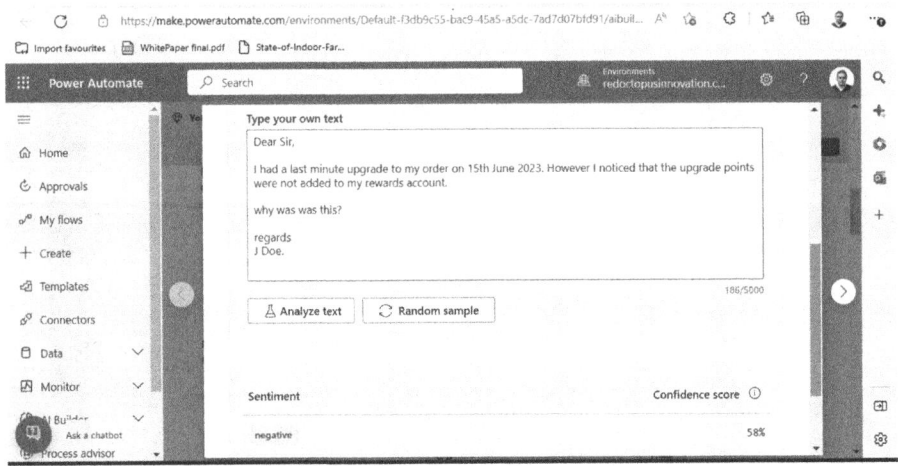

Figure 8-53. Sentiment Analysis 2

By changing a few words on the earlier message, the sentiment has changed from a negative to a positive rating. It does flag that by blindly pursuing the recommendation, it could lead to problems. From the broad understanding of machine learning algorithms, feel free to push back to your developers to understand the sentiment algorithm and how it could be improved. Don't just trust the algorithm will produce the right answer!

Can you think of the reasons why the change in confidence occurred?

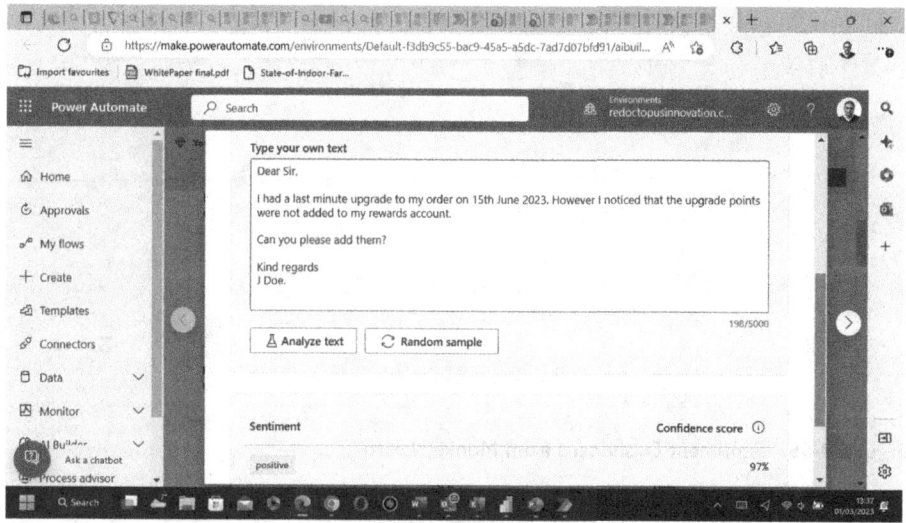

Figure 8-54. A positive sentiment by changing a few words

The problem most likely lies in the source data. Perhaps the bias to certain key words from the sentiment word table is not quite right. On testing, it doesn't mean you have to agree with the model output and this is where we need to query the output. There are many other free AI0505driven sentiment analysis tools available online like MonkeyLearn, Hubspot, and Brandwatch that you may want to try before making a decision on which one you prefer. They may have different biases or source word inputs.

A challenge with no-code can be the inability to track back and work out why the tool gave a particular response. Fortunately with sentiment tools it is quite clear.

Many of the of the other tools have data visualization tools to help in analysis too. Here is a screenshot of a Sentiment Dashboard from MonkeyLearn.

Figure 8-55. Sentiment Dashboard from Monkey Learn

Human-Like Conversations with Natural Language Processing Tools

ChatGPT is a natural language processing tool driven by AI technology that allows you to have human-like conversations and much more with a chatbot. There really hasn't been this much excitement in tech since the iPhone and the hype is permeating the main stream. The language model can answer questions, and assist you with tasks such as composing emails, essays, and code. It doesn't know what it is saying, it is basically using a predictive model trained on a data set of lots of words to predict the next word when prompted correctly. The technology is smarter than humans in generating text and it can analyze a 500 word book in a matter of seconds!

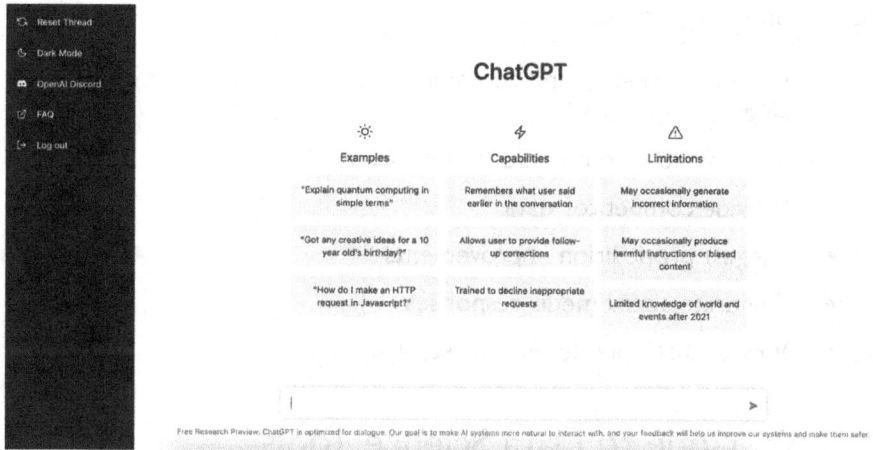

Figure 8-56. ChatGPT3 Examples, Capabilities and Limitations as Described by ChatGPT

You can try ChatGPT simply by visiting chat.openai.com and creating an OpenAI account. Once you sign in, you are able to start chatting away with ChatGPT. Try and get your conversation started by asking a question.

Microsoft recently announced that OpenAI's next-level chatbot tech is going to be integrated into both Bing and Microsoft's web browser Edge. As a counter, Google Bard is an AI chatbot, similar to ChatGPT and just like ChatGPT, it is powered by a language model to converse with users.

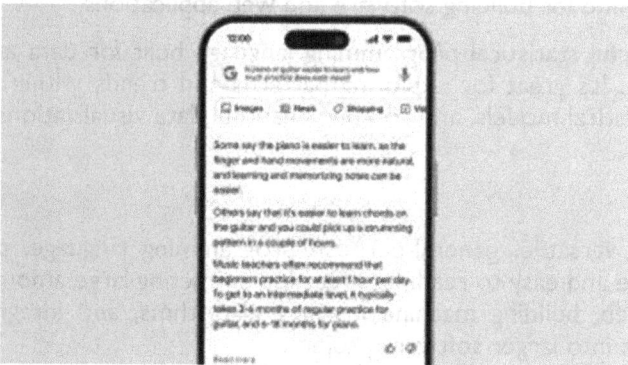

Figure 8-57. Google Bard

Can you think of ways it can help Landis Car Hire company improve its operations?

Here are some suggestions:

- Provide marketing and communications material in many languages
- Identify most common questions from clients
- Provide competitor data
- Suggest proposition improvements
- Generate social media responses
- Virtual customer service assistant

From No-Code to Data Science Tools

Although you won't need to do the coding itself, having a broad understanding of the languages your data scientists counterparts will use can always help.

Programming Languages Used for Large Scale Data Science Projects

R

At a high level, R is a programming language designed specifically for working with data. Python is a general-purpose programming language, used widely for data science and for building software and web applications.

R is a powerful statistical programming language built for data analysis and data science. It's great for exploring patterns and trends within your data, building statistical models, and creating beautiful data visualizations.

Python

Python is a versatile, general-purpose programming language, praised for being concise and easy to read. It's great for extracting large amounts of data from the web, building machine learning algorithms, and integrating data science tasks into larger software projects.

For any large data science project, you need to download separate packages. Some key packages to know are pandas and Numpy for data manipulation, Matplotlib and seaborn for visualizing data, and SciPy, scikit-learn and statsmodels for hypothesis testing and model fitting.

With many libraries being created for data science, Python has become a growing language within the data science world.

SQL

SQL (can be pronounced "sequel" or S.Q.L.) is a language used by data scientists to query data bases. The query could be for finding data, updating, deleting information. It is used in conjunction with R and Python so a data scientist might write an SQL query to pull specific data from a company database based on conditions outlined in the query. Then, they can use their Python or R skills to perform deeper analysis using the dataset their SQL query fetched.

Comparison of Packages Used by Data Scientists

While we may not need to get too involved in the data science exercise itself, there are packages that are commonly used that may get discussed in any data science engagement, Here is a high level list of the most common packages and their application.

Factors	Data Mining	Machine Learning
1. Scope	Data mining is used to find out how different attributes of a data set are related to each other through patterns and data visualization techniques.	Machine learning is used for making predictions of the outcome such as price estimate or time duration approximation.
	The goal of data mining is to find out relationship between 2 or more attributes of a dataset and use this to predict outcomes or actions.	It automatically learns the model with experience over time. It provides real time feedback.
2. Working	Data mining is the technique of digging deep into data to take out useful information.	Machine learning is method of improving complex algorithms to make machines near to perfect by iteratively feeding it with trained dataset.
3. Uses	Data mining is more often used in research field such as web mining, text mining, fraud detection.	Machine learning has more uses in making recommendations of products, prices, estimating the time required for delivery, etc.

(continued)

Factors	Data Mining	Machine Learning
4. Concept	The concept behind mining is to extract information using techniques and find out the trends and patterns.	Machine learning runs on the concept that machines learn from existing data and learns and improves by itself. Machine learning uses data mining methods and algorithms to build models on logic behind data which predict the future outcome. The algorithms are built on Math and programming languages.
5. Method	Data mining will perform analysis in Batch format at a particular time to produce results rather than on continuous basis.	Machine learning uses the data mining technique to improve its algorithms and change its behavior to future inputs. Thus data mining acts as an input source for machine learning.

Machine learning algorithms will continuously run and improve the performance of system automatically, also analyze when the failure can occur.

When there is some new data or change in trend, the machine will incorporate the changes without need to reprogram or human interference. |
| 6. Nature | Data mining requires human intervention for applying techniques to extract information. | Machine learning is different from Data Mining as machine learning learns automatically. |
| 7. Learning Capability | Data mining requires the analysis to be initiated by human thus it is a manual technique. | Machine learning is a step ahead of data mining as it uses the same techniques used by data mining to automatically learn and adapt to changes. It is more accurate then data mining. |

(continued)

Factors	Data Mining	Machine Learning
8. Implementation	Data mining involves building models on which data mining techniques are applied. Models like CRISP-DM model are built.	Machine learning is implemented by using Machine Learning algorithms in artificial intelligence, neural network, neuro fuzzy systems and decision tree, etc.
	Data mining process uses database, data mining engine, and pattern evaluation for knowledge discovery.	Machine learning uses neural networks and automated algorithms to predict outcomes.
9. Accuracy	Accuracy of data mining depends on how data is collected.	Machine learning algorithms are proved to be more accurate than Data Mining techniques
	Data mining produces accurate results which are used by machine learning making machine learning produce better results.	
	Since data mining requires human intervention, it may miss important relationships.	
10. Applications	Relative to machine learning, data mining can produce results on lesser volume of data.	Machine learning algorithm need data to be fed in standard format, due to which the algorithms available are limited.
		To analyze data using machine learning, data from multiple sources should be moved from native format to standard format for the machine to understand.
		Also it requires large amounts of data for accurate results
11. Examples	Places where data mining is used is in identifying sales patterns or trends, by cellular companies for customer retention and so on.	Machine learning is used in running marketing campaigns, for medical diagnosis, image recognition, etc.

Way Forward

Through various case examples and an immersion into big data, data mining, and algorithms, we have covered the fundamentals of digital transformation.

The rise of app-driven and automated culture has opened new ways for how we can all work with data. The tools and statistical methods employed by data scientists can often appear unfamiliar to those without technical backgrounds. Fortunately, there are tools now available to bridge the comprehension gap between data scientists' methods and non-technical individuals. This not only enables us to produce descriptive reports but also empowers us to make predictions and recommendations ourselves. The tutorial highlights a light on a few of the tools available, but try to explore new tools as they come along. Figure 8-1 shows a snapshot of the categories of these tools.

Embracing statistical methods can greatly enhance our ability to work with data. Utilizing these practical user-friendly tools while having a basic grasp of statistics allows us to explore new data-driven opportunities. However, it's important to note that many of these tools operate on a no-code basis, which can pose challenges in terms of transparency and interpretability. As we've seen with sentiment analysis, algorithmic biases can influence the outcomes, making it essential for non-technical stakeholders to be willing to raise concerns and seek clarification.

In the upcoming section, we will delve into the ethical use of data and algorithms, their consequences, and the imperative for non-technical executives when leading digital transformation engagements.

Balancing Digital Transformation with Ethical Values

Introduction

Over the previous chapters, we have looked at how digital transformation has rewritten the rules of how we conduct ourselves in business and in our daily lives. We have discussed the power of data and how data mining and algorithms can help us retrieve, process, predict, and prescribe to help us stay ahead.

© Attul Sehgal 2024
A. Sehgal, *Demystifying Digital Transformation*,
https://doi.org/10.1007/978-1-4842-9499-4_9

How social media can help consumers hit back at traditional big brand through building their own following and how building digital platforms has allowed new companies to create new business opportunities to established market places.

We know that digital transformation is not just for digital natives but also for traditional brands that can adapt themselves to create real transformations like DBS Bank and Domino Pizza, but there are many casualties who do not respond to change like Blockbuster, HMV or Kodak. We saw that with lots of data available, there are many different types of algorithms we can use to build effective insights. Like linear regression helps us to predict, clustering algorithms to classify objects, or neural networks to learn from random data and prescribe solutions.

By looking at digital roadmaps, we saw technologies can be hyped to produce real market excitement, but also can create distraction and confusion to business owners at the same time. In Chapter 4, we looked at ways to apply them to improving business outcomes. Big data as the driving force has slowly transformed the ways we build relationships, understand our markets, and work with our partners in ways never seen before. In fact, data, algorithms with mobile phones have gradually become very indispensable in how we manage our lives and think about the future. The way we can use data to help us make reliable decisions makes algorithm-driven technologies key tools for today.

Despite things being mathematically driven and needing programming skills, we have seen that there are "no code tools" that enable even non-technical business executives to be digitally driven, and more productive. These tools can help us engage more easily with our technical counterparts and make wiser decisions on new technology investment.

If you recall, we discussed at the beginning that digital transformation is more than just a technology overlay but cover many aspects including empowered customers, continuous data, rapid innovation, evolving propositions, and fluid competition. If applied correctly, it can deliver on the business problems we are trying to address. Today there is a high risk of digital transformation engagements failing to reach business expectations and, with the wrong data used in algorithms, can create wrong decisions that can affect people's lives. As business owners, should digital transformation really be at any cost? Who should look after our ethical values on use of data?

In this chapter, we will try to answer these questions by looking at a case example where society was affected by unfair outcomes from an algorithm, understanding how ethical principles are implemented today in our digital services, how big tech stacks up to being self-regulated, and understand how society is regulating data and AI.

Let's start by defining ethics and looking at how digital transformation (DX) accelerated over the recent pandemic.

DX Acceleration Over the Pandemic

The term "Ethics" is derived from the Greek word "ethos" which can mean custom, habit, character, or disposition. It covers the questions of how to live a good life, our rights and responsibilities, what is right or wrong, and what is good or bad. It is a basic principle for how we engage with each other. With data-driven decision-making, how should ethics play a role in our digital transformation engagements? Could legislation help us

- Ensure fairness for customers?
- Ensure big data is used responsibly?
- Competitors play on a level playing field?
- Innovation is tested before being put in front of real customers?
- Value propositions are more clearly thought out?

To start, let's look at how digital transformation positively helped society during the recent pandemic.

We cannot ignore the major effect the recent Covid pandemic had in accelerating digital transformation in our day-to-day lives, changing the mindsets of organizations and individuals who were actively encouraged to approach work and business relationships through remote digital techniques. We had to adapt using remote communication tools to stay connected with friends and family. Some of these digital apps became essential as we actively downloaded used symptom trackers and digital certificates to track our location and symptoms to alert others. Organizations realized that through these tools, they were able to be more autonomous, flexible, and manage worker's time more effectively despite the pandemic restrictions. From virtual offices, video conferencing tools, messaging, remote project management tools facilitated collaborative ways to engage and serve the customers during the lockdown and some of these are now firmly part of our post-pandemic world.

In fact, over the pandemic, it was shown that a typical employer could save an average of $11,000 per half-time telecommuter per year, in terms of increased productivity, lower real estate costs, reduced absenteeism, and turnover. (https://hub.jhu.edu/2020/07/27/digital-technology-in-business-joel-le-bon/)

The speed of digital transformation was phenomenal as organizations adapted digital strategies planned to take place over years to transformations happening in a matter of months – much to the delight of the service providers. We saw earlier the results of a McKinsey survey of the expected days needed by various companies to changes in digital transformation and what actually happened during the pandemic. (Source: `www.mckinsey.com/capabilities/ strategy-and-corporate-finance/our-insights/how-covid-19-has- pushed-companies-over-the-technology-tipping-point-and- transformed-business-forever`)

The graph showed that remote working was expected to take 454 days but actually took only 10.5 days. Online purchasing was expected to take 585 days, but only took 21.9 days. The ways that algorithms are used in business decision-making was supposed to take 635 days but actually took 25.4 days with an acceleration factor of 25!

It is clear that these changes were absolutely necessary for economies to survive while the pandemic played out. At the same time, were business owners running blind to the potential consequences of digital technology in our society?

Before we look at this:

- Did digital transformation improve your life during the pandemic?
- Were you comfortable with the speed of change?
- Did you trust the tools you were working with?

Your Algorithm Doesn't Know Me!

Figure 9-1. Protests Against an Algorithm and Its Use

We just saw how the recent pandemic created a sharp acceleration in efforts to introduce more digital tools but also introduce more digitally driven forms of decision-making. This was across all sectors, even in public services. In the UK, it provided a reason for government authorities to implement new digital systems as tools for the common good. However, something happened with one of these systems that attracted unwanted society backlash at the time which reverberated nationally, leading to the resignations of the business owners. Figure 9-1 shows one of the demonstrations that took place at the time.

Let's look into what happened.

Every year in the UK, around 700,000 teenage students take public exams that are assessed to decide on their future career. They are normally paper exams that are assessed by external examiners. During the pandemic, however, a whole cohort of Year 11 (16-yr-olds) and Year 13 (18-yr-olds) students were not able to take exams in exam halls because of the virus. Doing remote exams was not practical.

The UK Department of Education and a UK government agency, Ofqual, decided the most practical way was to issue predicted grades for each individual student using data-driven algorithms. The approach seemed quite straight-forward to the authorities. By mining the performance from the previous years of the particular school, the sociodemographic of the neighborhood, the exam subject and trends in previous years, and the teacher's individual assessment, the result could be computed. The scores would then be issued to the students as their final grade, thus removing the need to sit for exams.

The mined data inputs would be entered into a "black box" where an algorithm would compute the final grade decision. The method used is summarized in Figure 9-2, which shows how historical data is fed and then adjusted, then ranking applied to the education center, the subject taken, and then the individual. Deploying complex algorithms to decide on commercial decisions are nothing new. They are used industrially for issuing credit scores to customers, upselling products and mining data, but deciding on an individual's life decision is a big step.

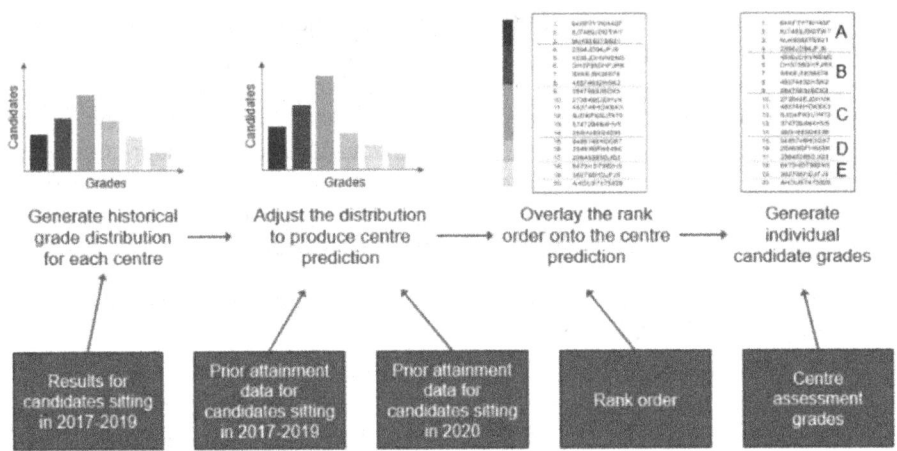

Figure 9-2. Process Overview

Eleven algorithms were considered for fairness and accuracy and an "ensemble algorithm" was selected. Ensemble algorithms have very high levels of accuracy and are a mixture of different machine learning algorithms. However, they present a challenge for being hard to detect any biased or incorrect calculation. Linear regression and decision trees could have been used but they have a much lower performance despite being easier to track back on the reasoning behind the decision. Figure 9-3 shows a broad comparison of some of the machine learning algorithms. At the end of the day, it could be a business decision on which algorithm would be used.

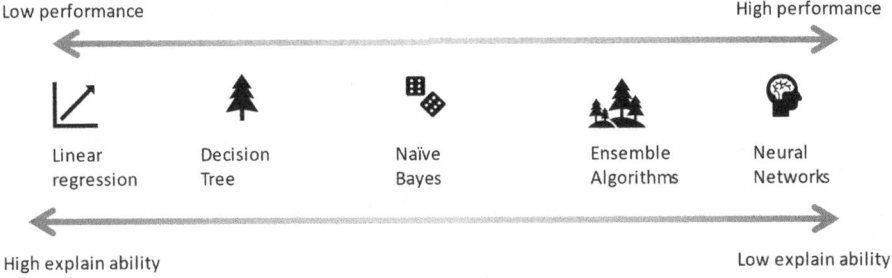

Figure 9-3. Performance and Explain-ability Comparison of Machine Learning Algorithms

From a data science point of view, the algorithm produced a fair result and did what it was supposed to do. The grades were not unduly high or low compared with previous years. However, there were some anomalies – less than a quarter of 1%. According to The Guardian's report, the process anomalies meant some bright children in deprived areas lost out in university places. The student and the algorithm: how the exam results fiasco threatened one pupil's future | Education | The Guardian

Ofqual was concerned enough about potential anomalies to send a memo to the Prime Minister's office, noting "the risks of disadvantage to outlier students". Despite these concerns, the approach was approved. The applicant volume had to be processed rapidly and accurately in time for the new academic year and this process was the way to do it. On scrutiny, some of the reasons were due to the same inherent biases found in the mined data similar to the Amazon example we discussed in Chapter 6.

When Ofqual published the grades for the academic year, the CEO of Ofqual stated: "Some students may think that, had they taken their exams, they would have achieved higher grades. We will never know." This triggered a public outcry with demonstrations like those shown in Figure 9-4. Once the algorithmic process had been decided, there is then a sense of powerlessness in challenging the algorithm. This created real problems with any appeals resulting from the published grades. Similar to the Amazon example, questions were raised on whether historical patterns on race and gender were then replicated in the data, giving the data set then an air of detached certainty and objectivity. (Source: www.aiimi.com/insights/2020-grading-algorithm-understanding-what-went-wrong) To have provided an appeals process, would it have been safer to have used a more explainable algorithm at the expense of accuracy like a decision tree?

Figure 9-4. Student Protests at Government Offices in London: Source: CNN

There were protests at schools and at government building. The BBC reported that the Prime Minister blamed everything on a "mutant algorithm." (www.bbc.co.uk/news/education-53923279) The overall impression was that the people in charge had implemented a solution without knowing what was really going on.

A real example was published for the case of a teenager achieving top grades at the age of 16, only to face parents who separate and has to relocate to a different postal area with a less academically successful school just before university exams, which highlights the problems of the algorithmic evaluation process. This situation underscores the critical human element which is needed.

Today algorithms are used in the background to make decisions on our lives without our knowledge, but this algorithmic process was played out in public view and so the consequences were highly visible. In this scenario, the business stakeholders, the Education Minister, and the Prime Minister took responsibility.

With such public pressure, the Education Secretary had to ditch the process and use teacher predictions for each student instead.

It was felt that the government's algorithm approach appeared to devalue things that are human. "What this has shown is that people really care about individual justice," says Reuben Binns, an associate professor of human-centered computing at the University of Oxford. People want the decisions about their lives to be personal and not based on historical data, over which they have no control. One size doesn't fit all and people are mostly concerned with their own individual results and the fairness of them. (The lessons we all must learn from the A-levels algorithm debacle | WIRED UK)

It has also opened up a new dialogue on how governments, local councils, police forces, should use algorithmic systems for decision making. In Nov 2021, the UK launched a standard for algorithmic transparency, which we will discuss later.

This fiasco ended in the government having to revert to a more traditional form of assessment and students getting a fair assessment with appeals if needed.

Unfortunately, this wasn't the first instance of algorithms being used unfairly in public services. Without regulation, our civil liberties are being slowly eroded through digital technology for many years. Here are some examples from 2018.

- In the United States, the American Civil Liberties Union (ACLU) released a report revealing that Amazon's facial recognition software, known as Rekognition, erroneously identified 28 out of the 435 members of Congress as criminals. Additionally, it was found that a disproportionate number of people of color (39%) were flagged as compared to white individuals (5%q). Although Amazon argued that ACLU did not use the software at the recommended tolerance level of 95%, but there is no legal requirement to adhere to this threshold. ACLU had set it at 80%. (Source: "Amazon's facial recognition AI confuses politicians with criminals" on thenextweb.com.)

- In the UK, the "The Verge" magazine reported that the police were comfortable in deploying facial recognition technology even with a 98% failure rate. London police chief "completely comfortable" using facial recognition with 98 percent error rate – The Verge

Doesn't the publicized racial profiling "side effect" mean that Amazon was probably launched/piloted too soon? How do our rights and responsibilities as humans play a part in the digital transformation today? What are the rules from regulators?

Are data firms allowed to push their new technologies without true regard for social responsibility? Would we allow this to happen in other sectors like pharmaceuticals? Approvals in this sector take place over many years to ensure any "side effects" are well understood.

Let's start by looking at the pioneers and their ethical values.

Understanding ethics from the 'Tech Giants'

From the examples given earlier, it seems too easy for data flaws that include bias, unfairness, gender, and ethnic discrimination to be used in commercial algorithms and data outputs that we then use as business owners without fully understanding the real consequences. Why do we trust big tech solutions more than our own intuition?

While this confusion exists, do Internet firms sell our data to any third party anywhere in the world, exploit tax loopholes and destroy local competitors in new markets, make us unhealthily addicted to our smartphones, dupe us into buying things online that we don't need, prioritize what we see on YouTube and Facebook, force us to use only Microsoft tools in our day-to-day and steal our private conversations?

To understand if this really is the case, let's start by seeing how big they are and how important they are for the US economy. Visualcapitalist.com published data from Henrik Bessembinder from Arizona State University in September 2023, that is shown in the following table. He analyzed the 28,114 publicly listed US companies over the last century (1926–2022) to identify the best performing stocks in modern history and the importance of big tech is pretty clear. The top 10 firms are shown in the following table with total lifetime wealth creation, the first month of being on the stock market to the end of December 2022. The performance of big tech is quite startling. Apple, Microsoft, Alphabet, and Amazon all figure in the top 5.

Rank	Company	Lifetime Wealth Creation	First Month	Last Month
1	APPLE	$2.7T	Jan-81	Dec-22
2	MICROSOFT	$2.1T	Apr-86	Dec-22
3	EXXON MOBIL	$1.2T	Jul-26	Dec-22
4	ALPHABET	$1.0T	Sep-04	Dec-22

(continued)

Rank	Company	Lifetime Wealth Creation	First Month	Last Month
5	AMAZON	$764B	Jun-97	Dec-22
6	BERKSHIRE HATHAWAY	$704B	Nov-76	Dec-22
7	JOHNSON & JOHNSON	$661B	Oct-44	Dec-22
8	WALMART	$629B	Dec-72	Dec-22
9	CHEVRON	$583B	Jul-26	Dec-22
10	PROCTER & GAMBLE	$581B	Sep-29	Dec-22

Imagine, on Aug 2, 2018, Apple hit a $1tn market capitalization just 42 years after it was founded! By comparison, it took 117 years for US Steel to become the first company to be valued at $1bn in 1901. Today, through its digital strategy, Apple's market value is higher than Turkey or Switzerland's GDP! Alphabet and Amazon were not far off in $1tn market capitalization either. There is a lot at stake to regulate big tech.

Other regions of the world, like the European Union, have sensed a problem and tried to rein back big tech. However, as President Barack Obama argued in 2016, European regulators were being too aggressive with regulation out of a desire to protect their companies that aren't as capable as Google. He told Re/code in February 2016, "We have owned the Internet. Our companies have created it, expanded it, perfected it, in ways they can't compete." While global regulatory uncertainties continue to be discussed, the market capitalization of big tech continues on an inexorable path.

Let's try and assess whether greater controls really need to be in place by applying our five levers to these companies:

- Value: Do they really practice what they preach in their brand story?

- Competition: Do they permit fair competition?

- Innovation: How much of their profits do they invest in R&D?

- Data: Are they open on how they use our data?

- Customer: Do they use our customer information responsibly?

1. Value – Do They Practice What They Preach?

"I just want you to know that, when we talk about war, we're really talking about peace."

————**George W. Bush (**Doublespeak Quotes (6 quotes) (goodreads.com))

The preceding quote from George W Bush is an example of saying something but doing something else. Doublespeak has been applied to big tech firms in the United States, causing regulators around the world to take notice. Let's look at some examples.

Google – "Don't Be Evil"

There is no doubt that big tech has a way of looking at the world and its problems since their inception is radically differently from the previous generation of firms. Here is Google's well-known simple brand message with a great ethical standpoint from Google. **DON'T BE EVIL.**

Figure 9-5. Google Don't Be Evil. Source: `https://crooksandliars.com/2014/01/hey-google-what-happened-dont-be-evil`

This mantra for corporate values really brings out honesty, fairness, exploitation, and why Google is different. In 2014, Larry Page, the CEO, expressed his frustration with peoples' lack of trust in "big data" companies like his own. "We get so worried about [data privacy] that we don't get the benefits," he said. Everything seems so simple – leave us alone and we can change the world.

The origin of the powerful phrase, according to the 2007 book, Founders at Work, by Jessica Livingston, came from the Gmail inventor, Paul Buchheit, who stated that he coined the phrase during a Google meeting on corporate values, as a way to *"jab at a lot of the other companies, especially our competitors, who at the time, in our opinion, were kind of exploiting the users to some extent."* "We will live up to our *"don't be evil"* principle by keeping user trust and not accepting payment for search results." In the meantime, as a result of customer belief, Figure 9-6 shows how the market cap of Google has grown since 2014.

Market cap history of Alphabet (Google) from 2014 to 2023

Figure 9-6. Growth of Alphabet since 2014

Let's look at some instances to see whether its ethical standpoint has been questioned:

- In 2012, Google settled a fine of $22.5M by breaking a 20-year privacy promise by tracking customers on the iPhone safari browser. It could target adverts to those users through the cookie. Cookies are small pieces of computer text that are used to collect information from computers. This indiscretion took place between 2011 and 2012. (Google Will Pay $22.5 Million to Settle FTC Charges it Misrepresented Privacy Assurances to Users of Apple's Safari Internet Browser | Federal Trade Commission)

- In 2019, this statement was issued by the Federal Trade Commission, "**Google** LLC and its subsidiary **YouTube**, LLC agreed to pay a **$170 million** civil penalty to the Federal Trade Commission and the New York Attorney General to settle allegations that the **YouTube** video sharing service illegally collected personal information from children without their parents' consent in violation of the **Children's** Online **Privacy** Protection Act Rule (COPPA)" (see later).

In September 2023, a North Carolina family filed a lawsuit against Google, alleging the company's failure to update its maps resulted in the death of their father, who drove off a collapsed bridge while relying on Google Maps for directions home the previous year.

Despite this, as Figure 9-6 shows, the market capitalization increased, as we all became dependent on their free products.

Meta (Facebook) – "Don't Tell Us What Is Ethically Correct"

In December 2015, Mark Zuckerberg, CEO of Meta who owns Facebook and his wife, Priscilla Chan, pledged to give away 99% of their Facebook stake over their lifetimes through the Chan Zuckerberg Institute. Its stated goals are "advancing human potential and promoting equality." The Tech Giant entrepreneurs see their products as not for profit but "gifts to humanity." (https://nonprofitquarterly.org/the-philanthropy-of-amazon-facebook-and-google/)

Mark Zuckerberg, saw social connection as a tool for political progress and democracy globally more than existing democratic infrastructures. In 2017, he said "In a lot of ways Facebook is more like a government than a traditional company. We have this large community of people, and more than other technology companies we're really setting policies." The perception here is that no local regulatory rules can apply and they have the principles to do what they believe is ethically right. We will see later on how their market performance ballooned globally. (`www.theguardian.com/technology/2017/ sep/19/facebooks-war-on-free-will`)

Microsoft – "Ethics Team Getting in the Way of Product Delivery"

Microsoft employees said that their ethics and society team was crucial in making sure the AI products they actually designed were instilled with the principles of responsibility the company had espoused. In April 2023, Microsoft released their ethics and society team as part of a wider layoff of staff. the ethics and society team had over 30 members. According to the Verge, it was from pressure to get AI products into customer hands at a higher speed. The ethics team had the job of saying "no" or "slow down" inside organizations that often don't want to hear it – or spelling out risks that could lead to legal headaches for the company if surfaced in legal discovery. (`www.theverge. com/2023/3/13/23638823/microsoft-ethics-society-team-responsible- ai-layoffs`)

2. Competition – Do Big Data Firms Compete Fairly?
Background

To ensure fair competition in the market, anti-trust laws are in place. They stop price fixing, restricting unfair competition all for the benefit of the customer by creating a level playing field. In 2020, it was found that big data firms who were dominating in their fields were at the same time, according to US lawmakers, suppressing the competition. In 2020, the US House Judiciary antitrust subcommittee accused Facebook, Google, Amazon, and Apple of "abuses of monopoly power" in a report on competition in digital markets. "These firms typically run the marketplace while also competing in it – a position that enables them to write one set of rules for others, while they play by another." (`https://judiciary.house.gov/uploadedfiles/ investigation_of_competition_in_digital_markets_majority_ staff_report_and_recommendations.pdf`)

As consumers, we only seem to wake up to this situation when major civil liberties issues arise and alert the broadcast media. But then the story dies down and governments don't take any action.

However, in the United States despite these reports, nothing has been done to address unfair competition. It is said the reason why US antitrust law fails to act is due to the "revolving door" of politics. For years, the big tech firms have been recruiting antitrust regulators from the Federal Trade Commission (FTC) and the Department of Justice (DOJ). Antitrust enforcers are disinclined to turn against their former and potential future employers. (Source: US Antitrust Against the Big Tech – The World Financial Review)

To protect their global interests in major markets, all big tech firms actively lobby hard. In the EU, figures in Figure 9-7 show the high lobbying investments that the tech giants have made in 2022.

Top 10 digital industry lobbyists

Tech firms ranked by how much they spend lobbying the EU Institutions.

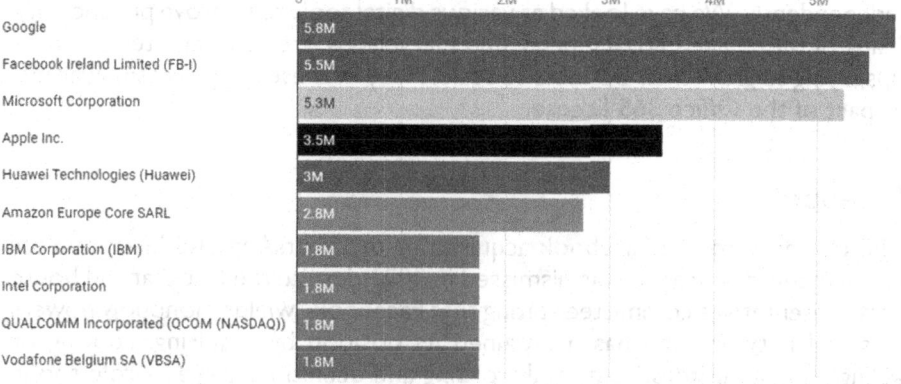

Chart: Corporate Europe Observatory & Lobbycontrol · Source: EU Transparency Register · Embed · Download image · Created with Datawrapper

Figure 9-7. Top Digital Lobbyists to EU t2022

The active lobbying has enabled the tech giants to achieve huge profits globally. It is hard to react as digital has no borders and so it is hard to get a common global understanding. The General Data Protection Register (GDPR) was a watershed (see later) in that it finally showed how different jurisdictions can finally work together to protect how companies use our data, but it took over eight years for it to be finally in law. The United States has been ineffective thus far.

To try and get an understanding on this, do you think Zoom or Spotify could be more successful on a different set of competition rules?

Here are some of the anti-trust cases that were unsuccessful

Microsoft

The first big tech anti-trust case emerged when 19 US states and the Justice Department tried to sue unsuccessfully Microsoft for bundling additional programs into its operating system. It meant that for customers who wanted to access a particular Microsoft application, the Microsoft Windows operating system was a prerequisite. The defense argument was that antitrust laws would stifle the success of domestic firms on a global level, hence making them less competitive. The defense won. This case was instrumental in creating a market environment favorable for the emergence of the biggest companies today, such as Google and Meta, to do the same.

Since then, Microsoft has been accused by its competitors of "abusing its market dominance" by bundling of apps within its Office 365 software as being an "illegal and anti-competitive practice." Most startups complain about Microsoft's tendency to "bundle" new features in its products, restricting the new start-ups with the ability to grow their own creations in the marketplace independently. We have looked at various digital tools to improve productivity. Many of these, like Miro, Lumen5, and Marvelapps, are tools created by start-ups trying to grow their business to scale. Many of these are not easily available as part of the Office 365 license.

Facebook

The challenge to the Facebook acquisitions of WhatsApp and Instagram for social media dominance was dismissed in 2021 despite the fact that the house of representatives committee stating that Facebook "wields monopoly powers in social network and has maintained its position by acquiring, copying or killing its competitors." But legal wording and definitions played a role too in the anti-trust failure on pretty basic points. It seem the challengers were not clear on what the monopoly referred to. (www.cnbc.com/2020/10/06/house-antitrust-committee-facebook-monopoly-buys-kills-competitors.html#:~:text=Facebook%20is%20entrenched%20as%20a%20monopoly%20due%20to,either%20acquiring%20them%2C%20copying%20them%20or%20killing%20them)

(https://techcrunch.com/2021/07/14/facebook-is-shook-asks-for-removal-of-ftc-chair-khan-from-antitrust-cases-against-it/)

Also a minor alteration to an algorithm has the potential to devastate smaller companies that depend on tech giants' platforms, and it can even disrupt emerging industries. The adjustments made to Facebook's algorithm in January 2018 to "prioritize posts that spark conversation and meaningful interaction between people" had a significant impact on the earnings of certain viral publishers that depended on the algorithm. (Source: www.marketingcharts.com/cross-media-and-traditional/content-marketing-106924)

Google

Similarly, a case was dismissed by the United States against Google for biasing search results. Google's ad business is under the microscope because the company owns every step in a complicated system that connects ad sellers and buyers. Rivals say the process gives Google an unfair edge over the market. However, the European Union has been far stronger fining Google – up to $9.3 billion – for its practices with online advertising and search over the last few years.

There are still ongoing anti-trust cases against Google for locking out competitors to become the default search engine on Apple and Samsung mobile devices. This could set new precedents. (www.cnet.com/tech/services-and-software/google-fined-1-7bn-for-abusive-online-ad-practices-in-the-eu/#link=%7B%22role%22:%22standard%22,%22href%22:%22www.cnet.com/news/google-fined-1-7bn-for-abusive-online-ad-practices-in-the-eu/%22,%22target%22:%22%22,%22absolute%22:%22%22,%22linkText%22:%22hit%20with%20a%20$1.7%20billion%20fine%22%7D)

Another point raised was in fair corporate income tax in the country where the big tech firms operate. Despite getting revenues in the region, big tech firms escape corporate income tax in those local countries through not having a physical presence there. It had meant that smaller sellers who pay local tax have not been able to compete at an equal level as the tech giants. According to a study by the Fair Tax foundation, the big six firms handed over $149bn less to global tax authorities than would be expected if they had paid headline rates where they operated; the researchers said the tech giants deliberately shift income to low-tax jurisdictions to pay less tax. (Source: www.theguardian.com/business/2021/feb/06/is-big-tech-now-just-too-big-to-stomach)

Evidence of hiding money in low tax jurisdictions came in 2017, when there was a data leak from a law firm called "Appleby" showing the offshore activities of wealthy individuals and companies. Apple was shifting huge cash piles to Jersey.

The Republican senator John McCain said: "Apple claims to be the largest US corporate taxpayer, but by sheer size and scale it is also among America's largest tax avoiders … [It] should not be shifting its profits overseas to avoid the payment of US tax, purposefully depriving the American people of revenue." (www.theguardian.com/news/2017/nov/06/apple-secretly-moved-jersey-ireland-tax-row-paradise-papers)

This does pose some important questions about transparency among big tech.

3. Data – Can Big Tech Really Be Trusted with Our Data?

Lack of transparency from big tech seems to be going on for many years without any regulations to make them more open. On average, a person in the United States has their details exposed 747 times a day, and in Europe, 376 times a day. This data is sent to nearly 5000 companies around the world. The global real-time bidding (RTB) market size grew from $10.85 billion in 2022 to $14.07 billion in 2023, at a compound annual growth rate (CAGR) of 29.7%. To understand what happens with our data, here is a quick summary of what happens when we sign up to one of the Internet services:

When we install a new application, the system requests the user's consent before accessing personal information. Generally, this practice is beneficial because certain information is essential for the app to function correctly. For instance, a navigation app relies on access to positioning data to determine your location. However, once an app obtains permission to collect this information, it can share the data with any entity chosen by the app's developer, potentially enabling third-party companies to track your whereabouts, speed of movement, and activities.

Similar to websites, many mobile apps are constructed by integrating various functions that have been pre-coded by other developers and companies, often referred to as third-party libraries. Most of these libraries also gather sensitive data and transmit it to their online servers or to entirely different companies. Successful library creators might then compile comprehensive digital profiles of users. For instance, a user might grant one app permission to access their location and another app permission to access their contacts. Initially, these permissions are separate, assigned to each individual app. However, if both apps employ the same third-party library and share distinct pieces of information, the developer of that library could potentially link these fragments together.

Unfortunately, users remain unaware of these connections because apps are not obligated to disclose the specific software libraries they utilize. Furthermore, users' online identities lack protection under the laws of their home countries. Data can be transferred across national borders, often ending up in countries with questionable privacy regulations. In such places, government agencies may gain potential access to this data, even if the users are located in regions with robust privacy laws, such as Germany.

According to science direct, a data profile is then built behind the scenes. A Real-Time Bidding (RTB) process operates on websites and apps when we use the service. It tracks what we are looking at, no matter how private or sensitive, and it records where we go.

Every day it broadcasts these data points about us to a host of companies continuously, enabling them to profile us.

www.sciencedirect.com/science/article/abs/pii/S016975529800110X?via%3Dihub.   www.theguardian.com/commentisfree/2022/mar/19/is-googles-domination-of-the-internet-finally-over-search-me.

www.digitalinformationworld.com/2022/05/study-shows-google-collects-most-data.html

www.iccl.ie/wp-content/uploads/2022/05/Mass-data-breach-of-Europe-and-US-data-1.pdf

www.reportlinker.com/p06443904/Real-Time-Bidding-RTB-Global-Market-Report.html?utm_source=GNW

4. Innovation – How Much of Their Profits Do They Invest in R&D?

The boldness of the "Silicon Six" firms like, Google, Facebook, Amazon, Netflix, Apple, and Microsoft to successfully drive rapid innovation, and deep customer engagement shows that old regulatory norms could not apply. Today, we live in a world of reality TV where scenarios are played out, people openly share more personal details of what they really think, helping others reflect on what they might do in a similar situation. Many people from all walks of life actively seek followers on social platforms and build up new friendships or like-minded individuals. Today, being less private and more open through digital has given people greater freedoms and they want that relationship extended to their brands, law makers, and their service providers?

Earlier we discussed tax avoidance, but Figure 9-8 shows that the tech giants are some of the highest investors into R&D which they use to offset their revenues and pay even lower tax. The figure shows a study from Strategy& carried out in 2018. and how Amazon, Alphabet, Microsoft, and Apple figure prominently as the highest investors into R&D.

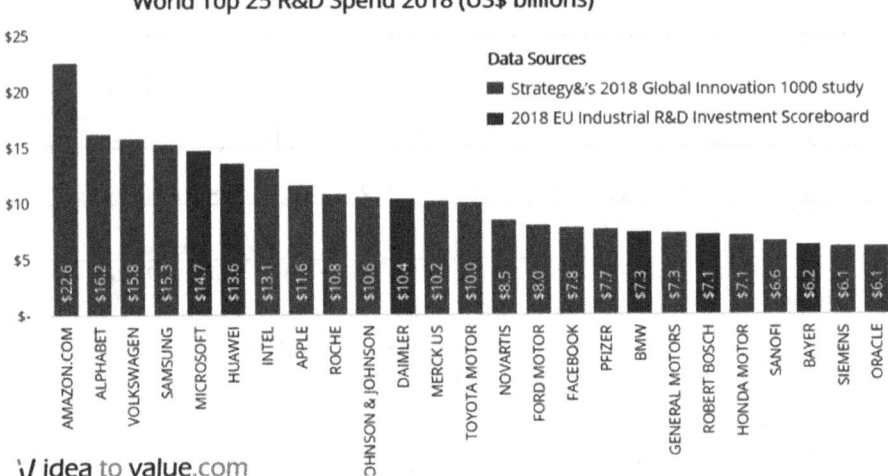

Figure 9-8. Investment into R&D of Leading Companies. Source: ideatovalue.com

Think of big techs' investment into revolutionizing electric cars or in Quantum Computing. Would these innovations ever have happened without the ability for big tech to offset revenues and reduce corporation tax? Aren't the tech giants just using their money more wisely?

If we look at one of the newer innovators, Tesla, Figure 9-9 shows the R&D investment of Tesla against the other car makers in 2015. Their deep investment created jobs and new opportunities and kick started green cars revolution.

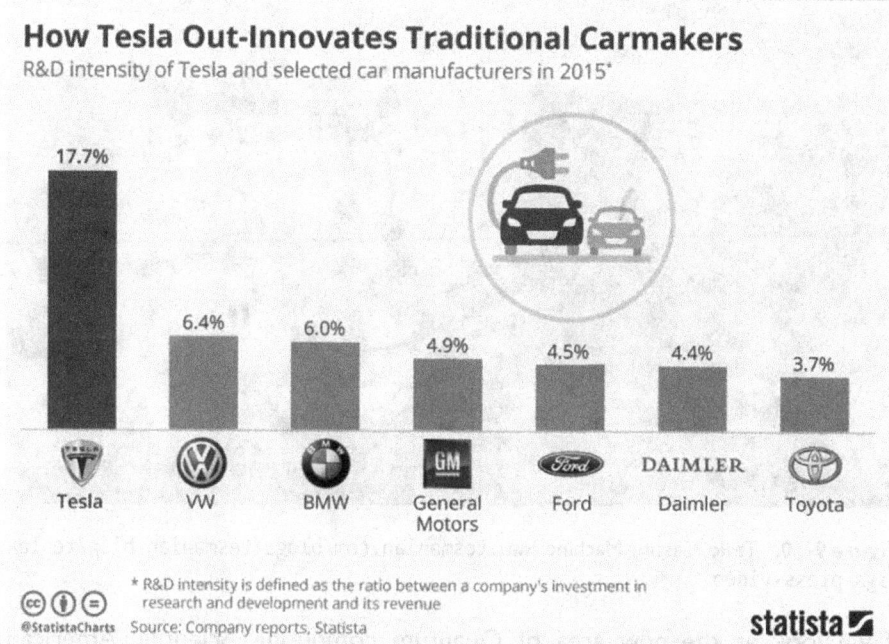

Figure 9-9. www.statista.com/chart/6312/r-d-spending-tesla-vs-carmakers/

By their sheer boldness, they have driven incumbents to innovate and revisit their operations. Tesla's determination to succeed has global automakers realizing that electric cars are the future, not just a fad. Tesla was the first US car company to go public since Ford in the 1950s.

Tesla's research was not only with electric batteries but also in the way cars are made. "With our giant casting machines, we are literally trying to make full-size cars in the same way that toy cars are made" Elon Musk, (18 January 2021). Would any of this have happened within the constraints of regulation and high tax burden?

Figure 9-10. Teslo, Casting Machine: www.tesmanian.com/blogs/tesmanian-blog/tesla-giga-press-video

If we look at the new area of Quantum computing, Scientific American published some breakthrough research from Google. Figure 9-11 shows the headline.

SCIENTIFIC
AMERICAN.

QUANTUM COMPUTING

Google's Quantum Computer Achieves Chemistry Milestone

A downsized version of the company's Sycamore chip performed a record-breaking simulation of a chemical reaction

By Neil Savage on September 4, 2020

Figure 9-11. Google and Quantum Milestone

The quantum research by Google can help improve agriculture yields, cure cancers, and many other transformations. A small 2000 QU BIT Quantum Machine cost: $15M. For real life use cases of quantum computing, Google says it will need to build a 1-million-qubit machine capable of performing reliable calculations without errors. That is a huge investment.

- Could any company and academic institution apart from the tech giants afford that?

- Is big tech more transparent, responsible and better at distributing their wealth than democratically elected governments?

5. Customer – Are We Treated "Fairly"?

Big tech does promote itself as reliable to consumers and can be self-regulated. Here are some of the forums set up by big tech to show social responsibility:

- Social media companies established the Global Internet Forum to Counter Terrorism in 2017, which they use to share information about terrorist threats on their services.

- In 2018, Facebook announced community guidelines that explain which content it does not publish. However, it doesn't share any statistics of the proportion of the content takedown or users that have been disabled as a result.

- In 2021, Meta then introduced an "Oversight Board" to oversee its content decisions. Mark Zuckerberg, the CEO, had initially proposed the concept of establishing this Oversight Board in 2018, a time when legislators globally were contemplating methods to regulate the social media platform. Critics argued that the company was devoid of any mechanisms for being held accountable for its moderation choices.

- In July 2023, Google, ChatGPT-maker OpenAI, Microsoft, and Anthropic introduced the Frontier Model Forum, which the companies say will advance AI safety research and technical evaluations for the next generation of AI systems. The group will establish an advisory board to guide its strategy and priorities. The CEO of OpenAI stated at the time, "What we are saying is if someone – us, somebody else, but probably us – makes a model that is as smart as all of human civilization, has the power of all human civilization, I think that deserves some regulation." Google and Microsoft were already founding members of Partnership on AI, a nonprofit created in 2016 to develop best practices around the responsible use of AI.

- In 2021, to self-regulate against dangerous content, YouTube released, a viewing statistic called the "violative view rate". It's role is to control the amount of content posted that violates YouTube's content policy. YouTube is able to take down 94% of content that breaks its rules with automated flagging systems, and that the large majority of those videos are caught before they get more than ten views. www.vox.com/recode/2021/4/6/22368809/youtube-violative-view-rate-content-moderation-guidelines-spam-hate-speech. www.theverge.com/2021/4/6/22368505/youtube-violative-view-rate-transparency-stat

- Microsoft maintains an Office for Responsible AI (ORA), which the company claims "puts Microsoft principles into practice by setting the company-wide rules for responsible AI through the implementation of our governance and public policy work." www.microsoft.com/en-us/ai/principles-and-approach?SilentAuth=1&f=255&MSPPError=-2147181526&activetab=pivot1%3aprimaryr5

The problem is the trade-off between protecting revenues, being innovative, ensure brand perception stays high and high customer engagement with self-regulation. Let's see how the customer trust has been eroded.

Google. "You think you are the customer, but in fact you are the product."

When Google launched, it competed against engines Lycos, Alta Vista, among others. It's strength was in the way that it objectively ranked searches upon relevance. There was no advertising incentive and customers believed them.

In 1998, the Google founders wrote, *"We expect that advertising funded search engines will be inherently biased towards the advertisers and away from the needs of the consumers… we believe the issue of advertising causes enough mixed incentives that it is crucial to have a competitive search engine that is transparent and in the academic realm."*

To raise revenue in 2000, they started gleaning words from the search text to identify relevant adverts to users. The user data is a product that Google deploys not only to improve on search results but to sell on to advertisers – it collects our data to sell on to advertisers. It builds up profiles based on demographics and interests for advertisers to target and bid for advertising space. If you use all the Google apps, it basically knows all about your life by linking all the data points together – approximately 39 data points in total.

Google, like the other big tech services, obtains user consent before providing any service. But the idea of consent on the Internet is not clear among all the techno and legal language. Is this deliberate?

To illustrate, Figure 9-12 shows an extract from a study carried by Costa, E. & D. Halper on the T's and C's of the big data firms on the time to read the terms and the reading age required. The Facebook terms take 34 minutes with a reading age of 18 years. However, the Facebook service is available for children from 13 and over!

Figure 2: Length and complexity of typical terms of service and privacy

Company		Time to Read	Reading age required
Instagram	terms of use and data policy	31 mins	18 years
Facebook	terms of service and privacy policy	34 mins	18 years
Whatsapp	terms of service and privacy policy	41 mins	21 years
Snapchat	terms of service and data policy	35 mins	16 years
Twitter	terms of service and privacy policy	46 mins	18 years

Figure 9-12. www.bi.team/wp-content/uploads/2019/04/BIT_The-behavioural-science-of-online-harm-and-manipulation-and-what-to-do-about-it_Single.pdf

If knowing how data is used be more transparent for users, would it stop anyone using these free services? To understand the "Google effect," let's look at Google Search Ads.

In 2021, Google search ads, its biggest revenue product, pulled in revenue of nearly $150 billion. According to Statcounter, which produces daily statistics of Internet usage, Google controls about 66% of browsers, 66% of desktop browsers, and the operating systems on 71% of mobile devices in the world. Ninety-two percent of Internet searches go through Google. Google runs code on approximately 85% of sites on the Web and inside as many as 94% of apps in the Play store. It collects data about users' every click, tap, query, and movement from all of these sources and more.

Google's search engine is so indispensable for our day-to-day that we cannot avoid it. It is not just Google Search but also the indispensable Google Maps product for GPS navigation. We discussed earlier on the Nicaragua invasion of Costa Rica based on Google Maps borders. In 2013, local residents repeatedly contacted Google to update its maps because a bridge mentioned on the application no longer existed, but to no avail. In 2022, a man drowned after using Google's outdated map to drive home. In September 2023, the victim's family filed a lawsuit: www.bbc.co.uk/news/world-us-canada-66873982.

It is not just commentators raising concerns about data, but big tech itself.

It was the CEO of Apple, in 2014, who said in a statement implying the other big tech firms, "We don't 'monetize' the information you store on your iPhone or in iCloud. And we don't read your email or your messages to get information to market to you. Our software and services are designed to make our devices better. Plain and simple. A few years ago, users of internet services began to realize that when an online service is free, you're not the customer. You're the product. But at Apple, we believe a great customer experience shouldn't come at the expense of your privacy."

Apple

Apple made a clear stance that its business was to sell great products and not to build a profile based on customers' email content or web browsing habits to sell to advertisers.

Apple has taken a different position with regard to ethics marketing. In response to the ways that customer data is exploited by other institutions, Apple took a stance of being the bastions of customer privacy as one of its values. In 2014, they posted the motto at CES in Las Vegas, "What happens on your IPhone Stays on your IPhone."

Figure 9-13. Apple Advert at CES Las Vegas. Source: liveatpc.com

This may come across as a clever marketing slogan, but Apple saw their role as in upholding the rights of individuals against the United States government who wanted to hack into an iPhone.

Apple had been asked to help break into a phone password found at the San Bernadino massacre in 2015, and they had refused to comply. The Silicon Six all backed Apple's stance. (www.theguardian.com/technology/2016/mar/03/silicon-valley-apple-fbi-encryption-airbnb-ebay-reddit-twitter) What is ethically correct? Apple protecting customer privacy and our phone data or the FBI protecting us from the "War on Terrorism"?

Since 2014, Apple has positioned its message further as the privacy champion, often challenging both Google and Facebook on how they exploit their own customer data for financial gain. (www.cnbc.com/2014/09/18/apples-tim-cook-takes-a-swipe-at-google-facebook.html) See later

Facebook – "The Social Engineering Company"

In 2014, Facebook published a series of social experiments carried out by the firm on its users. The experiments were all legal as Facebook asks users to relinquish the use of their data for "data analysis, testing and research" when they sign up to Facebook, so no explicit consent was actually needed. Everything We Know About Facebook's Secret Mood-Manipulation Experiment – The Atlantic. It revealed that in 2012, Facebook manipulated the feeds of 690,000 users to show more positive or negative news to affect users' moods. The ethical aspect was only noticed when the results became public. The study was described by the public as "disturbing." After all, it involved hundreds of thousands of users unknowingly participating in a study that may have made them either happier or more depressed than usual. It did not cause outcry because Facebook is offered for free and we sign up to Terms and Conditions. Consumers get benefits and so are responsible.

Then questions arise on whether a free product is good for our society's health. To illustrate, let's look at the evolution and social effects of the phenomenally successful Facebook social media platform.

Twitter – "Not Understanding Its Own Commercial Algorithms"

On March 18, 2023, Elon Musk tweeted about the algorithms used by his newly acquired company "Twitter." Figure 9-14 shows the tweet.

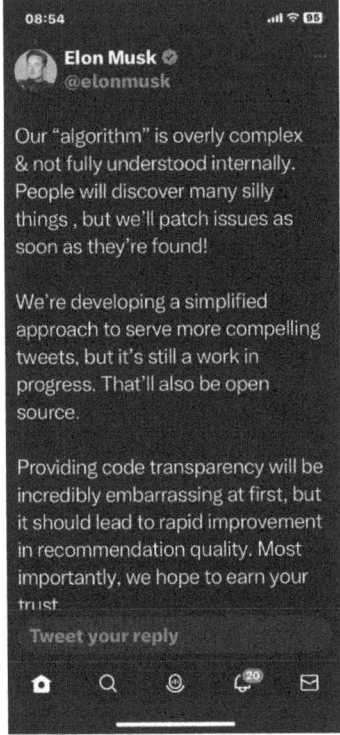

Figure 9-14. Tweet on Twitter's Algorithm. Source: Twitter

For how long have big tech firms like Twitter had commercial algorithms that influence society and people behavior that were "not fully understood internally"?

Influence of Social Media on How We Live Our Lives

I'm Nobody! Who are you?
Are you — Nobody — too?
Then there's a pair of us!
Don't tell! They'd advertise — you know!

How dreary — to be — Somebody!
How public — like a Frog —
To tell one's name — the livelong June —
To an admiring Bog

I'm Nobody! Who are you? Emily Dickinson

The poem may be summarized as being about how it is actually quite nice to be a Nobody rather than a Somebody – that anonymity is preferable to fame or public recognition. Well Emily Dickinson may be a famous poet, but she certainly could not predict the future! She definitely missed out on the dopamine rush when you get a lot of "likes" on social media!

It's nearly impossible to find someone who doesn't use a social media platform these days. Whether it's Facebook, Twitter, Instagram, or even LinkedIn, social media continues to evolve and take up a growing portion of our daily lives. At first, social media existed to help end users connect digitally with friends, colleagues, family members, and like-minded individuals they might never have met in person, but it is a way to make money, be an influencer, and live a digital life outside physical reality.

Figure 9-15. Social Media Companies. Source: https://www.vecteezy.com/vector-art/229578-social-media-icon-set

Who would have guessed even 20 years ago that around 2Bn people would be happy to share their interests, photos, family pictures, hobbies, personal opinions with a network of friends, acquaintances, and strangers. It has allowed us to reach out of our small network and join social groups to those of similar interests to form like-minded communities. The GWI global Internet survey in Jan 2023 produced some of the reasons why people use the platform (see Figure 9-16).

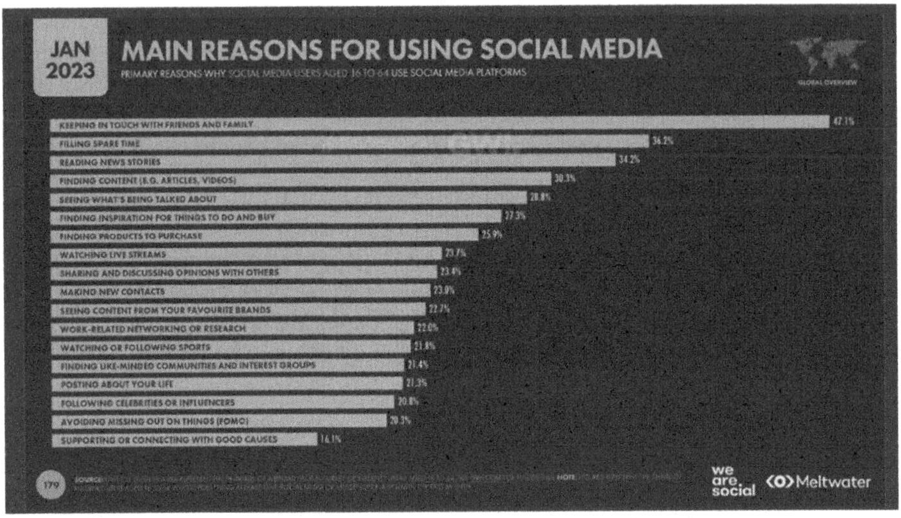

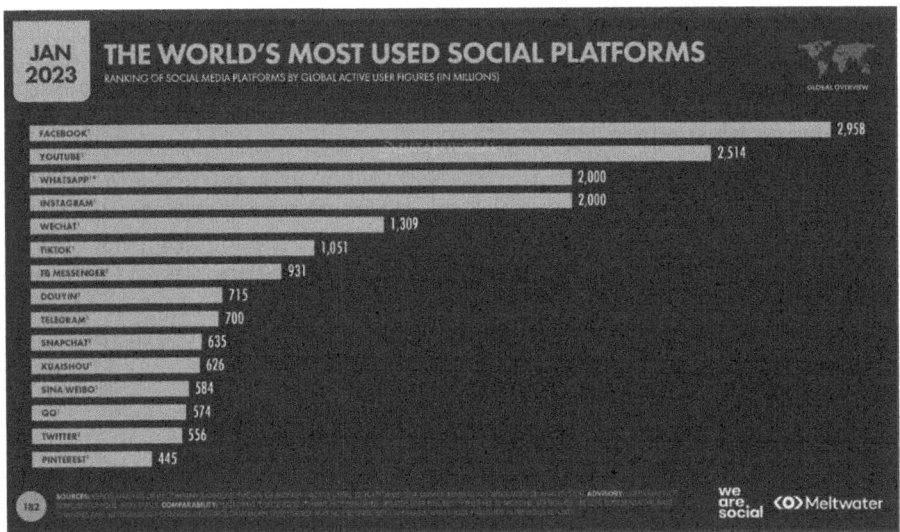

Figure 9-16. GWI Global Internet Survey 2022

Figure 9-17 shows the astounding global take-up of social media by users in 2023. It is quite strange then to think that it is the customer's user data that is the key product.

Figure 9-17. Active Users of Main Social Media Platforms Q3 2022

Facebook – The Richest Commercially Available Data Source on the Planet!

IAS insider summed it up as "Users don't just log in and browse on Facebook, they tell the platforms their name, and where they live, what they like and who they know, painting the most vivid picture currently possible for marketers looking to target specific consumers." Mining this information for marketing is through cookies. Cookies are small pieces of data which are stored in web browsers. Whether you are on Facebook or YouTube, cookies allow advertisers to know who you are and know that they want to target you because the data on you suggests you're interested in their products. Although Facebook says "We use this cookie information to help show you a personalized experience on that site as well as Facebook." It is very simple for advertisers to promote products on the Facebook platform. The segmentation features allow platform businesses to target any audience in four easy steps:

1. Advertiser chooses a business goal – like a product sell or brand awareness.

2. Advertiser selects the target audience.

3. Advertiser creates the advert.

4. Facebook shows the advert to the target audience.

The platform is so versatile that advertisers and agencies can target based on user many details that the user has, for example, the likes, number of followers, age, marriage status, location, sex, hobbies, even a recent Facebook update. All of these points are measurable thanks to analytics provided by the social media platforms (Facebook Insights, Twitter Analytics, LinkedIn Page Analytics, etc).

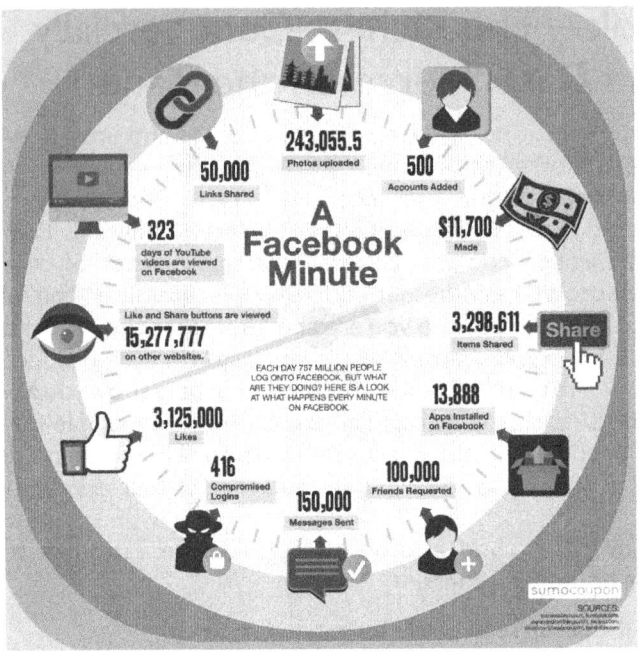

Figure 9-18. User Information Generated in a Facebook Minute. Source: `https://jumper-media.co/facebook-ads-for-small-business/`

Jumper media showed the activity generated by users in a Facebook minute. The granularity of the Facebook insights product is so rich for advertisers. Imagine a Facebook user who updates their feed while travelling from Paris to Amsterdam over lunchtime; the platform can target a relevant advert related to their feed when they arrive at their destination. Facebook is consistently introducing new features to drive even more customer data. tunities for advertisers.

The features introduced over time are shown in Figure 9-19.

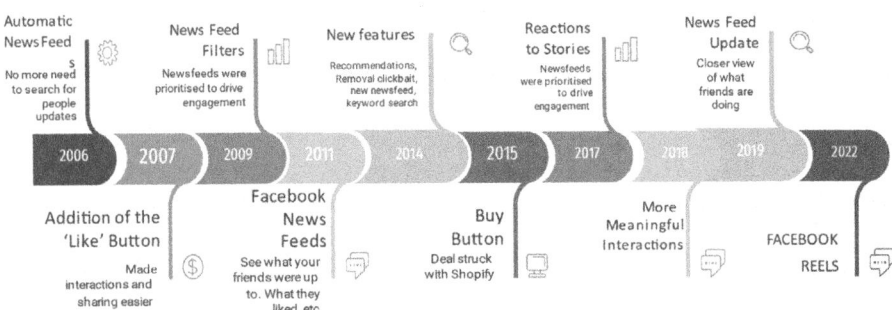

Figure 9-19. Evolution of Facebook Features: Source: Learn How the Facebook Algorithm Works in 2023 [UPDATED] (socialchamp.io)

Figure 9-20 illustrates the addictive nature of these features by seeing the average number of hours spent by users per month on the platform.

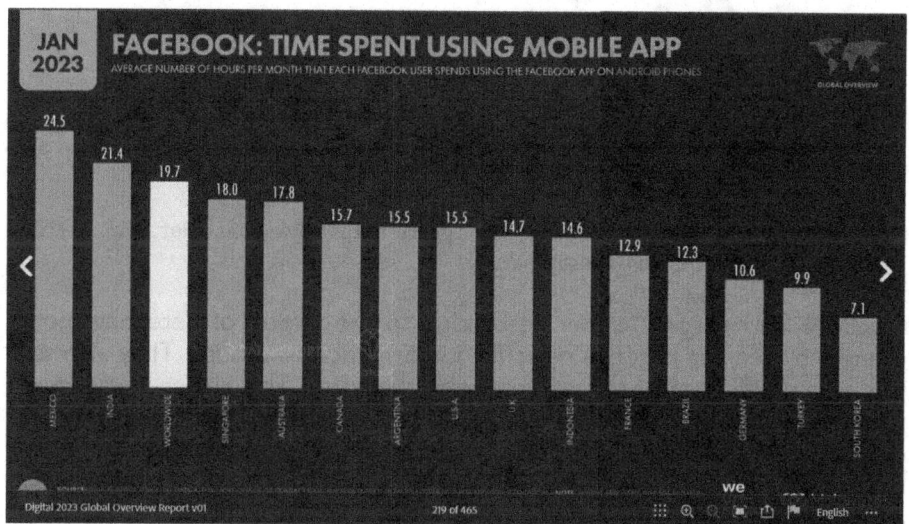

Figure 9-20. Hours of Engagement on Facebook from Around the World

As we discussed earlier, one of the consequences of this platform is the phenomenon of digital influencers. We saw how Cristiano Ronaldo has millions followers on Facebook and this feed influences his follower network thus redefining our relationship with established commercial brands. The more shock generated by people's activities increases the engagement on social media. It is not just celebrities who benefit. Politicians who are on tight budgets can use shock tactics to drive interest and awareness through social media thus saving money on media advertising. This mixture of addictive features and shock tactics by brands can lead to emotional contagion in the real world.

It was not clear the effect of likes and influencers had until a Facebook study, published 2012 *Nature*, showed the large-scale effect that the online world can have on real-world behavior. (Source: It published the results of the Facebook experiment that boosts US voter turnout | Nature).

About 340,000 extra people turned out to vote in the 2010 US congressional elections because of a single election-day Facebook message, estimate researchers who ran an experiment involving 61 million users of the social network. The results showed that those who got the informational message voted at the same rate as those who saw no message at all. But those who saw the social message were 2% more likely to click the "I voted" button and 0.3% more likely to seek information about a polling place than those who received the informational message and 0.4% more likely to head to the polls than either group.

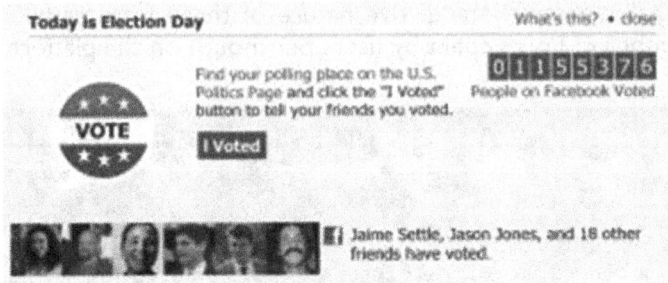

Figure 9-21. The "I voted" Facebook Message. Source: https://www.dailydot.com/unclick/facebook-i-voted-election-message-study/

Facebook carried out further research into the effects of detecting mood changes by sending negative news feed information to groups. They also saw the heightened level of engagement with their site. This higher engagement then drove the algorithm to fuel more of these news feeds changing the emotion set of users – emotional contagion. Things went a bit further, when in 2018 Facebook explained to Congress how they mined customer's data for a client called Cambridge Analytica who was sponsored by people of a political persuasion to influence the mindsets of voters in key elections around the world, namely, the UK Brexit referendum and the US election. By understanding the emotion set of a target audience the platform fueled viewpoints by posting extreme news articles with endless scrolling that created a cycle of higher engagement and emotional contagion which changed people's behavior.

In May 2020, the Wall Street Journal published a report which stated that Facebook's powerful algorithm is exploiting the "human brain's attraction to divisiveness" and, if not fixed, would continue to divide users even more, as a way to increase user engagement. Facebook's news feed algorithm has since been blamed for fanning sectarian hatred, steering users toward extremism and conspiracy theories, and incentivizing politicians to take more divisive stands.(www.wsj.com/articles/facebook-knows-it-encourages-division-top-executives-nixed-solutions-11590507499)

The issue that flies in the face of self-regulation, is that Facebook knew that they were doing something wrong but on the other hand, were protected under US law. Facebook and other social media were accused of inciting terrorism and other extremes. Some of the headlines are in Figure 9-22.

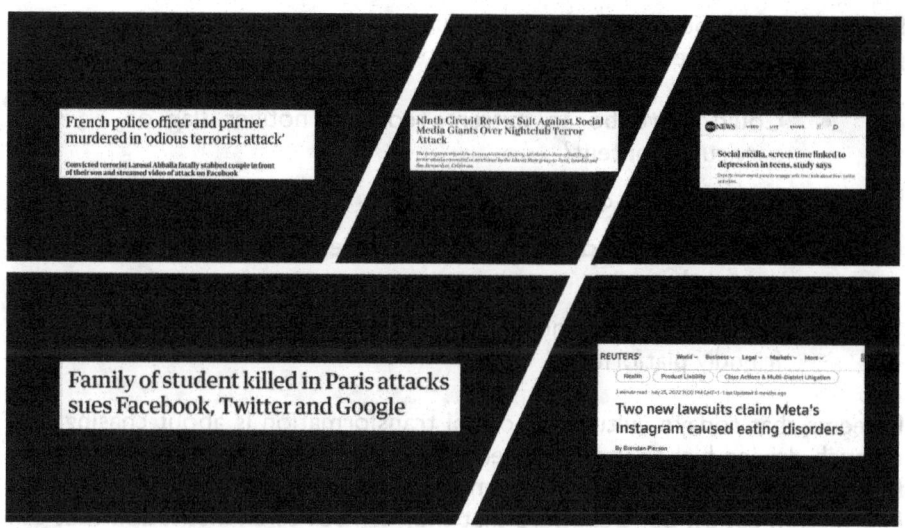

Figure 9-22. Social Media Inciting Hate

On November 10, 2021, CNN published a poll that reported 3 out 4 adults think Facebook is making society worse, however, as Figure 9-23 shows, while Facebook take-up has flattened slightly, overall social media usage by customers is on the rise. Are we just hooked?

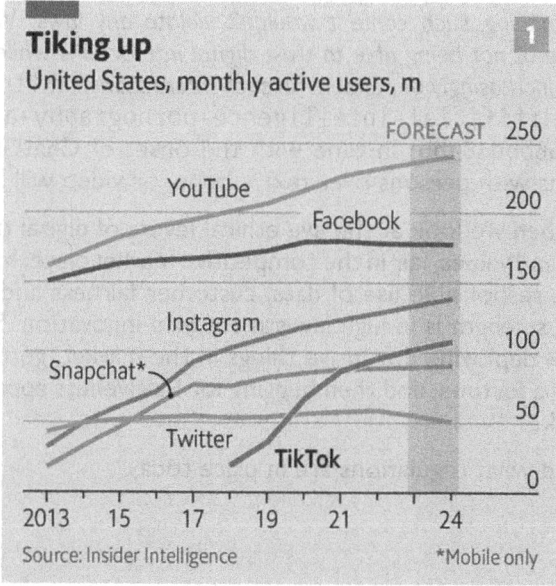

Figure 9-23. Social Media on the Rise. Source: www.economist.com/business/2023/03/21/how-tiktok-broke-social-media

Despite being protected under law, what self-regulation could have been in place to protect users?

- Could there be an extreme content notifier flag on particular content?
- Spread limiter of certain content?
- Further checks on advertisers and their reasons for the content?
- Could the government agencies promote more privacy-friendly platforms?

It seems that today's culture for digital transformation is about chasing ROI through driving higher user engagement through addictive features that are free for customers to use. Social media firms can create a highly detailed information set on our behaviors that they can sell to an institution that can exploit in many ways, all under the protection of US regulation.

Facebook was protected under law of not being responsible for the content shared and so it allowed misinformation, or "fake news" to pervade its user base without any recourse from official regulators.

The moral dilemmas raised here are difficult to ignore. According to Law professor and online abuse expert Danielle Citron, "*Machine learning models can also spit out images depicting child abuse or rape and, because no one was harmed in the making, such content wouldn't violate any laws. We seem to be arriving at a cycle of not being able to trust digital interactions while we are at the same time being increasingly dependent on such interactions.*" (https://medium. com/the-pub/artificial-intelligence-pornography-and-a-brave-new-world-6a66bbd483bb) In time with the onset of ChatGPT, even real-time interactions with persons over text, phone, or video will be faked, too.

It seems that when we look at the five ethical levers of digital transformation of consistent brand values, fair in the competitive market place, high investment into innovation, responsible use of data, customer fairness and transparency, the only ethical strength is in high investment into innovation. Should the Big Tech strategy of deploying disruptive things in the market, getting customers hooked, making a fortune, and then begging for forgiveness approach really be allowed to work?

Let's understand what regulations are in place today.

Regulation Today

Given the international reach of big data, it is hard to regulate companies on a global level. This section summarizes the regulatory position today in the United States and Europe with Big tech and the moves taken to address some of the issues raised. There are also numerous proposals that will dictate how data and algorithms will be used in the future. It seems leadership is coming from the EU that then reverberates to the United States and elsewhere.

The legislations and proposals covered are summarized in the timeline in Figure 9-25.

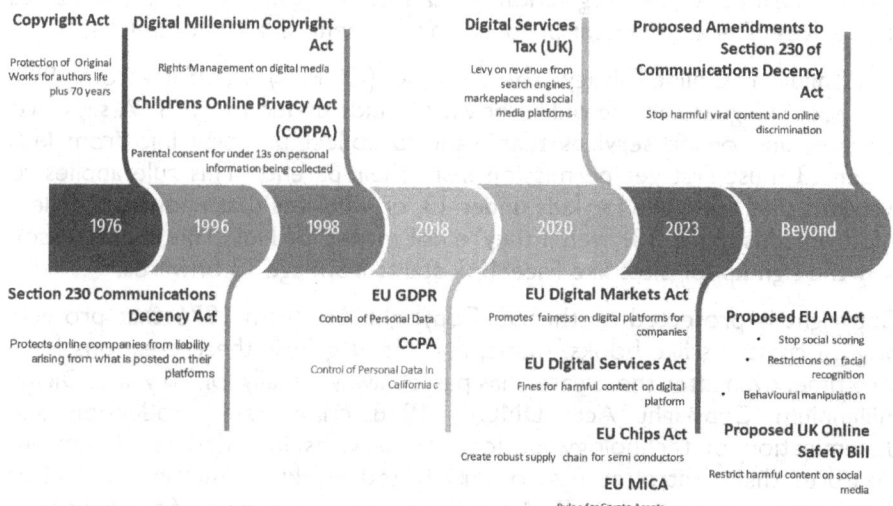

Figure 9-25. Overview of Key Legislation and Proposals from the United States, the EU, and the UK

The main US regulations stem from the passing of Section 230 of the communications decency act in 1996 (CDA). It was the first attempt by US congress to regulate the content of the Internet. In the United States, the First Amendment prohibits the government from restricting most forms of speech, which would include many proposals to force tech companies to moderate content. The CDA makes it clear that the Internet was a place where people could express themselves freely, even if their speech was offensive or harmful. This helped to create the vibrant and open online community that we know today. For example, it allows us to have reviewers sites, like Trustpilot, for people to voice their opinions without any recourse. Without Section 230, online platforms would have to pay for settlements and judgments if they were sued for content that their users posted. Today, a survey of American adults found that 67% of respondents check online reviews most of the time or every time they purchase a product, and 85% would be less likely to purchase products online that don't have reviews. Certain industries rely on reviews, with the same survey finding that reviews make respondents feel safer using ridesharing, vacation rental, and maintenance services, and that at least 40% wouldn't use such a service without user reviews every 60 seconds. One study sponsored by the Internet Association, a trade group of Internet companies, estimated that without the strong liability protections in Section 230, the United States could lose $440 million in gross domestic product (GDP) and 4.25 million jobs within a decade. However, Section 230 was created at a time before social media and it is being discussed as to how large social media platforms should treat political speech. In the meantime, any regulation is carried by the big tech companies themselves. The amendment proposals are presented later in the Chapter.

The Children's Online Privacy Protection Act (COPPA) is a US law from 1998. It's about safeguarding the online privacy of kids under 13. COPPA says that websites and online services that want to collect personal info from kids under 13 must first get permission from their parents. This rule applies to websites that are made for kids under 13, or websites that knowingly collect info from kids under 13, even if they're not meant for kids. This is one reason why the sign up for sites like Facebook starts from age 13 onwards.

Copyright is protected by the US Copyright Act from 1976 that protects original creations like books, music, and art. It guards these creations for a long time, even after the creator has passed away, usually for 70 years. Digital Millennium Copyright Act (DMCA) 1998 criminalizes production and dissemination of technology, devices, or services intended to circumvent measures that control access to copyrighted works (commonly known as digital rights management or DRM). It also criminalizes the act of circumventing an access control, whether or not there is actual infringement of copyright itself. In addition, the DMCA heightens the penalties for copyright infringement on the Internet.

This law is important because it helps creators keep their work safe and ensure distribution. But now, with Generative AI, people are asking if it's also breaking the rules by creating new things based in the original material in the public domain.

For the protection of customer data, the California Consumer Privacy Act (CCPA) is a state statute intended to enhance privacy rights and consumer protection for residents of California, United States. The CCPA is the first comprehensive privacy law in the United States. It gives consumers the right to know what personal data is being collected about them, know how their personal data is being used, say no to the sale of their personal data, access their personal data, request a business to delete any personal information about a consumer collected from that consumer and not be discriminated against for exercising their privacy rights.

The European Union has been seen as a regional leader in how the Internet is regulated today and how it will be regulated in the future. Here are some of the key rules in place. (Source : www.europarl.europa.eu/ for any updates on the regulations and proposals described)

The General Data Protection Regulation (GDPR) 2018. GDPR is a regulation in EU law on data protection and privacy in the EU and the European Economic Area (EEA). The GDPR aims primarily to give control back to citizens and residents over their personal data. It requires organizations to take a number of steps to protect personal data, with consequences of huge fines if they do not comply. Including obtaining consent from individuals before processing their personal data, minimizing the amount of personal data processed, giving individuals access to their personal data, rectifying inaccurate or incomplete personal data, deleting personal data upon request. The law also gives individuals a number of rights, including the right to restrict the processing of their personal data, object to the processing of their personal data, port their personal data to another organization. (Source: https://en.wikipedia.org/wiki/General_Data_Protection_Regulation)

Some of the more recent EU laws are as a response to some of the ethical issues raised in the previous section on fair competition. The Digital Markets Act : 2023 ensures a level playing field for all digital companies, regardless of their size. The regulation will lay down clear rules for big platforms – a list of "dos" and "don'ts" – which aim to stop them from imposing unfair conditions on businesses and consumers. Such practices include ranking services and products offered by the gatekeeper itself higher than similar services or products offered by third parties on the gatekeeper's platform, or not giving users the possibility of uninstalling any preinstalled software or app. In the UK, Digital Services Tax (DST) is a tax applied at a rate of 2% to specific types of revenue arising from specified digital services, including search engines, social media sites, and online marketplaces. The DST is not a tax on the online sales of goods, so it would only apply to revenues earned from intermediating those types of sales, not the underlying sale itself. The legislation is designed to be narrowly targeted and only apply to very large businesses. Proposals are being addressed to provide a similar levy across the European Union. The Digital Services Act (DSA) 2023 regulates big tech companies in the European Union (EU) to stop harmful content from spreading, restrict certain practices that target users, and share some of their internal information with regulators and researchers. These rules only apply to the 19 largest online platforms and those with more than 45 million customers in the EU. If a company breaks these rules, they could be fined up to 6% of their global earnings, and if they do it again, they might be banned from operating in Europe. Two of the companies being closely watched for these new regulations, Amazon and Zalando, are currently disputing their inclusion on the list in court. This means that if a platform like Facebook allows ads that promote hatred within the countries of the European Union, they would be breaking the law.

Other European Laws cover semi-conductor supply chains and cryptocurrencies.

The European Chips Act 2023, where the EU hopes to guarantee semi-conductors availability for critical applications. There was a global chips shortage in 2021 which disrupted supply chains, causing product shortages ranging from cars to medical devices, and in some cases, even forced factories to close. The production of microchips relies on an extremely complex and interdependent supply chain in which countries all over the world participate. For example, a large semiconductors firm may rely on as many as 16,000 highly specialized suppliers located in different countries. This makes the global supply chain vulnerable. By creating the Chips Act, the EU hopes to avoid this shortage in the future.

EU Markets in Crypto Assets Regulation (MiCA) 2023 – the primary aim of this regulation is to support financial stability, transparency, and protection for consumers and investors and create a level playing field for different market participants. This regulation applies to crypto-assets that are not currently governed by existing financial services laws. These rules focus on making transactions more transparent, ensuring disclosure, obtaining authorization, and overseeing these activities. Platforms dealing with crypto-assets must inform consumers about the risks involved in their operations. Additionally, the sale of new tokens will be subject to regulation. MiCA also addresses concerns related to the environmental impact of cryptocurrencies. Companies will be required to disclose their energy usage and how digital assets affect the environment. (Source: www.esma.europa.eu/esmas-activities/digital-finance-and-innovation/markets-crypto-assets-regulation-mica)

UK Announces the First Algorithmic Standards for Public Services

The UK Government addressed the issues of algorithmic bias through the publication of a national standard. It was the world's first national standard for algorithmic transparency. (Review into bias in algorithmic decision-making [publishing.service.gov.uk])

According to the UK government initiative, "any system must align with societal values and ethics. Factors such as privacy, transparency, and fairness. Firms should adopt best practices, such as collecting and processing data in a manner that upholds privacy, designing algorithms that are transparent and interpretable, and examining systems to prevent discrimination against certain groups." Unfortunately, it does not include education that would have stopped the UK exams case example discussed earlier.

Key recommendations within the report include:

- Organizations should be actively using data to identify and mitigate bias. They should make sure that they understand the capabilities and limitations of algorithmic tools that they are using, and carefully consider how they will ensure that individuals are fairly treated.

- Government should place a mandatory transparency obligation on all public sector organizations using algorithms that have an impact on significant decisions affecting individuals.

- Government should issue guidance that clarifies the application of the Equality Act to algorithmic decision-making. This should include guidance on the collection of protected characteristics data to measure bias and the lawfulness of bias mitigation techniques.

Proposals and Amendments Under Discussion from the United States and the EU

Each region has its own ideas on how to fix the Internet with regard to AI.

The EU is the most advanced as an institution with the EU AI act.

The UK, meanwhile, is attempting to use its new position outside the EU to fashion its own more flexible regime that would regulate the applications of AI by sector rather than the software underlying them. Both the American and British approaches are expected to be more pro-industry than the Brussels law, which has been fiercely criticized by the tech industry.

Any legislation could be used as a political football between regions. The most stringent restrictions on AI creators, however, might be introduced by China as it seeks to balance the goals between controlling the information split out by generative models and competing in the technology race with the United States.

The United States, in the meantime, is working with Big Tech on self-regulation. In July 2023, Representatives from Amazon, Anthropic, Google, Inflection, Meta, Microsoft, and OpenAI joined US President Joe Biden to announce:

- Security testing of their AI systems by internal and external experts before their release.

- Ensuring that people are able to spot AI by implementing watermarks.

- Publicly reporting AI capabilities and limitations on a regular basis.

- Researching the risks such as bias, discrimination, and the invasion of privacy

This was prompted to stem the flow of AI driven misinformation ahead of the 2024 US Presidential Election.

We will review the elements to the EU AI act and also list the suggested amendments to Section 230 of the Communications Decency Act.

Proposed EU AI Act

In April 2021, the European Commission proposed the first EU regulatory framework for artificial intelligence (AI). It should have far-reaching consequences if implemented. It defines AI quite broadly as

- Machine learning approaches, including supervised, unsupervised, and reinforcement learning, using a wide variety of methods, including deep learning

- Logic- and knowledge-based approaches, including knowledge representation, inductive (logic) programming, knowledge bases, inference and deductive engines, (symbolic) reasoning and expert systems

- Statistical approaches, Bayesian estimation, search and optimization methods

It says that AI systems that can be used in different applications are analyzed and classified according to the risk they pose to users. The different risk levels will mean regulation. Once approved, these will be the world's first rules on AI. Risk is according to three levels.

- Forbidden: Poses risks that are so high they are forbidden

- High: Poses significant impact on a person's life and ability to secure their livelihood or they can complicate a person's participation in society

- Low: certain transparency rules are required for AI systems

The following table shows some examples of the AI systems and where they would apply in the risk rating.

FORBIDDEN	HIGH	LOW
Manipulative Systems: techniques that are beyond a person's consciousness or that exploits any vulnerabilities of a specific group (age, physical or mental disability) in order to distort a person's behavior in a manner that causes harm to that person or another person.	**Social Systems:** These systems can, for example, determine access to services and benefits, be used in recruitment, or evaluate students. These can be put into service only if they comply with certain mandatory requirements that contain internal assessments and through reporting.	**General:** If an AI system interacts with people, it must notify the user that the user is interacting with an AI system.
Social scoring algorithms: an AI system used by public authorities that evaluates trustworthiness of natural persons that leads into "social scoring" of citizens.		**Sentiment Systems:** People must be informed if they are exposed to emotion recognition systems or systems that assign people to specific categories based on sex, age, hair color, tattoos, etc.
Real-time biometric systems: the use of a real-time system that identifies people from a distance in publicly accessible spaces for the purpose of law enforcement		**Deep Fakes**: Manipulated image, audio, or video content that resembles existing persons, places, or events that could falsely appear to be authentic or truthful (e.g., "deep fakes") has to clearly state that the content has been artificially generated.

An agreement was reached in December 2023, with the bans on prohibited AI coming into effect from June 2024, the transparency requirements by December 2024 and the full set of rules within two years.

The agreement also included measures to enhance copyright protection against generative AI and mandate greater transparency regarding the energy consumption of general-purpose AI systems. The prohibitions on certain AI applications will take effect in June 2024, while transparency requirements are slated for December 2024, and the comprehensive set of regulations will be finalized within two years. Entities found non-compliant will face penalties of 7% of their global revenue.

The aim is to reach an agreement by the end of 2023 for implementation by 2025.

The United States hasn't advanced any rules as yet for regulating AI, but it released recommendations in an AI "bill of rights" in October 2022. (www. whitehouse.gov/ostp/ai-bill-of-rights/)[1]

Suggested Amendments to Section 230

Both the US political parties have suggested revoking Section 230 or amending it.

Suggested Amendments include:

1. Implementing "circuit breakers" so that newly viral content is temporarily stopped from spreading while it is fact-checked.

2. Forcing social networks to disclose in the news feed why content has been recommended to a user.

3. Limiting the use of micro-targeting advertising messages.

4. Making it illegal to exclude people from content on the basis of race or religion, such as hiding a spare room advert from people of color.

5. Banning the use of so-called dark patterns – user interfaces designed to confuse or frustrate the user, such as making it hard to delete your account.

(Source: https://plato.stanford.edu/entries/ethics-ai/ and What Is Section 230? | Section 230 Explained | The Hartford; Bard; https://itif. org/publications/2021/02/22/overview-section-230-what-it-why-it-was-created-and-what-it-has-achieved/)

Why Does Regulation Take So Long to Become Law?

With the speed of innovation, regulatory timelines have not kept up. Here is the time for the EU AI Act.

---

[1] China has also issued several initiatives for AI governance which are probably the most advanced at the time of writing (Oct 2023). See: https://carnegieendowment.org/ 2022/01/04/china-s-new-ai-governance-initiatives-shouldn-t-be-ignored-pub-86127

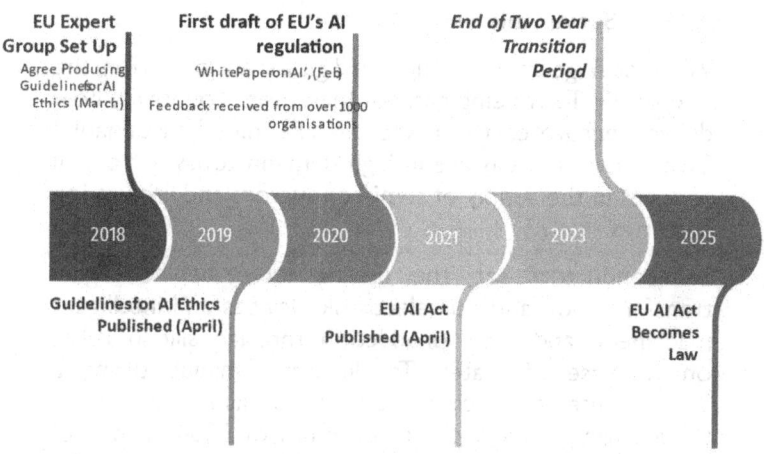

Figure 9-26. Timelines for EU Regulation – EU AI Act. Source: Author

It seems that regulation is chasing the innovation but really struggling to keep up. Getting the scope correct and agreement among members takes time, and in the meantime, technology keeps marching on.

However, with the prospect of investigation by regulators, big tech does take proactive steps to avoid scrutiny. For example, in August 2023, Microsoft said it would unbundle some of its apps to avoid an EU antitrust fine a month after the EU launched an investigation. (Source: www.reuters.com/technology/european-regulators-crack-down-big-tech-2023-10-03/)

Before moving to the next section.

- Are there ways that regulators could be better equipped to deal with the speed of innovation?

- Are there any other regulatory parallels outside digital transformation where technology is moving faster than the regulation? E-Cigarettes or E-Bike regulation?

Could Big Tech Just Better Regulate Themselves in the Meantime?

There is an argument that if the United States overregulates big tech in the country, then it could trigger problems for companies around the world through "tit-for-tat" regulation. We can see that they are working with the US government recommendations on managing AI. Is it better that big tech just uses its own ethics and morals to better regulate themselves? Here are some of the main points of concern.

- A More Sustainable Environment

  With the huge breakthroughs in digital transformation, the size of Big Tech being greater than most countries, how do you ensure earth's resources are mined sustainably? Two resource areas are in high demand today for digital services in the supply of semi-conductors and lithium ion batteries.

  Semiconductors are the driving force behind digital transformation and our electronic devices and intelligent machinery, and their production through silicon relies on the use of water. To illustrate, manufacturing a 30 cm integrated circuit board containing the chips for a smartphone needs a minimum of 2000 gallons of water. This substantial water requirement is due to the necessity of rinsing each chip with ultrapure water (UPW) to eliminate any impurities. To put it into perspective, it takes 1600 gallons of regular tap water to produce 1000 gallons of UPW. As we witness the proliferation of smart machines, it is anticipated that there will be an excess of 30 billion devices connected to the Internet so the production needs to be managed sustainably. It will be further driven by the rising demand for semi-conductors in automotive, computation, data storage, and wireless sectors.

  There are new sectors, like health care, emerging which are increasing their demand for semi-conductors. Ways to produce them ethically and sharing fairly, without creating supply shortages is key.

  There is an ever-increasing demand for lithium ion batteries because they are the most efficient and cost-effective type of battery available. Lithium-ion batteries store energy that powers mobile phones, electric cars, and electricity grids (when attached to wind turbines and photovoltaic cells). The "lithium triangle" comprises Argentina, Bolivia, and Chile. This region holds 54% of the world's "lithium resources." American car manufacturer Tesla's main mission is "to accelerate the world's transition to sustainable energy." The battery of a Tesla Model S, for example, uses around 12 kg of lithium. While Lithium is a naturally occurring element that is found in a variety of rocks and minerals, it still needs to be mined effectively. The demand for Lithium-Ion is rising exponentially and is expected to reach 9300 GW hours by 2030. Lithium is a very effective energy component when mined in a sustainable way.

- Managing space clutter

  Our activities on Earth have not only resulted in environmental pollution on Earth but is also being extended into space. Thousands of fragments, originating from defunct satellites, discarded rocket boosters, and weapons testing, have become trapped in orbit, leading to orbital congestion. This congestion poses multiple threats, including potential collisions with vital Earth-monitoring satellites, the release of harmful chemicals into the atmosphere during re-entry, which could further deplete the ozone layer, and complications for future space missions and exploration.

  The total number of LEO satellites should rise to about 24,500 over the next decade, with more than half of them for the three largest constellations, according to forecasts by Euroconsult. (Source: https://phys.org/news/2023-03-satellite-constellations-profit-geopolitics.html#:~:text=The%20total%20number%20of%20LEO%20satellites%20should%20rise,three%20largest%20constellations%2C%20according%20to%20forecasts%20by%20Euroconsult)

  As of September 30, 2019, there were more than 2200 satellites circling the Earth, primarily in low Earth orbit. The number of satellites is anticipated to increase significantly. Notably, companies such as SpaceX and Blue Origin are heavily investing in the production of low Earth orbit (LEO) satellites due to their superior data transmission capabilities compared to satellites in higher orbits. LEO satellites are also smaller and more cost-effective to manufacture. These satellites operate at altitudes ranging from 500 to 2000 kilometers.

  While the proliferation of LEO satellites offers the promise of delivering high-speed data and broadband services to remote areas worldwide, critics raise two concerns regarding the exponential growth of these smaller satellites. Firstly, the exact threshold for the number of LEO satellites that can coexist without a significant risk of collisions remains uncertain. Once a collision occurs, it could trigger a chain reaction leading to future collisions. Secondly, many astronomers are skeptical about the increasing number of LEO satellites as they believe these satellites will interfere with astronomical observations. Small satellites, like those from Elon Musk's Starlink project, have already been shown to reflect sunlight and disrupt astronomical studies. Starlink, for instance, has deployed over 3000 satellites into low Earth orbit since 2018, with plans to reach around 30,000 in total. Amazon's Kuiper project looks to launch over 3200 satellites.

The Sustainability Rating Association was set up in Lausanne, Switzerland to provide sustainability guidelines, and while the membership is growing, these groups are to date not members. (Source: `https://spacesustaina bilityrating.org/` and so they are acting independently.)

- Become ethical role models for the next generation of entrepreneurs

  There are questions if big tech firms can really "self-regulate" themselves as their actions also govern how the next generation of digital entrepreneurs behave. Since 2014, there have been some major ethical issues raised from the new generation of start-ups. From Figure 9-27, any idea who these founders are?

Figure 9-27. New Generation of Start-Up Founders

Conclusion

From earlier innovation curves, there was reasonably little regulation at the beginning, as the market steadily grew and the old markets faded, but eventually regulation caught up. This is not the case today. Through unchanged regulation and a market without borders, US big tech firms have become so big that they control the market where they play and can stifle new innovators. Today, things move so fast that by the time that a regulation is finally approved, the product or service has significantly changed and new considerations need to be considered. We are reliant on big tech to signal whether regulation is needed and regulate themselves under existing regulatory rules in the meantime. Despite having over 25 years to catch up, national regulators seem to be confused by the technology, the speed of change, and the ethical implications of new products, as they do not quite fit into existing defined regulatory categories. Different to the regulations of the past, we need regulation that crosses borders to ensure a fair competitive playing field, responsible use of data and social and environmental well-being. Unfortunately, there are differing political priorities that stop any global agreement and so things need to be considered across regions. While the United States has been slow to react, the EU has been a leader in getting cross-border regional consensus and its laws like GDPR, are being replicated globally. Its recommendations for AI could follow a similar route if they get implemented in 2025.

In the meantime, without any control gears in place, we are reliant on the values of the founders of large firms from the United States to regulate their new technology like AI on our behalf. We have seen how facial recognition tools have been used by the public sector to discriminate, and how social media can create emotional contagion. On the other hand, with low regulation, it allows an innovative field to be created and plays well with the younger generation who are disconnected with the traditional ways of "the law making institution knows best." They have shown that they can use these digital tools themselves to group together and respond if the values they hold dear are challenged.

While we scratch our heads on what to do, big tech continues to innovate, leaving new questions on our human values. The dawn of AI is causing new concerns as it can define new truths from what it draws from the Internet.

Unless business owners are more accountable, the potential negative effects of their future digital transformations on our society and our environment will increase.

The material presented in the earlier chapters as well as the points raised in this chapter lay the groundwork for developing a competency set that can effectively tackle these challenges.

Before moving on the final Chapter,

1. As you evaluate the free tools you use, do you believe application providers should be more forthcoming about where your data goes and how it is utilized with these free tools? If so, how would you recommend implementing greater transparency?

2. Could regulation pose a hindrance to innovation? Conversely, does big tech's lack of regulation stifle new innovators?

3. As Generative AI emerges, should we employ warning signs to guide its usage? Or would such measures be overly restrictive for such a new innovation?

Embrace Your Digital Journey with New Confidence

In hindsight, the journey of digital transformation appears less like a meticulously planned roadmap and more like an evolving narrative shaped by pivotal moments and technological advancements. From the enactment of Section 230 in 1997 that opened the door for virtual marketplaces and innovative messaging platforms to the disruptive impact of smartphones and social media in the next decade, businesses faced unprecedented challenges and opportunities. The resistance of some to embrace change led to their demise during the 2008 financial crisis, while forward-thinking pioneers thrived.

© Attul Sehgal 2024
A. Sehgal, *Demystifying Digital Transformation*,
https://doi.org/10.1007/978-1-4842-9499-4_10

The introduction of Bitcoin in 2009 showcased decentralized decision-making, setting the stage for a new era in payments. The shift to the cloud, accelerated by faster machine processing, transformed data management and fueled the hype around artificial intelligence. However, as big data firms prioritized profits over ethics, questions of bias and data usage ethics emerged.

The landscape shifted again with the 2019 pandemic, compelling businesses to rapidly adopt digital solutions for survival. Yet, despite the urgency, many struggled with the complexities of digital transformation, leading to a low success rate. Business managers faced unclear roles, and non-technical staff grappled with understanding the universal implications of the shift.

Now, with a clearer understanding of the broader effects and ethical challenges, it is time for non-technical business owners to play a more significant role. By addressing knowledge gaps and embracing ethical considerations, business owners can make informed decisions in the digitally transformed environment.

As we stand on the other side of the digital transformation wave, facing new challenges like generative AI, sustainability, and renewable energy, business owners can confidently lead technology decisions toward business success. Demystifying digital transformation empowers them to navigate the complexities of the digital landscape and harness its potential for positive outcomes. This book has sought to unlock digital transformation for non-technical executives, offering insights into tools that can enhance productivity and enable better business decisions.

So as we wrap up this journey, let's take a step back and see what we have covered.

As we wrap up this journey, it's clear that the challenge for non-technical business owners to be more effective is not straightforward. We have all had to, including myself, unravel the confusion created by the flood of technology hype, lack of alignment of business outcomes to technology, people stubbornly trapped in old ways of working, and the obsession with "shiny toy gadget syndrome" to produce successful digital solutions – so don't think you are alone.

We cannot ignore DX, and in many ways, we have been victims of DX. Our own data is used to suck us into a digital cycle culture where digital mastery is defined by the number of followers you have, the acronyms you know, the blogs you read, and the notifications you receive. The digital technology we are trying to harness is, as we speak, distracting our attention through news via clever engagement algorithms. We have no time to absorb anything before something else comes along to distract us. For non-technical executives trying to unravel this, without some adapting to our ways of working, technology becomes intimidating, forcing us to recoil to the tools we know and resort to expensive third parties who always have quick answers to our most pressing business problems.

This approach of understanding how we got here through classic case examples and immersion into digital tools, while not without its complexities, is brimming with huge potential to improve our way of working in the digital space. Despite the low success rates today, digital transformation can yield remarkable results when conducted in the right way, and the global investment in this endeavor is a testament to its huge significance in the future.

This book hopefully has served as a primer to steer you in the right direction and maximize your effectiveness in the digital realm on some of the key issues. Let's take a moment to reflect on our adventure by exploring the key questions we've answered in each chapter, as illustrated in Figure 10-1.

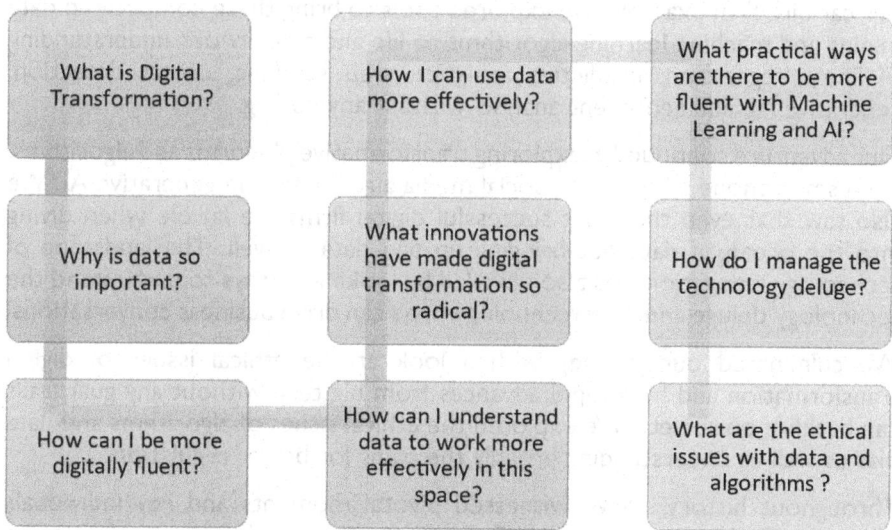

Figure 10-1. Key Questions Addressed in Each Chapter

Throughout these chapters, we've defined digital transformation as an integration effort that reshapes how we interact with customers, data, innovation, competition, and value propositions. Through classic case examples, we have highlighted how customers gain empowerment, data flows seamlessly, innovation becomes rapid and cost-effective, competition takes on dynamic forms, and value propositions continuously evolve.

The cycles of digital innovation have shortened, prompting us to adapt swiftly to newer technologies or be left behind. Data, a continuous process, has been a focal point of our exploration. As our journey deepened, we recognized the pivotal role of data in shaping business decisions. With an astonishing 175 zettabytes of data expected by 2026, this vast information reservoir can empower us to not only analyze the past but also predict outcomes and also create new revenue streams. Tools for data visualization have revolutionized our ability to quickly grasp trends and make recommendations with ease.

Despite significant investment into digital technology, our own outdated business tools have hindered our progress. But fear not – we've explored a range of new digital tools that enhance productivity and data competence. We brought these tools together in a creative exercise for a fictional car hire firm, showcasing the potential of whiteboarding, video production, UX design, and data visualization.

Shifting from technology-driven to insight-driven approaches, we've emphasized the importance of measurable business outcomes through a KPI-driven strategy for digital technology. Data and algorithms then took center stage as we explored their significance and practical execution, delving into the key machine learning and AI algorithms that power the digital age. Using our car hire firm example, we explored tools to bring these complicated data mining and machine learning algorithms to life and simplify our understanding of linear regression, predictive analytics, web scraping, object detection, generative AI, and sentiment analysis without any coding.

Our adventure continued in exploring transformative platforms and algorithms, from smartphone adoption to social media algorithms and generative AI. We also saw that even the most successful digital firms are fallible when diving into the ocean of data but bringing up bad data as well. The landscape of technology innovation was also unveiled by looking at ways to understand the technology deluge and how technology hype can drive business conversations.

We culminated our journey with a look at the ethical issues of digital transformation and how rapid advances from big tech without any guardrails can backfire on society. We explored the ethical issues of algorithms and data bias as well as understanding broadly the plans for better regulation.

Throughout history, we've witnessed pivotal moments and key individuals who shaped the landscape. We've brought classic digital transformation lessons to life through stories from McDonalds, Circuit City, Waze, IBM, Tesla, Domino's Pizza, Airbnb, Amazon, Meta, the UK Government, and many more that happened during key periods in the last 25 years.

As we stand at the present, the journey isn't over. The digital onslaught continues, but armed with newfound knowledge and confidence with exploring new toolsets, we're better equipped to sift through the noise. However many questions are still to be answered:

- Will intellectual property rights be impinged upon with the scramble for big data to service data hungry algorithms?

- Could web 3.0 rewrite the fairness rules for consumers?

- Should we really rely on algorithms that cannot explain themselves?

- Will regulators restrict AI?

While these challenges persist – aligning from clear business outcomes to technology, breaking free from old work methods, and taking lesson from the past – the potential for transformation is boundless.

Use this book as your springboard to building confidence in managing and exploring digital innovation. Here are some key takeaways highlighted in Figure 10-2 and described as follows:

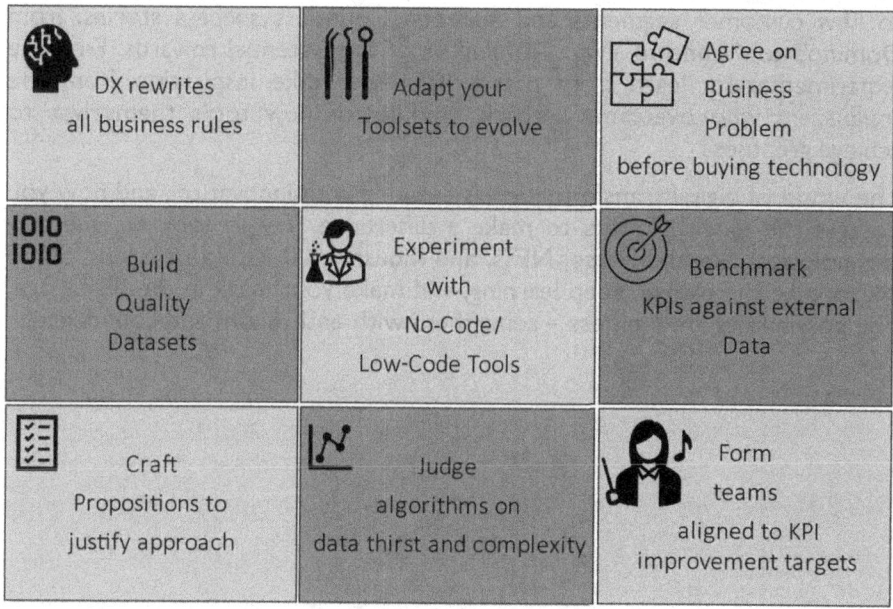

Figure 10-2. Key Takeaways to Thrive in the Digital Age

- Digital transformation is not just a technical overlay but a rewriting of business rules.

- Continue to embrace innovation and adapt your toolsets accordingly.

- Prioritize the business challenge before the technology – don't let the hype distract you.

- Harness the power of quality datasets to address your business problems.

- Continuously experiment with no-code/low-code AI tools to keep pace with advancements.

- Focus on improving benchmarks through a KPI-driven approach to business problems.

- Scope problems for improvement and craft robust propositions to justify technology.

- Judge algorithms based on data availability and complexity.

- Form teams aligned with KPI targets for successful pilot projects.

Successful digital transformation can revolutionize your business and lead you to new customer segments and markets. Countless success stories, from Domino's to Airbnb to Waze, remind us of the potential rewards. Embrace experimentation, learn from past pitfalls, and take inspiration from the trailblazers who overcame setbacks and learnt new tools themselves to achieve greatness.

The world of digital transformation is teeming with innovation, and now you possess the extra toolsets to make a difference. Try to look at emerging technologies, like Metaverse, NFTs, and Industry 4.0 with a new lens. So go ahead, take the plunge, keep learning, and make your mark in the digital age. The possibilities are limitless – seize them with enthusiasm and confidence!

A

Coding Languages Used in Data Science

From our discussion of Data Mining and Algorithms in Chapter 5, here is a comparison of the coding languages you will come across in data engagements.

Coding Languages

Data analysts utilize SQL (Structured Query Language) for database communication, but when it comes to data cleaning, manipulation, analysis, and visualization, Python or R can provide simpler solutions.

High-level programming languages are designed with human readability and comprehension in mind, while low-level languages are easily understood by machines. Examples of high-level languages include Python, C++, C#, and Java. When code is written in a high-level language, it is converted into low-level machine code that computers can recognize and execute.

© Attul Sehgal 2024
A. Sehgal, *Demystifying Digital Transformation*,
https://doi.org/10.1007/978-1-4842-9499-4

Python is a versatile, high-level programming language renowned for its intuitive syntax that resembles natural language. Python code can be applied to various tasks, with three popular applications being

- Data science and analysis
- Web application development
- Automation and scripting

R is a software environment and statistical programming language specifically tailored for statistical computing and data visualization. The capabilities of R can be broadly categorized into three areas:

- Data manipulation
- Statistical analysis
- Data visualization
- Comparison between Python and R

Python's primary advantage lies in its ability to implement machine learning on a large scale. If the results of your analysis need to be integrated into another application or website, Python is the optimal choice. On the other hand, R is a programming language and environment designed for statistical computing and graphics.

Python is better for...	R is better for...
Handling massive amounts of data	Creating graphics and data visualizations
Building deep learning models	Building statistical models
Performing non-statistical tasks, like web scraping, saving to databases, and running workflows	Its robust ecosystem of statistical packages

Figure A-1. Benefits of Python vs. R

Business KPI Sources

The following visualization shows some of the sources for KPI benchmarks in various business areas. This will be helpful as a start when finding industry benchmarks for the business outcomes approach discussed in Chapter 4.

A. Sehgal, *Demystifying Digital Transformation*,
https://doi.org/10.1007/978-1-4842-9499-4

Figure B-1. Business KPI Benchmarks: Credits: Dr Joerg Storm (www.passionfroot.me)

Sample Business Outcomes Data Set for US Local Government Public Safety

Business KPI Reduce Crime (all figures per 100,000)	Industry Average	Industry Leader	State	Public Data Source
Crime Rate	52	0.01%	New Hampshire	https://www.statista.com/statistics/202703/crime-rate-in-the-usa-by-type-of-crime/
Closure Rate (Clearance Rate)	0.01%	N/A	N/A	https://www.statista.com/statistics/194213/crime-clearance-rate-by-type-in-the-us/
Number of Violent Crime Incidents	431.7	374.7	N/A	https://en.wikipedia.org/wiki/Crime_in_the_United_States
Number of Property Crimes	2883.13	1744.1	New York	https://en.wikipedia.org/wiki/Crime_in_the_United_States
Recidivism Rate (over 5 rs)	77%	27.70%	Oregon (2008)	https://www.recidivism.com/rates/; https://atlascorps.org/recidivism-united-states-overview/
Improve Response Time				
Response Time (detroit)	8-11 minutes	N/A	N/A	https://www.bridgemi.com/detroit-bankruptcy-and-beyond/benchmark-public-safety-0
Fatality Rate (by all causes)	731.9	N/A	N/A	https://www.statista.com/statistics/189670/death-rates-for-all-causes-in-the-us-since-1950/
Maximise Resource Efficiency				
Crime Rate (per 100,000)	52	0.01%	N/A	https://www.statista.com/statistics/202703/crime-rate-in-the-usa-by-type-of-crime/
Closure (Clearance) Rate	0.012%	N/A	N/A	
Number of Violent Crime Incidents	431.7	374.7	N/A	
Number of Property Crimes	2883.13	1744.1	New York	
Response Time	8-11 minutes	N/A	N/A	https://www.bridgemi.com/detroit-bankruptcy-and-beyond/benchmark-public-safety-0
Vacancy Rates	77%	28%	N/A	https://www.recidivism.com/rates/; https://atlascorps.org/recidivism-united-states-overview/

Figure B-2. Local Government Figures

Sonnet About Digital Transformation in the Form of Shakespearean Tragedy Using ChatGPT 3.5

A. Sehgal, *Demystifying Digital Transformation*,
https://doi.org/10.1007/978-1-4842-9499-4

The application of Generative AI allows executives to try areas they would not normally do to explore particular topics. These can help in the richness of the output. Here is a sonnet on Digital Transformation. The important element to the result is how the question is formed and so the human is in control. Try versions yourself and see how the response changes.

"Write me a Shakespeare tragedy sonnet about digital transformation with the words customer, competition, innovation, data and value."

Oh, digital realm, where transformation lies, Where customers seek value with longing eyes. Competition fierce, a battle to be won, Innovation's cry echoes, it can't be undone.

Amidst this tempest, data takes its throne, A treasure trove of insights yet unknown. In bits and bytes, the secrets lie concealed, Waiting to be harnessed, their worth revealed.

The customer, a king, demands their due, Their needs, desires, paramount and true. But in this digital realm, they're adrift, Lost in a sea of choices, a challenging shift.

And as the tides of progress ever flow, The value sought becomes harder to bestow. Yet 'tis our duty to navigate this storm, To craft experiences that transform and inform.

Oh, digital transformation, a tragic tale, A quest for value, where fortunes may fail. But in this tapestry, we strive to find, The perfect harmony, the sweetest bind.

So let us, like Shakespeare's characters, endure, Embrace this era, seek wisdom and procure, A tale of tragedy turned to victory, Where digital realms thrive with harmony.

Table C-1. Data Mining Methods

Tool	Description
Anova (Analysis of Variance): Single Factor	This tool determines if there is a relationship between two datasets by performing a simple analysis of variance.
Anova (Analysis of Variance): Two Factor with Replication	This tool determines if there is a relationship between two datasets by performing an analysis of variance when each data set has more than one observable data point.
Anova (Analysis of Variance): Two-Factor without Replication	This tool determines if there is a relationship between two data sets by performing an analysis of variance. There is only a single observable data point for each pair.
Correlation	Tells you how strongly two variables are related to each other.
Covariance	The Covariance analysis tool calculates the average of the product of deviations of values from the means of each data set.
Descriptive Statistics	Generates a report of univariate statistics for the selected data. Statistics generated include: Mean, Standard Error, Median, Mode, Standard Deviation, Sample Variance, Kurtosis, Skewness, Range, Minimum, Maximum, Sum, Count, Largest, Smallest, and Confidence Level.
Exponential Smoothing	Smooths out irregularities (peaks and valleys) in data, to easily recognize trends. More recent data is weighted more heavily.
F-Test Two Sample for Variances	This analysis tool compares the variances between two groups of data.
Fourier Analysis	This tool solves problems in linear systems and analyzes periodic data by using the Fast Fourier Transform (FFT) method to transform data. The Fourier Analysis tool also supports inverse transformations, where the inverse of transformed data returns the original data.
Histogram	The Histogram analysis tool counts occurrences in each of several data bins. It calculates individual and cumulative frequencies for a cell range of data and data bins. The output is a table and column chart by the frequency of occurrences.
Moving Average	Calculates a moving average to allow you to smooth out a data series that contains peaks and outliers. Used for forecasting trends in sales, inventory, call volume, etc.

(continued)

Table C-1. *(continued)*

Tool	Description
Random Number Generation	Creates a number of several types of random numbers, including Uniform, Normal, Bernoulli, Poisson, Patterned, and Discrete. More flexible than the RAND and RANDBETWEEN functions.
Rank and Percentile	Creates a table which ranks numbers from highest to lowest and provides a percentile value of each number relative to the other numbers within the data set.
Regression	Uses the function LINEST to analyze how a single dependent variable is affected by the values of one or more independent variables. Creates a table of statistics that result from least-squares regression.
Sampling	Samples a population randomly or periodically, as desired.
t-test: Paired Two Sample for Means	Paired two-sample student's t-test. Each Two-Sample t-test analysis tool tests for equality of the population means that underlie each sample. The paired two-sample form of the t-test is used when there is a natural pairing of observations in the samples – for example, when a sample group is tested twice, before and after an experiment. There is no assumption that the variances of both populations are equal.
t-test: Two Sample assuming equal Variances	This analysis tool performs a two-sample student's t-test. This t-test form is based on the assumption that the two paired data sets came from distributions with the same variances. It is also known as a "homoscedastic t-test". This t-test can be used to determine if the two samples are likely to have come from distributions with equal population means.
t-test: Two Sample assuming unequal Variances	This t-test form assumes that the two datasets are from distributions where the variances are unequal. This is called a "heteroscedastic t-test."
Z-Test: Two Sample for Means	The Two Sample for Means analysis tool performs a two sample z-Test for means with known variances. This analysis tool is used to test the null hypothesis that there is no difference between two population means against either one-sided or two-sided alternative hypotheses. If mean variances are not known, use the Z.TEST function instead

I

Index

© Attul Sehgal 2024
A. Sehgal, *Demystifying Digital Transformation*,
https://doi.org/10.1007/978-1-4842-9499-4

Printed in the United States
by Baker & Taylor Publisher Services